COMPUTER ORGANIZATION AND ASSEMBLY LANGUAGE PROGRAMMING

JAMES L. PETERSON

UNIVERSITY OF TEXAS AT AUSTIN

ACADEMIC PRESS
NEW YORK   SAN FRANCISCO   LONDON
A Subsidiary of Harcourt Brace Jovanovich, Publishers

ACADEMIC PRESS, INC.
111 FIFTH AVENUE, NEW YORK, NEW YORK 10003

UNITED KINGDOM EDITION PUBLISHED BY
ACADEMIC PRESS, INC. (LONDON) LTD.
24/28 OVAL ROAD, LONDON NW1

ISBN: 0–12–552250–9
LIBRARY OF CONGRESS CATALOG CARD NUMBER: 77–91331

PRINTED IN THE UNITED STATES OF AMERICA

CONTENTS

4
ASSEMBLY LANGUAGE PROGRAMMING TECHNIQUES   132

5
INPUT/OUTPUT PROGRAMMING   161

6
SUBROUTINES AND PARAMETERS   196

PREFACE

This book has been designed and used as a text for a second course in computer programming. It has developed from class notes for a course offered at the University of Texas at Austin to undergraduate students. These students have had one previous programming course and should know, from that first course, the basic operation of computers, in general, and have some basic skills in converting problem statements into programs in a higher level language, such as Fortran. The second course, and this text, assumes that the student knows how to program, i.e., how to find an algorithm to solve a problem and convert that algorithm into a program.

The purpose of this book is to teach the student about lower level computer programming: machine language and assembly language, and how these languages are used in the typical computer system. This is meant to give the student a basic understanding of the fundamental concepts of the organization and operation of a computer. Even if the student never again programs in assembly language (and we would hope that they never have to!) it is important that they understand what the computer is doing at the machine language level. A good understanding of computer organization translates into a better understanding of the features and limitations of all computer facilities, since all systems must eventually rest on the underlying hardware machine.

The content of this text follows the recommendations of the ACM Curriculum 68 for Course B2 ''Computers and Programming.'' After a brief review of the general concepts of computers in Chapter 1, the remainder of the text uses the MIX computer to provide an example machine for illustrating computer organization and programming. Chapter 2 and Chapter 3 present the architecture of the MIX computer, its machine language and the MIXAL assembly language. Programming techniques in assembly language are covered in Chapters 4 and 5 with Chapter 5 concentrating mostly on input/output programming. The use and implementation of the subroutine concept is investigated in Chapter 6.

Systems programs are considered in the next three chapters. Chapter 7 explores loaders, while Chapter 8 discusses assemblers. In Chapter 7 the code for a simple, but real, absolute loader is given; in Chapter 8, the code for a MIXAL assembler is given. These two programs provide an opportunity for the student to see and study a real loader and assembler, and not simply the concepts in the abstract. Chapter 9 briefly discusses other system programs, macro assemblers, compilers, interpreters, and operating systems.

From these chapters, the basic concepts of assembly language programming and programs should be evident to the student. Chapter 10 then proceeds to present a brief description of several other computers, to introduce the student to both the similarities and differences among computer systems.

In our one-semester course, these concepts are reinforced by numerous programming assignments. The early assignments emphasize basic programming techniques such as simple arithmetic, input/output, character manipulation and array handling. The later assignments have included writing either a relocatable loader and two-pass assembler for a subset of the MIX computer, or writing an interpreter and one-pass load-and-go assembler for a simple minicomputer (16 instructions, four general registers, etc.). All of these assignments are programmed in MIXAL. The last assignment is to write a simple program in the new assembly language of their own assembler. Thus, students should see that they know how to program in assembly language, in general, and not simply in MIXAL.

The major question in your mind now is undoubtedly: Why MIX? MIX is a pseudo computer, not a real one. This is at once both its major drawback and its major advantage. The major drawback to MIX is, of course, that it is not real; this implies that the use and programming of the MIX computer will include a certain air of artificiality which may annoy and confuse some students.

However, from an educational point of view, MIX is ideal. It is simple, easy to understand, and yet typical of many computers. Machine and assembly languages are different for each computer. However, the techniques of assembly language programming are largely machine independent. Thus, learning one assembly language provides the basis for quickly and easily learning any other assembly language. This is emphasized by the descriptions of other computers in Chapter 10.

Also consider the alternative to teaching MIX: teaching the structure and language of a real computer. As Knuth has written, in the Preface to Volume 1 of *The Art of Computer Programming* (Addison-Wesley, Reading, Mass., 1973),

> "Given the decision to use a machine-oriented language, which language should be used? I could have chosen the language of a particular machine X, but then those people who do not possess machine X would think this book is only for X-people. Furthermore, machine X probably has a lot of idiosyncrasies which are completely irrelevant to the material in this book, yet which must be explained; and in two years the manufacturer of machine X will put out machine X + 1 or machine 10X, and machine X will no longer be of interest to anyone".

Knuth continues that it is very unlikely that programmers will only use one computer in their life. Each new machine can be easily learned once the first machine is understood, but the ability to change smoothly from one computer to another is an important skill for a programmer. Thus, teaching first MIX and then another, real, computer is preferable, since it immediately forces the student to understand how to move from machine to machine. In my own, so far short career, I have programmed on several different computers (IBM 1620, CDC 3600, CDC 6500, PDP-11/20, HP 2116, CDC 1700, IBM 360/370, DEC-10, SDS Sigma 5, Nova 3/D).

From an economic viewpoint also, the MIX machine is an advantage over a real computer. It is often said that a simulated machine is much more expensive than a real machine, and for production computation this is undeniably true. However, for a student environment, most of the computer time is in assembly and debugging, *not* execution. The simple MIXAL assembler, written as a cross assembler for the machine at hand, generating load-and-go code for a simulator with good trace, dump, and error detection facilities will provide a much better instructional tool at a lower price than most real assemblers with their extensive pseudo instructions, macros, relocatable code, and operating system input/output, most of which cannot and need not be used in an introductory course.

The construction of a MIXAL assembler/simulator is, although nontrivial, within the range of a senior year or early graduate student project. The complexities are derived mainly from the need for an event driven simulator to allow CPU and I/O overlap, and the need to provide the best possible debugging facilities. Properly written, the design and code for these systems would be easily transported over the years to new computer systems.

One further benefit from the use of MIX is the ability to easily pick up and use *The Art of Computer Programming* books by D. E. Knuth. These are very handy in later courses as references and texts. More can be learned from them with a good knowledge of MIX.

In summary, we feel that MIX is preferable to any real machine for teaching a beginning course in machine language, assembly language and computer organization. The major problem we have faced in using MIX has been the lack of an adequate text, a problem which we hope has now been solved.

I would especially like to express my gratitude to the reviewers—Stan Benton, Montclair State College; Michel Boillot, Pensacola Junior College; Werner Rheinboldt, University of Maryland; and Robert C. Uzgalis, University of California—Los Angeles; whose comments and suggestions helped greatly in guiding the manuscript to its final form.

Austin, Texas   James Peterson
August 11, 1977

COMPUTER ORGANIZATION AND ASSEMBLY LANGUAGE PROGRAMMING

1
BASIC COMPUTER ORGANIZATION

Computers, like automobiles, television, and telephones, are becoming more and more an integral part of our society. As such, more and more people come into regular contact with computers. Most of these people know how to use their computers only for specific purposes, although an increasing number of people know how to program them, and hence are able to solve new problems by using computers. Most of these people know how to program in a higher-level language, such as Basic, Fortran, Cobol, Algol, or PL/I. We assume that you know how to program in one of these languages.

However, although many people know how to use automobiles, televisions, telephones, and now computers, few people really understand how they work internally. Thus, there is a need for automotive engineers, electronics specialists, and assembly language programmers. There is a need for people who understand how a computer system works, and why it is designed the way that it is. In the case of computers, there are two major components to understand: the hardware (electronics), and the software (programs). It is the latter, the software, that we are mainly concerned with in this book. However, we also consider how the hardware operates, from a programmer's point of view, to make clear how it influences the software.

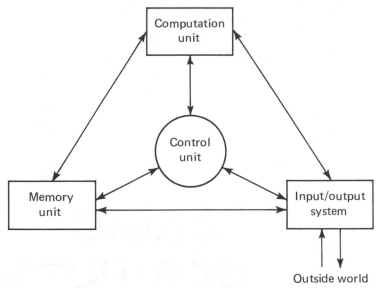

FIGURE 1.1 Basic components of a computer.

This chapter reviews the basic organization of computers, to provide a background for the software considerations of later chapters. You should be familiar with most of this material already, but this review will assure that we all agree on the basic information.

We can understand a computer by studying each of its components separately and by examining how they fit together to form a computing system. The four basic components of a computer are shown in Figure 1.1. These four elements are: (a) *a memory unit*, (b) *a computation unit*, (c) *an input and output system*, and (d) *a control unit*. The arrows between the different components in Figure 1.1 illustrate that information *may* travel freely between any two components of the computer. Some information paths may be missing in some computers. For example, in many systems there is no direct connection between the computation unit and the input/output system.

The memory unit functions as a storage device in the computer, storing data and programs for the computer. The computation unit does the actual computing of the computer—the additions, subtractions, multiplications, divisions, comparisons, and so on. The input/output (I/O) system allows the computer to communicate with the outside world, to accept new data and programs and to deliver the results of the computer's work back to the outside world. The control unit uses the programs stored in the computer's memory to determine the proper sequence of operations to be performed by the computer. The control unit issues commands to the other components of the system directing the memory unit to pass information to and from the computation unit and the I/O system, telling the computation unit what operation to perform and where to put the results, and so forth.

Each of these components is discussed in more detail below. Every computer must have these four basic components, although the organization of a specific computer may structure and utilize them in its own manner. We are therefore presenting *general* organizational features of computers, at the moment. In Chapters 2, 3, and 10 we consider specific computers and their organization.

1.1 THE MEMORY UNIT

A very necessary capability for a computer is the ability to store, and retrieve, information. Memory size and speed are often the limiting factors in the operation of modern computers. For many of today's computing problems it is essential that the computer be able to quickly access large amounts of data stored in memory.

We consider the memory unit from two different points of view. We first consider the *physical* organization of a memory unit. This will give us a foundation from which we can investigate the *logical* organization of the memory unit.

Physical organization of computer memory

For the past twenty years, the *magnetic core* has been the major form of computer memory. More recently, *semiconductor memories* have been developed to the point that most new computer memories are likely to be semiconductor memories rather than core memories. The major deciding factors between the two have been speed and cost. Semiconductor memories are undeniably faster, but until recently have also been more expensive.

Core memories have been used for many years and will undoubtedly continue to be used widely. They have been the main form of computer main memory for almost twenty years. Since semiconductor memories have been trying to replace core memories, they have been built to look very much like core

FIGURE 1.2   A magnetic core (much enlarged).

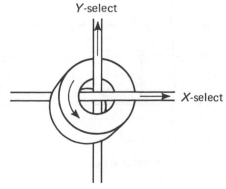

Y-select

X-select

memories, from a functional point of view. Therefore, we present some basic aspects of computer memories in terms of core memories first, and then we consider semiconductor memories.

Core memories

Figure 1.2 is a drawing of a magnetic core. Cores are very small (from 0.02 to 0.05 inches in diameter) doughnut-shaped pieces of metallic ferrite materials which are mainly iron oxide. They have the useful property of being able to be easily magnetized in either of two directions: clockwise or counterclockwise. A core can be magnetized by passing an electrical current along the wire through the hole in the center of the core for a short time. Current in one direction ($+$) will magnetize the core in one direction (clockwise), and current in the opposite direction ($-$) will magnetize the core in the opposite direction (counterclockwise). Once the core has been magnetized in a given direction, it will remain magnetized in that direction for an indefinitely long time (unless it is deliberately remagnetized in the opposite direction, of course). This allows a core to store either of two *states*, which can be arbitrarily assigned the symbols 0 and 1 (or + and −, or A and B, etc.).

FIGURE 1.3   Core plane showing X-select and Y-select wires and sense wire.

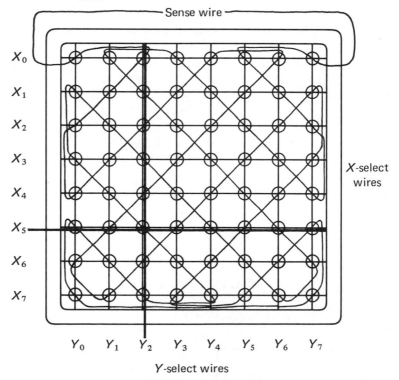

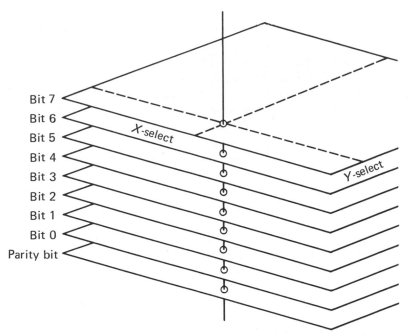

Bit 7
Bit 6
Bit 5
Bit 4
Bit 3
Bit 2
Bit 1
Bit 0
Parity bit

X-select

Y-select

FIGURE 1.4 Core planes stacked to form a memory module; one bit from each core plane forms a word (or byte).

The magnetic core was chosen as the basic storage unit because of several desirable physical properties. It can be easily and quickly switched from one state to the other by passing an electrical current through the core. A positive current will put the core in one state, while a negative current will put the core in the other state. The *switching time* of a core depends again upon the size and composition of the core, but is typically in the range 0.25 to 2.5 microseconds (10^{-6} seconds). The switching time is the time it takes the core to switch from one state to the other.

Individual cores are organized into larger units called *core planes*. A core plane is a two-dimensional rectangular array of cores. Figure 1.3 illustrates the basic design of a core plane. A specific core can be selected by choosing a specific X-select and Y-select wire. For example, in Figure 1.3 the core at the intersection of the X_5 and the Y_2 wires has been "selected."

Cores can be written by setting their magnetic state to one of the two possible states. They can be read by sensing their current state. Core memories have *destructive readout*; that is, reading a core can be accomplished only by disturbing the state of the core. It is necessary to rewrite the information back to the core to preserve it. This defines a *read-write cycle* for the memory. Whenever a core is read, it is immediately rewritten. For a write, the "old" information is read out, and the "new" information is written instead. The *cycle time* for a memory is at least twice its switching time, and typical core memory cycle times are 0.5 to 5 microseconds. Notice that the *access time* (time to read information) is generally only half the cycle time.

Core planes are "stacked," one on top of another, to form *memory modules*. All the cores selected by a specific pair of X and Y wires (one core from each core plane) are used to form a *word* of memory. To read or write a word from memory, one core from each core plane is read and written, simultaneously. The specific core in each core plane is selected by a *memory address register* which specifies the X-select and Y-select wires to be used. The result from a read is put into a *memory data register*. The contents of this register are then used to restore the selected word. In a write operation, the result of the read operation is not used to set the memory data register, but is simply discarded. The word in memory is then written from the memory data register.

The memory address register and the memory data register, along with a single read or write line, are the interface of the memory module to the rest of the computer system (Figure 1.5). To read from memory, another component of the computer system puts the address of the desired word in the memory address register, puts "READ" on the read-write selector, and waits for the first half of the read-write cycle. After this first half, the contents of the addressed word are in the memory data register and may be used. They are also written back into memory to restore the cores of that word. For a write, the contents of the word to

FIGURE 1.5   Memory module appearance to rest of system.

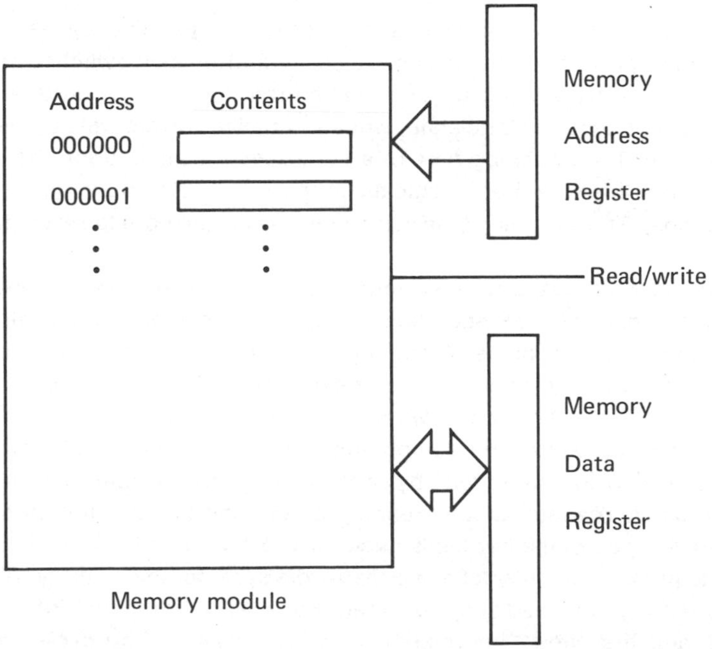

be written are put in the memory data register, and the read-write wire is set to "WRITE". After the entire read-write cycle is over, the addressed word will have its new contents.

Semiconductor memory

The basic element in a core memory is the core. The parameters of the core define the parameters of the memory. Specifically, the size of the core determines its switching time, and switching time defines access time and cycle time. To achieve faster memories, it is necessary to make the cores smaller and smaller. There is a practical limit, given current manufacturing techniques, to the size, and hence, speed, of core memories.

Semiconductor memories use electrical rather than magnetic means to store information. The basic element of a semiconductor memory is often called a *flip-flop*. Like the core, it has two basic states: on/off, or 0/1, or $+/-$, and so on. The basic idea is to replace the magnetic cores of a memory with the electrical flip-flops. However, the functional view of memory is the same. Each memory module has a memory address register, a memory data register, and a read-write function selector. The difference lies in how the information is stored in the memory module. Many different kinds of semiconductor memories have been developed.

Bipolar memories are the fastest memories available, with switching times as low as 100 nanoseconds (10^{-9} seconds). *MOS* (metallic-oxide semiconductor) memories are slower (500 to 1000 nanoseconds) but cheaper. These memories are made on "chips" which correspond roughly to a core plane. Memory modules are constructed by placing a number of chips on a memory board.

One major problem with semiconductor memories is the *volatility* of the stored information. In core memories, information is stored magnetically, while semiconductor memories store information electrically. If the power to a semiconductor memory is turned off, the contents of the memory are lost. This means that power is never intentionally turned off, unless all useful information has been stored elsewhere. However, if power is cut off due to an accident, a power failure, or a "brown-out," the consequences can be a major catastrophe. A temporary alternate power supply (such as a battery) can solve this problem, and most systems now have this protection.

Another form of this same volatility exhibits itself in some semiconductor memories. *Static* memories use transistor-like memory elements which store information by the "on" or "off" state of the transistor. *Dynamic* memories store information by the presence or absence of an electrical charge on a capacitor. The problem is that the electrical charge will leak off over time, and so dynamic memories must be *refreshed* at regular intervals. Refreshing a memory requires reading every word and writing it back in place. Special circuitry is used to constantly refresh a dynamic memory.

Almost the opposite of a dynamic memory is a *read-only memory* (ROM). Read-only memories are very static. In fact, as their name implies, they cannot be written (except maybe the first time, and even that is often difficult). Read-only memories are used for special functions; information is stored once and never changed. For example, read-only memories are often used to store bootstrap loaders (Chapter 7) and interpreters (Chapter 9), programs which are supplied with the computer and are not meant to ever be changed. Most hand calculators are small computers with a special program, stored in ROM, which is executed over and over.

Some read-only memories can in fact be rewritten, but while access time for reading may be only 100 nanoseconds, writing may take several microseconds. These memories are called programmable read-only memories (PROMs) and electrically programmable read-only memories (EPROMS), among others.

Even more advanced forms of semiconductor memories which may be used in the near future include magnetic bubbles and charge-coupled devices (CCDs). The important fact about all of these forms of memory, however, is that despite their various types of physical construction, their interface to the rest of the computer system is the same: an address register, a data register, and a read-write signal. Memory modules can be constructed in many different ways and with many different materials: cores, semiconductors, thin magnetic films, magnetic bubbles, and so on. However, because of the uniform and simple interface to the rest of the computing system, we need not be overly concerned with the physical organization of the memory unit. We need only consider its logical organization.

Logical organization of computer memory

All (current) computer memories are composed of basic units which can be in either of two possible states. By arbitrarily assigning a label to each of these two states, we can store information in these memory devices. Traditionally, we assign the label 0 to one of these states and 1 to the other state. The actual assignment is important only to the computer hardware designers and builders. We do not care if a 0 is assigned to a clockwise magnetized core and 1 to a counterclockwise magnetized core, or vice-versa. What we do want is that if we say to write a 1 into a specific cell, then a subsequent read of that cell returns a 1, and if we write a 0, we will then read a 0. We can then consider memory to store 0s and 1s and may ignore how they are physically stored.

Each 0 or 1 is called a *binary digit*, or a *bit*. Each bit can be either a 0 or a 1. A *word* is a fixed number of bits. The number of bits per word varies from computer to computer. Some small computers have only 8 bits per word, while others have as many as 64 bits per word. Typical numbers of bits per word are 12, 16, 18, 24, 32, 36, 48, and 60, with 16 and 32 being the most common. Each word of memory has an *address*. The address of a word is the *bit pattern* which must be put into the memory address register in order to select that word in the memory module. In general, every possible bit pattern in the memory address register will select a different word in memory. Thus, the maximum size of the

TABLE 1.1　Typical Memory Sizes
and Address Sizes

Number of bits in the memory address register	Memory size (in words)
12	4,096
15	32,768
16	65,536
18	262,144
20	1,048,576
24	16,777,216
n	2^n

memory unit (number of different words) depends upon the size of the memory address register (number of bits).

If there are n bits in the memory address register, how many words can there be in memory? With only one bit ($n = 1$), there are only two possible addresses: 0 and 1. With two bits, there are four possible addresses: 00, 01, 10, and 11. If we have three bits, there are eight possible addresses: 000, 001, 010, 011, 100, 101, 110, and 111. In general, every additional bit in the memory address register doubles the number of possible addresses, so with n bits there are 2^n possible addresses. Table 1.1 gives some typical memory sizes and the number of bits in the memory address register.

Consider a computer with a 32-bit word and a 16-bit address. This computer could have up to 65,536 different 32-bit words. The purchaser of the computer may not have been able to afford to buy all 65,536 words, however. Memory modules are generally made in sizes of 4096, 8192, 16,384 or 32,768 words. Since $2^{10} = 1024$ is almost 1000, these are often referred to as 4K, 8K, 16K, or 32K memories. (The K stands for *kilo*, meaning 1000. The next size of memory, containing 65,536 words, is referred to as either 64K or 65K.) To get a larger memory, several modules are purchased and combined to form the memory unit. For example, a 64K memory may be made up of four 16K memory modules. The address size for a specific computer only places an upper limit on the amount of memory which can be attached to the computer.

An n-bit word can be drawn as,

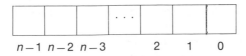

$$n-1 \quad n-2 \quad n-3 \qquad 2 \quad 1 \quad 0$$

To be able to refer to specific bits, we number them. Different people number their bits differently. Some number from left to right, others from right to left. Some number their bits from 0 to $n - 1$, others from 1 to n. We will number our bits from 0 to $n - 1$ from right to left. This will be convenient in Section 1.2 when we discuss number systems. The right-hand bits are called the *low-order* bits, while the left-hand bits are called *high-order* bits.

Many computers consider their words to be composed of *bytes*. A byte is a part of a word composed of a fixed number (usually 6 or 8) of bits. A 32-bit word could be composed of four 8-bit bytes. These would be bits 0–7, 8–15, 16–23, and 24–31. The usefulness of byte-sized quantities will become apparent in Section 1.3, when we discuss I/O and character codes.

In addition to the words of the memory unit, a computer will probably have a small number of high-speed *registers*. These are generally either the same size as a word of memory or the size of an address. Most registers are referred to by a name, rather than an address. For example, the memory address register might be called the MAR, and the memory data register the MDR. Typical other registers may include an accumulator (A register) of the computation unit, and the program counter (P register) of the control unit. These registers provide memory for the computer, but they are used for special purposes.

Memory for a computer consists of a large number of fixed-length words. Each word is composed of a fixed number of bits. Words can be stored at specific locations in the memory unit and later read from that location. Each location in memory is one word and has its own unique address. A machine with n-bit addresses can have up to 2^n different memory locations.

EXERCISES

   a.   Name two forms of physical memory. How do they differ?

   b.   What is the function of the memory address register? What is the function of the memory data register?

   c.   If we have 12-bit addresses, how much memory can the computer address? How much with 15-bit addresses? With 24-bit addresses?

   d.   Why is the cycle time of a memory at least twice the switching time? Show the relationship between cycle time, switching time, and access time.

   e.   How many different bit patterns can be represented in an n-bit word?

   f.   How many individual bits are needed to build a memory module of 4K of 16-bit words? If the memory module costs $3,000, what is the cost per bit?

   g.   The obvious improvement upon a memory module with two-state storage units would be a three-state storage unit. This would allow information to be coded in ternary. Each ternary digit (trit) could represent three values (0, 1, 2). How many different values can be stored in an n-trit word? How many different words can be addressed by an n-trit address?

   h.   Consider a computer system with two memory modules, A and B, each with 4096 words. The total amount of memory is thus 8192 words, and requires a 13-bit address. If half the words are in module A and half the words are in module B, then 1 bit is needed to determine which memory module has a specific word, and the remaining 12 bits address one of the words within the selected module. If the high-order bit of the address is used to select module A or module B, which addresses are in which module? Which words are in which module if the low-order bit is used to select the module?

i.   What is the difference between dynamic and static semiconductor memory?

j.   Is a read-only memory volatile? Why?

1.2 THE COMPUTATION UNIT

The computation unit contains the electronic circuitry which manipulates the data in the computer. It is here that numbers are added, subtracted, multiplied, divided, and compared. The computation unit is commonly called the *arithmetic and logic unit* (ALU).

Since the main function of the computation unit is to manipulate numbers, the design of the computation unit is determined mainly by the way in which numbers are represented within the computer. Once the scheme for representing numbers has been decided upon, the construction of the computation unit is an exercise in electronic switching theory.

The representation of numbers

Mathematicians have emphasized that a number is a *concept*. The concept of a specific number can be *represented* by a *numeral*. A numeral is simply a convenient means of recording and manipulating numbers. The specific manner in which numbers are represented has varied from culture to culture and from time to time. Early representations of numbers by piles of sticks gave way to making marks in an organized manner (I, II, III, IIII, IIIII, . . .). This method in turn eventually was replaced by Roman numerals (I, II, III, IV, V, . . .) and finally by Arabic numerals (1, 2, 3, 4, 5, . . .). Notice that we have Roman *numerals* and Arabic *numerals*, not Roman numbers or Arabic numbers. The symbols which are used to represent numbers are called *digits*.

The choice of a number system depends on many things. One important factor is the *convenience* of expressing and operating on the numerals. Another important idea is the *expressive power* of the system (Roman numerals, for example, have no representation for zero, or for fractions). A third determining factor is *convention*. A representation of a number is used both to remember numbers and to communicate them. In order for the communication to succeed, all parties must agree on how numbers are to be represented.

Computers, of course, have only two symbols which can be used as digits. These two digits are the 0 and the 1 symbols which can be stored in the com-

puter's memory unit. We are limited to representing our numbers only as combinations of these symbols. Remember that with n bits we can represent 2^n different bit patterns. Each of these bit patterns can be used to represent a different
number. (If we were to use more than one bit pattern to represent a number, or
one bit pattern to represent more than one number, using the numbers might be
more difficult.)

The correspondence between numbers and bit patterns can be quite arbitrary. For example, to represent the eight numbers 0, 1, . . ., 7, we could use

Number	Bit pattern
0	110
1	101
2	001
3	100
4	010
5	111
6	011
7	000

or any other pairing of numbers with bit patterns. However, we should realize that
if we assign bit patterns to numbers with no underlying plan, the circuitry of the
computation unit to perform operations on our numerals may become very, very
complex (and expensive).

We are defining a *mapping*, P, from bit patterns to numbers. The computation unit must be designed so that the mapping, P, is an *isomorphism* under the
operations of addition, subtraction, multiplication, and division, and under rela-
tions such as "less than", "equal to", and "greater than". This means that if a
bit pattern X and a bit pattern Y are presented to the computation unit for
addition and the bit pattern Z is the result, then we want $P(X) + P(Y) = P(Z)$.
That is, the number $P(Z)$, represented by the bit pattern Z, should be the sum of
the number $P(X)$, represented by the bit pattern X, and the number $P(Y)$, represented by the bit pattern Y.

This requirement, plus the desire to keep the cost of the computer down, has
resulted in almost all computers representing their numbers in a *positional
notation*. Everyone should be familiar with *positional* (or *place*) *notation* from our
familiar decimal (base 10) number system. In a positional notation, the value of a
digit depends upon its place in the numeral. For example, the digit 2 has different
values in the three numbers 274, 126, and 592, meaning two hundreds, two tens,
and two units, respectively.

In a binary (base 2) place notation, the concepts are the same, but each
place can have only two possible digits, 0 or 1, rather than ten (0 through 9) as
in the decimal (base 10) place notation. Because of this, the value of the places
increases more slowly than with the decimal system. Each place is worth only

twice the value of the place to its right, rather than ten times the value as in the decimal system. The rightmost place represents the number of units; the next rightmost, the number of twos; the next, the number of fours; and so forth. Counting in the binary positional number system proceeds

0,	1,	10,	11,	100,	101,	110,	111,	1000,	1001,	. . .
0,	1,	2,	3,	4	5,	6,	7,	8,	9,	. . .

The decimal system

We stopped at 9 above, because at 10 two major methods of representing numbers in a computer show their differences. One method, the binary system (discussed in the following section), continues as above. The other system, the decimal system uses the above bit patterns to represent the digits from 0 to 9, and then uses these digits to represent all other numbers. The decimal system represents numbers in the familiar decimal place system, replacing the digits 0 through 9 with 0000, 0001, 0010, 0011, 0100, 0101, 0110, 0111, 1000, 1001, respectively. This is known as a *binary coded decimal* (BCD) representation. For example, the numbers 314,159 and 271,823 are represented in BCD by

$$314,159_{10} = 0011 \quad 0001 \quad 0100 \quad 0001 \quad 0101 \quad 1001_{BCD}$$
$$271,823_{10} = 0010 \quad 0111 \quad 0001 \quad 1000 \quad 0010 \quad 0011_{BCD}$$

The subscripts indicate what kind of representation scheme is being used. The 10 means standard base 10 positional notation; BCD means a binary coded decimal representation. The blanks between digits in the BCD representation would not be stored, but are only put in to make the number easier to understand.

To add these numbers, we add each digit of the addend to the corresponding digit of the augend to give the sum digit. Each digit is represented in binary, so binary arithmetic is used. For binary addition, the addition table is

$0 + 0 = 0$
$1 + 0 = 1$
$0 + 1 = 1$
$1 + 1 = 0$ with a *carry* into the next higher place

Thus, adding the two numbers 314,159 (base 10) and 271,823 (base 10) is

```
  0011 0001 0100 0001 0101 1001 (BCD)
+ 0010 0111 0001 1000 0010 0011 (BCD)
─────────────────────────────────────
  0101 1000 0101 1001 0111 1100 (BCD)
```

Notice that in the low-order digit we have added 1001 (9) and 0011 (3) to yield a sum digit of 1100. This is the binary equivalent of 12 ($1 \times 8 + 1 \times 4 + 0 \times 2 +$

0×1), but it is not a decimal digit. To correct this, we must subtract 10 and add a carry into the next higher place to give

0101	1000	0101	1001	0111	1100	(BCD)
				+0001	−1010	(correction)
0101	1000	0101	1001	1000	0010	(BCD)

This is then the number 585,982 (base 10). Checking, we see that

$$\begin{array}{r} 314,159 \\ +\ 271,823 \\ \hline 585,982 \end{array}$$

which agrees.

The decimal number system has been used in many computers, particularly the earlier machines. It has several distinct advantages over competing number systems. Its greatest advantage is its similarity to the representation of numbers used by most people. Numbers can be easily read into the machine and output again. Its major disadvantages tend to outweigh these considerations, however. Compared to the binary number systems which we discuss next, the computation unit circuitry for addition, and so forth, is much more complicated (and hence more expensive). Furthermore, it uses only 10 of the 16 possible bit patterns in 4 bits ($2^4 = 16$), so that it wastes memory. To represent the numbers from 0 to 99,999,999 would take 32 bits (4 bits per digit times 8 digits) in BCD, while only 27 bits provide many more than 100,000,000 different bit patterns ($2^{27} = 134,217,728$). At $.05 per bit, this means each word costs ($.05 per bit times 5 bits) $.25 more for decimal than for binary, and a memory module of 4096 words would cost an extra thousand dollars.

For certain applications, however, these considerations are not as important. An electronic calculator, for example, normally uses a decimal number representation scheme, since a calculator uses very little memory, but must be compatible with human operators. Also, as the price of computer memory and logic hardware decreases, so will the cost disadvantage of decimal machines.

The binary number system

In the binary number system, numbers are represented by a sequence of *binary digits* (bits). Each bit has a value determined by its position in the number. The sequence of bits

$$X_n X_{n-1} \cdots X_2 X_1 X_0 \qquad 0 \le X_i \le 1$$

represents the number

$$X_0 + 2X_1 + 4X_2 + 8X_3 + \cdots + 2^{n-1} X_{n-1} + 2^n X_n$$

The binary number system assigns the following bit patterns to represent the corresponding numbers.

Binary number	Decimal number
0	0
1	1
10	2
11	3
100	4
101	5
110	6
111	7
1000	8
1001	9
1010	10
1011	11
1100	12
1101	13
1110	14
1111	15
10000	16
10001	17
10010	18
. . .	. . .

The largest number which can be represented in n bits is 111 . . . 111 (n bits of 1) which is

$$1 + 2 + 4 + \cdots + 2^{n-1} = 2^n - 1$$

In a word of n bits, each bit pattern corresponds to one of the numbers 0 to $2^n - 1$, thus allowing the representation of 2^n different numbers.

Binary arithmetic is quite simple. The addition table is simply

$0 + 0 = 0$
$0 + 1 = 1$
$1 + 0 = 1$
$1 + 1 = 0$ with a carry of 1

Adding two binary numbers is simply

```
  1 1 1 1   1 1 1 1       1         carries
  0 1 1 0 1 0 1 1 1 1 0 0 0 1 0 1   addend
+ 0 0 0 1 1 0 0 1 0 1 0 1 0 1 0 0   augend
  1 0 0 0 0 1 0 1 0 0 0 1 1 0 0 1   sum
```

Notice how the carries may *propagate*, with one carry causing the sum in the next column to result in a carry also. If we change bit 11 of the addend from a one to a zero, for example, the resulting sum is

```
                    1  1  1  1              1              carries
          0  1  1  0  0  0  1  1  1  1  0  0  0  1  0  1   addend
      +   0  0  0  1  1  0  0  1  0  1  0  1  0  1  0  0   augend
      ─────────────────────────────────────────────────
          0  1  1  1  1  1  0  1  0  0  0  1  1  0  0  1   sum
```

The value of the high-order bit of a sum depends upon the value of all lower-order bits. Since the value of the high-order bit is greatest, it is called the *most significant bit*. The low-order bit is the *least significant bit*.

The hardware to build a computational unit for a binary machine is quite simple and easy to design and build. The major disadvantage with binary systems is their inconvenience and unfamiliarity to humans (Quick! Is 010101110010 [base 2] greater or less than 1394 [base 10]?). The large number of symbols (zeros and ones) which must be used to represent even "small" numbers is also cumbersome. Hence, very few programmers prefer to work in binary. But the computer *must* work completely in binary. It has no choice, due to the binary nature of computer hardware. What is needed is a quick and easy way to convert between binary and decimal. Unfortunately, there is no quick and easy conversion algorithm between these two bases.

Conversions between bases

In an arbitrary base B ($B > 0$) a sequence of digits

$$X_n X_{n-1} \cdots X_2 X_1 X_0 \qquad (0 \le X_i < B)$$

represents the number

$$X_0 + B \times X_1 + B^2 \times X_2 + \cdots + B^{n-1} \times X_{n-1} + B^n \times X_n$$

Now if we wish to express the number in another base, A, we can do it in either of two ways, depending upon whether we want to use the arithmetic of base A or of base B. For example, if we wish to convert a number from binary (base $B = 2$) to decimal (base $A = 10$), we want to use decimal arithmetic (base A). If we wish to convert from decimal (base $B = 10$) to binary (base $A = 2$), we want to use decimal arithmetic (base B). The computer, on the other hand, always wants to use binary arithmetic. Thus, we need two different algorithms for conversion.

To convert from binary to decimal, we use the equation given above to calculate the decimal representation of the binary number. For example,

$$
\begin{aligned}
0110101001 \text{ (base 2)} &= 0 \times 2^9 + 1 \times 2^8 + 1 \times 2^7 + 0 \times 2^6 + 1 \times 2^5 \\
&\quad + 0 \times 2^4 + 1 \times 2^3 + 0 \times 2^2 + 0 \times 2^1 + 1 \times 2^0 \\
&= 0 \times 512 + 1 \times 256 + 1 \times 128 + 0 \times 64 + 1 \times 32 \\
&\quad + 0 \times 16 + 1 \times 8 + 0 \times 4 + 0 \times 2 + 1 \times 1 \\
&= 256 + 128 + 32 + 8 + 1 \\
&= 433 \text{ (base 10)} \\
1000101100 \text{ (base 2)} &= 1 \times 2^9 + 1 \times 2^5 + 1 \times 2^3 + 1 \times 2^2 \\
&= 512 + 32 + 8 + 4 \\
&= 556 \text{ (base 10)}
\end{aligned}
$$

TABLE 1.2 Powers of Two

2^n	n	2^n	n
1	0	8192	13
2	1	16,384	14
4	2	32,768	15
8	3	65,536	16
16	4	131,072	17
32	5	262,144	18
64	6	524,288	19
128	7	1,048,576	20
256	8	2,097,152	21
512	9	4,194,304	22
1024	10	8,388,608	23
2048	11	16,777,216	24
4096	12	33,554,432	25

For large numbers, a table of powers of two (such as Table 1.2) is obviously useful. You should, of course, memorize the small powers of two, up to about 2^{10} or 2^{11}.

To convert from decimal to binary requires a different approach. For a number x, we have the equation

$$x = X_0 + 2X_1 + 4X_2 + 8X_3 + \ldots + 2^n X_n$$

where $2^{n+1} > x$, and we wish to determine the values of the bits

$$X_n X_{n-1} \ldots X_3 X_2 X_1 X_0$$

which are the binary representation of the number x. It is convenient to rewrite this equation as

$$x = X_0 + 2(X_1 + 2(X_2 + \ldots + 2(X_{n-2} + 2(X_{n-1} + 2X_n)) \ldots))$$

From this we notice that

1. X_0 is 1 if x is odd; X_0 is 0 if x is even.
2. X_0 is the remainder resulting from dividing x by 2.
3. The integer part of $x/2$ specifies the values of the remaining bits.

From this we can now derive the values of the bits in the binary representation of x by repeated division by 2. The remainder of the ith division is the ith bit. For example, 47,132 (base 10) is converted to binary by

$$47132 \div 2 = 23566 \quad \text{remainder is } 0$$
$$23566 \div 2 = 11783 \quad \text{remainder is } 0$$
$$11783 \div 2 = 5891 \quad \text{remainder is } 1$$
$$5891 \div 2 = 2945 \quad \text{remainder is } 1$$

$$2945 \div 2 = 1472 \quad \text{remainder is 1}$$
$$1472 \div 2 = 736 \quad \text{remainder is 0}$$
$$736 \div 2 = 368 \quad \text{remainder is 0}$$
$$368 \div 2 = 184 \quad \text{remainder is 0}$$
$$184 \div 2 = 92 \quad \text{remainder is 0}$$
$$92 \div 2 = 46 \quad \text{remainder is 0}$$
$$46 \div 2 = 23 \quad \text{remainder is 0}$$
$$23 \div 2 = 11 \quad \text{remainder is 1}$$
$$11 \div 2 = 5 \quad \text{remainder is 1}$$
$$5 \div 2 = 2 \quad \text{remainder is 1}$$
$$2 \div 2 = 1 \quad \text{remainder is 0}$$
$$1 \div 2 = 0 \quad \text{remainder is 1}$$

Reading up from the bottom, 47,132 (base 10) = 1011100000011100 (base 2).

A different algorithm can be used when a table of the powers of two can be used. Suppose we want to convert 747 (base 10) to binary. Looking in the table, we see that the first power of two that is less than 747 is 512 (= 2^9). Since $747 - 512 = 235$

$$747 \text{ (base 10)} = 512 + 235$$
$$= 512 + 128 + 107$$
$$= 512 + 128 + 64 + 43$$
$$= 512 + 128 + 64 + 32 + 11$$
$$= 512 + 128 + 64 + 32 + 8 + 3$$
$$= 512 + 128 + 64 + 32 + 8 + 2 + 1$$
$$= 2^9 + 2^7 + 2^6 + 2^5 + 2^3 + 2^1 + 2^0$$
$$= 1011101011 \text{ (base 2)}$$

The octal and hexadecimal number systems

As we said earlier, there is no conversion method between binary and decimal that is so quick and simple that it can be done in your head. A simple observation leads, however, to two reasonable alternatives to using binary. Consider the expansion of the 12-bit binary number

$$x = X_{11}X_{10}X_9X_8 \ldots X_2X_1X_0$$
$$x = X_0 + 2X_1 + 4X_2 + 8X_3 + 16X_4 + 32X_5 + 64X_6 + 128X_7$$
$$+ 256X_8 + 512X_9 + 1024X_{10} + 2048X_{11} \hspace{2cm} [1]$$
$$= (X_0 + 2X_1 + 4X_2) + 8(X_3 + 2X_4 + 4X_5)$$
$$+ 8^2(X_6 + 2X_7 + 4X_8) + 8^3(X_9 + 2X_{10} + 4X_{11}) \hspace{1cm} [2]$$
$$= (X_0 + 2X_1 + 4X_2 + 8X_3) + 16(X_4 + 2X_5 + 4X_6 + 8X_7)$$
$$+ 16^2(X_8 + 2X_9 + 4X_{10} + 8X_{11}) \hspace{2cm} [3]$$

Notice that in equation [2] each of the parenthesized quantities represents a value from 0 to 7, an *octal digit* (base 8). The equation is of the form

$$x = Y_0 + 8Y_1 + 8^2Y_2 + 8^3Y_3$$

where the parenthesized groups of bits define the octal digits for the representation of the number x in base 8 (octal). Similarly, equation [3] is of the form

$$x = Z_0 + 16Z_1 + 16^2Z_2$$

and each Z_i is in the range 0 to 15, a *hexadecimal digit* (base 16).

As a direct result of the fact that $8 = 2^3$ and $16 = 2^4$, we can easily convert between binary and octal or binary and hexadecimal. To convert a binary number to octal, start at the right-hand side (low-order bits) and group the bits, three bits per group. Add leading zeros as necessary to make the number of bits a multiple of three. To convert to hexadecimal, group four bits per group, with leading zeros as necessary to make the total number of bits a multiple of four. Then convert each group as follows.

Binary	Octal	Binary	Octal
000	0	100	4
001	1	101	5
010	2	110	6
011	3	111	7

Binary	Hexadecimal	Binary	Hexadecimal
0000	0	1000	8
0001	1	1001	9
0010	2	1010	A (10)
0011	3	1011	B (11)
0100	4	1100	C (12)
0101	5	1101	D (13)
0110	6	1110	E (14)
0111	7	1111	F (15)

Notice that we use the first six letters of the alphabet in order to have 16 different possible hexadecimal digits, since there are only 10 decimal digits and we need 16 for hexadecimal.

As an example of the conversion from octal to binary, consider

```
1 1 1   0 0 0   1 1 0   0 1 0   1 0 0   1 1 0   (base 2)
   7       0       6       2       4       6     (base 8)
```

```
0 1 1   1 1 0   0 1 1   0 1 0   1 1 1   0 0 1   0 1 0   (base 2)
   3       6       3       2       7       1       2    (base 8)
```

In this last case, we have added a leading zero in order to convert from binary to octal. For conversion to hexadecimal we have,

```
0 0 1 1   1 0 0 0   1 1 0 0   1 0 1 0   0 1 1 0   (base 2)
    3         8         C         A         6      (base 16)
```

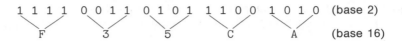

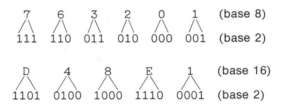

Conversion from hexadecimal to binary or from octal to binary is simply the reverse of the above transformation.

Because these conversions can be done easily and quickly, bit patterns are almost never given in binary, but in octal or hexadecimal. Addition in these systems is basically the same as in base 10, except that carries occur whenever a sum exceeds 8 (in octal) or 16 (in hexadecimal).

The choice between using octal or hexadecimal is largely a matter of personal taste. There are some objective measures which can be used to compare them. Hexadecimal obviously will use fewer characters to represent a bit string. For a 32-bit number, for example, only 8 hexadecimal digits are needed, while 11 octal digits would be necessary. Machine word lengths (the number of bits per word) tend to be powers of 2, and 4 bits per hexadecimal digit gives an integral number of hexadecimal digits per word, in these cases. Thus, for machines with word lengths of 12, 16, 24, 32, 48, 60, or 64 bits, hexadecimal is a convenient choice.

Octal, on the other hand, has the advantage of being "closer" to base ten than hexadecimal. Machines with 12, 18, 24, 36, 48, or 60 bits per word have an integral number of octal digits per word. Only eight conversions between octal and binary need to be memorized (as opposed to 16 for hexadecimal). Also, all octal digits are decimal digits, so octal numbers *look* like numbers (not like half-word, half-number hybrids). Still, this means octal can be mistaken for decimal, while a hexadecimal number is more likely to have a digit which is not a decimal digit.

Most decisions to use either octal or hexadecimal as the primary way to represent binary numbers are determined by personal bias. We use octal, in this text.

One advantage of octal mentioned above was that it was "close" to base 10. This can be very useful when quick order-of-magnitude type comparisons are needed with binary numbers and decimal numbers. Table 1.3 gives a short table of octal numbers and their decimal equivalents. Notice that until about 1000 (octal) = 512 (base 10), octal numbers and decimal numbers are very similar in magnitude. Even with 18-bit numbers, octal numbers are only about 4 times

TABLE 1.3 A Table of Octal Numbers and Their
Decimal Equivalents

Octal	Decimal	Octal	Decimal
10	8	1 000	512
40	32	4 000	2 048
100	64	10 000	4 096
200	128	100 000	32 768
400	256	1 000 000	262 144

smaller than they should be. Hence, a *very* crude way to interpret a binary
number is to convert it to octal, and then treat that octal number as a decimal
number.

Of course, this crude conversion gives only order-of-magnitude results. To
know exactly the value of an octal number, we need to follow the same multiplicative algorithm which we saw earlier for base 2, but now we are working with
base 8, so the multiplicative factor is eight. For example

$$1742 \text{ (octal)} = 1 \times 8^3 + 7 \times 8^2 + 4 \times 8 + 2 \times 1$$
$$= 512 + 448 + 32 + 2$$
$$= 994 \text{ (base 10)}$$

$$40653 \text{ (octal)} = 4 \times 8^4 + 0 \times 8^3 + 6 \times 8^2 + 5 \times 8 + 3 \times 1$$
$$= 16384 + 0 + 384 + 40 + 3$$
$$= 16811 \text{ (base 10)}$$

This can be done quite easily by the use of a table such as Table 1.4. This table
gives, for each octal digit, the value of that digit for each of the places in a
six-digit octal number. This also illustrates that the value of a given digit depends
upon which position in the number it occupies. To utilize the table for the octal

TABLE 1.4 Table of the Value of an Octal Digit
in a Given Position

	Digit position					
Digit	6	5	4	3	2	1
0	0	0	0	0	0	0
1	32 768	4 096	512	64	8	1
2	65 536	8 192	1 024	128	16	2
3	98 304	12 288	1 536	192	24	3
4	131 072	16 384	2 048	256	32	4
5	163 840	20 480	2 560	320	40	5
6	196 608	24 576	3 072	384	48	6
7	229 376	28 672	3 584	448	56	7

number 574, for example, we look up the entry for digit 5, place 3 (320), and add to that the value for digit 7, place 2 (56), and add to that the value of digit 4, place 1 (4), to give 574 (octal) = 320 + 56 + 4 = 380 (base 10).

A different method of conversion is to express the original equation of a conversion as

$$x = X_0 + BX_1 + B^2X_2 + B^3X_3 + \ldots + B^nX_n$$
$$= X_0 + B(X_1 + B(X_2 + B(X_3 + \ldots + BX_n \ldots)))$$

Using this form of the conversion equation, we can convert 3756 (octal) to decimal by

$$3756 \text{ (octal)} = 6 + 8(5 + 8(7 + 8 \cdot 3))$$
$$= 6 + 8(5 + 8 \cdot 31)$$
$$= 6 + 8 \times 253$$
$$= 2030 \text{ (base 10)}$$

To convert back from decimal to octal, we repeatedly divide the decimal number by 8. The remainder at each step is the octal digit, with low-order digits produced first. Thus, converting 2030 (base 10) to octal gives

$$2030 \div 8 = 253, \quad \text{remainder} = 6$$
$$253 \div 8 = 31, \quad \text{remainder} = 5$$
$$31 \div 8 = 3, \quad \text{remainder} = 7$$
$$3 \div 8 = 0, \quad \text{remainder} = 3$$

and so 2030 (base 10) = 3756 (octal).

Similar algorithms can be used to convert between decimal and hexadecimal.

Computer addition

Now that we are familiar with the use of the different number systems, how do we use this information to represent numbers in the computer? A number is represented by setting the bits in a word of the computer memory to the binary representation of the number. To perform arithmetic operations on two numbers (for example, to add them), the words containing the binary representation of the two numbers are read from memory, or registers, and copied to the computation unit. The computation unit is instructed (by the control unit) as to which operation is to be performed, and when the operation is complete the result is stored back in memory or a register.

The different operations which the computation unit may be asked to do vary from computer to computer, but almost every computer can at least add two numbers. Like reading or writing information in memory, the operations done by the computation unit take time. Generally the computation unit operates somewhat faster than the memory cycle time. The time to do an addition (the *add time*) varies from machine to machine due to different hardware designs and compo-nents, and also due to different word lengths. Longer words mean longer waiting for carries to propagate. Add times typically are from 0.3 to 2 microseconds.

Addition of two n-bit words may produce a number requiring $n + 1$ bits for its representation. This is too large to fit into one computer word and is known as *overflow*. For example, if we were working with a 6-bit computer word, we could represent the numbers from 000000 (base 2) (00 (octal) = 0 (base 10)) up to 111111 (base 2) (77 (octal) = 63 (base 10)). If we add 010110 (base 2) (26 (octal)) to 100101 (base 2) (45 (octal)), we have a sum of

```
0 1 0 1 1 0   (26 (octal))
1 0 0 1 0 1   (45 (octal))
1 1 1 0 1 1   (73 (octal))
```

which is fine, but if we add 101010 (base 2) (52 (octal)) to 110001 (base 2) (61 (octal))

```
1 0 1 0 1 0    (52 (octal))
1 1 0 0 0 1    (61 (octal))
1 0 1 1 0 1 1  (133 (octal))
```

and we have a carry into a seventh bit position, which does not exist in a six-bit word. This is overflow and means that the result of the addition is too large to fit into one computer word. Since only a fixed number of bits are available in a word, we can only represent a fixed range of numbers. With n bits, we can represent all (and *only*) the integers from 0 to 2^{n-1}.

Subtraction of binary numbers is similar to addition, except that we may generate a "borrow" of 1 from the next higher place rather than a "carry". For example

```
    10          (borrows)
  1 0 0 1 1 1   (47 (octal))
− 0 1 0 1 0 1   (25 (octal))
  0 1 0 0 1 0   (22 (octal))
```

In this example, a borrow occurred from the high-order bit to the next highest order bit (bit 5 to bit 4).

Representation of negative numbers

The possibility of subtraction brings up the problem of the representation of *negative numbers.* So far we have considered only the problem of representing positive numbers, and have seen that there are at least two methods of representation: decimal and binary. Negative numbers may also be stored and manipulated in the computer as well. Several methods of representing negative numbers, in addition to positive numbers, are used in computers. We consider here four representation schemes

1. Sign and magnitude
2. Ones' complement
3. Two's complement
4. Biased, or excess, notation

Sign and magnitude

In the early designs of computers the representation of numbers was in BCD because the algorithms for decimal arithmetic were familiar to the designers, builders, and users of the computer. For much the same reasons, a *sign and magnitude* representation of negative numbers was used. To represent positive and negative numbers, all we need is a sign ($+$ or $-$) and the absolute value of the number (its magnitude). Thus, positive 5 is represented by $+5$ and negative 5 by -5. The same scheme can be used in binary, octal, decimal, or any other number system. Positive 100110 (base 2) is represented by +100110 (base 2) and negative 100110 (base 2) is represented by –100110 (base 2). The sign can be represented by encoding a $+$ as a 0 and a $-$ as a 1 and attaching this *sign bit* to the front of the word. The decision to make a $+$ a 0 bit, and $-$ a 1 bit is arbitrary, but was done to represent zero by 00 . . . 000. An n-bit word has a high-order sign bit and $n - 1$ bits to represent the magnitude of the number. The range of numbers which can be represented is

$$-2^{n-1} + 1, \cdots, 0, \cdots, 2^{n-1} - 1$$

For $n = 16$, this is $-32,767$ (base 10) to $+32,767$ (base 10); for $n = 32$, from $-4,294,967,295$ (base 10) to $+4,294,967,295$ (base 10).

Notice that this method of specifying negative numbers can also be used for a BCD representation of numbers. To represent the numbers from $-999,999,999$ (base 10) to $+999,999,999$ (base 10), we would use a 1-bit sign bit and 9 BCD digits of 4 bits each, so our word length would be 37 bits.

A quirk of sign and magnitude for binary numbers is the existence of 100...000 as a signed number. The sign bit is 1, so the number has a negative sign, but the magnitude is zero. This number is known as *minus zero*, (-0), or *negative zero*, and is the negative of *positive zero*.

The major problem with sign and magnitude notation, however, is the complexity of the computational unit necessary to operate on sign and magnitude numbers. If we wish to add two numbers, we must first examine their signs, and if they differ, subtract one from the other rather than adding. This means we must have both adding and subtracting devices (adders and subtracters) in our computation unit. These units are very similar in design, so this may double the cost of the computation unit, over those with only adders. If we could find an easy way to simply add two numbers, rather than having to subtract for different signs, and a way to find the negative of a number, then we could utilize the fact that $x - y = x + (-y)$ and dispense with the subtracter (or the adder, since $x + y = x - (-y)$).

Ones' complement notation

Ones' complement notation was devised to make the adding of two numbers with different signs the same as for two numbers with the same sign. The *complement* of a binary number is the number which results from changing all 0s to 1s and all 1s to 0s in the original number. For example, in a 12-bit machine, the complement of 0110100111010011 is 1001011000101100, and the complement of 1110111101011011 is 0001000010100100. The complement of 00...000 is 11...111 and the complement of 11...111 is 00...000. In octal, the complement of each octal digit is

| | | Complement | |
Octal	Binary	Binary	Octal
0	000	111	7
1	001	110	6
2	010	101	5
3	011	100	4
4	100	011	3
5	101	010	2
6	110	001	1
7	111	000	0

The complement of a number is very easy to create. Also notice that the complement of the complement of a number is the original number, a very important property for a method of representing negatives. The ones' complement notation represents the negative of a number by its complement. Thus, for an 8-bit word, the number 100 (base 10) is represented by 01100100, and negative 100 (base 10) by 10011011. The high-order bit is still treated as the sign bit and not as a part of the number. A 0 sign bit is a positive number, and a 1 sign bit is a negative number.

To evaluate the usefulness of this scheme for representing negative numbers, consider each of the four possible combinations of signs for adding two numbers, 33 (base 10) and 21 (base 10), in 8-bit binary

```
+33    0 0 1 0 0 0 0 1
+21    0 0 0 1 0 1 0 1
+54    0 0 1 1 0 1 1 0 = 54 (base 10)

+33      0 0 1 0 0 0 0 1
−21      1 1 1 0 1 0 1 0
+12    1 0 0 0 0 1 0 1 1 = 11 (base 10) plus a carry
```

```
-33        1 1 0 1 1 1 1 0
+21        0 0 0 1 0 1 0 1
-12        1 1 1 1 0 0 1 1  = -12 (base 10)
```

```
-33        1 1 0 1 1 1 1 0
-21        1 1 1 0 1 0 1 0
-54        1 1 1 0 0 1 0 0 0  = -55 (base 10) plus a carry
```

In two of our four examples, the addition works fine, but in the other two cases our answers are incorrect in two ways: (1) we have a carry out of the high-order bit, and (2) our answer is one too small. Putting these two problems together, and using one to solve the other, it can be shown that ones' complement arithmetic requires an *end-around carry*. That is, if a carry is generated out of the high order (sign) bit, this carry is taken around to the low order bit and added back in. Thus, for the two cases which were in error above, we have

```
+33        0 0 1 0 0 0 0 1
-21        1 1 1 0 1 0 1 0
+12       (1)0 0 0 0 1 0 1 1
                         → + 1      end-around carry
           0 0 0 0 1 1 0 0  = 12 (base 10)
```

```
-33        1 1 0 1 1 1 1 0
-21        1 1 1 0 1 0 1 0
-54       (1)1 1 0 0 1 0 0 0
                         → + 1      end-around carry
           1 1 0 0 1 0 0 1  = -54 (base 10)
```

Overflow is still possible, of course, although the method of detecting it is different from the method used for unsigned integers. Before considering overflow, notice that,

1. Overflow can now occur because a number becomes too large (positive) or too small (negative), and
2. The addition of two numbers of opposite sign can never cause overflow.

Now consider the addition of two positive numbers and two negative numbers which cause overflow. For an 8-bit word (7 bits plus sign), we can represent the range of integers from -127 to $+127$, so

```
+100       0 1 1 0 0 1 0 0
+ 28       0 0 0 1 1 1 0 0
+128       1 0 0 0 0 0 0 0  = -127 (base 10)
```

```
-100       1 0 0 1 1 0 1 1
- 28       1 1 1 0 0 0 1 1
-128     1 0 1 1 1 1 1 1 0
                         + 1      end-around carry
           0 1 1 1 1 1 1 1  = +127 (base 10)
```

There are several ways to state the condition for overflow. One method is to notice that the sign of the output is different from the sign of the inputs. Overflow occurs in ones' complement if—and only if—the signs of the inputs are both the same and differ from the sign of the output. Another statement of this is that overflow occurs if there is a carry into the sign bit and no carry out of the sign bit (no end-around carry), or if there is no carry into the sign bit and there is a carry out (the carry out of the sign bit differs from the carry into the sign bit).

Ones' complement allows simple arithmetic with negative numbers. It does suffer from one problem that sign and magnitude notation has: negative zero. The complement of zero (00 . . . 000) is negative zero (11 . . . 111). Because of the end-around carry, the properties of negative zero are the same as the properties of positive zero, as far as arithmetic is concerned. For example, 307 (octal) + (−0) on a 10-bit word is

```
    0 0 1 1 0 0 0 1 1 1
  + 1 1 1 1 1 1 1 1 1 1
    1 0 0 1 1 0 0 0 1 1 0
                    + 1   end-around carry
    0 0 1 1 0 0 0 1 1 1   = 307 (octal)
```

But the hardware to test for zero must check for both representations of zero, making it more complicated.

Two's complement notation

To correct the problem of negative zero, *two's complement arithmetic* is used. The ones' complement arithmetic is fine except for negative zero, so to eliminate it, two's complement notation moves all negative numbers "up" by one. The two's complement negative of a number is formed by complementing all bits and then adding one. The two's complement of 342 (octal) on a 12-bit machine is

```
  0 0 0 0 1 1 1 0 0 0 1 0
  1 1 1 1 0 0 0 1 1 1 0 1   complement
                    + 1     plus one
  1 1 1 1 0 0 0 1 1 1 1 0   two's complement negative
```

(The high-order bit is still the sign bit). If we consider the four cases of addition given above for ones' complement arithmetic on an 8-bit machine, we have the following (notice that negative numbers are represented differently from ones' complement):

```
  +33     0 0 1 0 0 0 0 1
  +21     0 0 0 1 0 1 0 1
  +54     0 0 1 1 0 1 1 0 = 54 (base 10)

  +33     0 0 1 0 0 0 0 1
  −21     1 1 1 0 1 0 1 1
  +12     1 0 0 0 0 1 1 0 0 = 12 (base 10) plus a carry
```

```
−33        1 1 0 1 1 1 1 1
+21        0 0 0 1 0 1 0 1
−12        1 1 1 1 0 1 0 0 = −12 (base 10)

−33        1 1 0 1 1 1 1 1
−21        1 1 1 0 1 0 1 1
−54      1 1 1 0 0 1 0 1 0 = −54 (base 10) plus a carry
```

We see that with two's complement arithmetic an end-around carry is not needed. A carry out of the sign bit is simply ignored. Since an end-around carry might have produced carry propagation throughout the entire word, this feature may result in faster adders, as well as simpler ones. (This complexity is simply transferred to the part of the computation unit which produces the negative of a number.)

Negative zero has disappeared, since

```
zero              00000000000000000
complement        11111111111111111
add 1                           +1
                 100000000000000000 = 0   (discard carry)
```

Overflow is detected in the same way as in ones' complement; if the signs of the inputs are equal, but differ from the sign of the output, or if the carry into the sign differs from the carry out of the sign.

A new "quirk" has appeared to replace minus zero, however. The range of numbers which can be represented in n bits for ones' complement notation is

$$-2^{n-1} + 1 \text{ to } 2^{n-1} - 1$$

For two's complement, the range is

$$-2^{n-1} \text{ to } +2^{n-1} - 1$$

(Since we shifted all the negative numbers up by one, we gained one new negative number at the bottom.) Notice that although -2^{n-1} is representable, its negative $+2^{n-1}$ is not. If we try to negate -2^{n-1}, we have (using 8-bits per word as an example)

```
−128              1 0 0 0 0 0 0 0
complement        0 1 1 1 1 1 1 1
add 1                         + 1
                  1 0 0 0 0 0 0 0 = −128 (base 10)
```

We add two positive numbers and get a negative number: overflow. Overflow must be checked both when addition is done and when a negative is formed.

Biased or excess notation

Another scheme for representing negative numbers is excess 2^{n-1} notation. In this scheme, the range of numbers from -2^{n-1} to $2^{n-1} - 1$ is represented by *biasing* each number by 2^{n-1}. Biasing is done by adding the bias (2^{n-1} in this case) to the number to be biased. This transforms the represented numbers to the range 0 to $2^n - 1$. These biased numbers can be represented in the normal n-bit unsigned binary notation. Excess notation is identical to two's complement notation, but with the sign bit complemented (a 0 sign bit means a negative number, a 1 sign bit a positive number; the opposite of a normal sign bit).

The major advantage of excess notation is with comparisons. For the normal sign bit definition ($0 = +, 1 = -$), signed and unsigned numbers must be compared differently. If 0100 and 1011 are unsigned integers, then $1011 > 0100$, but if they are signed, then $0100 > 1011$, since 0100 is positive and 1011 is negative. By reversing the sign bit definition, both signed and unsigned numbers can be compared in the same way, since $1 > 0$ and $+ > -$. (On the other hand, the adder now has to treat the sign bit differently from the other bits when addition is being done.)

All of these schemes (sign and magnitude, ones' complement, two's complement, and excess) are used for the representation of numbers in some computer system. They are simply convenient methods of defining the mapping from bit patterns to the integers which we wish to represent in the computer. Different notations assign the bit patterns to suit different purposes. Table 1.5 illustrates how a 4-bit word is interpreted differently for each of the schemes we have discussed. The bit pattern is the same; only the interpretation of its meaning

TABLE 1.5 Interpretation of a 4-Bit Number as Five Different Number Representation Schemes.

	Unsigned	Sign and magnitude	One's complement	Two's complement	Excess 8
0000	0	0	0	0	-8
0001	1	1	1	1	-7
0010	2	2	2	2	-6
0011	3	3	3	3	-5
0100	4	4	4	4	-4
0101	5	5	5	5	-3
0110	6	6	6	6	-2
0111	7	7	7	7	-1
1000	8	-0	-7	-8	0
1001	9	-1	-6	-7	1
1010	10	-2	-5	-6	2
1011	11	-3	-4	-5	3
1100	12	-4	-3	-4	4
1101	13	-5	-2	-3	5
1110	14	-6	-1	-2	6
1111	15	-7	-0	-1	7

differs. Most computer systems use only one of these methods for representing integers so that the same interpretation can be applied to all words.

Addition and subtraction are two very common operations in a computer, and the computation unit provides the ability to perform these operations on binary numbers. As we hinted earlier, most computers do not provide separate adding and subtracting devices, but only an adder (or subtracter) and a device to complement or negate numbers. This requires that subtraction be done by negation and addition (or that addition be done by negation and subtraction).

Multiplication and division

Multiplication and division do not occur as frequently as addition and sub-traction, so many of the smaller computers do not provide hardware to multiply or divide, but require that the programmer implement multiplication by repeated additions,and division by repeated subtraction. Larger computers, however, do generally provide multiplication and division hardware. Both of these functions normally take more time to perform than addition.

In addition to the increased time required for multiplication, the problem of overflow becomes more important. When two n-bit numbers are added, overflow may occur because the result may generate a carry out of the high-order bit. The largest number which can be represented in an unsigned n-bit number is $2^n - 1$, and so the sum of any two numbers can be no larger than $2^n - 1 + 2^n - 1 = 2^{n+1} - 2$, which requires $n + 1$ bits for its representation. For multiplication, the largest possible result is $(2^n - 1) \times (2^n - 1) = 2^{2n} - 2^{n+1} + 1$ which requires $2n$ bits, or *twice* as many bits. In decimal, for example, $99 \times 99 = 9801$, so the product of two two-digit numbers may be a four-digit number. To represent the entire product, a *double-length register* is used. This is commonly done by using two single-length registers and considering them as one long register with twice the normal number of bits. If the result of a multiplication is to be used further, with addition, subtraction, or further multiplication, the high-order bits had best be all zeros (or all ones, if the product is negative and represented in ones' complement or two's complement). Otherwise, the product is a number which is too large to be represented in one word of memory and hence cannot be operated on by the normal arithmetic operations.

For division, the opposite phenomenon occurs. A $2n$-bit dividend divided by an n-bit divisor may result in an n-bit quotient plus an n-bit remainder. For example, the four-digit number 1478 divided by the two-digit number 55 yields the two-digit quotient 26 and the two-digit remainder 48. Thus, many computa-tion units require a double-length dividend and produce two single-length re-sults, the quotient and the remainder. If a single length dividend is desired, it is extended to a double-length representation for the division. For sign and magni-tude, this involves simply inserting additional high-order (leading) zeros. For ones' complement, two's complement, and excess notation, this is done by *sign extension*. The sign bit is replicated as the new high-order bits. For example, in ones' complement, a 6-bit representation of 13 (base 10) is 001101 (base 2), while a 12-bit representation is 000000001101 (base 2). For -13 (base 10), we have 110010 for a 6-bit representation and 111111110010 for a 12-bit representation. Only the high order 6 bits differ between the 6-bit and 12-bit representations, and each of these bits is the same as the sign bit. If the quotient which results from a division exceeds the normal word length, it can be treated either as overflow or as a double-length quotient, according to how the computation unit is built. The remainder of a division by an n-bit divisor is never more than n-bits.

Fractions and fixed-point numbers

The divide operation discussed above is often called an *integer divide*, since it divides one integer by another and produces an integer quotient and integer remainder. An alternative way to represent the result would be to give the quotient as a *fraction*. How do we represent fractions? In common decimal mathematical notation, fractions can be represented in two different forms, as a/b or as a decimal fraction, $0.xxxx \ldots xx$. A decimal fraction is another example of positional notation, but with weights of negative powers of ten (the base) associated with the places. For example

$$0.357 = 3 \times 10^{-1} + 5 \times 10^{-2} + 7 \times 10^{-3}$$

Similarly, we can define *binary fractions* as a sequence of binary digits after a *binary point*. A binary point looks like a decimal point, but the base of the numbers is 2, not 10. Thus,

$$0.1011 \text{ (base 2)} = 1 \times 2^{-1} + 0 \times 2^{-2} + 1 \times 2^{-3} + 1 \times 2^{-4}$$
$$= 0.5 + 0.125 + 0.0625$$
$$= 0.6875 \text{ (base 10)}.$$

Integers and fractions can be combined, as in

$$1100.011 \text{ (base 2)} = 1 \times 2^3 + 1 \times 2^2 + 0 \times 2^1 + 0 \times 2^0$$
$$+ 0 \times 2^{-1} + 1 \times 2^{-2} + 1 \times 2^{-3}$$
$$= 12.375 \text{ (base 10)}$$

Conversion from binary fractions to decimal can be done in several ways. One method is, as demonstrated above, to expand the number as a sum of products of powers of two and simply evaluate the resulting expression. A table of negative powers of two can help. Alternatively, common powers of two can be factored out, as in (using $2^{-1} = \frac{1}{2}$)

$$0.01101 \text{ (base 2)} = (0 + (1 + (1 + (0 + 1/2)/2)/2)/2)/2$$
$$= (0 + (1 + (1 + (0 + 0.5)/2)/2)/2)/2$$
$$= (0 + (1 + (1 + 0.25)/2)/2)/2)$$
$$= (0 + (1 + 0.625)/2)/2$$
$$= (0 + 0.8125)/2$$
$$= 0.40625 \text{ (base 10)}$$

Or, considering that multiplication by two simply shifts the binary point by one place to the right, we can convert by

$$
\begin{aligned}
0.101111 \text{ (base 2)} &= 0.101111 \times 2^6 \times 2^{-6} \\
&= 101111 \times 2^{-6} \\
&= 47/2^6 \\
&= 47/64 \\
&= 0.734375 \quad \text{(base 10)}
\end{aligned}
$$

Conversion from decimal fractions to binary is easily done by a simple iterative multiplication scheme. Assume we have a fraction, x, which we wish to express in binary. Then we wish to solve for the bits in

$$ x = X_{-1}2^{-1} + X_{-2}2^{-2} + X_{-3}2^{-3} + \cdots + X_{-m}2^{-m} $$

We can immediately derive that

$$ 2 \times x = X_{-1} + X_{-2}2^{-1} + X_{-3}2^{-2} + \cdots + X_{-m}2^{-m+1} $$

and the first bit (X_{-1}) is the integer part of the result. Separating this from the remaining fraction, we can derive the second bit by multiplying by two again, and so on. Thus, for 0.435 (base 10), we have

$$
\begin{array}{lll}
2 \times 0.435 = 0.87 & \text{first bit} = 0 \\
2 \times 0.87 \;= 1.74 & \text{next bit} = 1 \\
2 \times 0.74 \;= 1.48 & = 1 \\
2 \times 0.48 \;= 0.96 & = 0 \\
2 \times 0.96 \;= 1.92 & = 1 \\
2 \times 0.92 \;= 1.84 & = 1 \\
2 \times 0.84 \;= 1.68 & = 1 \\
2 \times 0.68 \;= 1.36 & = 1 \\
2 \times 0.36 \;= 0.72 & = 0 \\
2 \times 0.72 \;= 1.44 & = 1 \\
\quad \cdots & \quad \cdots
\end{array}
$$

and so on. Thus,

$$ 0.435 \text{ (base 10)} = 0.0110111\underline{101011100001010001111} $$

where the underlined portion repeats forever, in the same way that the decimal fraction for $1/3 = 0.3333333333333333\underline{3}$. This illustrates both the conversion process and that not all decimal numbers can be exactly represented in a finite number of bits. Some nonrepeating decimal fractions are *repeating fractions* in binary, just as the fraction $1/3$ is a repeating fraction in decimal. No matter how many bits we allow in a word to represent a binary fraction, we may not be able to represent some decimal fractions exactly. By adding more and more bits, we can come closer and closer, but we may always be incorrect by some small amount.

For 0.435, for example, if we allow only two bits of *precision*, then we can represent only $0.00, 0.01, 0.10,$ and 0.11 (base 2) (0, 0.25, 0.5 and 0.75 [base

10]) and we would chose 0.10 as the closest approximation to 0.435. With 9 bits, we can represent 0.011011110 (base 2) (= 0.43359375 [base 10]) and 0.011011111 (base 2) (= 0.435536875 [base 10]) but not 0.435. Obviously, as we keep increasing the number of bits used, the precision of our numbers gets better and better. In fact, if the closest binary fraction of n bits is used to represent a decimal fraction, the *round-off error* in representation is less than 2^{-n-1}. With 9 bits to represent 0.435, the closest representation is 0.011011111 (base 2) (= 0.435546875 (base 10)) and the error is

$$0.435546875 - 0.435 = 0.000546875 < 0.0009765625 = 2^{-10}$$

When the position of the binary point is assumed to be in the same location for all numbers, the resulting representation is called a *fixed-point number*. Integers are a special case of fixed-point numbers where the binary point is assumed to be just to the right of the low-order bit. Fixed-point numbers can always be treated as if they were just integers whenever addition or subtraction is done because of the distributive law of multiplication over addition. If a and b have the binary point n bits from the right, then $a \times 2^n$ and $b \times 2^n$ are integers and

$$a + b = (a + b) \times 2^n \times 2^{-n}$$
$$= (a \times 2^n + b \times 2^n) \times 2^{-n}$$

(This is just saying that when you add dollars and cents, you do not have to add the cents by any special rule, but can just add as if the decimal point is not there, and then replace the decimal point after the addition.)

Floating point representation

A different way to represent fractions allows the position of the binary point to vary from one number to another. This is called *floating point* representation. If this is done, then we need to know both the fraction and where the binary point is. So a floating point number consists of two parts, one part to give the magnitude of the number and the other to indicate the location of the binary point. Binary floating point numbers are generally thought of as equivalent to *scientific notation* for decimal numbers. Scientific notation, as you remember, represents a number as a fraction times a power of 10. Thus, Avogadro's number is expressed as 6.0225×10^{23}, rather than as 602250000000000000000000. Planck's constant is 1.0545×10^{-27}, rather than 0.0000000000000000000000000010545. Similarly, we can express numbers in binary as 0.101101×2^{15} to represent 101101000000000 (base 2), and 0.111101×2^{-3} to represent 0.000111101 (base 2).

For each floating point number, we need to store only two numbers: the *exponent* (or *characteristic*) and the *fraction* (or *mantissa*). The same base can be used for all floating point numbers and need not be stored. The most popular base for floating point numbers is 2 (for obvious reasons), but some machines use 8 or 16 as the base for the exponent. The choice of exponent base is influenced by considerations of range and precision, and can in turn affect the choice of octal or hexadecimal for writing numbers.

To represent a floating point number, we have two numbers to store. Notice that both numbers can be treated as signed integers. Both numbers are commonly packed into one word for machines with large enough word sizes. For example, on the CDC 3600, a floating point number is stored as

sw	se	exponent	fraction

where, *sw* is the sign of the number (ones' complement)
   se is the sign of the exponent (excess 1024)
   exponent is a 10-bit biased exponent
   fraction is a 36-bit fraction

This notation allows a range of numbers from approximately

2^{-1024} to 2^{+1023} $(10^{-307}$ to $10^{+307})$

On the IBM 360/370 machines, a floating point number is represented by

sf	se	exponent	fraction

where *sf* is the sign of the fraction (sign and magnitude)
   se is the sign of the exponent (excess 64)
   exponent is a 6-bit exponent
   fraction is a 24-bit fraction

The IBM 360/370 uses 16 as the base of the exponent, so that the range of numbers which can be represented is approximately

16^{-64} to 16^{+63} $(10^{-77}$ to $10^{+75})$

The number of bits allocated to the fraction determines the *precision* of the number. Remember that the round-off error in an *n*-bit fraction is less than 2^{-n-1}, so the 36-bit fraction of the CDC 3600 means an error of less than 2^{-37} (about 11 decimal digits of accuracy), while the 24-bit fraction of the IBM 360/370 gives only about 6 decimal digits of accuracy. For more places of accuracy, more bits are needed to represent the fraction, and some machines use two words to represent a floating point number, with the second word being considered an extension of the fraction of the first word, as (for the IBM 360/370)

sf	se	exponent	56-bit fraction

First 32-bit word   Second 32-bit word

By increasing the number of bits used to represent the fraction in this way, the round-off error is less than 2^{-57}, giving about 16 decimal digits of accuracy. This latter form is known as a *double precision* floating point number, while the normal, one-word format is called *single precision*.

The exponents are generally stored as *biased* integers, using the excess 2^{n-1} representation, while the fraction is stored in either ones' or two's complement, or even sign and magnitude. The interpretation of a bit pattern as a floating point number can be quite complex. For example, on the CDC 3600, the exponent is stored as a biased, excess 1024 number, while the fraction is stored in ones' complement. To make things even more complex, if the fraction is negative, the entire word (including the exponent) is complemented. Thus, if the word

10111111101101010111111111111111111111111111111111

is to be interpreted as a floating point number on the CDC 3600, we first note that the sign bit is 1, so the number is negative. To determine its magnitude, we first complement the entire word to get

01000000010010100000000000000000000000000000000000

Then we extract the exponent (10000000100) and the fraction (1010000...0). The exponent is 1028, which is $+4$, since it is biased by 1024. The binary point is assumed to lie just to the left of the fraction so the fraction is $0.101000...0$. The number represented is then $0.101 \times 2^4 = 1010$ (base 2) $= 10$ (base 10). Since the original number was negative, the bit pattern given above represents -10 (base 10).

As another example, try

00111111111011110000000 . . . 00

The sign is positive. The exponent is 01111111101 (base 2) $=$ 1021 (base 10), which with a bias of 1024 gives a *true exponent* of -3. The fraction is $0.111000...0$. The entire number is $0.111 \times 2^{-3} = 0.000111 = 0.109375$ (base 10).

There are several ways to store the number 0.111×2^{-3} as a floating point number. We could store it as 0.111×2^{-3}, or 0.0111×2^{-2} or 0.000111×2^0 or $0.0000000000111 \times 2^7$. Which representation do we use? All we are doing in the alternative definitions is introducing leading zeros. Leading zeros make no contribution to the accuracy of our number; they are not *significant digits*. Zeros *after* the first nonzero digit can be significant. Thus, the trailing zeros on $0.1110000000 \times 2^{-3}$ distinguish this number from $0.1110000001 \times 2^{-3}$, or $0.1110000010 \times 2^{-3}$. If we have only a limited number of bits to represent a floating point number, we want to store only the significant digits, not the leading zeros. This is accomplished by shifting our fraction and adjusting the exponent so that the first digit after the binary point is nonzero. This is the *normalized* form of a floating point number. Only zero has no one bits. It is treated as a special case with both an exponent and fraction of zero.

In general, for a base B of the exponent of a floating point number, the number is normalized if the first digit (in base B) after the radix point is nonzero. For a base 16 exponent, only the first hexadecimal digit of the fraction need be nonzero; the first bits may be zero, as in the normalized number

$$0.1A8_{16} \times 16^4 = 0.000110101000_2 \times 16^4$$

For a general base B, this means that a floating point number

$$frac \times B^{exp} \qquad 0 \le frac < 1$$

is normalized if either (i) it is zero, or (ii) the exponent, exp, has been adjusted so that the fraction, $frac$, satisfies

$$1/B \le frac < 1$$

Floating point arithmetic

Arithmetic with floating point numbers is more complex than with integer or fixed-point numbers. Addition consists of several steps. First, the binary points of the two numbers must be *aligned*. This is done by shifting the number with the *smaller* exponent to the right until exponents are equal. As an example, to add

$$0.111010100 \times 2^4$$
$$+\ 0.111000111 \times 2^2$$

we first align the binary points by shifting the number with the smaller exponent right as many places as the difference in exponents, in this case, two places:

$$
\begin{array}{ll}
0.111010100 & \times\ 2^4 \\
+\ 0.00111000111 & \times\ 2^4 \\
\hline
1.00100010111 & \times\ 2^4
\end{array}
$$

This result will need to be *postnormalized* to place the binary point before the first significant digit. Also, we see that the result has more bits than the original operands. Since we cannot store these bits (having only a fixed number of bits per word), something must be done with them. One approach is to just ignore them. This is called *truncation*, and in this case yields the answer 0.100100010×2^5 (truncated to nine bits for the fractional part). Truncation always results in a number which is less than or equal to the correct answer (in absolute value). Hence any inaccuracy in computation caused by the limited number of bits used to represent numbers tends to accumulate, and the accuracy of the result of repeated operations may be quite limited.

An alternate policy is to *round* the result by adding 1 to the least significant digit if the first bit which cannot be kept is 1. This results in an addition like

0. Original operands 0.111010100 $\times\ 2^4$

    $+\ 0.111000111$ $\times\ 2^2$

1. Align operands 0.111010100 $\times\ 2^4$

    $+\ 0.00111000111$ $\times\ 2^4$

2. Add 1.00100010111 $\times\ 2^4$

3. Round result $+0.00000001$

    1.00100011111 $\times\ 2^4$

4. Normalize result 0.100100011 $\times\ 2^5$

Another problem for floating point numbers is *overflow*. Just as with integers, the addition of two large (in magnitude) numbers may produce a number which is too large to be represented in the machine. For example, if we have a 7-bit biased exponent and a 24-bit fraction, and try to add two numbers like

$$0111111111000000000000000000000000$$
$$+\ 0111111111000000000000000000000000$$

we get (since the exponents are equal, no alignment is necessary)

1. Operands $0.110000\ .\ .\ .\ 00$ $\times\ 2^{63}$

    $+\ 0.100000\ .\ .\ .\ 00$ $\times\ 2^{63}$

2. Add $1.010000\ .\ .\ .\ 00$ $\times\ 2^{63}$

3. Normalize $0.101000\ .\ .\ .\ 00$ $\times\ 2^{64}$

The biased exponent is 64 plus the bias of $64 = 128$, which cannot be represented in 7 bits (0 to 127). This is *exponent overflow*. For floating point numbers, a number which is too large to represent results in a requirement for an exponent which is too large to represent, so overflow occurs due to overflow of the exponent.

A similar problem can happen when the difference between two very small numbers is being computed. For example, the difference between $0.101000000 \times 2^{-63}$ and $0.101000001 \times 2^{-63}$ is only $0.000000001 \times 2^{-63}$, or when normalized, $0.100000000 \times 2^{-71}$. If we are limited to a seven-bit biased exponent, this exponent is too large (in a negative direction) to be represented. This is *exponent underflow*. Normal practice for exponent underflow is to replace the result with zero, since although this is not the correct answer, it is very close to the correct answer.

The fraction of a floating point number cannot overflow, since this is corrected by adjusting the exponent, in postnormalization. Adjusting the exponent may cause exponent overflow or underflow, however.

The representation of floating point numbers is different for almost every computer. The variations which are possible include,

1. The base of the exponent part (2, 8, 10, 16).
2. How the exponent is represented (sign and magnitude, ones' complement, two's complement, biased).

3. How the fraction is represented (sign and magnitude, ones' complement, two's complement, biased).
4. Where the binary point is assumed to be (to the left of the high-order bit of the fraction, just to the right of the high-order bit of the fraction, to the right of the low-order bit).
5. The number of bits used for exponent.
6. The number of bits used for fraction.
7. How the parts are assembled (where the exponent is, where the sign bits are, where the fraction is).
8. Other miscellaneous points (not storing the first bit of the normalized fraction, since it is always 1, whether the exponent is complemented for negative fractions, etc.).

On many computers with a small word length, several words are used to represent a floating point number. For example, on the HP2100, a floating point number is represented by two words by

sf	23-bit fraction stored in two words	7-bit exponent	se

First word	Second word
sf = sign of fraction	se = sign of exponent

Both exponent and fraction are represented in two's complement notation. The binary point is assumed to be between the sign for the fraction and the high-order bit of the fraction.

Summary

Numbers can be represented in a computer in many ways. The basic unit of representation is the binary digit, or bit. Each number is represented by an encoding in terms of the bits of a computer word. Numbers can be represented in decimal by the binary coded decimal (BCD) scheme or in a binary positional notation. If the latter scheme is used, it is necessary to be able to convert between binary and decimal. Octal and hexadecimal schemes are sometimes used.

Since only a fixed-number of bits are allowed, overflow may occur. If subtraction is possible as well as addition, then negative numbers may result. Negative numbers can be represented in sign and magnitude, ones' complement, two's complement, or excess notation.

When multiplication and division are possible also, then fractions may need to be stored as well as integers. These can be stored as either fixed point or floating point numbers. Floating point numbers are represented by encoding a pair of numbers representing an exponent and a fractional part in a normalized form. Exponent overflow and exponent underflow may occur as the result of operating on floating point numbers. Some numbers cannot be represented exactly as binary fractions with a given number of bits, so the precision and accuracy of the results of computation should be considered. This is influenced by the use of either truncated or rounded arithmetic.

EXERCISES

1. What is the difference between a number, a numeral, and a digit?
2. What is the largest unsigned number that can be represented in 16 bits?
3. If n bits can represent 2^n different numbers, why is the largest unsigned number only $2^n - 1$ and not 2^n?
4. Represent 41,972 in BCD.
5. In what base is 13426?
6. What number(s) have the same representation in octal, binary, and decimal?
7. What hexadecimal numbers of four digits or less can also be interpreted as English words?
8. Add the following numbers:

   Binary
   ```
    1011010      1001000111       11101011
   +0101011    +    110010      +100100101
   ```

   Octal
   ```
    567674          77651         3472010
   +776571       +1623507       +    7743
   ```

   Hexadecimal
   ```
    143AF          F9A8C7B          4FF58
   +2E135       +    9A67B        +141508
   ```

9. Convert the following numbers between the indicated bases so that each row of the table is the same number represented in each base.

Binary	Decimal	Octal	Hexadecimal
1101	13	15	D
100110010	____	____	____
____	____	144	____
____	144	____	____
101101	____	____	____
____	____	____	CAB
____	____	127	____
____	43	____	____
____	____	____	144

10. How many octal digits are necessary to represent 35 bits? How many binary digits can be represented by this number of octal digits? Is there a difference between the 35 bits we started with and the answer to the second question? Why?

11. Define a base 4 representation. Show how to convert from binary to base 4 and back.

12. Show how Table 1.4 can be used to convert from decimal to octal.

13. Consider any three-digit number, abc. Show that abc represents a smaller number if it is interpreted as an octal number, as compared to interpreting it as a decimal number. That is, show that abc (base 8) $\leq abc$ (base 10).

14. Show that a binary number can be multiplied by 2 by shifting all bits left one bit. What should be shifted into the low-order bit, zero or one? Show that a binary number can be divided by 2 by shifting all bits right one bit. What is the significance of the value of the bit shifted out of the low-order bit?

15. Represent the following decimal numbers in (a) sign and magnitude, (b) two's complement, (c) ones' complement, and (d) excess-128, for an eight-bit machine (seven bits plus sign).

    93   -93 -13 -14 47   128 -128 0 -0

16. What range of numbers can be represented in 8 bits with an excess-3 notation?

17. Write all possible bit patterns for a three-bit word. Interpret each of these bit patterns as a signed number in sign and magnitude, two's complement, ones' complement, and excess-4 notation, and also as unsigned numbers.

18. What is an end-around carry? Why is it needed?

19. How can a number represented in n bits be transformed into the same number, but represented in $2n$ bits? Consider if the number is interpreted as unsigned, sign and magnitude, two's complement, or excess notation.

20. Show that the complement of the complement of a number in two's complement notation is the original number again.

21. How is overflow detected for ones' complement arithmetic? For two's complement arithmetic?

22. Does division of a double-length dividend by a single-length divisor always yield a single-length quotient? A single-length remainder?

23. In converting from a decimal fraction to a binary fraction, why do we always eventually arrive at a repeating pattern? What is the maximum length of the pattern, for a decimal with at most n decimal fraction places?

24. Not every decimal fraction can be represented exactly by a finite number of binary digits. Why can every binary fraction be represented exactly by a finite number of decimal digits?

25. Convert 10101.111010 (base 2) to decimal.
26. Define overflow and underflow.
27. What is a normalized floating point number (in contrast to an un-normalized floating point number)?
28. Convert 3.1416 to a normalized binary floating point number, assuming that the high-order bit is the sign for the number, followed by a 7-bit signed excess-64 exponent for a power of two, followed by a 16-bit fraction with the binary point between the exponent and the fraction (i.e., the fraction is less than 1 and greater than or equal to 0.5). Assuming that 0111110111000000000000000 is a floating point number in this same representation, convert it to decimal.
29. Why would the exponent of a floating point number be represented in an excess notation, while the entire number uses two's complement?
30. Can BCD be used to represent fractions? Fixed-point or floating point?

1.3 THE INPUT/OUTPUT SYSTEM

The largest memory unit and fastest computation unit in the world would be useless if there was no way to get information into the computer or to get results back from the computer. In fact, the usefulness of many present computers is severely limited by the way in which new programs and data can be put into and results displayed from the computer. Thus, the input/output (I/O) system is an integral component of a computer system. We will see that there exist a large number of radically different devices which the computer may use for this purpose. This makes it very difficult to discuss all aspects of an I/O system. In this section, we consider first some general concepts important to an understanding of I/O, and then some specific common I/O devices.

The function of an I/O system is to allow communication between the computer system and its environment. This may mean communication with people (operators, programmers, users) and also with other machines. These other machines may be other computers (such as in a computer network), laboratory measuring devices, manufacturing equipment, switching equipment, or almost anything which can produce or receive electrical signals. Computers interact with other machines by sending electrical signals on cables. The cables are attached to the computer by *interface boards* which plug into slots in the computer chassis. Interface boards are flat pieces of plastic which contain the electronic circuitry to convert between the binary words of the computer and the electrical signals which go to and from the devices. Some devices are used for both input and output, while others are only input devices or output devices. For each different kind of device, a new interface board is needed.

The organization of the I/O system within the computer itself varies from machine to machine. We examine some specific organizations later. Generally, each computer manufacturer provides a collection of I/O devices which are specifically designed for use with its particular line of computers. These devices

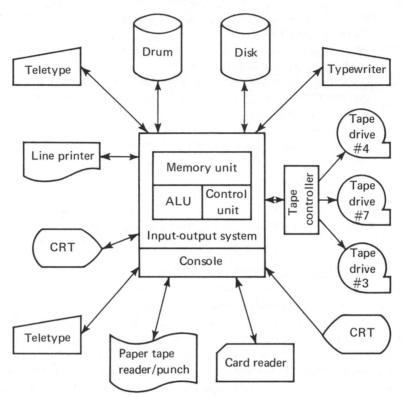

FIGURE 1.6 Block diagram of computer system and peripheral devices.

are mainly *incompatible* with the I/O system of other computers. However, with a suitable interface, almost any device can be attached to any computer. Thus, there is a growing number of independent vendors of I/O devices. These independent manufacturers often design their devices so that they are *plug-to-plug* compatible with a popular computing system (such as the IBM 360/370 system, or the PDP-11). This means that, with their interface, their I/O device looks the same to the computer as the original manufacturer's device and can be just plugged right in. (Of course, the device is faster, cheaper, or has more functions than the original manufacturer's device.)

Figure 1.6 illustrates a typical block diagram of a computer system which has a large number and variety of I/O devices. Since I/O devices are the interface between the machine and its users, they are called *peripheral devices* to distinguish them from the central computer.

Character codes

In the same way that information is encoded in the memory unit (as 0s and 1s), and the computation unit (as fixed-point integers or floating point numbers), it is also encoded in the I/O system. Unlike the memory unit and computation unit, it is often not encoded in the same way for all peripheral devices. Much of the information in the I/O system is not numbers, but digits, letters, and punctuation, or *characters*. For instance, when a computer is handling billing information, the information is both amounts paid and owed, and the names and addresses of the people involved. These names and addresses must be represented in an encoding which the computer can store and manipulate. This is done by defining a *character code*. A character code is a list of the characters which can be represented and the bit pattern which is used to represent each character. Although characters can be assigned bit patterns in arbitrary ways, most computers and peripheral devices use one of three standard character codes: BCD, ASCII, or EBCDIC.

What is needed for a character code? We certainly want to be able to represent all 26 letters, 10 digits, and some special characters, such as a blank, comma, period, left and right parenthesis, plus sign, minus sign, and equals sign. A 48-character set is generally considered a minimal set, meaning that at least 6 bits must be used per character ($2^5 = 32 < 48 < 64 = 2^6$). The BCD (Binary Coded Decimal) character code uses 6 bits per character to define a 64-character set, including (upper case only) letters, digits, and some special characters. Table 1.6 lists a BCD character code. This is *a* rather than *the* BCD code, because there are several BCD codes, varying from machine to machine. Most of these codes agree on the representation of the letters and numbers, but many special characters will have different representations.

TABLE 1.6 A BCD Character Code (Code Given in Octal)

Character	BCD	Character	BCD	Character	BCD	Character	BCD
0	00	+	20	−	40	blank	60
1	01	A	21	J	41	/	61
2	02	B	22	K	42	S	62
3	03	C	23	L	43	T	63
4	04	D	24	M	44	U	64
5	05	E	25	N	45	V	65
6	06	F	26	O	46	W	66
7	07	G	27	P	47	X	67
8	10	H	30	Q	50	Y	70
9	11	I	31	R	51	Z	71
:	12	<	32	V	52	]	72
=	13	.	33	$	53	,	73
'	14	)	34	*	54	(	74
⩽	15	⩾	35	↑	55	→	75
%	16	¬	36	↓	56	≡	76
[	17	;	37	>	57	∧	77

Although BCD is satisfactory for many purposes, it is too small a set of characters if upper and lower case letters and additional special characters are desired. This means at least a seven-bit code. The American Standard Code for Information Interchange (ASCII) is a seven-bit character code which allows representation of upper and lower case letters, the decimal digits, a wide variety of special symbols, and a collection of *control characters* for use in telecommu-

TABLE 1.7 The ASCII Character Code

ASCII	Character	ASCII	Character	ASCII	Character	ASCII	Character
000	NULL	040	blank	100	@	140	'
001	SOH	041	!	101	A	141	a
002	STX	042	"	102	B	142	b
003	ETX	043	#	103	C	143	c
004	EOT	044	$	104	D	144	d
005	ENQ	045	%	105	E	145	e
006	ACK	046	&	106	F	146	f
007	BELL	047	'	107	G	147	g
010	BS	050	(	110	H	150	h
011	HT	051	)	111	I	151	i
012	LF	052	*	112	J	152	j
013	VT	053	+	113	K	153	k
014	FF	054	,	114	L	154	l
015	CR	055	−	115	M	155	m
016	SO	056	.	116	N	156	n
017	SI	057	/	117	O	157	o
020	DLE	060	0	120	P	160	p
021	DC1	061	1	121	Q	161	q
022	DC2	062	2	122	R	162	r
023	DC3	063	3	123	S	163	s
024	DC4	064	4	124	T	164	t
025	NACK	065	5	125	U	165	u
026	SYNC	066	6	126	V	166	v
027	ETB	067	7	127	W	167	w
030	CNCL	070	8	130	X	170	x
031	EM	071	9	131	Y	171	y
032	SS	072	:	132	Z	172	z
033	ESC	073	;	133	[	173	{
034	FS	074	<	134	\	174	|
035	GS	075	=	135	]	175	}
036	RS	076	>	136	∧	176	¬
037	US	077	?	137	_	177	DEL

nications. Table 1.7 gives the ASCII character code (in octal). The two- and three-letter codes (000 to 037) are control codes, mainly for use on computer typewriter-like terminals. BEL, for example, rings a bell on a teletype.

Seven bits provide for up to 128 different characters—enough to satisfy most computer users. But 7 is an awkward number, since it is not a power or multiple of 2. Thus, many computers use an eight-bit character code. Since ASCII has an acceptable character set, the question is what to do with the extra bit. Mostly it is just left as a zero, or a one, and ignored, but for many applications it can be used to increase the reliability of the computer. For this use, the extra bit is used as a *parity* bit and helps to detect incorrect information.

Incorrect information can be introduced into a computer in several ways. If information is sent across wires (like telephone lines) from one location to another, static and interference can cause the information to be received incorrectly. If it is stored magnetically for a long period of time, it may change due to flaws in the magnetic medium or external magnetic fields (caused by static electricity or electrical storms, for example). Or an electronic component in the computer itself may break and cause incorrect results. In all these cases, the potential damage done by the changing of even one bit is great. For example, if the bit number 2 of the first "E" in "PETERSON" were to switch from a 1 to a 0, the "E" would change into an "A" ("E" = 1000101 $\geq$ 1000001 = "A"), and a Mr. Paterson might be billed, paid, credited, or shot instead of Mr. Peterson!

Parity allows this kind of error (a change of one bit) to be *detected*. Once the error is detected, the appropriate steps to correct the error are not immediately obvious, but that is another problem. Parity can be either *even* or *odd*. For odd parity, the extra bit is set so that the total number of 1 bits in the code for a character is an odd number. Thus, for the characters given below, the parity bit is as shown.

Character	ASCII code	Parity	ASCII with Odd Parity
A	1000001	1	11000001
E	1000101	0	01000101
R	1010010	0	01010010
Z	1011010	1	11011010
4	0110100	0	00110100
,	0101100	0	00101100
(blank)	0100000	1	10100000

For even parity, the parity bit is set so that the total number of one bits per character is even. Thus, an even parity bit is the complement of an odd parity bit.

Now suppose the same error described above happened, but the character is represented in odd parity. An "E" is represented by the bit pattern 01000101 and after bit 2 changes, the pattern is 01000001. This is no longer an "A" (11000001), and in fact, is not a legal bit pattern at all, since it has an even number of 1 bits. Since we are using odd parity, this is an error, and is called a *parity error.* Although we know that the character is illegal, we do not know what the original character was. It might have been an "E", but it could also have been an "I" (01001001) whose bit 3 changed, or an "A" whose parity bit changed. Also, notice that if two bits change, the parity of the result is still correct. Hence, parity bits allow us to detect some, but not all, errors. Hopefully, the more common errors will be detected.

Adding parity bits to the 7-bit ASCII code gives an 8-bit code, but only 128 characters are available. With 8 bits, up to 256 characters are possible. Although this many characters are not needed now, they undoubtedly will be someday. For this and other reasons, a third code, EBCDIC (Extended Binary Coded Decimal Interchange Code) is used by IBM for their 360/370 computers and peripherals. Table 1.8 lists some of this code. This code, as its name indicates, is similar to the BCD code.

Why are there different character codes? Part of the reason is historical. The original BCD code was defined to allow easy translation from the Hollerith punched card code (see Table 1.9) to the BCD code. This explains the strange grouping of 0–9, A–I, J–R, and S–Z. Special characters sort of filled in the left-over spaces. ASCII was defined with telecommunications in mind, so the letters, digits, and so forth can be put wherever convenient, trying to keep control characters, letters, digits, and so on together as much as possible to allow easy programming. EBCDIC tries to combine both of these features into its code.

What difference does it make which code is used? Within the computer, very little. Some codes are more convenient than others for some purposes. For simple English text, a BCD code requires only six bits per character rather than eight bits per character for ASCII with parity or EBCDIC; thus, only 3/4 as many bits are needed to store a given sequence of characters. We could store one character per word, but this would be intolerably wasteful of memory for large words, or long strings of characters. Hence, several characters are normally *packed* in each word. The number of bits needed to represent a character is called a *byte*. On a 24-bit machine, for example, each word has 4 6-bit bytes, or 3 8-bit bytes. The character code often influences the length of word (or vice versa). Hence 16-bit computers almost always use an 8-bit byte with an 8-bit ASCII code. The CDC 6600, with its 60-bit words, uses a 6-bit character code, while if its words had been 64 bits long, it probably would have used an 8-bit code. The IBM 360/370, with 32-bit words, uses the 8-bit byte with an EBCDIC code.

The character code also influences another function of the machine. It is often convenient to output lists of names in alphabetical order. It is convenient within the computer to consider each character as the unsigned integer number defined by its character code. Thus, "A" $<$ "B" $<$ "C" $< \cdots$ in all the character codes. But what about the digits, special symbols, and blanks? If the character code is used for names containing combinations of letters, digits, and special characters (like 3M, IBM 360, I/O), the alphabetical order may not be obvious

TABLE 1.8 An Abridged Listing of the EBCDIC Character Code

EBCDIC	Character[a]	EBCDIC	Character	EBCDIC	Character	EBCDIC	Character
00	NULL	40	blank	80		C0	
01	SOH			81	a	C1	A
02	STX			82	b	C2	B
03	ETX			83	c	C3	C
04	PF	4A	¢	84	d	C4	D
05	HT	4B	.	85	e	C5	E
06	LC	4C	<	86	f	C6	F
07	DEL	4D	(	87	g	C7	G
08		4E	+	88	h	C8	H
09		4F	|	89	i	C9	I
11	DC1			91	j	D1	J
12	DC2			92	k	D2	K
13	TM			93	l	D3	L
14	RES	5A	!	94	m	D4	M
15	NL	5B	$	95	n	D5	N
16	BS	5G	*	96	o	D6	O
17	IL	5D	)	97	p	D7	P
18	CAN	5E	;	98	q	D8	Q
19	EM	5F	¬	99	r	D9	R
21	SOS			A1	s	E1	S
22	FS			A2	t	E2	T
23				A3	u	E3	U
24	BYP	6A		A4	v	E4	V
25	LF	6B	,	A5	w	E5	W
26	ETB	6C	%	A6	x	E6	X
27	ESC	6D	_	A7	y	E7	Y
28		6E	>	A8	z	E8	Z
29		6F	?	A9		E9	
30				B0		F0	0
31				B1		F1	1
32	SYN			B2		F2	2
33				B3		F3	3
34	PN	7A	:	B4		F4	4
35	RS	7B	#	B5		F5	5
36	UC	7C	@	B6		F6	6
37	EOT	7D	´	B7		F7	7
38		7E	=	B8		F8	8
39		7F	"	B9		F9	9

[a] An empty character means no character has been assigned to that character code, yet. Other characters are not listed. Character code is given in hexadecimal.

and is generally left up to the character code. Thus, on some machines A1 is before AA alphabetically, while on others A1 is after AA. The order of the characters in the character code is called the *collating sequence*. If the character code in use matches our expectation for the collating sequence, then no problems arise. If not, then placing words in alphabetical order may become very complicated (or we adjust our expectations to what is easy for the computer).

The character code can also influence the ease of using various peripheral devices. A computer which is set up to use a six-bit BCD code may not be able to easily use an I/O device using ASCII or EBCDIC. Being able to use only a character set of 64 characters can limit how concepts are expressed to the computer, if these concepts are naturally expressed in terms of characters or symbols not available on the machine.

Specific I/O devices

Many different I/O devices are currently in use with computer systems. Despite this wide variety, however, there are certain classes of devices which are common to many computer installations. In order to be able to understand the constraints which are placed on the computer by its peripheral devices, we consider the typical characteristics of the common I/O devices. Individual devices will differ, and specific information can be obtained only from the vendors' manuals.

The console

Although most people do not consider the console of a computer as an input or output device, it can be a very useful means of communicating with a computer. The console generally consists of a collection of display lights, switches, and buttons. It is designed for utility and, sometimes, impressiveness. Typically, at least the following features are available on the computer console:

1. An ON/OFF switch for turning the computer power on and off. For some small computers, the electrical power to the computer is turned off whenever it is not needed. For larger computers, power may never be turned off.
2. A GO/HALT button, which starts and stops the execution of instructions. This is often called a RUN or EXECUTE switch.
3. A switch register. This is a set of switches which can be set to one of two positions (0/1) and can be read by the computer. It is often used to define addresses or contents of words.
4. A set of display lights, which can be used to display the contents of selected words of memory or registers. One light is provided for each bit in a word or address and indicates by its on/off state whether the corresponding bit is 1 or 0.
5. A set of status lights, which indicate whether the power is on or off,

whether the computer is running or halted, and perhaps other state information.

6.   A set of control switches, which allow the state of the computer and its memory to be manipulated. Common control buttons include a button which when pushed will read the console switches as an address and remember that address (LOAD ADDRESS); a button which will display in the status lights the contents of an addressed location of memory (DIS-PLAY/EXAMINE); a button which will store the switch register value into an addressed location of memory (DEPOSIT/STORE); a button to allow a program to be executed one instruction at a time, one instruction executed every time the button is pushed (SINGLE STEP); and so on.

The console is normally designed so that an operator sitting at the console has total control over the entire computer. The display lights allow the operator to monitor the contents of all memory locations and registers. Using the switch register to give addresses and data, the operator may change the contents of selected memory locations or registers.

In the early days of computing, a programmer normally debugged programs by sitting at the console and following them through, step by step, instruction by instruction. But as computers became more expensive, this was no longer possible, and programmers had to learn to debug programs from listings and dumps of memory. The console is generally used now only by the operator. Even the operator seldom uses the console display much for most computers, using instead a *console typewriter*. The console typewriter is really two devices in one. An input device, the *keyboard*, is basically a set of typewriter keys. When the operator depresses one of the keys, the character code corresponding to that character is sent to the computer. This allows the operator to input information to a program in the computer.

FIGURE 1.7   A typical operator's console for a small computer.

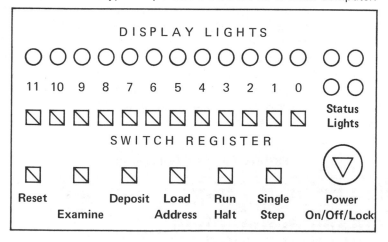

The computer can send information back by outputting to the other part of the console typewriter, the *printer*. When a character code is sent to the printer by the computer, the printer selects the appropriate symbol and prints it on the printer paper. Normally, the operator wants the characters typed on the keyboard printed also. This can be done either by a direct link from the keyboard to the printer, or by having the computer *echo print* every character that is typed in.

For many early computers and some modern small computers, the console typewriter is the only I/O device available. These devices tend to be relatively slow (from 10 to 100 characters printed per second) and hence may severely limit the usefulness of the computer. Typical is the ASR-33 Teletypewriter (TTY), which operates at 10 characters per second and uses the ASCII character code. These machines are slow, mainly because of their mechanical construction, but they are also very inexpensive (about $1,000) and hence fairly popular.

Paper tape

One problem with using a console typewriter to input a program or data is that if an error occurs, or if it is necessary to run the program again with more data, the entire program or data must be typed again. To prevent having to type the input many times, it can be put on a machine-readable medium. One such medium is *paper tape*. Paper tape is normally one inch wide and slightly thicker than a normal piece of paper. It is as long as necessary. Up to eight holes can be punched across the tape. Each hole is in one of the eight *channels* which run along the tape. Between the third and fourth channels is the *sprocket hole*. The sprocket hole serves several functions. It provides a means for a mechanical paper tape reader to move the tape (like the sprocket holes on the edges of a piece of movie film). It also defines where information is on the tape. Some systems use tape with 5, 6 or 7 channels rather than 8.

Information is encoded onto the tape by punching holes in the tape. Holes correspond to 1-bits and the absences of holes to 0-bits. Normally, ASCII is used to represent the characters to be punched on the tape. Thus, each character needs seven or eight bits (depending upon whether or not parity is used). Each character is punched as a set of holes across the width of the tape, one bit per channel. For each character, a sprocket hole is also punched. The sprocket hole thus defines when a character should be looked for. Without the sprocket holes, a sequence of NULL characters with an ASCII code of 00000000 (with even parity) would be just a space of blank tape, and it would be difficult to determine how many NULL characters are on the tape.

FIGURE 1.8   Sample paper tape.

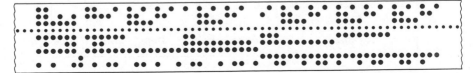

Paper tape is input to a computer by a *paper tape reader*. There are two varieties of these devices. One is electromechanical and reads the tape by using little pins which sense the presence or absence of a hole by pressing against the tape. If a hole is there, the pin moves through the tape and connects a switch; if no hole is in the tape, the pin is held back and the switch stays open. A sprocket wheel moves the tape forward one character at a time for the sensing pins. These readers operate at about 10 to 50 characters per second and are often attached to Teletypes. The ASR-33 and ASR-35 normally come with a paper tape reader attached to them, which allows input to be either from the keyboard or from paper tape.

The other paper tape readers are optical and read the tape by a set of eight photocells. The tape is moved between the photocells and a bright light. A special photocell is put under the sprocket hole to control when the other photocells are used to sense a hole or nonhole. By using a friction drive (rubber wheels, as in a tape recorder), paper tape can be read by an optical paper tape reader at speeds of up to 1000 characters per second.

Paper tape can be punched either by a special typewriter-like device (for example, a Teletype with paper tape punch attachment) which punches one eight-bit character for each key which is depressed at the keyboard, or by a computer using a paper tape punch I/O device. A computer-controlled paper tape punch can punch paper tape at a rate of about 200 characters per second.

The computer can use a paper tape punch as an output device, but, since people tend to be relatively poor at reading paper tape, it is used mainly to create output which can be easily read back into a computer at a later time. Thus, paper tape can be considered as an input medium, an output medium, and a *storage* medium.

Punched cards

One of the major problems with paper tape is the difficulty of correcting an error in the information on the tape. Programs often must be fed into the computer many times, with minor changes each time, before they are correct. Computer-punched paper tape can be wrong sometimes. Even if the tape is correct, it may become torn, or badly worn in a few spots. Generally, this requires punching a complete new paper tape.

Punched cards do not have this problem. Each card is a piece of cardboard about $3\frac{1}{2}$ inches wide by $7\frac{1}{2}$ inches long (the size of the dollar bill around 1900, according to computer folklore). The card is divided into 80 columns, spaced along the card. Each column has 12 rows. A small rectangular hole can be punched into any row of any column. A character can be encoded into any column by the right pattern of holes. Figure 1.9 illustrates a punched card with the letters, digits, and some special characters in a *Hollerith punched card code*. Both the columns and the rows are numbered: the columns from 1 to 80; the rows by 12, 11, 0, 1, 2, . . . , 9, from the top to bottom. A punched card code gives for each character which rows are to be punched. Table 1.9 gives one common punched card code, the Hollerith code.

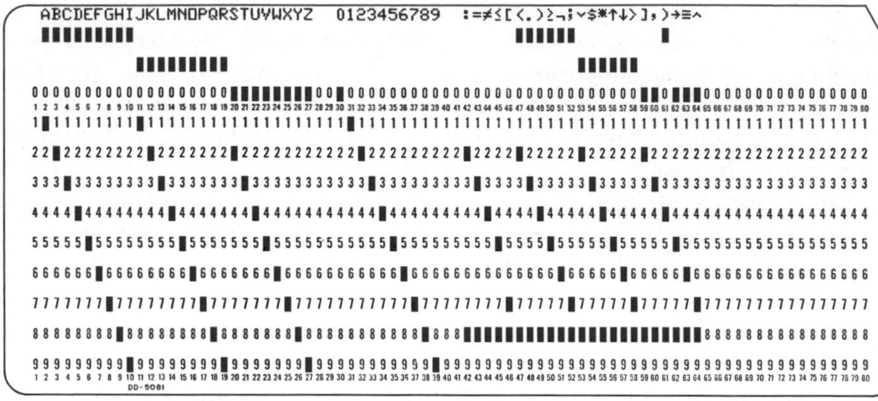

FIGURE 1.9 Sample punched computer card.

Cards are prepared by using a *card punch* or *keypunch* machine. Several companies manufacture these devices, but the most common ones are the IBM model 026 and the IBM model 029 keypunches. These machines have a type-writer-like keyboard with additional keys to control the flow of cards through the machine. The keypunch operator types his or her program onto the cards, one line of the program per card. If a mistake is made, the card is simply discarded and a new one punched. In addition to punching the code representing a character in a column, the keypunch prints the character on the top of the card

TABLE 1.9 A Hollerith Punched Card Character Code

Character	Hollerith	Character	Hollerith	Character	Hollerith	Character	Hollerith
blank	no punch	+	12	−	11		
0	0	A	12-1	J	11-1	/	0-1
1	1	B	12-2	K	11-2	S	0-2
2	2	C	12-3	L	11-3	T	0-3
3	3	D	12-4	M	11-4	U	0-4
4	4	E	12-5	N	11-5	V	0-5
5	5	F	12-6	O	11-6	W	0-6
6	6	G	12-7	P	11-7	X	0-7
7	7	H	12-8	Q	11-8	Y	0-8
8	8	I	12-9	R	11-9	Z	0-9
9	9	<	12-2-8	$\vee$	11-2-8	]	0-2-8
:	2-8	.	12-3-8	$	11-3-8	,	0-3-8
=	3-8	)	12-4-8	*	11-4-8	)	0-4-8
'	4-8	$\geq$	12-5-8	↑	11-5-8	→	0-5-8
$\leq$	5-8	¬	12-6-8	↓	11-6-8	≡	0-6-8
%	6-8	;	12-7-8	>	11-7-8	$\wedge$	0-7-8

(above row 12), making it relatively easy for a human to read the information on a card also.

Punched cards have been used for a long time, well before the invention of computers. Their first use in data processing operations was in the 1890 U.S. census. The population had been increasing so fast that data from the 1880 census took nearly eight years to process by hand, and it was projected that the processing of the 1890 census would not be finished before it was time for the 1900 census. Herman Hollerith invented the techniques used for encoding information onto punched cards and the machines to process them. He later founded a company which eventually merged with others to become the International Business Machines Corporation.

In addition to the keypunch, there are many other machines which can be used to process information punched on cards, without the help of a computer. Card sorters, duplicators, listers, verifiers, and interpreters are the more common pieces of simple card processing machines. More sophisticated machines include the collator (which can merge two card decks into one) and the tabulator, or accounting machine, which can perform simple computations to produce totals and subtotals for reports.

Because of this long history, the basic punched card code is standard for letters, digits, and certain special characters (such as "$", ".", and ","). For the more recent special characters, however, different punches are used by different computer systems. Even the codes for the IBM 026 and the IBM 029 keypunches may differ. This is one of the problems in moving a program or data from one computer to another.

Cards are read by an input device called a *card reader*. Each card is read, one at a time, and the information for each column is sent to the computer. Cards can be read either in an alphabetic mode, where each column is interpreted as a character according to a Hollerith code, or in *column binary mode*, where each column is interpreted as 12 binary digits (hole = 1, no hole = 0) and these 12 bits are sent to the computer with no interpretation as characters, digits, etc.

Cards can be read either by an optical card reader, which uses a set of photocells to detect the holes in each row, or by using a metallic *brush* (one brush for each row) which contacts a charged metal plate behind the card if there is a hole, or is insulated from it by the card if there is no hole. Either technique produces an electric current for a hole (1) and no current for no hole (0). Card readers can read from 200 to 1000 cards per minute or, at 80 characters per card and 60 seconds per minute, from 250 to 1300 characters per second.

Cards can be punched by hand, or if the information is already in the computer, by a computer card punch output device. A computer-controlled card punch will punch either the alphanumeric Hollerith code or column binary in a form which can be read back into a computer later, but often without the printing on the top of the card to allow a person to read it. Card punches operate at a speed of about 200 cards per minute (250 characters per second).

Line printers

In addition to being able to get information into a computer by using a Teletype, paper tape, or punched cards, it is sometimes useful to be able to get information out of the computer. The printer of a Teletype can be used for this purpose, but it is normally quite slow. A card punch can be used, but this requires running the punched cards through another machine to print the information punched in them on paper, or on the cards themselves. The most common form of computer output device is the *line printer*. A line printer is a printer which prints, not one character at a time, but an entire line at a time. The length (or width) of a line varies from 80 to 136 characters. Each character is 1/10 inch wide, so the paper for a line printer varies from about 10 inches to 15 inches across. On each edge is a set of sprocket holes to allow the line printer to easily and accurately move the paper for each line to be printed. A page of computer paper typically has 66 to 88 lines for printing (6 or 8 lines per inch, on 11-inch paper) and each page is serrated to allow easy separation.

The line printer prints each character much the same as a typewriter would. An ink-impregnated ribbon extends along the length of the page. On one side of the ribbon is the paper; on the other, the metallic image of the character. An electrically controlled hammer (solenoid) strikes the type for the selected character, printing the character. The major difference is that where a typewriter prints one character at a time, the line printer prints all the characters at once. Sometimes they "cheat" and print first all the odd columns, then all the even columns. Some of the more inexpensive line printers separately print the first twenty characters, then the next twenty, and so forth.

The character type pieces are organized in two ways. One is as a set of type wheels (one for each character position on the line) which rotate until the correct character is opposite the paper and then print that character. With this system, it is somewhat difficult to assure that each character is positioned exactly right, so some vertical displacement sometimes occurs, which produces an output line that wiggles slightly across the page. An alternative method organizes the characters in a long circular horizontal chain which rotates at high speed along the length of the print line. When the proper character is between the hammer and the ribbon for a particular print position, the hammer fires, to print the character. This may cause some horizontal displacement, so that the character spacing is not exact, but the eye tends not to notice this. To prevent having to wait too long for a given character to appear, characters are repeated on the chain at regular intervals, so that four copies of an "A" may appear on the chain.

Normal computer paper can be used in the line printer, or special *forms* may be used to print checks, reports, letters, bills, books, and so on. Unlike the other devices we have seen, there is no input device which corresponds naturally with this output device. The line printer is mainly used to present the results of a computer program to users for their reading.

Nonmechanical printers are also in use. These devices employ heat or radiation to "print" on specially processed paper and can print at speeds of up to 30,000 lines per minute.

Other input and output devices

The devices and media which we have just seen are by far the most common input and output devices in use with computers today, but they are by no means the only devices. An increasingly common output device is the *cathode-ray tube* (CRT), commonly connected with a keyboard to replace a console typewriter or Teletype. A CRT is basically an oscilloscope or TV tube with additional electronics to allow it to interface with the computer. This device uses an electron beam to "draw" pictures on the phosphorus-coated screen, or simply to display characters. A screen can typically display 24 lines of 80 characters and imitates a Teletype by "scrolling" (a new line appears at the bottom, pushing all other lines up, and the top line disappears). CRTs are quiet, fast, and easy to use, since they are completely electronic, but they suffer from their inability to produce "hard copy" (printed copy) which can be kept for reference.

CRTs were originally connected to computers to serve as graphic output devices, for plotting functions, charts, and diagrams. Another device used for this same purpose, but capable of giving hard copy output, is the *plotter*. A plotter controls the movement of an ink pen over a piece of paper. The paper is either stationary on a flat surface, with the pen moving back and forth across it, or the paper moves along the surface of a cylinder, called a drum, and the pen can move left and right as the paper goes back and forth. The pen can either move in a "down" position, where the pen is touching the paper and a line is left as the pen moves, or in an "up" position, with no line being drawn. Plotters can be quite useful in displaying the results of a computation in an easily understood visual manner.

In addition to output devices, there are additional input devices. *Mark sense* card readers and page readers use a reflective light photocell to be able to read marks made with the standard, number 2 pencil on special mark sense forms. This eliminates the need for a keypunch, since rather than punching a hole in the form, it is only necessary to mark where the hole should be. *Optical character readers* are being developed which can read some types of printed characters.

IBM has introduced a 96-character punched card that is only one-third the size of a Hollerith card, but which uses 3 sets of 6 rows of 32 columns to represent up to 96 characters. Each set of 6 rows encodes a character in a 6-bit BCD code and are read in column binary mode.

Television cameras, loudspeakers, mechanical arms, toy trains, robots, and other strange devices have been attached to computers to allow communication between them and their environment, although mainly for research purposes. A large variety of devices can be attached to a computer to provide it with input and output facilities.

Magnetic tape

Very early in the use of computers, it became obvious that there simply was not enough core memory to store all the information which we wanted to process. Punching the information out on paper tape or cards was both expensive (since the medium could not be reused) and slow. A fast, relatively inexpensive means of storing large amounts of data was needed. The magnetic tape was the answer.

Magnetic tape is a long (2400 feet) reel of a flexible plastic, about $\frac{1}{2}$ inch in width and coated with an iron oxide. Information is recorded by magnetizing little spots on the tape, allowing one bit of information to be recorded per spot. As with paper tape, the tape is recorded in channels, or tracks. Tapes are recorded as either seven- or nine-track tapes. This allows seven or nine bits to be recorded vertically along the width of the tape, accommodating a six- or eight-bit character code plus a parity bit. Each set of seven or nine tracks is called a *frame*. Along the length of the tape, information can be recorded at low density (200 bits per inch), medium density (556 bits per inch), high density (800 bits per inch) or hyper density (1600 bits per inch). The wording "bits per inch" (bpi) really means "frames per inch". Since each bit along the tape is 7 or 9 bits high, each bit along the tape can represent one character and hence, at high density, we can store 800 characters per inch of tape. If an entire tape were used to store information at 800 bpi, 23,040,000 characters could be recorded. In practice, however, it is best not to record too close to either end of the tape, and it is not practical to record information continuously on the tape.

A magnetic tape is mounted on a magnetic tape drive or tape transport to be read or written. In order to work properly, the tape must be travelling past the read-write heads of the tape drive at a fixed speed. This requires some time for the tape to "get up to speed" before reading or writing, and to stop after reading or writing. With only 1/800 inch per character, the tape drive cannot stop between characters. Thus, tape is written in blocks, or *records*, of information, which are read or written at one time and separated by *inter-record gaps*. An inter-record gap is simply a span of blank tape, typically about 3/4-inch long. The inter-record gap allows enough space for the tape drive to stop after one record and get started again before the next record. This can considerably reduce the amount of information on a tape, however.

For example, if we copy 80 character card images to a tape, one card image per record, then at 800 bpi, a card image will take only 0.1 inch of tape. Separating each record by an inter-record gap of 0.75 inch means that less than 1/8 of the tape is being used to store information. This allows the storage of about 30,000 cards per tape.

Most tape drives have the same functions that an audio tape recorder has. They can read or write, rewind, fast forward (called *skipping* forward), or skip backwards. Some tape drives can also read and write tape backwards.

Magnetic tape can be reused; that is, written and then rewritten. One prob-

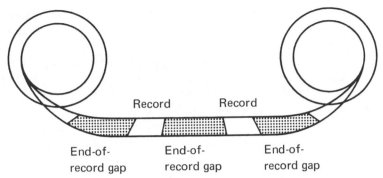

Record   Record

End-of-   End-of-   End-of-
record gap   record gap   record gap

FIGURE 1.10   Magnetic tape—information is recorded in variable-length records which are separated by inter-record gaps.

lem with normal tape drives, however, is that to write on the tape, the information which was there must be erased first. This is done automatically by an erase head that erases the tape in front of the write head, which writes the new information on the tape. The old information which was written on the tape in front of the space just written may be partially erased. Thus, magnetic tape cannot be read beyond the end of the most recent write on the tape. New or corrected information can only be added to the end of a tape. If it must be added in the middle, the entire tape must be recopied.

Another feature of magnetic tape is that the only way to determine where the information is on the tape (as opposed to just blank tape) is by having at least one 1 bit in each frame on the tape. Blank tape looks just like a character of all zeros. (This is like a paper tape with no sprocket hole.) Because of this, either odd parity must be used, or the all-zero code cannot be recorded on the tape. For the BCD code, if this code is written in even parity it is automatically converted to a 12 (octal) code, and all 12 (octal) codes are read back in as a 00 (octal) code. Thus, the character ":", which normally corresponds to a 12 (octal) code cannot be stored on a magnetic tape. In fact, there are two separate BCD codes: *internal BCD*, used for representing characters in memory; and *external BCD*, used for representing characters on tape. This is of little importance except to cause additional difficulty and confusion in the transporting of data or programs from one computer installation to another.

Tapes can be recorded in either even or odd parity. The parity bit is of great value with magnetic tapes, since the likelihood of a parity error on a magnetic tape is nonnegligible. The actual error rate per bit is quite small, but one tape can easily store a million characters, which is 7 or 9 million bits. Also, tapes are susceptible to damage from heat, dust, magnetic fields, or simple wear and tear. Whenever working with magnetic tapes, you should consider the possiblity of parity errors.

Many computer systems store large amounts of data on tape and have extensive tape libraries. Hundreds or thousands of tapes may be mounted on the tape drives for use and then dismounted and put back in the library. Tapes are a *removable* storage media, since they can be removed from the actual tape drive and stored separately from the computer.

In addition to the large storage capacity of magnetic tapes, they can be read or written at very high speeds. It takes from 1 to 20 milliseconds to get the tape up to speed. Then 3000 to 20,000 characters per second can be transferred between the tape and core memory.

How are magnetic tapes used? Mainly, they are used as auxiliary storage devices for the computer, storing large amounts of information, either temporarily or permanently. But they are also used as input and output devices. Because of the large speed difference between card readers and line printers on the one hand and the computer on the other, the computer can spend much of its time waiting on these devices. To prevent this, these devices are sometimes run *off-line*. The card reader reads onto a magnetic tape, rather than directly into the computer. When the tape is full, it is taken over and mounted on a tape drive connected to the computer. The computer reads and processes the data on the input tape, producing output on an output tape. The output tape is then taken to a line printer, which is driven not by the computer but by a tape drive, and the contents of the tape is copied to the line printer. This mode of operation can be quite successful in some situations. Several manufacturers have gone one step further and provide an ability to prepare data directly on a magnetic tape by using a *magnetic keyrecorder*. This device is similar in operation to a keypunch, but it outputs the typed data onto a magnetic tape instead of punched cards.

Magnetic disks and drums

One annoyance in using tapes is that they must be accessed *sequentially*. If we are at the rear of the tape and need some information from the front of the tape, we must rewind the tape. If we then want to continue writing, we must skip forward to the end of the recorded information to be able to write. On some problems, we must be able to store large amounts of data and be able to access it randomly and quickly. For these problems, magnetic tape is insufficient.

A *magnetic disk* is a form of auxiliary storage which is better than tape for these problems. A disk is very similar to a long-playing phonograph record but is made of a flat, circular metallic plate coated with ferromagnetic material. It is used in a disk drive, where it rotates at very high speeds (several thousand rpm) at all times. A read-write head is attached to an arm (like a phonograph needle) and can be positioned over any part of the disk's surface.The surface of the disk is logically divided into tracks, each track being a concentric circle. There are typically 200 tracks per disk surface, and 2 surfaces per disk (top and bottom). Several disks are attached to a spindle (like a stack of records) separated by 1 or 2 inches of space (to allow the read-write heads to move between them). All the disks rotate simultaneously, and each surface (top and bottom of each disk platter) has its own read-write head attached to a moveable arm. All the arms are ganged together and move together.

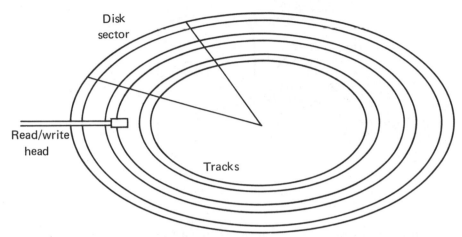

FIGURE 1.11   A magnetic moving head disk. Each disk has about 200 tracks of 12 sectors per track.

In order to read or write from a specific location on the disk, the arm is moved to position the read-write heads over the correct track. When the right spot rotates under the read-write heads, the transfer of information between disk system and computer can begin. It normally takes between 20 and 600 milliseconds to position the heads depending upon how far the arm has to move and whose disk you are working with. After this *seek time*, there is the *latency time* (while waiting for the right spot to rotate under the heads), then the *transfer time* (while the reading or writing is done). Transfer rates for disks range from 100,000 to 1,000,000 characters per second. Disks can store up to 200 million characters, but typically store from 10 to 30 million characters. As with a phonograph record, the entire surface of the disk is not used, since we do not want too get to close to the edge or the middle.

Several variations on this basic design are used. Some disk systems have removable disk packs; that is, one set of disks can be taken off the disk drive and another mounted. This allows disk packs to be used as very high speed, large-capacity tapes. Unlike tapes, however, disks take considerably longer to get up to speed, and to slow down after use, so they are changed only infrequently. Some disk systems are designed as nonremovable devices.

If still faster access to data is needed, it is possible to eliminate the seek time by using a disk system with fixed (i.e., nonmoving) read-write heads. This requires one head for each track. One large system has 5000 separate read-write heads. With this approach, only the latency time and transfer time are important. Since read-write heads are rather expensive, a fixed head device can be very expensive. A compromise between these two extremes is to have several heads per surface—for example, two independent movable arms, one for the inner half of the tracks on each surface, the other for the outer half of the tracks.

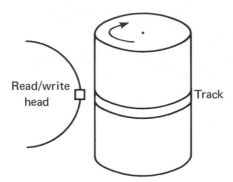

FIGURE 1.12   A magnetic drum.

Similar to the design of the head-per-track disk is the *magnetic drum*. A drum is shaped like a cylinder and the outside surface is coated with a magnetic material. The drum rotates at high speed at all times like the disk. Similar to the disk, the recording surface of the drum is made up of tracks. Each track generally has its own read-write head. The transfer rate of a drum is usually higher than for a disk (up to 1.5 million characters per second), but the capacity is lower (from 1 to 10 million characters). Drums are nonremovable.

Other auxiliary storage devices

Just as there is a wide variety of input devices and output devices, so there is also a variety of auxiliary storage devices. Magnetic tape is being used both in the normal $\frac{1}{2}$-inch magnetic tape reels and in more convenient (but smaller and slower) cassettes and cartridges. Small "floppy" disks are available that can be used very much like a flexible phonograph record. All these media are providing relatively cheap, convenient, mass storage for small computer systems.

For larger computer systems there are more exotic memory systems. Magnetic core storage is available in bulk, for use as an auxiliary storage device. Large (about a million words of memory) core memories can be built whose access times are greater than normal memory but for which sequential blocks of memory can be transferred between the bulk memory and normal memory at normal memory speeds.

Optical memories have been in use at a few computer sites for a number of years. One system used an electron beam to record on photographic film, which was then automatically developed and stored. When needed, it could be automatically retrieved and read by use of another electron beam and a photocell. Access times were on the order of seconds to minutes, but this was still faster than finding and mounting a tape. Recently, a similar system using a laser beam to burn small holes in plastic chips has been developed which provides a very large storage capacity (over a billion characters). Other new memories are being developed.

It is not possible to go into the details of all the various input/output/storage devices that are available. However, several of these devices will be referred to later in this book, and, since every computer installation will have its own devices, you should be aware both of typical devices (typewriter-like terminals, CRTs, paper tape reader/punch, card reader/punch, line printers, magnetic tapes, disks, and drums) and their general characteristics, as well as the great variety of devices a computer may use.

EXERCISES

a. Name five different I/O devices. What are their media?
b. How many bits are used in the BCD character code? In EBCDIC? In ASCII?
c. Give two definitions of BCD.
d. Why is a six-bit character code unsatisfactory? Why is a seven-bit code inconvenient?
e. At 200 bpi, how many bits of actual information are stored in 1 inch of 7-track magnetic tape?
f. Why are there 7- and 9-track tapes?
g. Suppose we wish to store 7-bit ASCII on a magnetic tape, one character per frame, with odd parity, and there are no 8-track computer tapes. What kind of tape do we use?
h. What is a parity bit? Explain odd and even parity, and how parity is used to detect errors in data transmission.
i. What is a typical set of functions and displays for a computer console?
j. Why are there sprocket holes on paper tape? Does the same problem occur on magnetic tape, and if so, why are there no sprocket holes on magnetic tape?
k. If each column of a punched card has 12 rows and each row can either be punched or not, how many different bit patterns can be punched in one column? Can you suggest a more efficent way to represent information on punched cards than the Hollerith punched card code?
l. Recording 80 character card images at 800 bpi with inter-record gaps of 0.75 inch results in less than 1/8 of the tape being used for information. How much tape is used at 200 bpi? At 1600 bpi? Which of these recording densities would be best?
m. What is the difference between a disk and a drum? Between a moving head device and a fixed-head device?
n. Define seek time, latency time, and transfer time for fixed head and moving head disks and drums.

1.4 THE CONTROL UNIT

Each of the components of the computer system which we have discussed so far has supplied one of the necessary functions of a computer. The memory unit provides the ability to store and retrieve words quickly. The computation unit can interpret these words as numbers and perform arithmetic functions on them. The input/output system can read information into the computer or write information from the computer. But how does the memory unit know what to store, and in what location of memory? How does the computation unit know which operation to perform? How does the I/O system know when and what to transfer in or out of the computer? Obviously, the system needs some coordination between the components. This is the function of the control unit.

The control unit directs the memory unit to store information or read that information back and send it to the computation unit. It instructs the computation unit to perform a specific operation and what to do with the result (send it back to memory or to a register). The control unit directs the I/O system to transfer information and tells it where the information is and where it should go. The control unit supervises the operation of the entire computer system.

How does the control unit know what to do? In some *special purpose* computers, the control unit is built to perform one specific task and is designed to do this and only this. For *general purpose* computers, the specification of what the control unit is to do is supplied by a *program*. A program is a sequence of instructions to the computer which the control unit uses to control the operation of the memory unit, the computation unit, and the I/O system. The control unit executes continuously the following *instruction execution cycle*:

1. Fetch the next instruction from memory.
2. Execute that instruction by sending appropriate signals to the other components of the system.
3. Then go back to step 1 and repeat the sequence for the next instruction.

Instructions are stored as words in memory, in the same way that data is stored. In order to locate the word in memory which is the next instruction to be executed, the address of the memory location which is storing that instruction is needed. This address is stored in a register in the control unit, called the *program counter* or *instruction address register*. The name of this register varies from computer to computer. In order to fetch the next instruction to be executed, this address is sent to the memory unit by copying it into the memory address register. The memory unit is then ordered to read, and when the read portion of the read-write cycle is over, the result has appeared in the memory data register. This is copied back to the control unit and put into an *instruction register*. The instruction address register is then incremented to the address of the next location in memory. Under normal circumstances, this will be the address of the next instruction to be fetched.

There are many different instructions that most computers can execute. The set of instructions which a computer can execute is called its *instruction set*, or *instruction repertoire*. Each computer tends to have its own instruction set, although many computers have similar or compatible repertoires. Since instructions are stored in memory, they must be encoded into a binary representation. As with all the other encodings of information, the decision as to how the encoding is done is strictly arbitrary; it can be done in many different ways. Some ways make the subsequent construction of the control unit easier, others make it more difficult. We consider now some of the general systematic methods used to encode instructions, but this general review does not cover all the many different ways instructions are represented.

One of the first problems is to decide what is an instruction. One approach is to consider every operation which differs from another in any way to be a different, unique, instruction. Thus, storing a zero word in location 21 of the memory is a different instruction from storing a zero word in location 47. More commonly, these are considered to be the same instruction, with the address of the location to be set to zero treated as an *operand*. Some instructions may have several operands. For example, an "add" instruction may have three operands: the location of the augend, the location of the addend, and the location in which the sum is to be put. Thus, a specific instruction is made up of an operation and a number (perhaps zero) of operands. The operations are assigned *operation codes* (opcodes), which are generally binary numbers. The operands are specified by the address of a location in memory, an integer number, or a register name.

The different components of an instruction are specified by different portions of the computer word which specifies a particular instruction. A word is composed of *fields*, one field specifying the opcode, and the others specifying modifications of the operation, or operands of the instruction. The *instruction format* defines where each field is in a word, how large it is, and what it is used for. For example, on the HP2100, the instruction format is

D/I	opcode	Z/C	operand address

where,

> D/I (bit 15) and Z/C (bit 10) are one-bit fields
> which modify how the operand address is computed;
> *opcode* is a 4-bit opcode (16 instructions); and
> *operand address* is 10 bits long.

Example:
0010110010101110
D/I = 0   *opcode* = 0101   Z/C = 1
operand address = 0010101110

The number of bits which are available for the opcode field determines the number of different instructions which can be in a computer instruction set.

Thus, the HP2100 can have up to 16 different instructions because it has a 4-bit opcode field.

Some machines have different instruction formats for different opcodes. For example, on the IBM 7090, five different instruction formats were used, with the decision between different formats made on the basis of the opcode. This allows different operations to have a varying number and kind of operands. For example, an instruction which halts the computer need have no operand, while an instruction which stores a zero in a memory location needs one operand, which is the address of the memory location, and an add instruction like the one described above may need three operands. In addition to being of different formats, instructions may also be of different *lengths*, with some instructions occupying two or three words of memory, rather than just one.

When a computer is being designed, the specification of the instruction set is one of the major problems that must be considered. The desire to have a large set of instructions must be balanced against the difficulty of building the control hardware to execute those instructions. The instruction set is sometimes tailored to be able to efficiently solve specific kinds of problems. On the IBM 360, for example, two different, but similar, instruction sets—the business instruction set and the scientific instruction set—were developed. Most of the instructions were the same in both sets, but some additional instructions for character handling and decimal arithmetic were included in the business set, while floating point operations were added to the scientific set. The instruction set is one of the major differences between computers.

On the other hand, although specific instructions vary from computer to computer, almost every computer has similar instructions. Instructions can be grouped into classes of similar instructions. Typical classes are

1. *Load and Store Instructions*. These instructions transfer words between the registers of the computer and the memory unit. The address of the memory location to be used and the register involved are specified as operands.
2. *Arithmetic Instructions*. These instructions specify an arithmetic operation (such as addition, subtraction, multiplication, or division), its operands, and where to put the result.
3. *Input/Output Instructions*. This class of instructions causes the I/O system to begin operation, halt operation, or allows the state of the I/O devices to be tested. Operands may include a memory address, a device number, and a function (input, output, test, rewind, and so on).
4. *Comparison, Test, and Jump Instructions*. Sometimes it is necessary to execute two different sequences of instructions, depending upon properties of the data. These instructions allow the program to specify a condition to test and a new memory address where execution of the next instruction should continue if the condition is true.
5. *Other, Miscellaneous Instructions*. This group includes all the instruc-

tions which will not fit conveniently into any other group. It includes instructions like the instruction to halt the computer and the "no operation" instruction.

These classes of instructions are by no means well-defined or complete. Some instructions may belong to several classes (like the instruction which tests the status of an I/O device and is hence both an I/O instruction and a Test instruction). The classes could also be further refined into more specific sets of instructions, but this could result in a very large number of classes. These classes should give you an idea of the types of instructions which are typical.

For all computers, the basic instruction execution cycle is the same. With the additional information about instructions we have now gained, we can give a better statement of the instruction execution cycle which the control unit follows:

1. Fetch the next instruction.
2. Decode the instruction.
3. Fetch the operands (if any) needed for the instruction.
4. Execute the instruction.
5. Go back to step 1 and repeat for the next instruction.

An even more detailed statement of the instruction cycle can be given for any specific machine, but this general outline is the same for all machines.

EXERCISES

a. What are the four basic components of a computer?
b. What is the function of the control unit?
c. What is the basic instruction execution cycle for all stored-program computers?
d. What is the difference between a general purpose and a special purpose computer? How does each know what to do next?
e. What is the use of a program counter or instruction address?
f. Suppose a computer has 37 different instructions. How many bits would be in its opcode field?

1.5 SUMMARY

So far we have been considering general principles that apply to all computers. As we have seen, there are many decisions which need to be made in the design of a computer. The basic parts of a computer are the memory unit, the computation unit, the input/output system, and the control unit, but in any given computer these units will be designed and built in a specific way. The specific design of both the components of a computer and their interconnections defines the *architecture* of the computer. The architecture of a computer defines what registers are used and for what, what the pathways in the computer are for, data and instruction formats, and how the basic units are connected.

Most books for a course on assembly language programming have introductory chapters discussing the general structure of computers. Ullman (1976) and Gear (1974) are such books. More complete and detailed information is contained in Sloan (1976), Tanenbaum (1976), and Stone (1975). These books are concerned solely with the organization and architecture of computer systems.

In order to learn how the architecture affects the ways computers are used, what computers can do, and how they do it, a specific computer design, the MIX computer, is examined (Chapters 2 and 3). After the background information necessary for a good understanding of this particular computer is presented, some other computer designs are presented (Chapter 10) to illustrate how these systems are different from and similar to the MIX computer.

2

THE MIX COMPUTER SYSTEM

The MIX computer system first appeared in 1968, although prototype models were undoubtedly in use before this. The MIX machine was designed to be both powerful and simple. It incorporates many of the useful and common features of a large class of computers. Although you may never have an opportunity to program in MIX machine language after this text, the MIX machine is so similar to many other computers that you will be able to learn and program the machine language for any new computer easily if you are able to program well for the MIX computer.

Although we will talk about *the* MIX computer, there is not just *one* MIX computer, but rather a family of computers. The basic machine, the MIX 1009, is available in a number of models. The choice of which model should be used is an important decision and is affected by the problems for which the computer will be programmed and the funds available (the bigger models cost more). All MIX machines have the same basic instruction set and architecture. This basic machine is the MIX 1009. To this basic machine can be added I/O devices, additional memory, and additional instructions to increase the speed, capacity, and convenience of the basic machine. We shall introduce some of these extensions as we discuss the MIX machine, in order to show how the capabilities of the machine can be increased. Most of our discussion is applicable to all MIX computers, with one exception.

The original design of the MIX machine reveals a certain ambiguity as to whether it is a binary machine or a decimal machine. This is to its credit, since, as we have seen, both systems have their advantages and disadvantages. With the rapid technological changes which are occurring in the design and use of computer hardware, a machine which is too closely tied to a particular hardware technology may rapidly become obsolete. The MIX machine was designed to be a flexible computer which can be implemented in many different hardware technologies. Thus, it will be able to evolve and improve while maintaining compatibility of programs which are written for different models of the computer. Most programs can be written so that they will work properly on any MIX machine, be it binary, decimal, hexadecimal, or any other underlying number system. MIX programs should be written to execute correctly for a variety of memories, computation units, and I/O devices.

There are certain properties of a specific model of the MIX machine which can be exploited, however, to increase considerably the efficiency and clarity of a program. It is important, for example, that the techniques for handling binary data be well understood, since so many computers are binary. Because of these considerations, we will sometimes use, not the basic MIX 1009 computer, but the MIX 1009B binary computer for our examples.

The MIX 1009B is a binary MIX computer with the same basic architecture as the MIX 1009, but with an explicitly binary representation of instructions and data. The instruction set has been extended to include instructions which exploit the binary data representation. These instructions are seldom needed, so most programs for the MIX 1009B computer will execute correctly on the MIX 1009D decimal computer as well as the basic MIX 1009 computer. Programs which use only the instructions which are available on all three machines are using the *common* instruction set. We state when the binary nature of the MIX 1009B computer is used in any of our programs.

A considerable amount of our early discussion of the MIX computer will deal with the *representation* of data and instructions in the computer. Since more computers represent information in binary than in decimal, we will likewise use binary to show our data representations. The contents of memory and encodings will thus be presented in binary (octal, actually).

2.1 THE MIX COMPUTER ARCHITECTURE

We turn now to examining the basic architecture of the MIX computer. The presentation of the specific properties of the MIX computer follows the general presentation of Chapter 1. We consider first the memory unit and registers of the MIX machine, its number representation scheme, its input/output system, character code, and instruction set. After a brief introduction to the instruction set, we turn to a description of the MIXAL assembly language for the MIX computers. Chapter 3 presents a very detailed discussion of the instruction set for the MIX computer.

The MIX architecture

The basic MIX machine has *4000 words* of memory. These are addressed by the addresses 0, 1, 2, . . . , 3999. Each word of memory consists of *five bytes plus a sign*. Each byte is six bits (on a binary machine). Thus, a MIX word is 31 bits, consisting of a one-bit sign and 5 six-bit bytes. Bytes are numbered from 0 to 5, left to right, with "byte" 0 being the sign bit.

sign	byte	byte	byte	byte	byte

Byte 0   1   2   3   4   5

The MIX machine has nine registers. The *A (accumulator) register* and the *X (extension) register* are both five bytes plus sign, like the words of memory. The A register is called rA; the X register, rX. Six *index registers* are named I1, I2, I3, I4, I5, I6. Index registers are only two bytes plus sign. The *J (jump) register* is only two bytes and is identified by rJ. In addition to these nine registers, the MIX

FIGURE 2.1 The MIX memory (4000 words; 5 bytes plus sign).

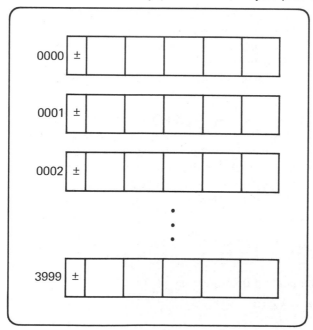

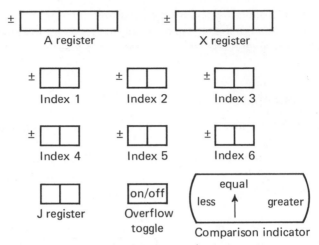

FIGURE 2.2 The MIX registers.

machine has an *overflow toggle* (OT) and a *comparison indicator* (CI). The overflow toggle is one bit, being either ON or OFF, while the comparison indicator has three states: LESS, EQUAL, and GREATER. The usage of these registers will become clear later.

Numbers are represented in *sign and magnitude notation*. With six bits per byte

one byte can represent 0 through 63.
two bytes can represent 0 through 4095.
three bytes can represent 0 through 262,143.
four bytes can represent 0 through 16,777,215.
five bytes can represent 0 through 1,073,741,823.

With a sign bit, the A register, the X register and each MIX memory word can represent the range of integers from $-1{,}073{,}741{,}823$ to $+1{,}073{,}741{,}823$. Index registers can represent any number in the range -4095 to $+4095$. The J register can represent only 0 to 4095, since it has no sign bit.

Floating point numbers are represented by storing a biased (excess 32) base 64 exponent in byte 1 (the high-order byte) and the fractional part in bytes 2 through 5. The MIX word

$\pm$	e	f_1	f_2	f_3	f_4

represents the floating point number

$$\pm 0.f_1 f_2 f_3 f_4 \times 64^{e-32}$$

A floating point number is normalized when (a) it is zero, or (b) the leading fractional digit (f_1) is not zero. This representation allows a range of floating point numbers from about 64^{-32} to 64^{31} (about 10^{-58} to 10^{56}) with an accuracy of about five or six decimal places.

Double precision floating point numbers on the MIX computer extend both the range and accuracy of representation by using two MIX words as

$\pm$	e_1	e_2	f_1	f_2	f_3	$\cdot$	f_4	f_5	f_6	f_7	f_8

which represents

$$\pm 0.f_1 f_2 f_3 f_4 f_5 f_6 f_7 f_8 \times 64^{e_1 e_2 - 2048}$$

The sign of the number is determined by the sign of the first word; the sign bit of the second word is ignored. This representation gives about 12 places of accuracy and a range from approximately 10^{-3700} to 10^{3700}.

The MIX machine has provision for several different input/output devices. The basic MIX machine has room for up to 20 separate devices. These are nominally used for eight magnetic tape units, eight disk or drum units, a card reader, a card punch, a line printer, and a typewriter/paper tape device. Each device is identified by a unit number from 0 to 19. This corresponds to the slot in the MIX computer chassis in which the interface card for the device is plugged in. The disks, drums, and tapes store information in 100-word fixed length

TABLE 2.1 The Mix Character Set

Character	MIX[a]	Character	MIX	Character	MIX	Character	MIX
blank	00	M	14	Y	28	(	42
A	01	N	15	Z	29	)	43
B	02	O	16	0	30	+	44
C	03	P	17	1	31	–	45
D	04	Q	18	2	32	*	46
E	05	R	19	3	33	/	47
F	06	Φ	20	4	34	=	48
G	07	Π	21	5	35	$	49
H	08	S	22	6	36	<	50
I	09	T	23	7	37	>	51
Θ	10	U	24	8	38	@	52
J	11	V	25	9	39	;	53
K	12	W	26	.	40	:	54
L	13	X	27	,	41	'	55

[a] Codes are given in decimal.

records. The card reader, card punch, line printer, and typewriter/paper tape units are character oriented and use the MIX character code shown in Table 2.1. Each byte of a MIX word can store one character, so each word can store 5 characters. The card reader and card punch have 16 word (80 character) records, while the line printer uses 24 words per record (120 characters). The typewriter/paper tape unit transmits 70 characters (14 words) at a time.

The instruction set of the MIX machine is represented in the following format

±	A	A	I	F	C

Byte   0   1   2   3   4   5

Byte 5, C, is the *operation code* (opcode) specifying the basic operation. F (byte 4) is a modifier byte which gives additional information about the operation to be performed. The ±AA field (bytes 0, 1, and 2) is the operand for the operation, and I (byte 3) modifies the operand.

There are eight classes of instructions for the MIX machine. *Loading Operators* copy information from memory into the registers, while the *storing operators* copy from the registers back to memory. These are necessary because all *arithmetic operations* operate on the registers. A set of *immediate operators* allow the registers to be modified by small constants. Data can be tested by a set of *comparison operators* which set the comparison indicator. *Jump instructions* can transfer control to different instructions based upon the comparison indicator or the state of the registers. *Input/Output operations* allow information to flow between memory and the input/output devices. A set of *miscellaneous operations* includes instructions to move information from memory to memory, shift information in the registers, and convert between the character code and binary representation of numbers.

The MIX instruction set, briefly

An assembly language or machine language programmer must be very familiar with the instruction set of the machine which is being used. However, often some of the instructions are used only rarely, in certain special circumstances. Some instructions may also be rather complex. Because of this an assembly language programmer always programs with a computer reference manual at hand. The computer reference manual lists all the instructions for the computer and exactly what they do. In Chapter 3, we give a reference manual for the MIX computer. This is a rather technical and lengthy description of the MIX instruction set and may require several readings before it is completely understood. This is normal. Whenever you are programming, you may want to refer to the description of the MIX instruction set often.

Each instruction is specified by its numeric opcode (C) and the opcode modifier (F). The computer hardware interprets the contents of the C and F fields of the instruction and performs the instruction specified. Thus, if the opcode is

10 (octal) and the F field is 05, then the hardware knows that it is to take the contents of the location specified by the address part of the instruction and copy it into the A register.

It is difficult to memorize all the different numeric opcodes of a computer and their corresponding instruction. Because of this, assembly language programmers do not use the numeric opcode of an instruction to identify the instruction but use a short name which tries to describe the effect of the instruction. This is a *symbolic opcode*. It is also called a *mnemonic opcode*. For example, the instruction which copies the contents of a memory location into the A register is denoted by "LDA" which stands for "*LoaD* the *A* register". Machine language programs are developed with symbolic opcodes, rather than numeric opcodes. After the program is written, it is necessary only to look up in a table the corresponding numeric opcode for each symbolic opcode, in order to produce the final machine language program (in binary).

The choice of which symbolic opcodes stand for which numeric opcodes is completely arbitrary. However, most symbolic opcodes are a natural abbreviation for the machine instruction in order to make them easier to remember. Also, since programmers want to be able to talk to each other about their programs, everyone who is working with a given machine generally uses the same symbolic opcodes. The symbolic opcodes are almost always assigned by the computer manufacturer and everyone uses these standard symbolic opcodes.

We give now a brief description of the MIX instruction set.

There are 16 *loading operators*. These loading operators are used to copy the contents of a memory location (or the negative of the contents) into the registers of the MIX machine. The address of the location to be copied from is specified by the address part of the instruction. There is a separate instruction to allow loading of the A register, the X register, and the six index registers, and another separate instruction for loading the negative of the contents of a memory location into each of these eight registers.

In addition to being able to load from memory into the registers, we need to be able to store information from the registers into memory. The *storing operators* allow this to be done. These storing operators are almost the opposite of the loading operators. The contents of the A register, the X register, and the six index registers can be stored into any memory location. In addition to these instructions, we can also store the J register. Another special store instruction allows us to easily set any memory location to zero, a very important value in programming.

Being able to move information between memory and the registers is of little use if we cannot do useful computations with the information. The *arithmetic operators* provide the four standard arithmetic operations of addition, subtraction, multiplication and division for both integers (ADD, SUB, MUL, DIV) and floating point numbers (FADD, FSUB, FMUL, FDIV). These operations are all binary operations; that is, they operate on two operands. But notice that we have only one address per instruction, and hence we can only specify one operand per instruction. This problem is resolved by defining all arithmetic operations to perform their operation on the A register and the memory location given in the instruction, leaving their result in the A register. Thus, an ADD instruction adds the contents of the memory location specified by the address part of the instruction to the A register, and the sum is left in the A register. The A register is often called the *accumulator* because of this.

In addition to being able to modify the A register by full-word addition and subtraction, it is often desirable to be able to modify the A register, the X register, and index registers by "small" integers. Commonly, it is necessary to add or subtract 1, for example. This capability can, of course, be achieved by storing a word in memory whose contents are an integer 1, and then adding or subtracting by using ADD or SUB, but the MIX machine provides a more convenient method with its *immediate operators*. For the normal arithmetic operators, the address field of the instruction specifies the address of a location in memory whose contents are the operand for the instruction. These operations are called *memory reference* instructions. With immediate operators, the address field specifies the operand itself. This means that the operand must be the same size as an address, so it is limited to being in the range -4095 to $+4095$, a "small" integer. Immediate operators allow the operand to be entered directly into the A, X, or index registers; or for the negative of the operand to be entered (in analogy to the "load" and "load negative" instructions) or for the operand to be added (an increment) or subtracted (a decrement) from the registers.

In addition to being able to perform computations on the registers, it is necessary in programming to be able to compare results in order to perform different computations for different types of input. The *comparison operators* are used to compare the contents of a register to the contents of a memory location and set the comparison indicator to indicate the result of the comparison. The comparison indicator has three possible values: LESS, EQUAL, and GREATER. The value of the comparison indicator changes only when a compare instruction is executed. There are instructions to compare a memory location to the A, X, or index registers as integers, or to the A register as a floating point number.

Once the comparison is done, we may wish to execute one of two different sequences of instructions, depending upon the result of the comparison. The *jump operators* allow the program to transfer control to a different location if the condition tested for is true, or to continue execution at the next location if the condition is false. Jump instructions allow the comparison indicator to be used to cause a jump, or to jump on the positive, negative, or zero state of the A, X, or index registers. Two special remarks need to be made about the jump operators. If a jump is made (for any of the jump instructions except JSJ), then the J register is set equal to the address of the instruction which immediately follows the jump instruction. This allows us to determine where we would have been if we had not jumped and is useful for subroutine calls. The JOV and JNOV instructions allow us to test the state of the overflow toggle and, in addition, always leave the overflow toggle *off*.

Any sequence of instructions which performs some useful computation must have input data and output results. The input/output instructions start the movement of data between the memory of the MIX computer and an external I/O device. The I/O system for the MIX machine is very simple and is controlled by only five instructions. The use of these instructions is covered in more detail in Chapter 5.

There are a few instructions that are left over, which do not fit comfortably into any of the above categories. These include operators which convert from character code to binary (NUM), and from binary to character code (CHAR), which copy a block of words starting at one location in memory to another location in memory (MOVE), and which shift the contents of the A and X registers left or right. These last instructions are the shift instructions and can shift the A register end-off, or the A and X register (as a unit) end-off or circularly. The sign bits are not affected by any of the shift instructions.

There are also a few control operations, such as HLT, which halts the computer, and NOP, which does nothing.

This very brief description of the MIX instruction set should give you an idea of the types of instructions which are available on the MIX machine, and the level of detail which is necessary when working in machine language. In fact, the level of detail needed to write programs in machine language is quite great, and in order to be able to program well for a computer it is necessary to understand the *internal* structure of the computer. The next chapter is a reference section which describes, in detail, the actual operation of the MIX computer.

Once you are familiar with the architecture and instruction set of the MIX computer, you can begin to program. In this section we present two ways to program: machine language and assembly language. These two programming languages are very similar and are often confused for each other. There is, however, a definite difference between the two, and almost no one voluntarily programs in machine language. After giving an example of machine language programming, we present the MIX assembly language, MIXAL, to provide the assembly language which is used in the remainder of this text.

2.2 MACHINE LANGUAGE

Machine language is the only language which the MIX machine can execute: *binary*. Every instruction must be encoded in the proper numeric binary representation in order for the MIX computer to understand it. All computers can speak only machine language and, to make things worse, the machine language for most computers is different for each computer. The machine language is defined by the instruction set and instruction format of the computer.

For example, in MIX, the instruction to load the X register with the contents of location 1453 is, in binary

+001100101011000000000101001111

or, in octal

+1453000517

(Although the computer machine language must be in binary, we shall express it in octal for convenience.)

A program in machine language is a set of addresses of instructions and data and the contents of these memory locations. To illustrate machine language programming, let us write a machine language program for a very simple problem, such as adding two numbers and printing their sum.

Even solving this very simple problem requires careful thought. How are the two numbers to be input? What should the output look like? Where does our program go in memory? These questions are actually relatively minor, compared with the actual programming, and so they will be answered later. We will basically assume that the two numbers to be added are on an input card and the sum will be printed on the line printer. The general outline of our program is given by the following algorithm.

Step I   Input the two numbers (IN)
Step II   Add the two numbers (ADD)
Step III   Output the sum (OUT)
Step IV   Stop (HLT)

This is an algorithm for solving our problem, but it leaves a lot unsaid. In most higher level languages (such as Fortran, PL/I, Algol, and Pascal), each of the above steps could be expressed as a single statement in the higher-level language. In machine language, however, things are more difficult.

After each step of the above program, we have listed the (symbolic) opcode in MIX which will do roughly what we want. Upon careful examination, however, we find that these instructions are not quite sufficient. First, the IN and OUT instructions only start an I/O operation; the numbers will not be input or output until the device is not busy again. Also, both the card reader and line printer use a character code representation of data, while the ADD instruction must have its data in numeric binary. Thus, we must *refine* our statement of what is to be done in steps I and III, for the input and output. Our second version of a solution to this problem is, then,

Step I   Input the two numbers

      I.1   Begin reading the numbers (IN)
      I.2   Wait until input complete (JBUS or JRED)
      I.3   Convert the two numbers to binary from character code (NUM)

Step II   Add the two numbers (ADD)

Step III   Output the sum

      III.1   Convert the sum to character code (CHAR)
      III.2   Begin the output of the sum (OUT)
      III.3   Wait until output complete (JRED or JBUS)

Step IV   Stop (HLT)

This improves our solution, making it closer to actual machine language instructions, but there are still some problems.

When working with data in a computer, there are two properties of the data which must be kept in mind. One is the *type* of the data; that is, how it is represented. Data can be represented in many ways. The number 5, for example, can be represented as an integer number (+0000000005), as a floating point number (+4105000000), in character code (+3636363643), in character code for the Roman numeral representation (+3100000000), and so on. The same piece of data may exist in different representations at different times in the computer. For example, a CHAR instruction will convert a binary integer representation into a character code representation. Thus, the type of a piece of data is a dynamic property of the data; it may change with the execution of the program.

The other property which must be kept in mind when programming is the location of the data: where is it stored? Data may be stored in memory (which location?), in a register (which register?), or on an I/O device (which unit and where on that unit?). Data may exist in several places at the same time. After a LDA instruction, the data is in both the A register and in memory. Data may also exist in several different places, in different representations at the same time or at different times. It should be remembered that each piece of memory in a computer has one and only one value at any given time, so that two different items or two different representations of the same item cannot exist in the same location at the same time. The most common location for data is in one of the registers or in memory. Since the registers are needed for performing arithmetic, data is often kept in memory and loaded into a register only when needed.

But, to get back to the problem at hand, the algorithm above does not consider the problem of where our data is stored, or the effect of our operations upon these storage locations. We now should add whatever instructions are needed to put information in the right place for our instructions.

First, we note that the IN instruction will read our card into memory, while the NUM instruction wants its operands to be in the A and X register. Thus, our program for step I.3 needs to be refined. We need to convert the first number, then the second number, from character code to numeric.

I.3   Convert the two numbers to binary from character code

    a.   Load first 5 bytes of character code of the first number into A register, second 5 bytes into X register (LDA, LDX)

    b.   Convert to numeric (NUM)

    c.   Store first number back into memory to free registers for next conversion (STA)

    d.   Load first 5 bytes of second number into A register, second 5 into X (LDA, LDX)

    e.   Convert to numeric (NUM)

    f.   Store second number in memory (STA)

This code now moves the two numbers from memory back into memory in a converted form. Now to do the ADD, we need to load one number into the A register and add the other to it.

Step II   Add the two numbers

II.1   Load first number into A register (LDA)
II.2   Add second number (ADD)
II.3   Store sum back in memory (STA)

The conversion for output uses the CHAR instruction. This instruction assumes that its operand is in the A register and puts the character code representation of this number back into the A and X registers. The OUT for step III.2 assumes that the sum (in character code) is in memory. This means we need to refine III.1, as

III.1   Convert sum to character code

a.   Load sum from memory (LDA)
b.   Convert to character code (CHAR)
c.   Store both A and X register into memory for output (STA, STX)

After these refinements, our entire algorithm looks like:

Step I   Input the two numbers.

I.1   Begin reading the numbers (IN)
I.2   Wait until input complete (JBUS or JRED)
I.3   Convert the two numbers to binary

a.   Load first number into A and X registers (LDA, LDX)
b.   Convert to numeric (NUM)
c.   Store first number (STA)
d.   Load next number into A and X (LDA, LDX)
e.   Convert to numeric (NUM)
f.   Store second number back in memory (STA)

Step II   Add the two numbers

II.1   Load first number from memory (LDA)
II.2   Add the second number (ADD)
II.3   Store sum back in memory (STA)

Step III   Output the sum

III.1   Convert sum to character code

a.   Load sum from memory (LDA)
b.   Convert to character code (CHAR)

     c. Store A and X registers for output (STA, STX)

III.2 Begin the output of the sum (OUT)

III.3 Wait until output is complete (JBUS or JRED)

Step IV Stop (HLT)

This gives us a complete set of instructions for our program. Looking them over, we should notice at once that some of the instructions are not needed. Specifically, the STA in step II.3 is followed by an LDA in step III.1a of the same information. Since the STA of step II.3 does not change the contents of the A register, we can drop the LDA altogether. As soon as we do this, we notice that the store in II.3 is now no longer needed either. Hence, we eliminate both the STA in II.3 and the LDA in III.1a.

Similarly, if we consider that addition is commutative (i.e., $a + b = b + a$), we realize that, since the NUM of step I.3e leaves its result in the A register and the ADD wants one of its operands in the A register, we can eliminate the STA in I.3f and the load in II.1, changing II.2 to adding the first number (from memory) to the second (in the A register).

These types of considerations are known as *local optimizations*, since we are improving the program (in terms of number of instructions, execution time, and number of data locations needed) by making only small changes in the program. These small changes only affect a small amount of the program, and take advantage of the local, temporary flow of data within the computer. This is in contrast to *global optimization*, which tries to improve the program by considering the entire program at once.

The next problem we need to face is: Where do we put our data? This is called *storage allocation*. It is necessary to use memory for our input, our output, and the temporary storage of the first number in memory. (Notice that our local optimization eliminated the need for memory to store either the second number or the sum.) For the input card, we will need 16 memory locations; the output line will require 24 memory locations. We need one location to store one of the numbers. If we start our program at location 0000 of memory, then we can allocate memory for our data either before or after our instructions. If we put our data before the program, then we can reserve locations 0000 to 0017 for the input card, 0020 for the number, and 0021 to 0050 for the output line image. Our instructions then begin at location 0051, and continue to (counting 16 instructions) 0070. Alternatively, we can put our 16 instructions at locations 0000 to 0017, our card image at 0020 to 0037, our first number at 0040, and our line image from 0041 to 0070. Since it makes no difference, we flip a coin, and it comes up, . . . tails! So we will put our data before our instructions.

Now, we can write what instruction goes into each memory location. We assume that the two numbers we are to add will be right-justified in columns 1 to 10 and 11 to 20 of the input card. We put the output sum in columns 1 to 10 of the line printer image.

```
0000–0017    Card image
     0020    Storage location for one number
0021–0050    Line printer line image
     0051    Begin input into locations 0000 to 0017 from card reader
             (IN)
     0052    Wait until the card reader is done by jumping to this instruc-
             tion until card reader is not busy (JBUS)
     0053    Load first five columns of card from 0000 into A (LDA)
     0054    Load second five columns from 0001 into X (LDX)
     0055    Convert to numeric (NUM)
     0056    Store first number in 0020 (STA)
     0057    Load first five bytes of second number, columns 11–15, from
             location 0002 into A (LDA)
     0060    Load columns 16–20 from location 0003 into X (LDX)
     0061    Convert to number (NUM)
     0062    Add first number (in 0020) to A register (ADD)
     0063    Convert the sum (in A) to character code (CHAR)
     0064    Store first 5 bytes of sum in location 0021 (STA)
     0065    Store second 5 bytes of sum in location 0022 (STX)
     0066    Begin output of line image in locations 0021 to 0050 to line
             printer (OUT)
     0067    Wait until output is complete by jumping to this instruction
             until line printer is ready (JBUS)
     0070    Stop (HLT)
```

Now that we have our program designed, we can convert this into machine language. This involves giving the (octal) machine language representation of each instruction. For the first one, we have an IN instruction, whose opcode is 44. The F field is the device which is the card reader, device number 16 (20 octal). The address field is the address of the first location to read into, in this case 0000. So our first instruction is

```
0051    +0000 00 20 44
```

Our next instruction is a JBUS (opcode = 42) to location 0052 for device 16, or

```
0052    +0052 00 20 42
```

Continuing, we can write our entire program, in machine language, as follows. On each line we give the address of the instruction, the numeric octal representation of the instruction, and a short comment about what the instruction should do.

```
0051    +0000 00 20 44    Begin reading a card
0052    +0052 00 20 42    Wait until read done
0053    +0000 00 05 10    Put part of number in A
0054    +0001 00 05 17    Put rest in X
```

0055	+0000 00 00 05	Convert to numeric
0056	+0020 00 05 30	Store for later ADD
0057	+0002 00 05 10	Do the same for the
0060	+0003 00 05 17	Second number
0061	+0000 00 00 05	Convert to numeric
0062	+0020 00 05 01	Add the two numbers
0063	+0000 00 01 05	Convert sum to characters
0064	+0021 00 05 30	Store first 5 characters
0065	+0022 00 05 37	And second 5 characters
0066	+0021 00 22 45	Start print of sum
0067	+0067 00 22 42	Wait until print is done
0070	+0000 00 02 05	Stop

This is a MIX machine language program to read two numbers from a card and print their sum. It is difficult to follow, long, obscure, and probably wrong. The input numbers must be right-justified in columns 1 to 10 and 11 to 20 of the input card. Overflow is not considered. Only the sum is printed, not the input numbers and their sum. It is not a very easy way to add two numbers. If we only wanted to add two numbers, it would be better to do it by hand. However, if a million pairs of numbers are to be added, then a program similar to the above might be reasonable. It is in these cases that writing a computer program is worth the effort and trouble.

Machine language is hardly worth the effort, however. Any little change would require us to rewrite the entire program. To add an instruction to test for overflow, for example, requires inserting a JOV instruction right after the ADD instruction at location 0011. This would require all the addresses of instructions and data which follow the ADD to be increased by one, and result in changing many of the address fields in the program. Also the last step of actually converting our program into machine language was very simple from an intellectual point of view, but dull, monotonous, and error prone. (I made at least five errors in the first translation into machine code for this example.)

These problems, among others, make it very difficult to program in machine language. However, machine language is very powerful, in the sense that if the computer can possibly do a certain thing, it can be done in machine language simply by creating the correct instruction or instruction sequence. *Assembly language* is a computer programming language which allows the programmer to exercise *total* control over the computer, as can be done in machine language, but also relieves the programmer of some of the hassles of machine language.

2.3 INTRODUCTION TO ASSEMBLY LANGUAGE

One of these hassles is the final translation of the program from a descriptive (but detailed) statement of the program into the actual numeric binary machine language. Notice that our writing of the machine language program was divided into two steps. The first was the creative one, deciding what the steps of the solution would be, which instructions to use, where to allocate space for data and where to allocate space for the instructions, considering the type and location of the data.

The second step was the relatively trivial, mechanical process of translating the program which resulted from the first step into machine language. This translation step requires no creativity, only the ability to derive, from our description of the program, the four fields of each instruction and assemble them into one machine language statement. The only difficult part is determining from our description what the four fields (opcode, field, index and address) of the instruction should be. If we would accept writing this description in a special format— one that explicitly states each field—then the actual construction of each instruction would be very easy and could even be done by a computer. This is the basic idea behind an *assembler*.

An assembler is a computer program which translates from assembly language into machine language. Assembly language is a simple way of describing instructions for a machine language program which is more convenient than machine language. The assembler reads these descriptions and translates them into a machine language instruction. After this translation, called assembly, is complete, the resulting machine language program can be executed by the computer.

The assembler needs one assembly language statement for each machine language statement. For MIX, we must specify four fields for each instruction:

1. The opcode (byte 5)
2. The field specification (byte 4)
3. The indexing modes (byte 3)
4. The address field (bytes 0:2)

In the assembly language for MIX, these are defined by an assembly language statement of the form

$$opcode \qquad address, index(field)$$

From this assembly language statement, the assembler creates the following machine language instruction

address			index	field	opcode
0	1	2	3	4	5

Bytes

This is some help, but the assembler does more. Each of the fields is, in machine language, a binary number, and the assembly language must specify what these numbers are. People, and programmers, have difficulty working with numbers all the time, however, and are more comfortable with symbolic, word-like quantities. Thus, assembly language uses *symbolic* opcodes to specify the opcode of an instruction. The assembler has a table which gives, for each symbolic opcode, the corresponding numeric opcode. This allows the assembly language programmer to write

```
ST3    +1453,0(05)
```

and the assembler will automatically translate the symbolic opcode "ST3" into its numeric equivalent "33" and produce the machine language instruction

+1453	00	05	33

Another convenience provided by the assembler is the ability to express the address field of the instruction by a symbolic name, rather than an actual number. In our example of the last section, we had three data items: the number stored in memory, the input card, and the output line. Rather than giving numeric addresses for each of these, we can use a symbolic name (such as FIRSTNUM, CARD, LINE) to represent the numeric address and have the assembler automatically substitute the numeric address for the symbolic address during assembly. This allows us to write an assembly language statement like

```
CMPA  FOUR,0(05)
```

and the assembler will assemble the correct machine language statement, given that the symbol FOUR has been given a value. This requires some means of defining our symbolic addresses. The MIX assembler uses a *label* to specify the symbol which is used to address a location in memory. The label is written as the first item of an assembly language statement as in

```
       ENT1  14
LOOP   DEC1  1
       J1P   LOOP
```

LOOP is a label on the second statement and a symbolic address in the third.

Several other conveniences can be provided by the assembler. For most of our instructions, the index field will be 00 and the field specification will be 05. Rather than having to specify these fields for each instruction, the assembler allows these fields to not be specified; they are *optional*. If the contents of a field are not specified, its *default* value (00 for the index field and 05 for most field specifications) is used.

Another convenience is in the specification of numbers. Rather than requiring numbers to be specified in binary or octal, the assembler expects numbers to be written in decimal, and will convert these decimal numbers to binary for the programmer. This relieves the programmer of the burden of converting numbers (which are thought of in decimal) into octal for the program, but has the contrary result of requiring that numbers thought of in octal must be converted to decimal for the assembler (which then converts them back into octal for the machine language program).

There are many other properties of assemblers, and each assembler will be different from each other assembler in some way. This is because different computers have different instruction sets and instruction formats. Also, it is because assemblers are programs, written by programmers, and hence reflect how the writer of the assembler views how things should be done. Assembly language is defined by the assembler and may thus be full of arbitrary decisions. It is necessary to write programs in the conventions defined by the assembly language only if you want to use that assembler. If you do not want to write programs in the way that the assembler says they must be written, you should feel free to write in machine language, write your own assembler, or use some other assembler. Some computers do have several assemblers.

In this text, from now on, we use the MIX assembly language, MIXAL. We give now a definition of that language.

2.4 MIXAL: MIX ASSEMBLY LANGUAGE

The MIX assembler reads assembly language programs, normally prepared on punched cards, and produces a numeric machine language program and a listing of the input program. The listing is printed on a line printer and consists of the assembled machine language program and the original assembly language program. Each line of the output listing corresponds to one input card image.

TABLE 2.2   The Assembly Process

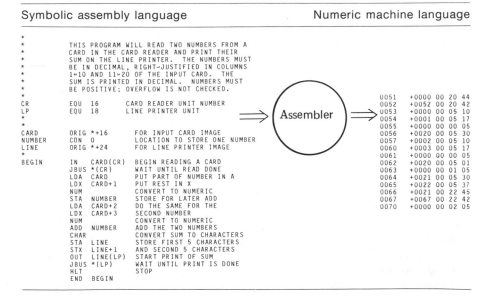

Symbolic assembly language			Numeric machine language

```
*
*           THIS PROGRAM WILL READ TWO NUMBERS FROM A
*           CARD IN THE CARD READER AND PRINT THEIR
*           SUM ON THE LINE PRINTER.  THE NUMBERS MUST
*           BE IN DECIMAL, RIGHT-JUSTIFIED IN COLUMNS
*           1-10 AND 11-20 OF THE INPUT CARD.  THE
*           SUM IS PRINTED IN DECIMAL.  NUMBERS MUST
*           BE POSITIVE; OVERFLOW IS NOT CHECKED.
*                                                          0051   +0000 00 20 44
CR          EQU  16        CARD READER UNIT NUMBER         0052   +0052 00 20 42
LP          EQU  18        LINE PRINTER UNIT               0053   +0000 00 05 10
*                                                          0054   +0001 00 05 17
*                                                          0055   +0000 00 00 05
CARD        ORIG *+16      FOR INPUT CARD IMAGE            0056   +0020 00 05 30
NUMBER      CON  0         LOCATION TO STORE ONE NUMBER    0057   +0002 00 05 10
LINE        ORIG *+24      FOR LINE PRINTER IMAGE          0060   +0003 00 05 17
*                                                          0061   +0000 00 00 05
BEGIN       IN   CARD(CR)  BEGIN READING A CARD            0062   +0020 00 05 01
            JBUS *(CR)     WAIT UNTIL READ DONE            0063   +0000 00 01 05
            LDA  CARD      PUT PART OF NUMBER IN A         0064   +0021 00 05 30
            LDX  CARD+1    PUT REST IN X                   0065   +0022 00 05 37
            NUM            CONVERT TO NUMERIC              0066   +0021 00 22 45
            STA  NUMBER    STORE FOR LATER ADD             0067   +0067 00 22 42
            LDA  CARD+2    DO THE SAME FOR THE             0070   +0000 00 02 05
            LDX  CARD+3    SECOND NUMBER
            NUM            CONVERT TO NUMERIC
            ADD  NUMBER    ADD THE TWO NUMBERS
            CHAR           CONVERT SUM TO CHARACTERS
            STA  LINE      STORE FIRST 5 CHARACTERS
            STX  LINE+1    AND SECOND 5 CHARACTERS
            OUT  LINE(LP)  START PRINT OF SUM
            JBUS *(LP)     WAIT UNTIL PRINT IS DONE
            HLT            STOP
            END  BEGIN
```

Assembler

Statement format

An assembly language program is made up of a sequence of assembly language *statements*. Each statement is one card or line image. There are two types of statements: comments and noncomments. If a MIXAL statement has an "*" in column 1 of the input card, it is a *comment card*. Comment cards are not used by the assembler to generate an instruction in the machine language program, but should be included by the assembly language programmer to describe, for himself and future programmers, what the program is doing and how. Comment cards are copied to the output listing of the program but have no other effect on the assembler.

Noncomment cards are all statements without an "*" in column 1. These are the statements which result in machine language instructions. These cards are prepared in an assembly language *statement format*. This format consists of four fields in the following order.

label   opcode   operand   comments

The label field is optional. If present it must begin in column 1, and consist of a *symbol*. A symbol in MIX is a string of one to ten letters or digits with at least one letter. Symbols are like variable names in other languages, but may be more general. Remember that most higher-level languages require that variable names begin with a letter. In MIXAL this is not necessary; it is only required that at least one letter exist in the symbol someplace, to allow the MIXAL assembler to differentiate between numbers and symbols.

After the label field is the opcode field. This field contains the symbolic opcode for the machine language instruction to be assembled. The symbolic opcodes which are used in MIXAL are listed in Appendixes B, C, and D.

The next field is the operand field. The operand field specifies the operand for the instruction. For most instructions (the memory reference instructions), this consists of three (optional) subfields: the address field, the indexing field, and the partial field specification. For immediate instructions, the operand field specifies the operand and any indexing. (The contents of byte 4 of the machine language instruction, the opcode modifier, is not a partial field specification, but identifies which of the immediate instructions is given.) The form of this field will be considered in more detail below.

The last of the four fields is the comment field. This field allows each and every statement in an assembly language program to be commented. This field should be used often, in a descriptive way, to aid the reader of a program to understand what a program is doing and how this particular instruction is being used to help the program work. Comments are very important to good programs, and particularly to assembly language programs.

The placement of the fields in an assembly language on an input card can be done in two general ways: *fixed-format* and *free-format*. A fixed-format assembler requires that each field be contained within specific columns of the input card. Some MIXAL assemblers are fixed-format, and for these assemblers, the input format is:

Columns	Field	Comments
1–10	Label	If a label is given, it must be left-justified, with blank fill (i.e., the symbol starts in column 1 and continues for as many columns as necessary, but no more than 10. The rest of the field is left blank).
12–15	Opcode	Each symbolic opcode has been defined so that it is 3 or 4 characters long, so no more than 4 columns are needed.
17–?	Operand	Starts in column 17 and continues for as many columns as needed, but not beyond column 80. This field is terminated by the first blank column.
?–80	Comment	Follows the operand field and is separated from it by at least one blank; continues to the end of the card.

Many assemblers reserve columns 73–80 for sequencing and identification information, so, for these assemblers, the operand and comment field may have to stop before column 73.

Column 11 (between the label and the opcode field) and column 16 (between the opcode and operand field) are left blank to improve the readability of the program, by insuring at least one blank between each field.

Notice how the comment field cannot be defined to occupy only certain columns, the way the label and opcode fields can. This is because the operand field may be of varying complexity and length. Normally, the operand field will be less than twenty columns in length, so one can almost always assign columns 17–36 for the operand and 38–80 for the comment field. Occasionally the operand may be longer, but most of the time it is shorter. Thus, the operand field is not terminated by a specific column but by the first occurrence of a blank, with the comment field being able to begin immediately after the delimiting blank. This idea can also be applied to the other fields of the statement, and is the basis of free-format input.

Since a blank cannot be a part of a symbol or a number, it can be used as a *delimiter*. For free-format input, the fields are separated by one or more blanks and are not constrained to begin in any specific set of columns. The label field starts in column 1, and ends with the first blank. The opcode field begins with the next nonblank character and is terminated by the first following blank. The operand field begins with the next nonblank and is terminated by the next blank; the rest of the card is the comment field. The label field is optional. If it is not present, the delimiting blank must still be included, so a blank in column 1 specifies that the label field is not present (or is blank). If column 1 is nonblank, then either it is a comment (* in column 1) or a label (symbol begins in column 1 and continues until the first blank).

Free-format input is almost always easier to prepare than fixed-format input, while it is easier for the assembler to input only fixed-format. Your assembler may be either. Notice, though, that a free-format assembler can accept programs which have been prepared in a fixed format, but not generally vice-versa. Also, fixed-format input produces a listing which is attractively laid out in columns. Thus, most assembly language programs are prepared in fixed-format. The use of a *program drum* on a keypunch or the *tab* mechanism of a typewriter or computer terminal can make it quite easy to prepare fixed-format assembly language programs.

Symbol definition and use

The major advantage of using an assembly language is the ability to use symbolic names rather than numeric constants. Two types of symbols are used: symbolic opcodes (defined by the assembler) and symbols defined by the user. The assembler has a table of each kind of symbol. The table contains, at least, the name of the symbol and its value. When the assembler is examining the opcode field of a statement, it searches the opcode table. If a symbolic opcode is found in the table which is equal to the symbolic opcode of the assembly language statement, then the value associated with that symbolic opcode is the numeric opcode and standard field specification for the assembled machine language statement.

Similarly, another table contains the user defined symbols and their (user-defined) values. The value of a symbol is normally an address. As the assembler reads the program, and translates it, card by card, into a machine language program, new symbols may be defined and put into this symbol table, along with their values. Then if a symbol is used, later in the program, the symbol table is

TABLE 2.3 A Symbol Table

Symbols	Values
ABCD	437
TR1	−1
5XY7KD3	263
ONE	100005
NOW	0
. . .	. . .

searched and the value of that symbol is used where the symbol occurs. Symbols may be defined only once, and so always have the same value once they are defined.

There are two ways to define symbols, with the EQU statement (which we will discuss later) and with the label field of an instruction. Since most symbols are symbolic addresses, they are used as the label for the location whose address is their value. Remember that each instruction in a machine language program goes in a specific memory location. To specify an instruction, it is necessary to give both its address and its numeric machine language representation. Most programs are placed in consecutive locations in memory, one after another. To minimize the need for the programmer to specify the address of every instruction, the assembler uses a special variable called the *location counter* to determine the address into which each assembled instruction should be put. After an instruction is assembled and printed on the output listing, the assembler reads in another card, and increments the location counter by one. It assembles that card, prints it, reads in the next one, increments its location counter, and so on, until the end of the assembly program is reached. The location counter is a variable in the assembler whose value is the address at which the current assembly language instruction is to be placed in memory. When a label is encountered on an assembly language statement, the symbol which is the label is entered into the symbol table with a value which is the current value of the location counter; that is, the address of the labelled instruction. As an example, consider the following sequence of instructions

```
LOOP            CMPA  TABLE,3    CHECK FOR ELEMENT IN TABLE
                INC3  1
                JNE   LOOP       IF NOT FOUND, TRY NEXT
```

If the location counter value is +2465 when the first card, with the label LOOP is assembled, then LOOP will be entered into the symbol table with a value of +2465. Later, this value will be retrieved to assemble the machine language instruction +2465001047 for the JNE LOOP statement which will be assembled for location 2467.

The major use of symbols is in the specification of the operand field of a MIXAL instruction. The operand field is composed of three fields: the address field, the index field, and the field specification. The contents of these fields can be specified in very general ways, but it is best to keep in mind that the resulting value for each subfield must be an integer number which is in the correct range for the part of the MIX instruction which it specifies. Thus, the address part must be in the range -4095 to $+4095$, and the index and field specification values must be in the range 0 to 63.

The basic components for specifying the operand of an instruction are of two types: numbers and symbols. A number can be considered a self-defining symbol, in that its value is represented by itself. All numbers are interpreted as decimal integers and must be less than the maximum integer which a MIX word can represent. When a number is used in an operand, the assembled instruction will use that number. The other basic component is a symbol. The value of a symbol is the value which has been stored in the symbol table for that symbol.

In addition to these two types of values, numbers and programmer-defined symbols—one other symbol can be used in operand field specifications. This is the symbol ''*''. * (pronounced star) has as its value the value of the location counter, the address of the instruction currently being assembled. This is useful in such situations as waiting for a device to finish an I/O operation, as in

```
IN    CARD(16)   READ A CARD
JBUS  *(16)      WAIT UNTIL IT IS READ
```

Any of these three (number, symbol, or *) may be used for the operand field of an assembly language statement. In addition to being used singly, they may be combined in *expressions*. An expression is any number of numbers, symbols, or *s, combined by any of the five binary operators +, −, *, /, :, with an optional leading plus or minus sign. The value of the expression is determined from the value of its components. The value of a number is that number; of a symbol, the value stored in the symbol table; and of *, the address of the current instruction. If these are combined by operators, the evaluation of the expressions ''$a + b$'', ''$a − b$'', ''$a * b$'', and ''a / b'', is the normal result of addition, subtraction, multiplication and (integer) division, on the MIX machine. The result of any expression evaluation may not exceed five bytes plus sign. The expression $a : b$ is evaluated as $(8 \times a) + b$. This is used mainly for specifying the contents of index fields and partial field specifications, but may be used more generally. (Notice that if a and b are $0 \leq a, b \leq 7$, then $a : b$ is the octal number whose ''eights'' digit is a and whose units digit is b).

The evaluation of expressions is strictly left to right. No parenthesis can be used to group subexpression evaluation and no operator has precedence over another. Thus, the expression

$$1+2-3*4/5$$

is evaluated as

$$((((1 + 2) - 3) \times 4) / 5) = 0$$

and $2*4-2*4 = 24$. Strictly left to right.

Examples:

```
4+5         equals 9
3+5*6       equals 48
7+2:6       equals 78
7+2:6+1     equals 79
```

Each subfield of the operand field of an assembly language statement may be an expression (with the constraint that the resulting value must be in the proper range). Each field may also be absent. The form of the operand field is "address,index(field)". If a particular subfield is absent, then its delimiter is also. Thus, if the index field is missing, zero is assumed and the comma separating the address and index fields is not present. If the field specification is missing, then the default is the standard field setting (0:5 for all memory reference instructions except STJ, for which it is 0:2). If the address is missing, it is assumed to be zero.

Assembler operation

The assembly process can now be described in considerable detail. It will be examined in more detail in Chapter 8, but a brief walk-through of the assembly process here will make it easier to understand assembly language programming. Each card is handled separately. First, a card is read. If column 1 is a "*", the card is copied to the printer, and we have completed this card and may start the next. For a noncomment card, the label field is examined. If it is nonblank, the symbol in the label field is entered into the symbol table with a value of the location counter. Next, the opcode is translated into its numeric form for byte (5:5) of the machine language instruction and the standard field setting defined for byte (4:4). The operand field expressions are evaluated, looking symbols up in the symbol table and using the value of the location counter for *, as needed. This specifies bytes (0:2), (3:3), and sometimes (4:4) of the instruction. All of these are assembled to form the machine language instruction which is output. The input assembly statement and the assembled machine language instruction are also printed on the line printer. Then the assembler increments the location counter, reads the next card, and repeats this entire process for the next card.

Several points still need to be considered. At several places in the assembler, errors can occur. Most of these are treated in a reasonable way. If a symbol is defined in the label field of a statement, and that symbol already exists in the symbol table, then the symbol is *doubly defined*, or more generally, *multiply defined*. The second definition is ignored and the output line is flagged to indicate the error. If the opcode cannot be found in the opcode table, it is an *undefined opcode* or an *illegal opcode* and is treated as a NOP instruction. If the operand field, or any of its subfields, is botched (by two operators next to each other, undefined symbols, results too large for the field, or results which exceed 5 bytes plus sign in an intermediate step), the default values are normally used. In all cases, the statement is flagged on the output listing and often the machine language program will not be executed.

One special case comes up in evaluating the address subfield of the operand. Suppose we wish to write the following

```
          JAP    POSITIVE
          ENTA   0
POSITIVE  STA    VR1
```

When the address field of the JAP is evaluated, the symbol is not yet defined. This is known as a *forward reference*. Forward references are allowed in MIXAL only because the assembler treats them as a special case. However, they can only be used by themselves; they cannot be used in expressions. They also cannot be used in the index, or partial field subfields. Forward references can only be used in the address field of an instruction, and not as part of an expression.

Pseudo-instructions

A number of questions can still be raised concerning the assembler operation. How does it stop? What is the initial value of the location counter? How are data values specified? These and other questions reveal the need to be able to give the assembler information other than simply the assembly language statements which are to be converted into machine language instructions. This control information could be specified in several ways, but for esthetic reasons it is felt to be nice if all input to the assembler has (roughly) the same format. Thus, a number of assembly instructions have been defined which resemble in their appearance the format of the machine instructions given above. These assembler instructions are not machine operations, so their symbolic notation cannot be called opcodes. However, their resemblance to opcodes has resulted in their being called *pseudo-instructions*. The MIXAL language has five pseudo-instructions: ORIG, CON, ALF, EQU, and END. The treatment of each of these is quite different from the treatment of the machine opcodes, and so we discuss each in some detail.

ORIG

The placement of machine language instructions in memory is controlled by the value of the location counter, . The location counter starts initially at zero, 0000, at the very beginning of the program and is normally increased by one after each machine language statement is generated. Occasionally, it is necessary to reset the location counter to another value. For example, if we wish our program to be placed in memory starting at location 3000, rather than at 0000. This can be accomplished by the ORIG pseudo-instruction. The format of the ORIG statement is

[label]   ORIG expression [comment]

The brackets [ ] around the label indicate it is optional. The label, if present, is given the value of the location counter *before* it is changed. Then the expression is evaluated and the location counter is set equal to the value of the expression. The expression cannot contain any forward references and must be a legal address (i.e., from 0 to 3999). The next assembled location will be assembled at the location whose address is the operand of the ORIG statement (*not* the expression plus one). For example

```
           ORIG  1000
P          LDA   Q
           ORIG  2000
Q          ENTA  P
R          STA   P
```

The symbol P will have the value 1000, the symbol Q will have the value 2000 and the symbol R will have the value 2001.

This statement can be used to reserve memory locations whose initial value is not important. For example

```
           ORIG  2140
ARRAY      ORIG  *+20
           LDA   ARRAY,3
```

The first ORIG sets the location counter to 2140. The label ARRAY is entered into the symbol table and given a value before the second ORIG takes effect, so its value will be 2140. For the second ORIG, the evaluation of the expression is * (whose current value is 2140) plus 20, or 2160, so the location counter * is reset to be 2160. The LDA then is assembled into location 2160, leaving 20 empty memory locations, addressable as ARRAY, ARRAY+1, ARRAY+2, . . . , ARRAY+19.

CON

A program is made up of two parts: instructions and data. We have already seen how instructions may be specified by using a symbolic opcode and expression. What about data? The ORIG statement can be used, as illustrated above, to reserve memory space for variables whose initial value is not important, but, sometimes, the initial value is important. For example, if we are running an index register, say I5, in a loop from 1 to 16, we need to be able to compare the contents of I5 with 16. There is no immediate compare instruction, so it is necessary to create a memory location someplace whose contents are 16. If we give this the label SIXTEEN, we can then write

```
           CMP5  SIXTEEN
```

To define the memory location whose initial contents are a specific number, we use the CON statement. The format of the CON statement is

```
[label]         CON    w-value      [comments]
```

The label, if present, is assigned the value of the address of the location counter. In this location will be put one word, then the location counter will be incremented for the next instruction and the next card read and assembled. The contents of the word are specified by the *w*-value. A *w*-value is used to describe a full-word MIX constant. In the simplest case, this is just an expression and the expression is put into the word which is assembled. However, we may want to define specific values for specific bytes or fields of the constant being assembled. As an example, suppose we wish to store two numbers in one MIX word, one number in bytes (1:2) and the other in bytes (4:5). If we want to put 17 into bytes (4:5) and 43 into bytes (1:2), we can write

            CON   17(4:5),43(1:2)

In general the form of a *w*-value is

    $expr_1(field_1),expr_2(field_2), \ldots , expr_k(field_k)$

The word which results is the result of taking a zero word of MIX memory and placing the value of $expr_1$ in $field_1$, then the value of $expr_2$ in $field_2$, then . . . , and finally the value of $expr_k$ in $field_k$. All expressions (and field expressions) must be evaluatable; that is, no forward references are allowed. Any field in the MIX word which is not set by any field will be zero; the sign bit will be "+" if not otherwise specified. If a field specification is absent, (0:5) is assumed. If an expression is absent, it is assumed zero. Remember that the evaluation of expressions and storage in fields is strictly left to right, so if the partial fields overlap, the rightmost one will be used. Thus, the result of

            ORIG 1736
    ABC   CON   100(3:4),23(4:5)

is the word

+	00	00	01	00	27

stored in location 1736 with label "ABC". Remember first that numbers in MIXAL are decimal, while the numbers given above for the MIX word are octal. The 100(3:4), puts an octal 0144 in bytes 3:4, but then the 23(4:5) puts a 0027 in bytes 4:5, erasing the 44 in byte 4 put there by the 100(3:4).

The CON pseudo-instruction affects only the initial value of the location defined by it. If we define

    PDQ   CON   13

and then write and execute the instructions

            ENTA   −5
            STA   PDQ

then the value of location labelled PDQ will not be 13 but −5. (The value was 13 until after the STA instruction was executed.)

ALF

In addition to wanting to define numeric constants, it is sometimes necessary to define alphanumeric character code constants. This is accomplished by the ALF instruction. Each word in MIX memory is made up of five bytes and each byte can hold one character. The ALF pseudo-instruction takes as its operand five characters and assembles one word whose contents will be the character code for these five characters. For example

Statement		Resulting MIX word
ALF	ABCDE	+0102030405
ALF	MIXAL	+1611330115
ALF	12345	+3740414243

The format of the ALF statement is

[label]   ALF   5 characters [comments]

The label, if present, is given a value of the address of this word.

For a fixed-format assembler, the five characters are the contents of columns 17–21 of the input card. For a free-format assembler, however, it is not so easy. In a free-format assembler, the fields are separated by one or more blanks, because for all instructions (except ALF) blanks are not important and cannot appear within a symbol or expression. For the ALF instruction, blanks can be very important. Suppose we want to construct two alphabetic constants, one of an A followed by four blanks, the other of one blank, then an A, followed by three blanks. In a free-format assembler, the leading blank of the second constant would be thought to be part of the delimiting blanks between the ALF pseudo-instruction and its operand string, and hence it would be ignored, unless ALF is treated specially. This problem is common to other assemblers and can be solved in several ways. The simplest is to state that the ALF pseudo-instruction is always followed by exactly two blanks and then the five characters to be put in the MIX word. (Two blanks allows the operand to start in the same column as everything else if a fixed-format is being used.) Thus, to create the two constants mentioned above we would write (where we are using a ".'' to represent a blank in order to emphasize the spacing)

            ALF..A....   +0100000000
            ALF...A...   +0001000000

Another approach is to introduce a special delimiter which is used to surround and delimit the five characters which are to be used for the ALF. For example, if a quote is the delimiter, then the two above constants are

            ALF "A   "
            ALF " A   "

Notice that the second delimiter is not really needed if there must always be exactly five characters in a MIX word. If this restriction is not made, the word is generally padded out with blanks to the right to fill a whole word. With this approach, special steps must be taken to allow the delimiter to appear within an ALF operand. (How do we do an ALF of three quotes?)

Other variations are also possible. The specific method used by your assembler may vary from those presented here. The ALF pseudo-instruction is one reason why a fixed-format input is often used; it avoids these problems.

EQU

We have already seen that one way to define a symbol is to place it in the label field of an instruction. The symbol so defined then has a value which is the address of the memory location for which that instruction is assembled. There are other times, however, when we wish to use symbols whose values do not correspond to memory addresses. These values may be device numbers (16 for the card reader; 18 for the line printer), lengths of tables or arrays, special values for flags or switches, or any of a number of other purposes. The EQU pseudo-instruction is a means of defining a symbol and putting it in the symbol table without affecting the location counter or assembling any code. The format of the EQU pseudo-instruction is

[label]   EQU   *w*-value   [comments]

If the label field is nonblank (it really does not make sense for it to be blank), the *w*-value in the operand field is evaluated to give a five-byte-plus-sign value. Then the symbol in the label field is entered into the symbol table with a value of the evaluated *w*-value. The *w*-value cannot have any forward references. The value of the location counter is unchanged. No machine language instruction is generated.

Examples:

```
CR              EQU    16
LP              EQU    18
N               EQU    4
M               EQU    3+2
P               EQU    M*N
```

END

Appropriately enough, the last pseudo-instruction is the END pseudo-instruction. The END pseudo-instruction signals to the assembler that the last assembly language statement has been read, and the program is now completely input. The assembler then terminates its operation, having completed the translation of the assembly language program into a machine language program. The format of the END statement is

[label]   END [*w*-value]   [comments]

If a label is given on the END card, it is given a value of the address of the first location beyond the end of the program. Thus, if the program ends with

```
                 JMP    LOOP
     LAST        END
```

and the JMP instruction is at location 3798, then the symbol LAST will have the value 3799. Notice that all references to it must be forward references.

If an operand (the *w*-value) is given on the END card, it is taken to be the address where execution of the program should begin. If no operand is given, the program will be started at location 0000.

If there are any undefined symbols in the program (i.e., forward references which never did appear as labels), the assembler will define them as CON 0 statements occurring just *before* the END card. Undefined symbols are generally considered programming errors and should be avoided, but if you do forget some, the assembler will assume that you meant to define them as the label of a CON 0 at the end of your program.

An example

As an example, we present the assembly language program which is equivalent to the machine language program presented in Section 2.2. This program reads two numbers from the card reader and prints their sum on the line printer. The assembler translates the following assembly language program into the machine language program of Section 2.2.

```
*
*                 THIS PROGRAM WILL READ TWO NUMBERS FROM A
*                 CARD IN THE CARD READER AND PRINT THEIR
*                 SUM ON THE LINE PRINTER. THE NUMBERS MUST
*                 BE IN DECIMAL, RIGHT-JUSTIFIED IN COLUMNS
*                 1-10 AND 11-20 OF THE INPUT CARD. THE
*                 SUM IS PRINTED IN DECIMAL. NUMBERS MUST
*                 BE POSITIVE; OVERFLOW IS NOT CHECKED.
*
CR            EQU    16       CARD READER UNIT NUMBER
LP            EQU    18       LINE PRINTER UNIT
*
*
CARD          ORIG   *+16     FOR INPUT CARD IMAGE
NUMBER        CON    0        LOCATION TO STORE ONE NUMBER
LINE          ORIG   *+24     FOR LINE PRINTER IMAGE
*
BEGIN         IN     CARD(CR) BEGIN READING A CARD
```

```
JBUS  *(CR)      WAIT UNTIL READ DONE
LDA   CARD       PUT PART OF NUMBER IN A
LDX   CARD+1     PUT REST IN X
NUM              CONVERT TO NUMERIC
STA   NUMBER     STORE FOR LATER ADD
LDA   CARD+2     DO THE SAME FOR THE
LDX   CARD+3     SECOND NUMBER
NUM              CONVERT TO NUMERIC
ADD   NUMBER     ADD THE TWO NUMBERS
CHAR             CONVERT SUM TO CHARACTERS
STA   LINE       STORE FIRST 5 CHARACTERS
STX   LINE+1     AND SECOND 5 CHARACTERS
OUT   LINE(LP)   START PRINT OF SUM
JBUS  *(LP)      WAIT UNTIL PRINT IS DONE
HLT              STOP
END   BEGIN
```

Literals and local symbols

Many of the features of assembly language are provided to make program-ming more convenient. The ability to use symbolic opcodes and operands, to specify numbers in decimal, and other features are both a convenience, and to some degree, necessary to make assembly language programming a reasonable task. In this section we discuss two more features of MIXAL which are conven-ient, but not as necessary; they simply make programming easier by allowing us to program in terms which are closer to the way in which we think of the programming task.

When we are programming, it is sometimes necessary to refer to a constant value which should be stored somewhere in memory. For example, if we have an index register, say 4, which is controlling the number of times that a loop is executed by ranging from 1 to 24, we would want to compare the register against the constant 24. We could do this by writing

```
CMP4  TWENTYFOUR
```

and elsewhere in our program, defining

```
TWENTYFOUR      CON   24
```

Instead of this three step process—thinking up a name, using that name in the instruction, and defining the memory location ourselves—we can let the assem-bler do it for us by the use of a *literal*. A literal is a symbol which is a special form, so that the assembler can tell that it is to be a constant value stored in memory someplace. The form of a literal is a *w*-value enclosed in a pair of equal signs, "=". The *w*-value must be less than 10 characters in length. In the example above, we could just write

```
CMP4  =24=
```

The assembler, when it finds a literal, stores it in the symbol table as a forward referenced symbol. When the END card is read, the symbol table is searched both for undefined symbols (as explained above) which are defined as CON 0 statements just before the END statement, and for literals. All literals are also defined as memory locations just before the END card. The contents of the memory location is the value of the w-value which defined the literal. If the literal symbol is =w=, this will result in the generation of an assembly language statement

```
CON    w           LITERAL =w=
```

and the address of this memory location will be used as the value of the literal symbol. For example, the program

```
           ORIG  0
BEGIN      LDA   =63(3:3)=(1:5)
           HLT
           END   BEGIN
```

is exactly equivalent to the program

```
           ORIG  0
BEGIN      LDA   LITERAL(1:5)
           HLT
LITERAL    CON   63(3:3)
           END   BEGIN
```

and will result in the generation of the following machine language program,

```
0000          +0002001510
0001          +0000000205
0002          +0000770000
```

The program begins at location 0000.

Literals are quite useful, since they allow the reader of an assembly language program to see at once both the instruction and the contents of the literal, instead of seeing a label and having to search throughout the program for that label to discover the contents of the location. Literals also help avoid accidentally forgetting to define symbols with a resultant CON 0 being generated instead.

Examples:
```
=100=
=N+1=
=BEGIN+3=
=ADDR(0:2)=
```

A second convenience in MIXAL is *local symbols*. For all loops or jumps, it is necessary to use a label in order to have an address to jump to. For short loops or branches this may result in a large number of labels, each of which must be unique. Normally, the label should be picked to reflect the meaning of the code which it labels, but often it becomes difficult to think of unique names which may describe code which is basically the same except for subtle differences. To solve this, MIXAL provides local symbols. Local symbols are the 10 symbols 0H, 1H, 2H, . . . , 9H. They are referenced by the symbols 0F, 1F, 2F, . . . , 9F when the local symbol is a forward reference, and by 0B, 1B, 2B, . . . , 9B when the local symbol is a backward reference. The H stands for "*Here*," the F for "*Forward*," and the B for "*Back*." The digit is used to allow 10 different local symbols. When a reference to iB is encountered (for $i = 0, 1, . . . , 9$), the assembler uses as the value of the local symbol the value of the *most recently* encountered iH symbol; when a reference to iF is encountered, the assembler treats it as a forward reference to the *next* iH symbol it finds. Because of this convention, the iH local symbols may be used many times in a program without resulting in multiply defined symbols. For example

```
              ORIG  1000
CARD          ORIG  *+16        RESERVE SPACE FOR INPUT CARD
*
3H            IN    CARD(16)    READ A CARD
1H            JBUS  1B(16)      WAIT UNTIL READ
              ENT1  0           WORD COUNTER 0..15
2H            ENT2  0           CHARACTER COUNTER 0..4
              LDA   CARD,1
1H            CMPA  =0=(1:1)    CHECK IF CHARACTER IS BLANK
              JE    1F
*
              SLA   1           SHIFT TO NEXT CHARACTER
              INC2  1           INCREASE COUNTER
              CMP2  =5=
              JL    1B          IF MORE CHARACTERS THIS WORD
              INC1  1
              CMP1  =16=
              JL    2B          OR MORE WORDS THIS CARD
              JMP   2F          NO BLANKS ON CARD
*
1H            HLT               BLANK FOUND, HALT
2H            JMP   3B          READ NEXT CARD
              END   3B
```

Remember that the label on a card is processed before the operand field, hence, in the following 5B refers to itself, while the 5F refers to the next instruction.

```
5H              LDA     ZED(1:5)
5H              JAN     5B
5H              JAP     5F
5H              STA     ZED
```

2.5 SUMMARY

The MIX computer is a small, general purpose computer whose architecture was defined by Knuth (1968). In this chapter, we first briefly described the architecture of the MIX computer, and then we presented an example of how machine language programs are written, showing the difficulty of programming in machine language.

An assembler is a program which translates from assembly language into machine language. With the exception of the assembler pseudo-instructions of ORIG, EQU, and END, each and every assembly language statement results in one machine language instruction or data value. The assembly language statement is composed of several fields in either a fixed-format or a free-format. The label field defines a symbol which may be used as the operand of other statements to reference the labelled instruction. The opcode and operand fields specify the machine language opcode, indexing, field specification, and address fields for the assembled instruction.

The assembler pseudo-instructions allow the location counter for assembly to be set (ORIG), numerical constants (CON) or alphanumeric character code constants (ALF) to be defined, symbols entered into the symbol table with a value other than an address (EQU), and define the end of the assembly program (END). Literals and local symbols make assembly language programming easier.

MIXAL was defined by Knuth (1968). However, each MIX computer system will have its own MIXAL assembler. This means that the operation and some of the specifics of your MIXAL assembler may differ from the assembler described here or in Knuth (1968). Check with your instructor for a manual or report describing your specific MIXAL assembler and its use.

Chapter 3 describes the MIX computer in more detail.

EXERCISES

1. How many words of memory does the MIX machine have? What are the addresses of these words?
2. What are the registers of the MIX machine?
3. What are the fields of a MIX instruction?
4. What I/O devices can be attached to a MIX computer?
5. How does a MIX 1009B differ from a MIX 1009D?
6. Name the six different types of MIX instructions.
7. List three advantages of assembly language over machine language.

8. Explain the difference between MIX and MIXAL.

9. What is the difference between an END and a HLT in MIXAL?

10. Contrast the following MIXAL instructions:

        LDA =5=   ENTA 5   LDA 5   ENTA =5=

11. What is the difference (if any) between a program counter and a location counter?

12. Contrast the use of an enter instruction (such as ENTA n) with the use of a load instruction with a literal operand (such as LDA $=n=$). What are the advantages of both?

13. What is the difference (if any) between the following two statements?

        ERG   EQU   1435
        ERG   CON   1435

14. What does the symbol * mean in MIXAL?

15. A programmer wanted to reserve space for a table of floating point numbers, FTAB. He needed double precision, so each entry in the table is two words long. He wrote the following code

        N   EQU   100   NUMBER OF WORDS IN TABLE
        FTAB   ORIG   *+2*N   RESERVE N TWO WORD ENTRIES

    But the program does not work. Can you suggest his error?

16. Consider the END card. If it has a label, the text says that all references to that label are forward references. Why?

17. Discuss what would happen if you stuck an ORIG *−100 card somewhere in the middle of a friend's MIXAL program.

18. Suppose we want the octal number +2145030000 to be in our program. Give three assembly language instructions which will generate this value.

19. In MIX there are many ways to do nothing at execution time: NOP, INCA 0, JSJ *+1, and so on. Give a way to do nothing at assembly time. For example, a comment card does nothing at assembly time. (We want an assembly language instruction that we could put any place in our program and which would not affect the generated machine language in any way.)

20. Literals cannot be involved in expressions in the address field of an instruction (i.e., LDA =47=+1). Why?

21. Write the equivalent of

        2H   EQU   10
        2H   MOVE   2F(2B)
        2H   EQU   2B−2

    without using any local symbols.

22. Some assembly language statements are instructions to the assembler

and are executed at assembly time, while others are instructions for the MIX machine and so are executed at execution time. When are the following statements executed?

```
        ORIG  100
        JMP   100
X       EQU   100
        ENTX  100
        HLT
        END
        JXN   OF
        ALF   TRACE
```

23. Suppose we had a defective MIXAL assembler which would allow labels only on EQU statements. How could we write a program where we wanted a statement equivalent to:

```
FIND            STJ   EXIT
```

24. Give the octal code and the symbol table which would result from the following MIXAL program (i.e., give the machine language for this assembly language).

```
        ORIG  100
X       ORIG  *+1
Y       EQU   X−10
BEGIN   LDA   X,1(0:2)
        STA   Y,7
        STJ   X+2
        HLT
        END   BEGIN
```

25. Suppose you are given the contents of some memory locations of the MIX computer. Can you reconstruct the assembly language program which asembled into these memory words? Is this assembly program unique? Explain.

26. Assume that a dump of locations 0 to 7 of MIX memory showed (all numbers are octal):

```
0000            +0004002044
0001            +0001002042
0002            +0004002245
0003            +0017040262
0004            +0000020406
0005            +3736000267
0006            +0015000406
0007            +0000000205
```

What is a possible assembly language program to have generated this MIX memory? This process is called deassembling.

27. What is the contents of the A register when the HLT instruction is executed below?

```
BEGIN           LDA    WORD
WORD            CON    5
                HLT
                END    BEGIN
```

28. Write a machine language program to input three numbers and print their product.

29. Write a machine language program to read three number from cards and print their maximum. What changes would be necessary to this program if we wanted to find the maximum of four numbers?

30. What does the MIXAL assembler do?

31. What are the default values for the fields of an assembly language statement?

32. What is the difference between a free-format and a fixed-format assembler?

33. Name five possible errors in a MIXAL program.

34. What is a forward reference?

35. Are both the ALF and the CON pseudo-instructions needed? Why are they both part of the assembly language?

3

A DETAILED
DESCRIPTION OF
THE MIX
COMPUTER

In this chapter, we give a detailed description of the instruction set of the MIX computer. This description considers the detailed specifications of the execution of each instruction. Much of assembly language programming is concerned with the small details of the computer organization and instruction set. Thus, it is necessary to be very familiar with the exact meaning of each instruction.

Before we can give a complete explanation of what the MIX instruction set is, we need to first look at how a program is executed by the computer. This is followed by a consideration of the common features of the execution of a large class of instructions—the memory reference instructions. Finally, we examine the complete instruction set.

3.1 INSTRUCTION INTERPRETATION AND EXECUTION

How does the MIX computer actually execute instructions? What does it do at what time and why? To answer these questions, it is necessary to look beneath the description of the MIX computer as a computer with 4000 words of memory and nine registers, an overflow toggle, comparison indicator, and I/O devices. We know that the basic instruction execution cycle is composed of the following four steps:

1. Fetch the next instruction.
2. Decode the instruction.
3. Fetch the operands (if any).
4. Execute the instruction.

All computers do nothing more than continuously repeat this basic instruction execution cycle. If we want to be able to truly *understand* the operation of the MIX machine, however, we need to know more about what is done in each of the above steps, and how it happens. This requires looking at the inside of the MIX computer and seeing how it is actually put together.

Figure 3.1 gives a block diagram of the internal structure of the MIX computer. Notice that the four basic components (memory, ALU, control unit, and I/O system) are present. There are also a number of registers which we did not tell you about in our earlier description of the MIX computer. These are the *internal registers* and are not directly accessible by the programmer. They are registers which have been used by the computer designers to build the MIX machine and are dedicated to specific internal functions; they are not meant to be used by the programmer. In fact, there are no instructions in the instruction set of the MIX machine which would allow them to be used.

Specifically the internal registers are,

1. MAR (memory address register) A two-byte register which holds the address of every referenced memory location.
2. MDR (memory data register) A five-byte-plus-sign register which contains the contents of memory locations (the data) which are read from or written to the memory.
3. P (program counter) The contents of the program counter is the address of the next (or current) instruction to be executed. The P register is two bytes, just enough to hold an address.
4. I (instruction register) The instruction register is used to hold the instruction which is being executed (five bytes plus sign). It is used by the control unit.

The instruction execution cycle for the MIX computer is quite simple. When the machine is started, the following steps are executed over and over again, until the computer executes a halt instruction, or someone presses the STOP button on the MIX console.

1. The first thing which must be done is to fetch the instruction to be executed. The P register has the address of the next instruction, so the contents of the P register are copied into the MAR register.

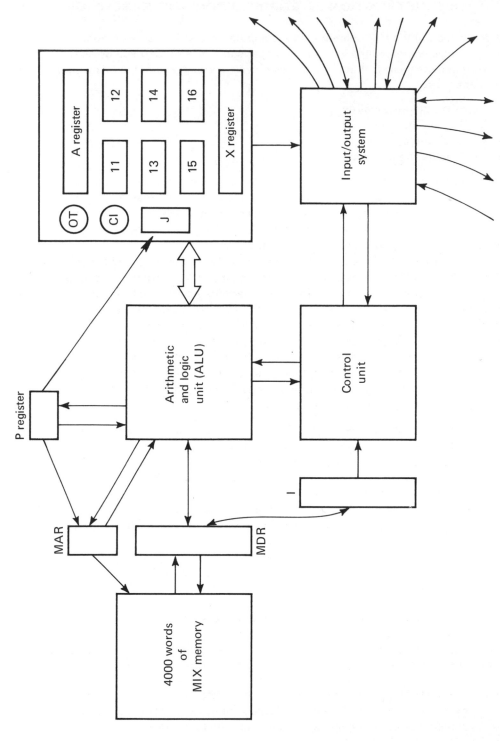

FIGURE 3.1 The internal registers of the MIX computer.

2. Next, the memory unit reads the contents of the memory location addressed by the contents of the MAR. These contents are put into the MDR.
3. When the read has been performed, the instruction which has been read into the MDR is copied into the I register so that it can be decoded into the control signals needed to execute the instruction.
4. Now that the current instruction has been fetched, the contents of the P register are increased by 1 to be ready to fetch the next instruction after the current one is executed.
5. Once the instruction has been fetched and copied into the I register and the P register incremented, the control unit can decode the instruction and start its execution.

Byte 5 of all MIX instructions is the opcode of the instruction and is examined first. Based upon the value of the opcode, the remainder of the instruction may be interpreted in different ways. For each of the different interpretations, the control unit performs different operations in order to execute the instruction.

There are two main types of instructions: those which specify an operand and those which need no operand. Instructions such as, HLT (halt the computer), NUM (convert the AX register from character code to numeric in the A register), NOP (no operation), and others need no operand. These instructions, determined by their opcode (C field, byte 5) and opcode modifier (F field, byte 4) are executed immediately, and the control unit returns to step 1 to fetch the next instruction (unless the instruction was a HLT, of course).

For operations with an operand, the operand must be determined. The operand is specified by the address field (bytes 0, 1, and 2) as modified by the I field (byte 3) of the instruction. The modification of the address field by the I field is called the *effective operand calculation* and is described in Section 3.2. This produces the *effective operand, m*. The effective operand is used in two ways. For immediate operations, jumps, and I/O instructions, the effective operand is the operand, a two-byte-plus-sign integer number. For memory reference instructions (the loading, storing, arithmetic, and comparison operations), the effective operand is the *address* of the operand. For these instructions, the control unit copies the effective operand into the MAR and fetches the contents of the addressed memory location into the MDR. This full-word (five bytes plus sign) quantity is then used as the operand.

In either case, memory reference or nonmemory reference, the instruction is

FIGURE 3.2 The MIX opcode format.

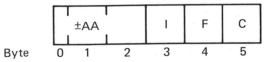

Byte   0   1   2   3   4   5

executed once the operand is obtained. Fetching an operand from memory for a memory reference instruction means that these instructions take longer to execute than the operations which use the effective address as their operand. Once the execution is complete the control unit returns to step 1 to repeat this sequence for the next instruction.

3.2 EFFECTIVE OPERAND CALCULATION

Most of the instructions for the MIX computer specify an operand in the address field (bytes 0 through 2) of the instruction. This operand is modified according to the contents of the I field (byte 3) of the instruction. Many, but not all, instructions use the resulting operand as an *address*. The immediate and the shift instructions treat the operand as an integer number. However, the load, store, compare, jump, arithmetic, and (some) I/O instructions treat the operand which results from the original operand and the modification specified by byte 3 as an address, *the effective address*. Because these instructions are more common, the standard terminology refers to the operand as an address. (Hence, bytes 0, 1, and 2 are called the address field instead of the operand field.) Thus, although we are concerned with the calculation of the effective operand and the operand is only used as an address most of the time, we present our discussion in terms of an *effective address calculation*. We denote the effective operand (or effective address) by m.

The I field of an instruction determines the *mode* of the effective address calculation. The simplest mode is *direct addressing*. Direct addressing is indicated by a zero value for the I field. In this case the effective address is equal to the address given in the instruction. No modification is needed. This is the most common and useful addressing mode.

The other addressing mode of every MIX computer is an *indexed* addressing mode. If the value of the I field is between 1 and 6 (inclusive) then the effective address is the sum of the contents of the address field of the instruction and the contents of the index register whose number is given in the I field. Letting AA be the contents of the address field, and i be the number given in the I field, then $m = $ AA $+$ contents of index register i.

FIGURE 3.3   Direct addressing (the effective address is the address field of the instruction).

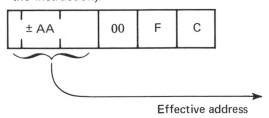

Effective address

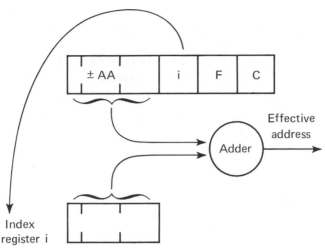

FIGURE 3.4 Indexing (the effective address is the sum of the contents of the address field of the instruction and the index register).

As an example, let the index registers have the (octal) values

I1 = +0100
I2 = +0200
I3 = −0001
I4 = +0001
I5 = −0500
I6 = +6666

Then for each of the following LDA (opcode = 10, F field = 05), instructions we have the effective address given

Instruction				Effective address	
AA	I	F	C	m	
+0013	00	05	10	+0013	no indexing (direct)
+1472	00	05	10	+1472	no indexing
+1472	01	05	10	+1572	indexing by I1
+0001	02	05	10	+0201	indexing by I2
+0014	03	05	10	+0013	indexing by I3
+0000	04	05	10	+0001	indexing by I4

Notice, however, that the indexing field is one byte (six bits) in size, and we have only specified the addressing mode for the values of the index field equal to 0, 1, 2, 3, 4, 5, 6. Many owners of MIX computers have bought an option for the CPU which increases the number and kind of addressing modes. This additional unit treats the index field as a pair of octal digits: *ab*. Each of these two digits specifies an addressing mode. The effective address calculation is performed by first modifying the address by the addressing mode specified by a and then using this effective address as the address to be modified by the addressing mode given by b. Since we have 3 bits per octal digit, we have 8 values for each of a and b, and 64 possible combination addressing modes. The interpretation of the addressing modes for each of the octal digits of the indexing field is

Digit	Mode
0	direct addressing (no modification)
1	indexing by I1
2	indexing by I2
3	indexing by I3
4	indexing by I4
5	indexing by I5
6	indexing by I6
7	indirect addressing

The first seven addressing modes have already been discussed. *Indirect addressing* ($a = 7$ or $b = 7$) is another addressing technique which is a common addressing mode for computers. With indirect addressing, the address which we already have (initially the address field of the instruction, AA) is not the effective address (as in direct addressing) but the address of a word in memory which contains (in its address field) the effective address.

Consider for a minute the difference between an immediate instruction and a memory reference instruction. If the address were +0100 for an immediate instruction, then the operand for the instruction is +0100. For a memory reference instruction, the operand is not +0100 but the contents of location +0100 in memory. For an indirect addressing mode, the operand is not +0100, nor is it the contents of location +0100. Rather, for indirect addressing, it is the contents of

FIGURE 3.5   Indirect addressing (the effective address is the contents of the address field of the memory location addressed by the address field of the instruction).

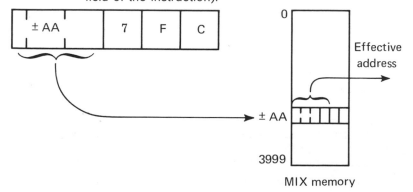

the memory location whose address is the contents of location +0100. Thus, in order for the MIX computer to execute the instruction, it requires either 0, 1, or 2 memory references:

(0) For an immediate instruction, the effective address is calculated and the instruction is executed immediately, using this number as operand.

(1) For a memory reference instruction, the effective address is calculated. This address is sent to the memory unit and the instruction is executed on the contents of the location addressed by the effective address.

(2) For a memory reference instruction with indirect addressing, the effective address is calculated first. This address is sent to the memory unit (first memory reference). The resulting word which is read from memory is not the operand but the address of the operand, so the contents of the fetched location are given back to the memory unit *as an address*, and this new location is read out (second memory reference). The instruction is then executed on the contents of this memory location.

The presence of two address modifier digits (*a* and *b*) in each instruction allows for three classes of effective addresses:

1. *No modification.* Both *a* and *b* are zero. The effective address is the address given in the instruction.

2. *Simple modification.* One of *a* or *b* is zero, but the other is nonzero. This results in either,

   i. *simple indexing* (if the nonzero indicator is between 1 and 6, inclusive). In this case, the effective address is the address field of the instruction plus the contents of the specified index register.

   ii. *simple indirection* (if the nonzero indicator is 7). The effective address is the effective address of the location whose address is given in the instruction.

3. *Complex modification.* Both *a* and *b* are nonzero. In this case, the address modification specified by *a* is performed first, resulting in a partially calculated effective address. This address is then modified by the address modification technique specified by b. The different combinations of indexing and indirection result in four kinds of complex address modifications:

   i. *double indexing.* If $1 \leq a \leq 6$ and $1 \leq b \leq 6$, then the effective address is the address (given in the instruction) plus the contents of the two index registers specified by *a* and *b*. For example, if

$$I1 = +0143$$
$$I2 = +0010$$
$$I3 = -1000$$

then the following LDA instructions have the listed effective addresses:

Instruction	Effective address
+0040 12 05 10	+0040 + 0143 + 0010 = +0213
+1000 32 05 10	+1000 − 1000 + 0010 = +0010
+3000 33 05 10	+3000 − 1000 − 1000 = +1000

ii. *preindexed indirection.* If $1 \leq a \leq 6$ and $b = 7$, the indexing operation is performed first and then this indexed address is used for indirection.

iii. *postindexed indirection.* If $a = 7$ and $1 \leq b \leq 6$, then the first address modification is indirection. The contents of the location specified by the address given in the instruction is fetched as the (partial) effective address for the indirection stage. Then the contents of the index register specified by b is added to the indirectly specified address to form the effective address.

iv. *double indirection.* If both $a = 7$ and $b = 7$, then the modification being specified is double indirection. Because of certain features of the MIX indirection feature (see below), this is *not* allowed. If an instruction attempts to use double indirection, the MIX machine will halt.

One major aspect of MIX indirect addressing has not been mentioned yet. Remember that there are 4000 memory locations in the MIX memory, addressed from 0000 to 7637. Thus, an address can be specified in two bytes. The address field of the instruction allows for two bytes plus a sign, while a word in memory is five bytes plus sign.

Which bytes of a memory word are used to specify an indirect address? There are two reasonable ways to specify a two-byte address in a five-byte memory word. One would be to use the lower two bytes (bytes 4 and 5) of the memory word, ignoring the high order bytes, or requiring them to be zero. The other method would be to interpret the memory word as if it were an instruction and use the upper two bytes (the address field of the instruction) as the indirectly specified address. This approach also makes it reasonable to allow the I field of the indirect word to modify the address field. This is the approach to indirect addressing taken by the MIX computer. The indirect address is used to fetch a word from memory. The effective address is then the result of applying the effective address calculation to this memory word. This may, of course, involve further indirection and/or indexing.

For example, assume that the (octal) contents of the following memory locations are

Location	Contents
1013	+0017 00 00 00
1014	+0200 01 00 00
1015	+0000 21 00 00

```
1016        +1013 07 00 00
1017        −0001 17 00 00
1020        +1017 71 00 00
```

and the contents of $I1 = +1017$ and $I2 = +0005$. Then, for an instruction such as +1013 00 05 10, no modification is specified ($a = 0$, $b = 0$), and the effective address is +1013. If the instruction were +1013 02 05 10, then indexing by index register 2 is specified, and the effective address is $+1013 + (I2) = +1013 + 0005 = 1020$.

For an instruction, +1013 07 05 10, indirection has been specified ($b = 7$). To calculate the effective address for this instruction, we must calculate the effective address of location 1013 of memory. The effective address of 1013 is an unmodified +0017 (since no modification is specified in byte 3 of location 1013). Thus, the effective address for the instruction is +0017. For an instruction +1014 07 05 10, we indirect through location +1014. This specifies an address of +0200 indexed by register I1, so the effective address is $+0200 + 1017 = 1217$. An indirect reference to location 1015 results in double indexing to give an effective address of $+0000 + (I2) + (I1) = +1024$.

For an instruction +1016 07 05 10, we have indirection through location 1016, so the effective address is the effective address of location 1016. The effective address of location 1016 specifies another level of indirection, through location 1013, so the effective address is +0017.

Consider the effective address calculation of the instruction +0000 17 05 10. This instruction does indexing first by I1 ($a = 1$). This gives a partially computed address of $+0000 + (I1) = +1017$. Then indirection occurs ($b = 7$), so we fetch location 1017 and apply the effective address calculation to it. Location 1017

FIGURE 3.6   Multiple levels of indirection (this example has three levels of indirection).

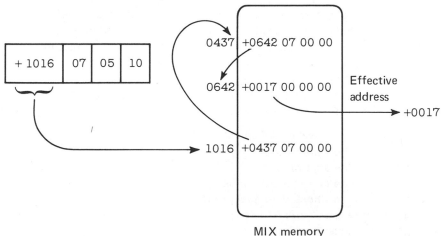

MIX memory

specifies preindexing of −0001 by I1, and then indirection again. The partially computed address is −0001 + (I1) = +1016. Going indirect through 1016 will take us (indirectly) to 1013 giving a final effective address of +0017 after three levels of indirection and two indexing operations.

An instruction like +1013 27 05 10 will result in four levels of indirection with both preindexing and postindexing, resulting eventually in an effective address of +1036.

The effective address calculation for the MIX computer can seem quite complex. It is based on the two simple techniques of indexing and indirection, which are used in many computers. The more complex forms of the effective address calculation seldom occur in programming. Most addresses are either direct or indexed with an occasional double indexing or simple one-level indirection. The other forms of effective address calculation must be used with great care, but can be quite useful in special circumstances. It is most important that you understand the effective address calculation procedure thoroughly in order to be able to read and write good MIX programs.

3.3 PARTIAL FIELD SPECIFICATIONS

For immediate instructions, the effective address calculation produces the operand which is to be used for the instruction. For memory reference instructions, however, the effective address is only the address of the operand and the operand must now be fetched from this location in memory. The contents of the addressed location is, of course, five bytes plus sign. Sometimes it is desirable to operate not on the entire memory word, but only on a part of a word (particularly when characters are being manipulated). To allow this, the F field (byte 4) of memory reference instructions is used to give a *field specification* which describes which part of the addressed memory location is to be used by the memory reference instruction.

A field specification specifies two byte numbers, which are the left and right byte numbers of the field. The field is the left byte and the right byte and all bytes in between. These are encoded into one byte in the same way that the I field (byte 3) encodes both a and b, as the two octal digits of a byte. If the F field is the two octal digits LR then L is the left byte number and R is the right byte number. Since the bytes are numbered 0 through 5, we must have $0 \leq L \leq R \leq 5$ to specify a valid field. The following list gives some examples of partial fields.

F field	Partial field specified
05	the whole word
00	the sign bit only
02	the first two bytes plus sign
15	the whole word except the sign
45	bytes 4 and 5
55	byte 5 only

To make it easier to specify partial fields, we use the colon ("`:`") to separate the left and right byte numbers of a partial field, as in 0:5, 0:0, 0:2, 1:5, 4:5, 5:5, and `L:R`.

Being able to specify only a part of a word of memory can be very useful, but it requires that the description of the instructions which can use partial fields be more complex, in order to describe how the partial fields are used. There are three ways that partial fields are used.

1. For the loading and arithmetic instructions, the partial field is treated as the low-order bytes of a complete five-byte-plus-sign word. The high-order bytes of the operand are treated as zero. If the sign byte is included in the field ($L = 0$), then it is used otherwise a positive sign (+) is used.
2. For a storing instruction, the low-order bytes of the register are stored into the specified field of the word. The remaining bytes of the memory location are unchanged. If the sign byte is included, then the sign of the register is stored in the sign of the memory location.
3. For a comparison instruction, the *same* specified field of both register and memory are compared.

As examples, consider a MIX memory with the contents of location 0452 = +1122334455 and 0453 = −0102030405. Then an instruction +0452 00 24 10

FIGURE 3.7 Partial field loading and storing (for loading, the *L:R* field of memory is copied into the low-order bytes of the register; for storing, the low-order bytes of the register are copied into the *L:R* field of memory).

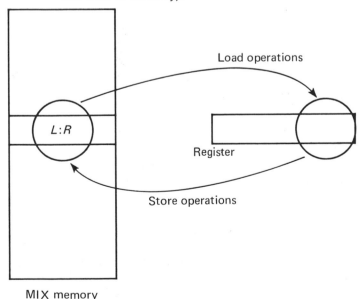

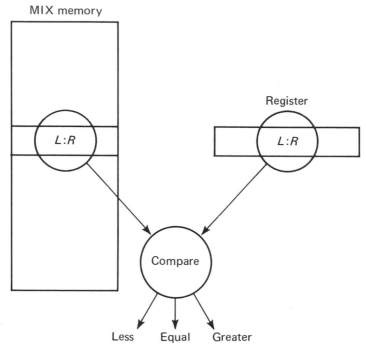

MIX memory

Register

L:R

L:R

Compare

Less   Equal   Greater

FIGURE 3.8   Comparing partial fields (the *same* fields of the register and memory word are compared and the comparison indicator is set).

will load into the A register (opcode = 10) from the contents of the effective address 0452 (no modification, since byte 3 is zero). A partial field is specified by byte 4 (= 2:4), so bytes 2, 3, and 4 of location 0452 will be copied into bytes 3, 4, and 5, respectively, of the A register. Bytes 1 and 2 of A will be set to zero, and the sign byte will be set "+". Thus, the A register will be +0000223344. If we then execute the instruction +0453 00 02 30, we will store (opcode = 30) the sign plus bytes 4 and 5 of the A register into the sign and bytes 1 and 2 (partial field specification in byte 4 of instruction = 0:2) of location 0453 (the effective address resulting from bytes 0:3 of the instruction), changing location 0453 from −0102030405 to +3344030405. The A register is not changed by the store.

For nonmemory reference instructions, the F field is not used to specify partial fields but is used to distinguish between instructions with the same numeric opcode in the C field. For example, an opcode of 64 specifies an immediate operation on register 4. The F field determines whether the instruction is an INC4 (F = 00), a DEC4 (F = 01), an ENT4 (F = 02), or an ENN4 (F = 03). For jump instructions, the F field determines which conditions will be tested for the jump. The F field specifies the I/O device unit number for I/O instructions.

Also, some field specifications which do not specify partial fields are used for memory reference instructions of special kinds. For example, a field of 06 is used with opcodes 01, 02, 03, and 04 (ADD, SUB, MUL, and DIV) to designate a floating point operation (FADD, FSUB, FMUL, FDIV). This allows the same opcode to be used for both integer and floating point operands, with the F field specifying which type of operand is meant.

This completes our description of the instruction execution steps for the MIX computer. We have presented the main ideas of a common instruction execution cycle, effective address calculation, and partial field specification. We now present a detailed description of the operation performed by each instruction.

3.4 LOADING OPERATORS

There are two kinds of loading operators in the MIX computer, the load (LD*) instruction and the load negative (LD*N) instruction. For both of these instructions, * specifies the register into which the new value will be loaded, and can be either A, 1, 2, 3, 4, 5, 6, or X, to refer to the appropriate register. The register is first set to zero with a positive sign. Then the bytes specified by the partial field specification in the F field are loaded into the register. In the case of the LD*N instructions, the sign is complemented (+ to −, − to +) *after* the loading operation. The contents of the memory location addressed by the effective address of the instruction are not changed. The previous value of the register is lost.

The index registers are only two bytes plus sign. The two bytes correspond

TABLE 3.1   Loading Instructions for the MIX Computer

Opcode	Field	Mnemonic	Instruction
10	*	LDA	load A with (*m*)
11	*	LD1	load I1 with (*m*)
12	*	LD2	load I2 with (*m*)
13	*	LD3	load I3 with (*m*)
14	*	LD4	load I4 with (*m*)
15	*	LD5	load I5 with (*m*)
16	*	LD6	load I6 with (*m*)
17	*	LDX	load X with (*m*)
20	*	LDAN	load A with negative of (*m*)
21	*	LD1N	load I1 with negative of (*m*)
22	*	LD2N	load I2 with negative of (*m*)
23	*	LD3N	load I3 with negative of (*m*)
24	*	LD4N	load I4 with negative of (*m*)
25	*	LD5N	load I5 with negative of (*m*)
26	*	LD6N	load I6 with negative of (*m*)
27	*	LDXN	load X with negative of (*m*)

to bytes 4 and 5 of a five-byte MIX word; bytes 1, 2, and 3 are missing. If an attempt is made to load nonzero information into these bytes, an error exists and the MIX machine will halt. To prevent this, it is wise to use a partial field specification for loading index registers, which results in only a two-byte-plus-sign field.

Partial field specifications for load instructions may or may not include the sign byte (byte 0). If it is included in the partial field specification, the sign of the memory word is loaded into the sign of the register; if not, the sign of the register is set to "+". The remaining bytes (nonsign) are loaded into the low-order bytes of the register being loaded. So, if L is not zero, the L:R bytes of memory location m are copied to the L$-$R$+$5:5 bytes of the destination register.

For the load negative (LD*N) instructions, the sign is complemented after the above load has been performed. Thus, if the field specification includes the sign byte of the memory word, the sign of the register will be the opposite. If the field specification does not include the sign, then the sign of the register will be "$-$".

3.5 STORING OPERATORS

The storing operators are almost the inverses of the loading operators. The store instructions are named ST*, where * = A, 1, 2, 3, 4, 5, 6, X specifies the register to be stored into the memory location specified by the effective address, m. The contents of the register are left unchanged.

If a partial field specification is used, only those bytes of the memory location addressed by the effective address are changed. If the sign byte is included in the partial field specification, the sign byte of the register is stored in the sign byte of the memory location. For $1 \leq L \leq R \leq 5$, the 5$-$R$+$L:5 bytes of the register are stored in the L:R bytes of the memory location. That is, the low order bytes of the register are stored into the partial field specified by the instruction. If a partial field specification for storing an index register includes bytes 1, 2, or 3 of the index register, zeros are stored for these bytes.

TABLE 3.2   Storing Instructions for the MIX Computer

Opcode	Field	Mnemonic	Instruction
30	*	STA	store A into location m
31	*	ST1	store I1 into location m
32	*	ST2	store I2 into location m
33	*	ST3	store I3 into location m
34	*	ST4	store I4 into location m
35	*	ST5	store I5 into location m
36	*	ST6	store I6 into location m
37	*	STX	store X into location m
40	*	STJ	store J register into location m
41	*	STZ	store zero into location m

In addition to store instructions for the arithmetic (A, X) and index registers, two special store instructions are available in the MIX instruction repertoire. STJ stores the J register into a memory location. The J register is always treated as having a positive sign, and bytes 1, 2, and 3 are zero. Partial fields can be used as with any of the other store instructions.

Since zero is an important value in computers, a special store instruction, STZ, can be used to store a (positive) zero in a memory location. Partial field specifications can be used to zero only selected bytes and to set sign bits to "+".

3.6 INTEGER ARITHMETIC INSTRUCTIONS

For ADD (and SUB), the partial field of the memory location specified by the effective address of the instruction is added to (or subtracted from) the contents of the A register. The contents of the memory location are unchanged.

If the result of an ADD or SUB instruction is too large to be stored in the A register, then overflow occurs, and the overflow toggle is turned on. The result in the A register is the lower five bytes of the result (plus the correct sign). Overflow occurs if the magnitude (either positive or negative) of the result is greater than 1,073,741,823. Since the largest numbers which could be added (or subtracted) would be 1,073,741,823 + 1,073,741,823 (or −1,073,741,823 − 1,073,741,823), the result can never be greater in magnitude than 2,147,483,646. So, only one bit is unable to fit into the A register. The value of this bit can be determined by testing the overflow toggle.

The MIX computer also provides integer multiplication and division operations. MUL multiplies the contents of the A register by the partial field contents of the memory location addressed by the effective address and places the result back in the A and X registers. The low-order five bytes are in the X register, and the high-order 5 bytes are in the A register. Both signs are set to the sign of the product.

The double register result is produced, since if two n-bit numbers are multiplied, the result can require $2n$ bits. Thus, for any two 30-bit numbers on the MIX machine, the product could be up to 60 bits long. The X register has been added to the MIX machine for this specific purpose. When a multiply instruction is

TABLE 3.3   Arithmetic Instructions for the MIX Computer

Opcode	Field	Mnemonic	Instruction
01	*	ADD	add (*m*) to register A
02	*	SUB	subtract (*m*) from A
03	*	MUL	multiply (*m*) by A, giving AX
04	*	DIV	divide (*m*) into AX, giving A (quotient) and X (remainder)

executed, the contents of the A register are multiplied by the contents of the addressed memory location and the result is placed in both register A and register X. The low-order bytes are put into the X register, and the high-order bytes are put into the A register. If the product of two numbers should never be too great to store in one word of MIX memory, then the A register should always be zero, after the multiplication.

Division is the inverse of multiplication, and so it expects a double register dividend in register A and register X (high-order bytes in the A register; low-order bytes in the X register; sign of A is used; sign of X is ignored) and returns both an integer quotient (in the A register) and an integer remainder (in the X register). If the dividend is only one word, the A register must be set to zero, and the dividend loaded into the X register, with the proper sign in the A register.

If the quotient is more than five bytes in magnitude (or the divisor is zero), the contents of A and X are undefined and the overflow toggle is turned on. The sign of the X register is the same as the original sign of the dividend (in the A register). The sign of the quotient (in the A register) is positive if both divisor and dividend had the same sign and negative if they did not. If we let AX be the 10-byte dividend and C be the divisor, then the new contents of the A and X registers are related by

$$AX = A \times C + X$$

with $0 \leq X < C$ (if $0 < C$), or $C < X \leq 0$ (if $C < 0$).

3.7 FLOATING POINT ARITHMETIC INSTRUCTIONS

The MIX computer instruction set provides for five floating point arithmetic instructions (FADD, FSUB, FMUL, FDIV, and FLOT). Floating point operators are similar to the integer operations in that the A register is used as an accumulator. The overflow toggle is also set if exponent overflow or underflow occurs. Because of the nature of floating point numbers, however, multiplication and division do not result in, or require, more bits in the fractional part of the floating

TABLE 3.4 Floating Point Instructions for the MIX Computer

Opcode	Field	Mnemonic	Instruction
01	06	FADD	add (*m*) to A as floating point numbers
02	06	FSUB	subtract (*m*) from A as floating point numbers
03	06	FMUL	floating point multiply of (*m*) by A; result in A
04	06	FDIV	floating point divide of (*m*) into A; quotient in A
56	06	FCMP	compare A and (*m*); set condition indicator
05	06	FLOT	convert the integer in A to floating point representation

point, but only an adjustment in the exponent. Thus, the X register is not used for floating point instructions. The floating point hardware works best on normalized numbers, and always returns a normalized result. The operator FLOT converts an integer number in the A register into the corresponding floating point representation and leaves this floating point number in the A register.

Most of our work in this text will deal with integer arithmetic, since (almost) all computers provide integer arithmetic operators, while floating point hardware is often not provided for the MIX machine. In fact, the floating point hardware for the MIX machine is not provided with the basic MIX 1009 computer but is an option available at extra cost. The instruction set has been defined with floating point operators included, however. If these instructions are included in a program which is run on a MIX computer without the floating point hardware option, they are treated as illegal instructions and will cause the MIX machine to halt.

3.8 COMPARISON OPERATORS

The comparison operators, CMP*, allow * to specify any of the eight registers A, 1, 2, 3, 4, 5, 6, X to be compared against the partial field in the memory location specified by the effective address. The *same bytes* of the register and memory are always compared. Thus, a CMPA with field specification 1:3 will compare bytes 1:3 of the A register to bytes 1:3 of memory. The values of any other bytes in memory or the register are not important. If the sign bit is not included, a positive sign is used.

The register is compared to memory and the comparison indicator is set to either GREATER, EQUAL, or LESS as,

GREATER	The register is greater than the memory location
EQUAL	The register is equal to the memory location
LESS	The register is less than the memory location

Remember that positive zero is equal to negative zero. Thus, a comparison with partial field (0:0) will always result in an EQUAL comparison indicator. Since bytes

TABLE 3.5 Comparison Instructions for the MIX Computer

Opcode	Field	Mnemonic	Instruction
70	L:R	CMPA	compare A and (m), set comparison indicator
71	L:R	CMP1	compare I1 and (m), set comparison indicator
72	L:R	CMP2	compare I2 and (m), set comparison indicator
73	L:R	CMP3	compare I3 and (m), set comparison indicator
74	L:R	CMP4	compare I4 and (m), set comparison indicator
75	L:R	CMP5	compare I5 and (m), set comparison indicator
76	L:R	CMP6	compare I6 and (m), set comparison indicator
77	L:R	CMPX	compare X and (m), set comparison indicator

1, 2, and 3 of all index registers are zero, using a field specification of (0:0), (0:1), (0:2), or (0:3) allows these bytes of memory to be compared with zero, to determine the positive, zero, or negative nature of memory.

3.9 JUMPS

The comparison operators are used to set the comparison indicator. The results of a comparison can be used to affect the flow of control in a program by a jump. Jump instructions will change the value of the program counter to the effective address if the test condition is satisfied. The following jump instructions test the current value of the comparison indicator.

JG   Jump if comparison indicator is GREATER
JE   Jump if comparison indicator is EQUAL
JL   Jump if comparison indicator is LESS
JLE   Jump if comparison indicator is LESS or EQUAL
JNE   Jump if comparison indicator is LESS or GREATER
JGE   Jump if comparison indicator is GREATER or EQUAL

These instructions do not change the value of the comparison indicator.
In addition, programs can test the state of the A register, X register, or index

TABLE 3.6   Jump Instructions for the MIX Computer[a]

Opcode	Field	Mnemonic	Instruction
47	00	JMP	jump to m
47	01	JSJ	jump to m (but do not change register J)
47	02	JOV	jump to m if overflow on, turn overflow off
47	03	JNOV	jump to m if overflow off, turn overflow off anyway
47	04	JL	jump to m if comparison indicator is less
47	05	JE	jump to m if comparison indicator is equal
47	06	JG	jump to m if comparison indicator is greater
47	07	JGE	jump to m if comparison indicator is greater or equal
47	10	JNE	jump to m if comparison indicator is not equal
47	11	JLE	jump to m if comparison indicator is less or equal
5*	00	J*N	jump to m if * is negative
5*	01	J*Z	jump to m if * is zero
5*	02	J*P	jump to m if * is positive
5*	03	J*NN	jump to m if * is nonnegative
5*	04	J*NZ	jump to m if * is nonzero
5*	05	J*NP	jump to m if * is nonpositive

[a] The * in the last six jump instructions can be replaced by either A, X, 1, 2, 3, 4, 5, or 6, giving 48 of these types of jump instructions.

registers directly and transfer control without the use of a comparison instruction by the following jumps, where * may be A, 1, 2, 3, 4, 5, 6, or X to specify the register being tested.

J*N	Jump if register * is negative (but not negative zero)
J*Z	Jump if register * is zero (positive zero or negative zero)
J*P	Jump if register * is positive (but not positive zero)
J*NN	Jump if register * is nonnegative (positive or zero)
J*NZ	Jump if register * is nonzero (positive or negative)
J*NP	Jump if register * is nonpositive (zero or negative)

In all these tests, negative zero and positive zero are zero, and are not considered to be positive or negative numbers.

JOV and JNOV will transfer control to the effective address if the overflow toggle is on (overflow) or off (no overflow), respectively. In either case, for both of these instructions, the overflow toggle is turned *off* after the instruction is executed.

JMP is an *unconditional* jump. It always transfers control to the effective address.

In all these cases, the J register is always set to the value of the program counter before the program counter is set to the effective address *if* the condition is satisfied and the jump occurs. (If the jump does not occur, both the J and P registers are unchanged.) Since the program counter is already advanced to point to the next instruction, the J register will always contain the address of the instruction which follows the most recent successful jump.

In certain cases this may not be desired. The JSJ instruction is an unconditional jump, but the value of the J register is not changed.

3.10 IMMEDIATE OPERATORS

The load, store, arithmetic, comparison and jump instructions all treat the effective address as an address of a location in memory. The immediate operators do not treat the effective address as an address but as a *signed integer*. This signed integer can be entered (placed, loaded) into a register (ENT*), added to a register (INC*), subtracted from a register (DEC*), or its negative entered into a register (ENN*). In any of these instructions, the register involved can be A, X, or any of the index registers.

The ENT* and ENN* instructions are directly analogous to the LD* and LD*N instructions allowing any register to be loaded with a small constant (in the range −4095 to +4095) directly from the instruction without needing to load from memory. Bytes 1 to 3 are always zero after an enter or enter negative instruction. The increment and decrement are similar to ADD and SUB but can affect any of the eight central registers by the addition or subtraction of a small constant (−4095 to +4095) without fetching it from memory. Overflow may occur and will

TABLE 3.7 Immediate Instructions for the MIX Computer

Opcode	Field	Mnemonic	Instruction
60	00	INCA	increment A by m
60	01	DECA	decrement A by m
60	02	ENTA	enter m into A
60	03	ENNA	enter negative of m into A
61	00	INC1	increment I1 by m
61	01	DEC1	decrement I1 by m
61	02	ENT1	enter m into I1
61	03	ENN1	enter negative of m into I1
62	00	INC2	increment I2 by m
62	01	DEC2	decrement I2 by m
62	02	ENT2	enter m into I2
62	03	ENN2	enter negative of m into I2
63	00	INC3	increment I3 by m
63	01	DEC3	decrement I3 by m
63	02	ENT3	enter m into I3
63	03	ENN3	enter negative of m into I3
64	00	INC4	increment I4 by m
64	01	DEC4	decrement I4 by m
64	02	ENT4	enter m into I4
64	03	ENN4	enter negative of m into I4
65	00	INC5	increment I5 by m
65	01	DEC5	decrement I5 by m
65	02	ENT5	enter m into I5
65	03	ENN5	enter negative of m into I5
66	00	INC6	increment I6 by m
66	01	DEC6	decrement I6 by m
66	02	ENT6	enter m into I6
66	03	ENN6	enter negative of m into I6
67	00	INCX	increment X by m
67	01	DECX	decrement X by m
67	02	ENTX	enter m into X
67	03	ENNX	enter negative of m into X

cause the overflow toggle to be set, in the case of the A or X register. The index registers cannot be set outside the range of −4095 to + 4095 (two bytes plus sign). An attempt to increment or decrement an index register outside this range is an error and will halt the computer.

3.11 INPUT/OUTPUT INSTRUCTIONS

The input/output system for the MIX machine is quite simple and uses only three instructions (IN, OUT, IOC). Byte 4 of the instruction specifies the device which is being used with the instruction.

The IN instruction starts the input of information from an input device. The address given as the operand of the instruction is the address of the first location of a group of contiguous memory words into which information from the device will be read. Each device always reads a *fixed* amount of information. Each of these items is called a *record*. For example, a record for a card reader is one card, or 80 characters. At 5 characters per word (one character per byte), a card reader record is 16 words long. The record length is 16 words. The record length for tape, disk, and drum units is 100 words.

When an IN instruction is executed, the device (specified in byte 4) is notified that it should read one record and put it in memory, starting at the memory location given by the effective address, *m*.

Most I/O devices are very slow relative to the central processing unit (CPU). The fastest card reader still takes about 50 milliseconds to read a card, while the CPU takes on the order of microseconds to execute an instruction. Thus, the IN instruction only *starts* to read the card and then it continues to the next instruction. The device will become busy for as long as it takes to input a record and then will again become ready (idle), waiting for the next IN instruction. Before the CPU can use the information which is being read in, it must be certain that the IN instruction which started the reading is complete. This will happen when the device becomes ready (not busy) again. To test this, two jump instructions exist. JBUS (jump if device is busy) will jump if the device (whose device number is in byte 4) is busy. If the device is not busy, execution continues to the next instruction. The JRED (jump if ready) will jump if the device is ready, that is, not

TABLE 3.8 Input/Output Instructions for the MIX Computer

Opcode	Field	Mnemonic	Instruction
42	N	JBUS	jump to location *m* if unit N is busy
43	N	IOC	issue I/O control signal to unit N
44	N	IN	start input transfer from unit N
45	N	OUT	start output transfer from unit N
46	N	JRED	jump to location *m* if unit N is ready

doing anything now and ready to perform an I/O operation if so instructed. Both of these instructions will change the J register if the jump occurs; otherwise, execution continues at the next instruction.

The OUT instruction is very similar to the IN. The device is requested to begin outputting information from the block of memory beginning at the memory location specified by the effective address. As with the IN instruction, the amount of information which is transferred is always exactly one record, the length of a record depending on the device. The line printer, for example, has 120 characters per line and a record length therefore of 24 words. The card punch has a record of 16 words.

Also, as with the IN instruction, the transfer of information caused by the OUT instruction is only *started* by the OUT instruction. It cannot be considered complete until a JBUS or JRED instruction indicates that the device is ready for another instruction. This is true with one exception. For both the IN and OUT instructions, if an I/O instruction occurs for a *busy* device (busy because of a previous I/O instruction which is not yet complete), then the CPU waits until the previous operation is complete before starting the new I/O operation and going on to the next instruction.

The IOC (Input/Output Control) instruction is provided in MIX to allow different I/O devices to be controlled. Each I/O device is unique in how it operates and although the basic functions which they perform are those of Input and Output, some devices can also do other functions. The IOC instruction instructs the I/O device to begin one of these additional functions. If the device is busy, the CPU waits until it is ready before executing the instruction and continuing. The effective address is a parameter to the device.

The greatest use of IOC comes with magnetic tapes. The IOC command is used to position a tape. The effective address, *m*, specifies how. If $m = 0$, the tape is rewound. If $m > 0$, the tape skips forward *m* records; if $m < 0$ then the tape skips backwards $-m$ records (or to the beginning of the tape, whichever comes first). For other devices, the effect of the IOC command depends on the device.

3.12 SHIFT INSTRUCTIONS

Six shift instructions are provided to shift information in the A and X registers. Three shift instructions shift left, and three shift right. The effective address specifies the number of bytes to shift. SLA and SRA are end-off shifts which affect only the A register, while SLAX and SRAX shift the A and X registers as one large 10-byte double register. (A is the high-order 5 bytes; X is the low-order 5 bytes.) Zeros are shifted in from the left (for a SRA or SRAX) or from the right (for an SLA or SLAX), since these are end-off shifts. The SRC and SLC shift the A and X registers (again as a double register) circularly with the bytes which are shifted off one end being shifted back in at the other end. The signs of the A and X registers are not changed by any shift instruction.

TABLE 3.9 Shift Instructions for the MIX Computer

Opcode	Field	Mnemonic	Instruction
06	00	SLA	shift A *m* bytes left, end-off
06	01	SRA	shift A *m* bytes right, end-off
06	02	SLAX	shift AX *m* bytes left, end-off
06	03	SRAX	shift AX *m* bytes right, end-off
06	04	SLC	shift AX *m* bytes left, circular
06	05	SRC	shift AX *m* bytes right, circular

3.13 MISCELLANEOUS COMMANDS

A number of commands do not fit easily into the categories of instructions presented above. These miscellaneous commands perform various important tasks.

The HLT instruction stops the computer. The computer can be restarted only by pushing the BEGIN button on the MIX console.

NOP is an instruction which does nothing. It is similar to a CONTINUE statement in Fortran.

MOVE is a very complicated but useful instruction. It copies the contents of a block of memory locations into another block of memory locations, effecting a memory-to-memory transfer capability. Byte 4 specifies the number of words to move, while the effective address specifies the address *from* which the contents should be copied. Index register 1 contains the address where the contents should be copied *to*. The copy is done one word at a time, and I1 is increased as the copy is executed, so that at the end of the move, I1 has been increased by the number of words moved. Words are moved one at a time, and the blocks of words being copied to and from can overlap.

The input/output system has many devices which treat information as alphabetic characters, not as numeric quantities, while the CPU operates only on numeric data, of course. To simplify the conversion between binary and character code, two conversion instructions, NUM and CHAR, are included in the MIX instruction set. The NUM operator converts the contents of the A and X register,

TABLE 3.10 Miscellaneous Instructions for the MIX Computer

Opcode	Field	Mnemonic	Instruction
05	00	NUM	10-byte decimal in AX converted to binary in A
05	01	CHAR	A is converted to 10-byte decimal characters in AX
05	02	HLT	halt the MIX machine
00	00	NOP	no operation
07	N	MOVE	move N words starting from *m* to (I1), add N to I1

considered as one large 10-byte register (A is high-order; X is low order), from a 10-character character code representation of an integer number (right justified, zero filled) to the binary representation of that number, and puts the numeric representation into the A register. The X register and the sign bytes of both registers remain unchanged. Each byte of the A and X register is the character code for one digit of the number. The digit specified by a byte is the remainder of the byte divided by 10. Thus, 00, 10, 20, . . ., 60 all are converted to the digit 0; 01, 11, 21, . . ., 61 convert to the digit 1; and 09, 19, 29, . . ., 59 convert to 9. Since the largest number which can be stored in one word is 1,073,741,823, there are (ten-character) numbers which cannot be converted to binary, and overflow results in these cases.

Conversion in the other direction, from numeric binary to character code is performed by the CHAR instruction. When the CHAR instruction is executed, the contents of the A register are converted from numeric binary into a 10 digit (decimal) character code (with leading zeros if necessary). The high-order 5 characters are put into the A register, and the low-order five characters are put into the X register. The signs of the A and X register are unchanged.

For both the NUM and the CHAR instructions, the effective address (bytes 0:3) of the instruction is ignored.

3.14 BINARY INSTRUCTIONS

As an option (at extra cost), purchasers of the binary MIX 1009B computer can have added to their instruction set several special instructions specifically designed for a binary machine. These instructions are only for binary computers and treat a MIX word not as 5 bytes plus sign, but as a word of 30 bits plus sign.

SRB and SLB shift the A and X register, treated as a double register, right or

TABLE 3.11   Binary Instructions for the MIX Computer

Opcode	Field	Mnemonic	Instruction
01	07	ORR	inclusive *or* of (*m*) with A
02	07	XOR	exclusive *or* of (*m*) with A
03	07	AND	logical *and* (*m*) into A
06	06	SLB	shift AX *m* bits left, end-off
06	07	SRB	shift AX *m* bits right, end-off
50	06	JAE	jump to *m* if Z is even
50	07	JAO	jump to *m* if A is odd
57	06	JXE	jump to *m* if X is even
57	07	JXO	jump to *m* if X is odd

left the number of *bits* specified by the effective address. A shift left of one bit is equivalent to multiplying by two; a shift left by two bits, multiplying by four; and so on. These shifts are end-off, with zeros shifted in.

The AND, ORR, and XOR operations are called *boolean instructions*. They perform the "logical", or boolean, operations on the A register and the contents of the memory location addressed by the effective address. These operations are those of "and", "or", and "exclusive-or". They are applied bitwise; so, for an AND instruction bit 0 of the A register is ANDed with bit 0 of memory and the result is put in bit 0 of the A register; bit 1 of the A register is ANDed with bit 1 of memory and put in bit 1 of the A register; and so on. The AND, ORR, and XOR functions on each of the four possible operand pairs (one from the A register, and the other from memory) are

Operand 1	Operand 2	AND	ORR	XOR
0	0	0	0	0
0	1	0	1	1
1	0	0	1	1
1	1	1	1	0

3.15 INSTRUCTION EXECUTION TIMES

One important property of a computer program is how long it takes to execute. This is determined to a large extent by the algorithm which the program uses, but also by which instructions it uses. Since arithmetic unit and control unit circuitry is electronic, it can operate at very high speeds, and so the time it takes to execute an instruction is determined mainly by how many memory references are made. The immediate, jump, NOP, NUM, and CHAR instructions all take one time unit, since only the instruction need be fetched from memory. The memory reference instructions (load, store, arithmetic, and compare instructions) need two memory references (one for the instruction and one for the operand), and so take two time units. MUL and DIV instructions are an exception, since they are so complex; MUL takes 10 time units and DIV takes 12. Shift instructions take two

TABLE 3.12 Execution Times for the Instructions
of the MIX Computer

Instructions	Time
·All load, store, compare, and shift instructions:	2 units
·The ADD and SUB arithmetic operations:	2 units
·The MUL arithmetic operation:	10 units
·The DIV arithmetic operation:	12 units
·The MOVE operation, to MOVE n words in memory:	$2n+1$ units
·All other instructions:	1 unit

time units, even though they only reference memory once. The MOVE instruction requires $2n + 1$ memory references to move n words, and so takes $2n + 1$ time units (one for the instruction fetch, and one to load and one to store each of the n words).

The IN, OUT, and IOC instructions only take one unit *plus* any time they must wait because of a busy device. This extra time is called the *interlock time* and is often on the order of thousands of time units.

The actual length of a time unit varies according to the technology used to build the MIX computer. Old MIX machines may have time units of 3 or 4 microseconds, while the newer models, using semiconductor memory, have time units of 500 to 800 nanoseconds. Since we wish to discuss all MIX machines, we discuss all execution timings in terms of the memory cycle time of the MIX machine, which we call one time unit.

3.16 SUMMARY

The MIX computer is a small general purpose computer whose design has been influenced by a number of contemporary computers. It has 4000 words of memory, with each memory location being composed of 5 bytes plus a sign. Registers include the A and X registers (five bytes plus sign), six index registers (two bytes plus sign), the J register (two bytes), overflow toggle (ON/OFF) and comparison indicator (GREATER/EQUAL/LESS). Instructions allow loading and storing registers, addition, subtraction, multiplication, division, shifts, immediate operations, compares, jumps, input/output, conversion between (decimal) character code and numeric binary, and a few miscellaneous commands. The operands for memory reference instructions may be partial fields of a memory location. The effective address may be given in the instruction with no modification, indexing, double indexing, indirection, preindexed indirection, or postindexed indirection. Binary MIX machines can be equipped with special binary instructions.

The MIX machine was originally defined by Knuth in the first volume of *The Art of Computer Programming*, Knuth (1968), and repeated in the second volume, Knuth (1969). A short paperback, entitled *MIX*, was published in 1970 to serve as a reference for the MIX system. This was a reprint of the defining pages of Knuth (1968). There may be a locally prepared manual or report which describes your particular MIX computer system; check with your instructor or computation center.

EXERCISES

   a.   Why does the MIX machine need the X register?
   b.   What are the contents of the A and X registers after a multiply? After a divide?

c. Why does it take longer to execute a load instruction than an enter instruction?

d. What is the difference between a memory reference instruction and an immediate instruction? Describe the instruction excution cycle for each on the MIX machine.

e. Describe the effective address calculation procedure without indirection.

f. How does (or doesn't) an increment of n differ from a decrement of $-n$? Why would both instructions be provided?

g. Write a single machine language instruction to do each of the following operations. Assume that your instruction will go in location 2734 (octal).

1. Put 10 (decimal) into index register I5.
2. Set the A register to zero.
3. Subtract the contents of I3 from the A register.
4. Put the sum of index registers I1 and I2 into I2.
5. Put the address of the current instruction into the A register.
6. Rewind tape unit 1.

h. What is double indexing? Give a MIX machine language instruction which uses double indexing by I1 and I2.

i. Most computers have a NOP (no operation) instruction. Why? Discuss its possible uses, if any. Can you think of any other instructions which have no more effect on the computer but add one to the program counter?

j. Appendices C and D list 159 different MIX instructions. How many bits are needed to represent 159 different things? How does MIX get by with only a six-bit opcode field?

k. For a load, store, and compare instruction with a partial field specification of L:R, which bytes of the register and which bytes of the memory location are affected and how?

l. Why are partial fields not allowed with immediate instructions?

m. Is the MOVE instruction necessary, or could its function be done with an appropriate combination of other instructions?

n. Give the instruction execution times for the MIX instruction set. If the MOVE instruction only moves n words, why does it take more than n time units?

4

ASSEMBLY LANGUAGE PROGRAMMING TECHNIQUES

In some sense, the programming process is independent of the language which is used for programming, but in a more realistic sense different languages encourage different programming techniques to be used. The machine which is being used for assembly language programming, since it affects the instruction set, also affects the type of programming which can be easily done. The result of this is that there is a body of general programming techniques which can be used for programming in assembly language for most machines, but the details must depend upon the particular machine being used. The basic concepts and techniques are the same for most computers. In this chapter we present some of these techniques to illustrate how to program in assembly language. By and large, many of these techniques will only be learned by their use, however, and as you program you will learn new techniques which are not presented here.

Writing a program is an art, and no one way to program is correct for all situations. Recent discussions have lead to general agreement on several points, however. First, an important distinction exists between *programming* and *coding*. Programming is the process of converting a vague description of a problem into a specific algorithm for solving the problem. This involves defining appropriate data structures, determining what information is to be input and output and the flow of control within the program.

Defining the flow of control can be helped by the use of *top-down programming* techniques. A top-down approach starts with a general statement of the problem and successively refines its components by considering each of these to be a separate problem. This is somewhat difficult to explain, but easier to illustrate. Look back at how the program to add two numbers together and print their sum, in Section 2.2, was developed. First the top-most level was defined: Input, Add, Output, Halt. Then each step at this level was examined and broken down into its components until each step of the program could be converted directly into machine language. Typically, the top-down refinement process continues until each step can be solved by a single machine language instruction, subroutine (see Chapter 6), or macro (see Chapter 9).

The translation of each step of a program into a machine readable format and machine instruction is *coding*. Coding is a necessary but not generally exciting activity.

The process of coding is itself composed of several steps. The data locations which are to be used must be decided upon and allocated. Then the instructions must be written to manipulate this data and perform the function for which the program is being written. In practice these two steps are often intermixed, with new variables being found to be needed as the result of newly written code. The data and the code must be well separated in the final program, however. A common mistake made by novice programmers is to allocate storage for variables as they find they are needed, as in

```
         LDA   B          COMPUTE B + C
         ADD   C
         STA   D          STORE IN D
D        CON   0          ALLOCATE STORAGE FOR D
         LDA   E
         SUB   D          NOW SUBTRACT (B+C) FROM E
```

What is the problem with this? In the assembly of this code, no problem develops; six words are assembled, the five instructions and the data value for D. But during the execution of the program, the program counter will be incremented by one after each instruction is executed in order to fetch the next instruction. This will result in the LDA being fetched and executed, then the ADD, then the STA and then the next location (containing the data value for D) will be fetched, decoded and executed *as an instruction*. The result of this is completely dependent upon the number stored in that location by the previous STA D instruction. For example, if B = 24 and C = 15, then their sum will be 39 and this will be stored in D as

+ 00 00 00 00 47

which is a JMP to +0000!

To prevent this kind of error, programmers use several methods. One method is to program with two sheets of paper, one for the instructions and a separate one for the variables and other data items. Then if new data items are discovered to be needed while writing instructions, the declarations for them are written on the appropriate sheet with other data items. Another approach is to first sit down and write all the code, ignoring the data declarations, and then after the instructions have been written, go back and write down data declarations and allocations for all variables which are used.

In either case, one arrives at the end with two lists, the instructions and the data. These are then combined to form the program. They can be combined in either of two ways: code and then data, or data and then code. In many instances the order is not important, but it is generally best, in MIXAL, to put your data before your code. This avoids many forward references and possible limitations on the use of symbols due to this. (Remember that forward references cannot be used in ORIG, EQU, or CON pseudo-instructions, in literals or in address expressions). Also the wise use of mnemonic variable names and comments can explain the use of the variables, preparing the reader of the program for the code which follows.

We do not generally present entire programs here, but only small fragments of code. This is because we wish to focus our attention on only specific aspects of the coding problem. This allows us to present coding techniques specifically applicable to that aspect of programming under study only. This may sometimes result in undefined symbols being used. It is assumed that the reader will be able to understand from their use how they should be defined. Most often it will be a simple variable which can be defined by a CON 0 or an ORIG *+1.

4.1 ARITHMETIC

Computers were originally built to automate arithmetic calculations, and many people still believe this is their major function. Thus the coding of arithmetic expressions is a logical place to start. (In fact, actual arithmetic computation is only a minor part of what computers do. Remember that in the machine language program of Section 2.2, only 1 instruction out of 16 was an arithmetic computation; the others were input/output, conversion, loads and stores, etc). Here we assume we have a set of integer numbers upon which we wish to compute some simple arithmetic expression.

To start, consider a simple addition. We wish to compute the sum of the value of the variables CAT and DOG and store the sum in the variable FIGHT. This code might look like

```
CAT        CON   0        DATA LOCATION FOR CAT
DOG        CON   0
FIGHT      CON   0
             . . .
```

(code to give CAT and DOG values)

```
  .   .   .
LDA   CAT
ADD   DOG
STA   FIGHT          SET FIGHT = CAT + DOG
```

If we wanted FIGHT = CAT − DOG, we have (assuming the data declarations above)

```
LDA   CAT
SUB   DOG
STA   FIGHT          SET FIGHT = CAT − DOG
```

For ZOO = DOG * CAT, the code needs to consider that the product of two 5-byte numbers will be a 10-byte number with the upper 5 bytes in the A register and the lower 5 bytes in the X register. If we expect that the product will always be no more than 5 bytes in magnitude, we can write

```
LDA   DOG
MUL   CAT          PUTS PRODUCT IN AX
STX   ZOO          ZOO = DOG*CAT LOWER 5 BYTES
```

Notice that this code fragment does not worry about overflow. If we fear that the product DOG*CAT may be too large for five bytes, we can write

```
LDA   CAT
MUL   DOG          AX = DOG * CAT
JANZ  TOOLARGE     CHECK FOR PRODUCT TOO BIG
STX   ZOO
```

For this code, if the product is greater than five bytes, the A register will have the upper five bytes, which will be nonzero. In this case the program will jump to the location whose label is TOOLARGE and execute the code there. If the A register is zero, the product is small enough to fit in five bytes (and is in the X register), so this is stored in the memory location ZOO. Remember, we still have to write the code for TOOLARGE. This code might be a simple

```
TOOLARGE        HLT  0            OVERFLOW, STOP
```

or more complicated (and better) code which prints a message saying what went wrong and informs the user of the program what steps can be taken to correct the problem (change data, rewrite program, or such).

Division must also be coded carefully. If we want RATIO = NMEN / NWOMEN, we need the dividend (NMEN in this case) as a 10-byte quantity in register AX for the DIV operator. Normally, this means putting the dividend in the X register and zero in the A register. This can be done in several ways. The major constraint in how it is done is that the sign of the dividend is the sign of the A register. Thus, if you know that your dividend is positive, division can be

```
LDX   NMEN
ENTA  0
DIV   NWOMEN    COMPUTE NMEN/NWOMEN
```

If the sign of the dividend can be either positive or negative, then code can be

```
LDA   NMEN(0:0) PUT SIGN IN A
LDX   NMEN       LOAD NUMBER IN X
DIV   NWOMEN     DIVIDE NMEN BY NWOMEN
```

which loads the sign into the A register (setting the rest to zero) and the rest of the dividend into the X register, or the code can be,

```
LDA   NMEN       LOAD NUMBER IN A
SRAX  5          SHIFT INTO X, LEAVING SIGN
DIV   NWOMEN     DIVIDE
```

In this case the number is loaded into the A register and shifted into X. SRAX is an end-off shift, so zeros are shifted into the A register and the old contents of the X register are lost. The sign bits do not participate in the shift, so the sign of the dividend remains in the sign bit of the A register.

   Once the division has been done, the quotient will be in the A register, and the remainder in the X register. Thus, these two quantities can be used, as desired, and the same code can be used to compute either the quotient or the remainder (or both). Remember that the DIV operator is an *integer* division. Fractions would require the use of floating point arithmetic.

   Once these basic operations are understood, it is possible to compute much more complicated expressions, like X1 = I + J*L1. This expression would be programmed to first perform the multiplication, then the addition. To do the multiplication, we would

```
LDA   J
MUL   L1         AX = L1*J
```

Now we have J*L1, but it is in the X register. The ADD operator only adds to the A register, so we must get our result into the A register for the addition. This could be done by

```
STX   TEMP
LDA   TEMP       TRANSFER FROM X TO A
```

where TEMP is a *temporary* variable, or we could simply

```
SLAX  5          SHIFT X INTO A
```

which is faster (2 time units instead of 4) and shorter (1 instruction instead of 2). Notice that we are taking advantage of the sign bits of the A and X registers as set by the MUL operator. Now we can add and store. Our complete code is then

```
LDA   J
MUL   L1          COMPUTE J*L1
SLAX  5           MOVE X TO A
ADD   I
STA   X1          X1 = I + J*L1
```

Even more complicated expressions may be computed. Consider the expression

$$((B+W)*Y) + 2 + ((L-M)*(-K))/Z$$

This is the sum of three terms. This means that at least one term must be stored in memory, in a temporary, while the other term is being computed. The addition by 2 can be done by either

```
ADD   =2=         INCREASE A BY 2
```

or

```
INCA  2           INCREASE A BY 2.
```

Since the latter is shorter and faster, we use it. (Shorter because although both instructions are the same length, the ADD also requires a literal, which is one memory location).

Since the first term is simpler, let us attack it first. We can write

```
LDA   B
ADD   W           A = B+W
MUL   Y           AX = (B+W)*Y
```

Now we can add the 2, but remember the result of the MUL will be in AX, so we

```
INCX  2           X = (B+W)*Y + 2
```

This is even better than we had thought, over the ADD approach, since it prevents having to move the product from the X register to the A register for the ADD. Now we need to store this while we compute the next term.

```
STX   TEMP        SAVE PARTIAL TERM
```

Next we compute $((L-M)*(-K))/Z$. This can be done easiest by noting that $((L-M)*(-K)) = ((M-L) * K)$, which removes one operation, and we can now write,

```
LDA   M
SUB   L           M-L
MUL   K           (M-L) * K
DIV   Z           ((M-L)*K) / Z.
```

Notice that the MUL leaves the AX register just right for a DIV. This is one reason for doing our multiply first. Another reason is due to the integer nature of the division. If $(M-L) = 100$, $K = 50$, and $Z = 100$, consider the result of computing $(M-L)*(K/Z)$ instead of $((M-L)*K)/Z$. For $(M-L)*(K/Z)$, $K/Z = 0$ and the product is 0, while for $((M-L)*K)/Z$, the product is 5000 and the quotient is 50. This illustrates the wide difference which can result from carelessness with the order of multiplication and division.

Once the division is done, we can add from our temporary, TEMP, to the quotient, which is conveniently in the A register. Our complete code is then

```
LDA   B         B
ADD   W         B+W
MUL   Y         (B+W)*Y
INCX  2         ((B+W)*Y)+2
STX   TEMP      TEMP = ((B+W) * Y) + 2
LDA   M         M
SUB   L         M-L
MUL   K         (M-L) * K
DIV   Z         ((M-L)*K) / Z
ADD   TEMP      ((B+W)*Y) + 2 + ((M-L)*K)/Z
```

Overflow is a problem which we have not considered in this code. Notice that at any (arithmetic) instruction overflow could occur (except for the DIV, but if $Z = 0$, this will act the same as overflow). One of the nice features of MIX is that the overflow toggle is turned on whenever overflow occurs, but is not turned off when it does not occur. This means that if it is off before we begin to execute this code, and is on after the code is executed then overflow has occurred somewhere in the expression. Often it is not important to know exactly where overflow has occurred, but only if it has occurred at any time during the evaluation of the expression. This can be tested by one test at the end of the expression computation as,

```
JOV   OVERFLOW
```

Remember that this will also turn the overflow toggle off so that it can be used for the next segment of code. This approach to testing overflow requires that the overflow toggle be off before the computation of the arithmetic expression is begun. How do we guarantee that it is off? The easiest way is to test for overflow whenever it may occur. This assures that as soon as it happens, it will be recognized and appropriate action taken. Alternatively, we will need to turn the overflow toggle off explicitly. Searching the list of machine instructions, we find that there is no instruction to turn off the overflow toggle. But consider

```
JOV   *+1.
```

This instruction will not jump if the overflow is off, and if it is on, it will turn the overflow off, and jump to *+1. In either case the next instruction will be at *+1, with the overflow toggle off.

4.2 JUMPS

The discussion of overflow brings up the subject of jumps and particularly *conditional jumps*. These instructions allow us to compute different functions based on the value of our data. Consider the absolute value function

if $n < 0$ then absolute value of $n = -n$
    otherwise absolute value of $n = n$.

To compute this we could write the following code

```
        LDA   N
        JANN  1F         IF NOT NEGATIVE LEAVE ALONE
        LDAN  N          BUT OTHERWISE LOAD -N
1H      EQU   *          A REGISTER HAS ABS OF N
```

When execution reaches the label 1H, the A register has the absolute value of N. The JANN will jump directly to 1H if the contents of the A register is positive or zero. If N was negative, then the LDAN would load the negative of N into the A register and then "drop through" to 1H.

Tests on the sign of a number or on the zero/nonzero nature of a number can be done by loading into a register and testing the register. The jump instructions allow the A and X registers and the index registers to be tested directly for positive, negative, zero, nonzero, nonpositive, and nonnegative states.

We can use these instructions to compute the sign function. The sign function of a number p is $+1$ if p is positive, zero if p is zero and -1 if p is negative. If we want to leave the sign function of p in the A register, we can write

```
        LDA   P
        JAZ   1F
        JAP   2F
        ENTA  -1         NEGATIVE NUMBER
        JMP   1F
2H      ENTA  +1         POSITIVE NUMBER
1H      EQU   *
```

Follow this code for each of the three cases ($p < 0$, $p = 0$, $p > 0$) to make sure that it is correct.

Comparisons between two numbers, and computations based on this comparison, generally use the CMPA or CMPX instruction. For example, to execute the code at FGREAT if $F > G$, or FLESS if $F < G$, we can write

```
        LDA   F
        CMPA  G
        JG    FGREAT
        JL    FLESS
```

What happens if F = G? In the above code, we "drop through" the tests. If we wanted to take the FGREAT path, then we should have written

```
        LDA    F
        CMPA   G
        JGE    FGREAT
        JL     FLESS
```

and the JL could have been replaced by a JMP.

To compute the maximum of two numbers P and W, we could write

```
        LDA    P
        CMPA   W
        JGE    1F
        LDA    W
1H      EQU    *
```

This code leaves the maximum of P and W in the A register.

4.3 LOOPS

Jumps are a very important part of computers. Code which does not have any jumps is called *straight-line code*, since it is executed in a linear manner, one statement after another. Jumps are used in two ways. One is to produce conditional execution of code similar to an IF statement. The other use of jumps is to create *loops*. Loops allow code to be repeated until some condition is met. The condition may be that a particular property holds, or that the loop has been executed a certain number of times. Both of these are programmed by the use of conditional jumps.

Suppose we wish to find a number i such that $i^2 \leq N < (i+1)^2$. We can do this by a loop which can be described as,

set i to 1.
if $i \times i > N$ then $i-1$ is our number
        otherwise set i to $i+1$
        and repeat the test again.

In MIXAL this would be

```
        ENTA   1
        STA    I          SET I TO 1
*
1H      LDA    I
        MUL    I          AX = I*I
        CMPX   N          COMPARE LOWER 5 BYTES
        JG     FOUND      IF GREATER, QUIT LOOP
*
```

```
              LDA   I
              INCA  1          SET I TO I+1
              STA   I
              JMP   1B         REPEAT LOOP
*
FOUND         LDA   I
              DECA  1          WANT I-1
```

This is a straightforward coding of the previous algorithm. We would hope that some local optimization would be able to improve that code, but the only obvious improvement is to move the label 1H back one location to the STA I in order to eliminate the second STA I before the JMP 1B.

Another kind of loop is the equivalent of the DO-loop of Fortran. In this kind of loop, we repeat execution of the loop a fixed number of times, as counted by an index variable. The DO-loop was specifically designed to allow its index variable to be stored in an index register. Thus the DO-loop

```
              DO 10 I = 1, N
              ⟨DO-loop body⟩
       10     CONTINUE
```

can be written in MIX code as (letting index register 3 be the index variable I)

```
              ENT3  1
1H            EQU   *
              ⟨MIX code for DO-loop body⟩
              INC3  1
              CMP3  N
              JLE   1B         CHECK FOR END OF LOOP
```

For example, to add the numbers from 1 to N, we could write

```
              ENT3  1          LOOP INDEX = 1..N
              ENTA  0          ACCUMULATOR OF SUM
1H            INCA  0,3        INCREASE A BY CONTENTS OF I3
              INC3  1          SET FOR NEXT LOOP
              CMP3  N          IF ANY
              JLE   1B
*                              A HAS SUM OF 1 TO N
```

Notice that since addition is commutative, we could also add our numbers backwards, from N to 1. The advantage of this is that our index can then be tested against zero, which eliminates the CMP3 instruction, making the code slightly shorter (and faster) as

```
              LD3   N
              ENTA  0          ACCUMULATOR FOR SUM
1H            INCA  0,3        A = A + INDEX 3
```

```
          DEC3 1
          J3P  1B         CHECK FOR END OF LOOP
*                         A HAS SUM OF 1 TO N.
```

Loops can be nested. When loops are nested, different index registers should be used to control the loops, of course.

4.4 ARRAYS

One of the primary reasons for the use of loops is the repetition of a piece of code on each element of an array. An array is a linear list of similar items which is indexed to specify any particular element. Arrays are represented in MIX programs by sequential locations in memory. Memory is allocated for an array by the ORIG pseudo-instruction. For example, an array of 100 integers can be declared by

```
BASE          ORIG *+100.
```

This statement moves the location counter of the assembly program ahead 100 locations, leaving 100 locations of memory for the array. The elements are accessed by BASE, BASE+1, BASE+2, . . . , BASE+99. The label (BASE in this case) is called the *base address*. To avoid having to write out each address separately, we use indexing to specify the address of each element in the array relative to the base address. To initialize an entire array to zero, we could use

FIGURE 4.1   Storage allocation and accessing for an array.

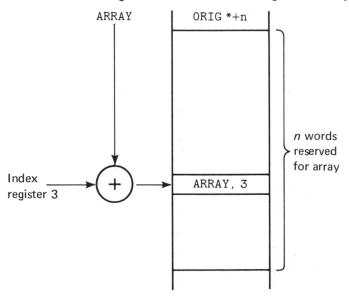

code such as

```
             ENT3  0           INDEX FOR ARRAY REFERENCING
1H           STZ   ARRAY,3     SET ELEMENT I3 TO ZERO
             INC3  1
             CMP3  =N=         CHECK FOR END OF ARRAY
             JL    1B
```

where the symbol N has been defined as the length of the array, as for example,

```
N            EQU   176         LENGTH OF ARRAY IS 176
```

and the array ARRAY has been defined as

```
ARRAY        ORIG  *+N.
```

Notice that an actual number may be used instead of the symbol. For example, for an array of length 238 called XRAY,

```
XRAY         ORIG  *+238       RESERVE SPACE FOR XRAY
             .  .  .
             ENT6  0           INDEX FOR LOOP AND SUBSCRIPT
7H           STZ   XRAY,6
             INC6  1
             CMP6  =238=       CHECK FOR END OF ZERO LOOP
             JL    7B
```

The symbol is used rather than the actual number because (a) it can be more descriptive, and (b) if the length of the array must be changed later, only the value of the symbol need be changed (one card) if a symbol is used, instead of many lines of code (one for every time the length of the array is used).

As with the loops seen above, the index variable can often be manipulated to make the code simpler by running the index towards zero, rather than a nonzero quantity. For an array 3DIM of length 27, for example, we could zero it by

```
3LENGTH      EQU   27          LENGTH OF 3DIM ARRAY
3DIM         ORIG  *+3LENGTH
             .  .  .
             ENT2  3LENGTH-1 LENGTH MINUS ONE
2H           STZ   3DIM,2      ZERO 3DIM
             DEC2  1
             J2NN  2B          CHECK FOR ENTIRE ARRAY DONE
```

We can also index our array by quantities other than 0 to (the length of the array minus one). If we want an array called YEAR which is indexed from 1900 to 1984, we can declare it as

```
YEAR         ORIG  *+85
```

Then the label YEAR refers to the first location of the array. We want this to correspond to an index value of 1900, so the correspondence between addresses and index values is

address	index value
YEAR	1900
YEAR+1	1901
YEAR+2	1902
. . .	. . .
YEAR+84	1984

If index register 3 has the index value, then the address expression to access that element of the array is YEAR−1900,3. This is the quantity YEAR−1900 plus the contents of register 3. Since the index value is between 1900 and 1984, we have

$$1900 \leq I3 \leq 1984,$$

and

$$YEAR \leq YEAR−1900+I3 \leq YEAR+84,$$

so our address will be in range. To illustrate it more concretely, suppose the array YEAR begins at location 1000 and continues to location 1084, then the address YEAR−1900, 3 is 1000 − 1900, 3 = −900, 3. From $1900 \leq 13 \leq 1984$, we have $1000 \leq −900, 3 \leq 1084$, again showing that the address which eventually results from the indexed address is correct.

The most common form of this type of array indexing is with arrays indexed from 1 to M, rather than 0 to M−1. For this case the address is (using index register 5 to hold the index value), ARRAY−1,5.

The types of processing which can be done on an array are almost endless, as are the variations of coding which can be used. For example, consider the array XRAY mentioned earlier, of length 238. XRAY can be zeroed by the code

```
        ENT5  238
2H      STZ   XRAY−1,5
        DEC5  1
        J5P   2B
```

Notice our index runs from 238 down to 1, as the locations zeroed vary from XRAY−1+238 down to XRAY−1+1.

Consider how long this code takes to execute. The ENT5 is executed once and takes 1 unit of MIX time. The STZ takes 2 units, DEC5 1 unit, and J5P 1 unit, with each of these being executed 238 times. The total time is then $1 + 238(2+1+1) = 953$ units.

Now consider the code

```
        ENT5  238
2H      STZ   XRAY−1,5
        STZ   XRAY−2,5   ZERO TWO ELEMENTS AT ONCE
        DEC5  2
        J5P   2B
```

This code zeros the array the same as the previous loop, but it does it two elements at a time. Notice that it is one instruction longer, but the loop is only executed 119 times (238/2) rather than 238 times. The execution time is then $1 + 119(2+2+1+1) = 715$ units, saving 238 units over our first code. (However, it should be pointed out that 238 units is much less than a millisecond, so unless this code was to be executed millions of times, the effort to save the computer time would take much longer than the savings). This is an example of a *space-time tradeoff*. We can trade one extra location in memory for 238 units of time (in this case). It is almost always possible to make a program run faster by making it more complex and hence longer in terms of the amount of space it uses. Similarly, it is generally possible to make a program use less space by making it take more time to execute. These tradeoffs (more time/less space; less time/more space) are most often the result of using different algorithms. Consideration of the time-versus-space tradeoffs of particular algorithms is very important when programming, since often the machine may have very limited memory available, or computer time is very expensive (or both).

Array loops need not be executed a fixed number of times. Suppose we have an array NAME ORIG *+500 and we want to search the first 37 entries for an entry whose value is in the A register, because we wish to know the index of such an item. Searching for an item in the A register can be

```
        ENT1  0           INDEX FOR SEARCH
4H      CMPA  NAME,1
        JE    FOUND       MATCH FOUND
        INC1  1           OTHERWISE INCREASE INDEX
        CMP1  =37=
        JL    4B          IF STILL MORE TO CHECK
```

If the code "drops through", then the item is not in the first 37 elements of the array; if the code jumps to the label FOUND (someplace else in the program), index register 1 has the index of the item in the array NAME.

Now a "smart" programmer comes along and says "I can speed that up by running my index from 37 down to 1 rather than from 0 to 36." He proceeds to write the code

```
        ENT1  37
4H      CMPA  NAME-1,1
        JE    FOUND
        DEC1  1
        J1P   4B
```

Now several questions arise. First, how much time has been saved? Only the loop is changed, and it now has a DEC1 instead of an INC1 (but these take the same time) and a J1P instead of a CMP1, JL (saving 2 units and 1 memory location, plus the literal). Since the loop is executed 38 times, this saves 76 units. (Consider how much real time this is). Another question is, does the code do the same thing? Well, no, not quite. Notice that if FOUND is reached in this version, the value of index register 1 is one more than the value of index register 1 from the first version. This means that either all references which were NAME,1 must now be changed to NAME−1,1, or we need to modify the code slightly to run our index from 36 to 0 rather than 37 to 1, as

```
         ENT1  36
4H       CMPA  NAME,1
         JE    FOUND
         DEC1  1
         J1NN  4B
```

This makes the code the same *except* in one, not necessarily unlikely case. Suppose there are two (or more) items in the array which are equal to the A register. Our first code, running the index register from 0 to 36, would find the entry that matched which had the lowest index, since it searches from smallest index to largest. The code above would find the match with the highest index. This may make a very large difference to the code at FOUND.

Another difference between these two pieces of code is in the average time that it takes them to execute. Notice that for this code two times are important: how long it takes to execute if the item is not found, and how long it takes to execute if an item is found. If the items searched for tend to be at the beginning of the table most of the time, then searching from the front will be faster (on average), while if the items searched for tend to be towards the end of the table, then the search from the back will be faster (on average). Most often we may not know where our searched for items will tend to be (front or back), and so the choice between these two techniques should be made on other considerations (such as indicated above). Notice however that our not knowing which code will be faster does not mean that they both will take the same time; one of them will be faster on average, we just do not know which. The problem of selecting efficient searching and sorting algorithms has received considerable attention and is the subject of many other books.

Arrays need not be constructed of only one-word elements. Multiple-word elements are also possible. These arrays are sometimes called *tables*. Each element of a table is a *record* with several *fields*. For example, the MIXAL assembler builds a symbol table which is used to translate symbols in an assembly language program into their values. This requires two parts to each item, the name and the value. The name may be up to 10 characters long, so we need two words for it, plus one word for the value. Thus each record is three words long, with a format such as

first 5 characters of name
second 5 characters of name
value of name

Suppose that the symbol table is an array of up to 500 such records declared by

```
SYMBOL          ORIG 3*500+*    SAVE 500 ENTRIES 3 WORDS EACH
```

and LENGTH is a variable whose value is the number (from 3 to 1500) which is the number of words in the symbol table. The table is originally empty (LENGTH = 0) and as each new symbol is entered into it, the length is increased by 3. LENGTH then has the index of the next empty spot in the symbol table. Then we can search the symbol table for a name whose first five characters are in the A register and whose second five characters are in the X register by

```
        ENT1  0
1H      CMPA  SYMBOL,1
        JNE   2F
        CMPX  SYMBOL+1,1   COMPARE SECOND HALF OF NAME
        JE    FOUND
2H      INC1  3            3 WORDS PER RECORD
        CMP1  LENGTH
        JL    1B
```

If the program drops through, the name in the AX register is not in the table; if control transfers to FOUND, the value of the name in AX is at SYMBOL+2,1.

One problem with the above might be if instead of LENGTH being the number of words in the table, suppose we only had NITEMS whose value was the number of records in the table. (So LENGTH = 3*NITEMS). From this we could compute the number of words by a multiplication or we could run our loop with two index registers, one for counting the number of items (1, 2, . . ., NITEMS) and the other for indexing the symbol table (0, 3, 6, . . ., 3*(NITEMS−1)). This can be coded as

```
        ENT1  1            COUNT NUMBER OF ITEMS
        ENT3  0            INDEX FOR SYMBOL TABLE
1H      CMP1  NITEMS       END OF TABLE?
        JG    NOTFOUND
        CMPA  SYMBOL,3     CHECK FIRST HALF
        JNE   2F
        CMPX  SYMBOL+1,3   CHECK SECOND HALF
        JE    FOUND
2H      INC3  3            NOT YET, INCREMENT INDEX
        INC1  1
        JMP   1B
```

Here we have made some other changes also. Control transfers to either FOUND or NOTFOUND, depending on whether the symbol is found or not. We have moved the test for completion of loop (I1 > NITEMS) to before the comparison to allow for a table with zero entries. If the item is found, SYMBOL+2,3 is the address of the value of the name in AX; if it is not found, I3 has the index of the first empty location in the table.

4.5 STACKS

One common use for an array is to implement a stack. A stack is a data structure along with a specific way of entering data onto and removing data from the stack. The classical example is a stack of plates or trays in a cafeteria. As plates are washed, they are added to the top of the stack; as they are needed they are removed from the top of the stack. This type of adding to the top and removing from the top mechanism is often very useful in computer systems (for example, with subroutines as explained in Chapter 6), and so we show here how a stack would be coded.

Two data structures are needed for a stack: an array, to store the stack and a variable to indicate the current number of items in the stack (top of stack pointer). As with tables, the items in a stack may be several words long, but for simplicity we assume that each item to be stacked is only one word. To provide storage for a stack, we define

```
TOP           CON  0          TOP OF STACK INDEX
STACK         ORIG *+LENGTH   SPACE FOR STACK
```

Notice that although the stack may have a variable number of elements in the stack, we must allocate a fixed amount of space for the stack. Thus, it is necessary to estimate the maximum size that the stack will ever grow to be, and allocate that much memory (or even a little more). This can be done by a LENGTH EQU n, where n is the amount of space wanted. By using a symbolic stack length indicator, we need only change the EQU statement if we decide we need more or less stack space.

FIGURE 4.2   Stack operations: the PUSH operation adds a new element to the top of the stack; the POP operation removes it.

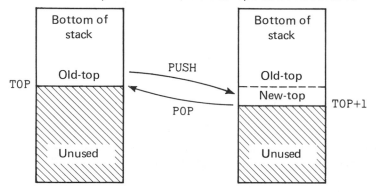

Two operations are possible on a stack: PUSH and POP (or STACK/UNSTACK, ADD/REMOVE, etc.). The PUSH operation involves adding a new element to the top of the stack. This requires storing the element on the top of the stack and increasing the number of elements by one. Assuming the element is in the A register and index I5 is not in use, the code for this would be,

```
        LD5    TOP             TOP OF STACK POINTER
        CMP5   =LENGTH=        CHECK IF STACK IS FULL
        JGE    OVERFLOW        IF SO, STACK OVERFLOW
*
        STA    STACK,5         STACK NEW ELEMENT
        INC5   1
        ST5    TOP             SET TOP = TOP + 1
*
```

This code checks to see that we do not store more elements in the stack than we have allocated space for. This type of error checking is good programming practice.

To remove an element from the stack and put it into the A register requires a similar sequence of code. This time we check to make sure that the stack is not empty before we remove an element from the stack. Also since the top-of-stack index (TOP) is the index of the next *empty* space in the stack array, we decrement it before loading the stack element.

```
        LD5    TOP
        DEC5   1               SET TOP = TOP + 1
        J5N    UNDERFLOW       CHECK IF STACK IS EMPTY
*
        LDA    STACK,5         LOAD TOP OF STACK
        ST5    TOP             RESTORE TOP INDEX
```

An additional function on a stack would be a test for an empty stack.

4.6 CHARACTER MANIPULATION

In addition to arrays of multiple-word items, arrays may be of partial-word elements, and particularly of single characters (one byte). The techniques which are used for manipulating arrays of characters (called strings) are very important. One character requires one byte for storage, thus it would be very wasteful to use an entire word to store only one character. Also, certain I/O devices, such as the card reader and line printer, use character strings which are *packed* five characters per word. For computational purposes, however, we wish to use the string one character at a time, generally. This requires *unpacking* the string and extracting one character from it. Two techniques are commonly used on the MIX computer: partial field specifications and shifting.

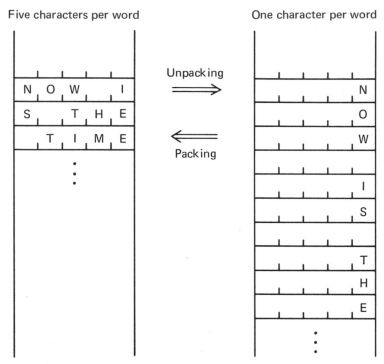

FIGURE 4.3   Packed and unpacked strings of characters (characters must be packed for input and output, but it is more convenient to program unpacked characters).

As an example, suppose we have an input card in the 16 locations CARD, CARD+1, . . ., CARD+15, and we wish to count the number of blank characters on the card. We want to examine each of the 5 bytes in each of the 16 words of the card. Letting index register 2 be our counter, we can write the following code to do this, using partial field specifications.

```
        ENT2  0               COUNTER FOR BLANKS
        ENT1  0               INDEX FOR WORDS, 0..15
1H      LDA   CARD,1(1:1)  CHECK FIRST BYTE
        CMPA  BLANK
        JNE   *+2
        INC2  1               FOUND A BLANK, COUNT IT
        LDA   CARD,1(2:2)  CHECK SECOND BYTE
        CMPA  BLANK
        JNE   *+2
        INC2  1
        LDA   CARD,1(3:3)  THIRD BYTE
        CMPA  BLANK
```

```
              JNE    *+2
              INC2   1
              LDA    CARD,1(4:4)  FOURTH BYTE
              CMPA   BLANK
              JNE    *+2
              INC2   1
              LDA    CARD,1(5:5)  FIFTH BYTE
              CMPA   BLANK
              JNE    *+2
              INC2   1
*                                 FINISHED WORD
              INC1   1            INDEX FOR NEXT WORD
              CMP1   =16=         CHECK FOR LAST WORD
              JL     1B
*                                 INDEX 2 HAS BLANK COUNT
```

This is a very simplistic approach which has its advantages but is very tiring in terms of writing code. The only varying portion is the field specification of the LDA instruction. There are several approaches to shortening the code. One is through *instruction modification*. In this approach we notice that the field specification is stored in byte 4 of the load instruction and we want this to be successively (1:1), (2:2), (3:3), (4:4), (5:5). The following code does this by keeping in index register 3 the partial field we want to use and changing the LDA instruction for each execution of the loop.

```
              ENT2   0            COUNTER OF BLANKS
              ENT1   0            INDEX FOR WORDS
1H            ENT3   1:1          FIRST BYTE
2H            ST3    *+1(4:4)     MODIFY LDA FIELD
              LDA    CARD,1(7:7)  PARTIAL FIELD SET AT *-1
              CMPA   BLANK
              JNE    *+2
              INC2   1            COUNT A BLANK
              INC3   1:1          INCREASE FIELD SPECIFICATION
              CMP3   =5:5=        CHECK END OF WORD
              JLE    2B
              INC1   1            IF END OF WORD, INCREASE INDEX
              CMP1   =16=         CHECK END OF CARD
              JL     1B
*                                 INDEX 2 HAS BLANK COUNT
```

This shortens the code but is more difficult to follow. The problem is that in debugging this code, the instructions which are executed are *not* the instructions which are written in the assembly program listing. You cannot tell by looking at the listing what the instruction which used to be LDA CARD,1(7:7) is in fact when it is executed. This makes it very difficult to debug a program and is considered a poor programming practice.

The more common approach to character manipulation is through shifting. Consider the word

If we load this into the A register, the (1:1) byte will have the first character we wish to use. Then if we SLA 1, we have

and the second character we want is now in the (1:1) byte. Another SLA 1 gives us

Another SLA 1 gives us

| D | E | 00 | 00 | 00 |

and finally a last SLA 1 gives

| E | 00 | 00 | 00 | 00 |

This allows us to examine each character in the (1:1) byte of the A register without needing to do partial loads. The code to count blanks using this technique can be

```
          ENT2  0               NUMBER OF BLANKS
          ENT1  0               WORD INDEX 0..15
7H        ENT3  5               BYTE COUNTER 5..0
          LDA   CARD,1          PICK UP 5 BYTES
1H        CMPA  BLANK(1:1)      BLANK HAS BLANK CHAR
          JNE   *+2
          INC2  1               FOUND A BLANK
          SLA   1               SHIFT NEXT BYTE INTO (1:1)
          DEC3  1               DECREASE BYTE COUNT
          J3P   1B              IF STILL MORE BYTES THIS WORD
          INC1  1               NEXT WORD
          CMP1  =16=            IF ANY LEFT
          JL    7B
*
                                INDEX 2 HAS BLANK COUNT
```

Other shift instructions can be used to vary the position of the character which we are processing. If we load into the X register and SLAX 1 before processing, Then the characters appear in byte (5:5) of the A register for processing as

| | | | | | | | S | T | U | V | W |

SLAX 1

| | | | | S | | T | U | V | W | 00 |

SLAX 1

| | | S | T | | | U | V | W | 00 | 00 |

Or we can load into the A register and shift circularly (SLC 1) into the X register.

This approach is fine for processing the characters sequentially from left to right, but what if we need only the 37th character from the card? The 37th character will be in word CARD+7, byte (2:2). How do we access it? First, how did we determine its location? Looking at the card as it is stored in memory

```
COLUMN OF CARD   1 2 3 4 5 6 7 8 9 10 . . . 80
WORD             0 0 0 0 0 1 1 1 1 1  . . . 15
BYTE             1 2 3 4 5 1 2 3 4 5  . . .  5
```

To obtain the word and byte number of a given column of the card, we notice that COLUMN NUMBER = BYTE NUMBER + 5*WORD NUMBER. If we divide the column number by 5, this almost gives us what we want in the quotient and remainder, but column 5 divided by 5 gives word 1 instead of word 0, so we subtract one from the column number first to give

```
WORD NUMBER = (COLUMN NUMBER-1) / 5
BYTE NUMBER = 1 + REMAINDER OF (COLUMN NUMBER-1)/5
```

Notice that the DIV instruction returns both of these numbers, one in the A register and the other in the X register.

Once we know the word number, we can use that as an index to load the appropriate word. Then, to get the correct byte we shift the loaded word so that the byte we want is in some convenient location (generally byte 1 or 5 of the A or X registers). For example, if we load into the X register and shift left the number of bytes which is the byte number (1, 2, 3, 4, or 5), the desired byte will be in byte 5 of the A register. To illustrate, suppose register I5 has the column number of the character we want. Then our code can be as follows. First, put the column number minus one in the X register and zero the A register for the DIV.

```
ENTA  0
ENTX  -1,5        COLUMN NUMBER MINUS ONE
DIV   =5=
```

Now the A register has the quotient and the X register has the remainder. Both of these need to go into index registers. Unfortunately, MIX does not provide convenient ways to move information from the A or X registers to the index registers, except via memory. One way to do this would be to store them in a temporary as

```
STA   TEMP
LD2   TEMP
STX   TEMP
LD3   TEMP
```

Another way is self-modifying code.

```
STA   *+1(0:2)
ENT2  0
STX   *+1(0:2)
ENT3  0
```

The address fields of the ENT2 and ENT3 instructions are modified at execution time to the values of the A and X registers, respectively. This saves one memory location (TEMP) and is only six time units instead of eight.

Once we have the word number in I2 and the byte number in I3, we can obtain the character we want by

```
LDX   CARD,2
SLAX  1,3
```

The character is now in byte 5 of the A register. We could have put it in byte 1 of the A register by

```
LDA   CARD,2
SLA   0,3
```

or by

```
LDX   CARD,2
SLAX  5,3
```

or by

```
LDA   CARD,2
SLC   10,3
```

among others.

Code such as the above allows us to specify characters by a character or column number, and hence ignore the packed nature of the characters in memory. However, notice that this takes a fair amount of computer time (the DIV instruction has the longest execution time of any instruction in MIX) and it also requires the use of both the A and X registers and two index registers. Thus, it may be better to break the processing of a card into two parts: first, unpack the card, and second, process the unpacked form. This allows the character number to be used as an index into the unpacked character array. After being processed, the data may need to be packed again for output.

Consider a program which reads a card and squeezes out all multiple blanks between the words on a card. The input might be English text which was prepared on a keypunch whose space bar sticks and sometimes inserts several blanks, between words. Our overall approach for the program could be to first read the card into a 16-word array CARD. Then it is unpacked into the 80-word array CHAR. From this array we move the card to an array OUTPUT without multiple blanks, and then finally pack it into an array called LINE for output (say to a card punch). Ignoring the actual input and output (which is the subject of Chapter 5), we can write the following code.

```
*
*                   DATA  ELEMENTS
*
CARD        ORIG  *+16      INPUT CARD IMAGE
CHAR        ORIG  *+80      UNPACKED INPUT IMAGE
OUTPUT      ORIG  *+80      UNPACKED COMPRESSED OUTPUT
LINE        ORIG  *+16      PACKED OUTPUT
*
*
                    <code to read into CARD>
*
*                   UNPACK THE CARD IMAGE OF 16 WORDS,
*                   5 CHARACTERS PER WORD FROM CARD INTO CHAR.
*                   UNPACKING IS DONE RIGHT TO LEFT TO ALLOW
*                   REGISTERS TO BE TESTED AGAINST ZERO.
*
*                   REGISTER USAGE
*
*                   I1 = WORD COUNTER FOR CARD 15..0
*                   I2 = BYTE COUNTER 4..0
*                   I3 = INDEX FOR CHAR 79..0
*                   A  = LOADED WORD SHIFTED TO GIVE THE RIGHT
*                        CHARACTER IN BYTE 5
*                   ENT3 79         CHARACTER COUNTER 79..0
                    ENT1 15         COUNTER OF WORDS 15..0
NEWWORD     LDA   CARD,1
                    ENT2 4          COUNTER OF BYTES 4..0
NEXTCHAR    STA   CHAR,3(5:5)
```

```
                    DEC3 1          DECREASE INDEX INTO CHAR
                    SRA  1          SHIFT WORD IN A RIGHT ONE
                    DEC2 1          ONE LESS BYTE
                    J2NN NEXTCHAR
                    DEC1 1          ONE LESS WORD
                    J1NN NEWWORD
*
*                   MOVE CHARACTERS FROM CHAR TO OUTPUT ONE AT A
*                   TIME. IF A BLANK IS FOUND, SET A FLAG TO
*                   PREVENT ANY MORE BLANKS FROM BEING STORED.  I1
*                   IS INDEX FOR CHAR, I2 INDEX FOR OUTPUT. FLAG
*                   FOR MULTIPLE BLANKS IS HELD IN REGISTER I3.
*                   CODE MAKES USE OF MIX CODE FOR BLANK BEING
*                   ZERO.
*
                    ENT1 -80        INDEX FOR CHAR -80..-1
                    ENT2 0          INDEX FOR OUTPUT 0..79
                    ENT3 STOREBLK   FIRST BLANK SHOULD BE STORED
*
ANOTHER             LDA  CHAR+80,1 LOAD NEXT CHARACTER
                    JMP  0,3        PROCESS THIS CHARACTER
*                                   AT STOREBLK OR NOSTORE.
STOREBLK            JANZ STORE      STORE ALL, BUT IF BLANK SET
                    ENT3 NOSTORE    TO SKIP ANY FUTURE BLANKS
                    JMP  STORE
*
NOSTORE             JAZ  SKIP       IF BLANK, SKIP IT
                    ENT3 STOREBLK   IF NOT SET TO STORE NEXT
*
STORE               STA  OUTPUT,2   STORE THE CHAR IN OUTPUT
                    INC2 1
SKIP                INC1 1          MOVE TO NEXT CHARACTER
                    J1N  ANOTHER
*
*                   LINE NOW COMPRESSED, MOVE TO LINE ARRAY.
*                   FIRST BLANK THE ENTIRE ARRAY
*
                    ENT1 LINE+1
                    STZ  LINE
                    MOVE LINE(15)  ZERO (BLANK) LINE ARRAY
*
*                   NOW PACK CHARACTERS BACK INTO ARRAY LINE FROM
*                   OUTPUT. I2 HAS THE LENGTH OF THE ARRAY OUTPUT.
*                   SINCE EXTRA BLANKS HAVE BEEN DELETED, MAY BE
```

```
*                  LESS THAN 80. I1 WILL INDEX THE PACKED WORDS
*                  OF LINE, I4 INDEXES OUTPUT. CHARACTERS WILL
*                  BE LOADED INTO BYTE 5 OF A, SHIFTED TO BYTE 1
*                  OF A AND THEN SHIFTED INTO THE X REGISTER.
*
                   ENT4  0
                   ENT1  0              WORDS OF LINE 0..15
PACKWORD           ENT3  4              NUMBER OF BYTES IN THIS WORD
*
PACKNEXT           LDA   OUTPUT,4(5:5)
                   INC4  1              FETCH NEXT CHARACTER NEXT TIME
                   SLA   4              SHIFT CHAR INTO BYTE 1
                   SLC   1              SHIFT INTO X
                   DEC2  1
                   J2NP  LASTONE        COUNTER OF CHARACTERS IN CHAR
                   DEC3  1              BYTE COUNT
                   J3NN  PACKNEXT
                   STX   LINE,1         WHEN 5 BYTES PACKED STORE IN
                   INC1  1              NEXT WORD INDEX
                   JMP   PACKWORD
*
LASTONE            SLC   0,3            JUSTIFY LAST PARTIAL WORD
                   STX   LINE,1
*
                   ⟨code to output LINE⟩
```

4.7 LEXICAL SCANNING

A very common form of character manipulation is *lexical analysis*. Many programs operate on character data which is constructed from free-format multicharacter words or symbols. The words or symbols are separated by blanks, special characters, or other delimiters. To operate on them, it is necessary to group together contiguous characters into words or symbols. This is lexical analysis, or lexical scanning.

For example, the entire text of this book has been stored on magnetic tape. To insure that there are no spelling errors, a program was written which produced a list of all of the different words in this book. This list was scanned for misspelled words. To produce the list, it was necessary to scan a line of characters and identify where each word began and ended. Then these individual characters were packed into a single item and stored in a table.

Assume that no single word or symbol (called a *token*) is more than 10 characters long. It could be packed into the A and X registers, using shift instructions as shown in the last section. Then, to find all the words on a card, we could write a program such as

```
*
*                 READ A CARD
*
NEXTCARD          ⟨code to read a card into the array CARD⟩
*
*                 UNPACK THE CARD INTO THE ONE CHARACTER PER WORD
*                 FORMAT IN THE ARRAY CHAR.
*
                  ⟨code to unpack CARD into CHAR⟩
*
*                 NOW SCAN THE CHARACTER ARRAY CHAR UNTIL THE FIRST
*                 ALPHABETIC CHARACTER IS FOUND. TREAT BLANKS (00)
*                 AND SPECIAL CHARACTERS (>39) AS DELIMITERS.
*
*                 INDEX REGISTER 6 POINTS TO THE END OF A TOKEN,
*                 WHILE INDEX REGISTER 5 POINTS TO THE BEGINNING.
*
                  ENT6  −1
*
*                 SKIP LEADING DELIMITERS FIRST
*
NEXTOKEN          INC6  1
                  CMP6  =80=      TEST END OF CARD
                  JGE   NEXTCARD
*
                  LDA   CHAR,6    GET NEXT CHARACTER
                  JAZ   NEXTOKEN  BLANK
                  CMPA  =40=      OR SPECIAL
                  JGE   NEXTOKEN
*
*                 FOUND NONBLANK, NONSPECIAL
*                 SET INDEX REGISTER 5
*                 THEN LOOK FOR NEXT BLANK OR SPECIAL
*
                  ENT5  0,6
*
1H                INC6  1         CHECK NEXT CHARACTER
                  LDA   CHAR,6
                  JAZ   ENDTOKEN  IF BLANK
                  CMPA  =40=
                  JL    1B        OR SPECIAL
```

```
*
*                   TOKEN IS IN CHAR,5 TO CHAR-1,6
*
ENDTOKEN           ⟨pack token into A and X register⟩
*
                   ⟨process new token⟩
*
                   JMP   NEXTOKEN   REPEAT WITH NEXT
*
```

4.8 SUMMARY

In this chapter, we have presented many different assembly language programming techniques. The techniques presented include how to compute arithmetic expressions, how to program conditionals and loops, examples of the use of arrays and tables, and some simple character manipulation techniques. Most of these concepts are easy and should quickly become a matter of habit. These are basic programming techniques; there are many others equally simple, and also a large number of more advanced techniques. The more practice you have in programming, the more skilled you will become at the art of assembly language programming. Additional programming concepts will be introduced throughout the remainder of this text.

Most assembly language programming techniques are developed by assembly language programmers by trial and error and are not written down for study. Many are passed from programmer to programmer informally, and many are picked up by reading the programs of a more experienced programmer. The program segments in the three volumes of *The Art of Computer Programming* by Knuth (1968, 1969, 1973) are good sources for MIX. Gear (1974) has a chapter on programming techniques, as does Eckhouse (1975). Stone and Siewiorek (1976) have many examples. In all cases except Knuth, however, these examples are for a computer other than the MIX computer. Thus, it is generally necessary to understand the computer instruction set and assembly language being used as the example language of that book before the programming techniques can be transferred to your MIX programs.

EXERCISES

a. What is the difference between programming and coding?

b. Write MIXAL code to compute the value of the expression, (J*LOGICAL)/PHYSICAL + BASE.

c. Write the MIXAL code to compute Z = Y+2*(W+V)/4-6*(10-W-V).

d. Section 4.2 gives a four-statement program to compute the absolute value of a number. This was done to illustrate the use of jumps. Can you give one statement which calculates the absolute value of a number?

e. Section 4.2 also gives a seven-statement program to compute the sign function. Can you give a shorter program to do the same, but without jumps?

f. Why would a programmer write

```
LABEL          EQU    *
```

rather than just attaching the label to the next instruction?

g. Write a code segment which simulates the MOVE instruction, but without using the MOVE instruction.

h. Why are some loops run backwards? Consider the two loops in Section 4.3 to compute the sum of the numbers from 1 to N. How much time does each take to execute for $N = 3$? For $N = 10$? For $N = n$?

i. How does an array differ from a table?

j. Consider the following code to index an array with a subscript in the range 400 to 800.

```
ARRAY          ORIG   *+401

               . . .
               LD1    INDEX
               DEC1   400
               LDA    ARRAY,1
```

Can you improve on this code? How is your code better?

k. What is a space-time tradeoff?

l. Write the code to add two double-precision integers in MIX. Define your data representation.

m. The stacks shown in Section 4.5 grow up, from low memory to high memory. Give the code for the PUSH and POP operations which would manipulate a stack which grows down from high memory to low memory.

n. Three different pieces of code were given to count the number of blanks on a card. How much time and how much space does each take?

o. Write a program to read a sequence of numbers and compute their maximum, minimum, and average. What problems arise in computing the average?

p. Write a program to read a set of numbers, calculate their sum, and then print the numbers and, for each number, its percentage of the sum. Do the printed percentages add up to 100? If not, why?

q. Write a program to read a text file and produce a table of all of the different words, and the number of times they occur. Consider printing the list either alphabetically or in order of decreasing frequency of words.

5

INPUT / OUTPUT
PROGRAMMING

A very important part of assembly language programming deals with the input and output of information to and from peripheral devices. The programming techniques of Chapter 4 deal mainly with the computing aspect of programming, but this aspect is useless unless data can be input for computation and the results of computation can be output for examination and use. In this chapter, we present some of the basic techniques for input/output programming.

As with the techniques of Chapter 4, the concepts discussed in this chapter are generally applicable to most computers. However, the specific instructions or instruction sequences for coding these techniques will vary with the instruction set, input/output system and devices available on a given computer. Each computer and each problem will need to be considered for its own properties.

5.1 BASIC I/O PROGRAMMING CONCEPTS

Input/output for most modern computers is *asynchronous*. This means that the timing of the operation of the central processor and each I/O device is independent. The central processor is internally *synchronous*; each action is controlled by the control unit and each action is performed at exact specific times as determined by a central clock in the CPU. Every operation in the CPU occurs at well-specified times and the duration of each operation is exactly specified in terms of the number of ticks of the clock needed for that operation.

With input/output devices, this is not true. The input/output instructions (IN, OUT, IOC) only *initiate* an operation; the actual operation takes an indeterminable time depending on the nature of the I/O device, its state, and the operation. This is caused by the physical nature of the I/O devices and the necessity of mechanical operation in order to perform I/O functions. Mechanical operations simply cannot be built to the rigid timing specifications that electronic circuits can be built to. This uncertainty requires careful consideration of the way in which I/O devices and the CPU interact. Physically, this is done by building, for each device, a *controller*. A controller is a piece of electronic circuitry which controls the attached I/O device for the CPU. A controller may well be a small computer (a microcomputer or minicomputer) programmed exclusively for this purpose, or it may be a special-purpose device designed and built specifically as a controller. The CPU sends commands to the controller to perform I/O, and the controller sees that it is actually done.

The actual input/output instructions for the MIX computer are limited to only three: IN, OUT, and IOC. For each of these, the F field of the instruction (byte 4) specifies the unit number of the device which is to be used for the I/O. The effective address calculated from bytes 0:3 (the address and index fields) is used as a parameter for the instruction. For the IN and OUT instructions, the effective address is the address of a *buffer* in memory which should be used in the transfer of information between the I/O device and memory. The IN instruction initiates the input of information into memory, storing in the memory locations beginning with the effective address and continuing for one record. The previous contents of the memory locations used by an IN instruction are destroyed by the storage of the new information. The OUT instruction sends information to an output device. The information is transferred from memory, beginning at the address specified by the effective address of the OUT instruction. Since the contents of memory are simply read and sent to the I/O device, the contents of memory remain unchanged.

For both the IN and OUT instructions, the amount of memory transferred is determined by the I/O device selected. Each IN or OUT instruction begins the transfer of one *record* of information. A record is the (physical) unit of information which is naturally handled by a device. The record for a card reader or card punch is one card; for a line printer, one line. Thus the size of a record for a card reader or card punch is 80 characters long; for a line printer, 120 characters long. Since 5 characters can fit in one word on the MIX computer, this requires 16 words of memory for a record of a card reader or card punch, and 24 words for a record of a line printer. The magnetic tape, disk, and drum devices for MIX computers all have records of 100 words. The typewriter and paper tape unit has 70-character (14-word) records.

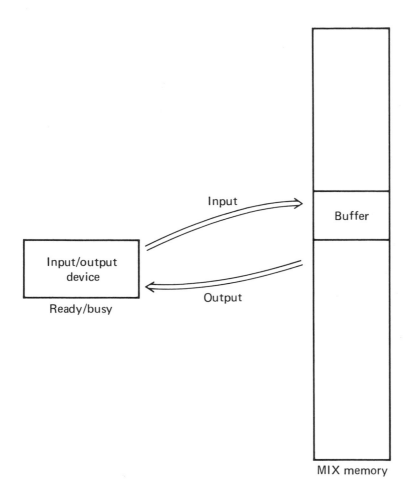

FIGURE 5.1   The relationship between an I/O device and an I/O buffer.

Note that these record lengths need not be true for all card readers, punches, line printers, tapes, disks, drums, or terminals. There exist card readers and punches which deal with cards of 51 or 96 characters instead of 80. Line printers have been built to handle lines of 80, 120, 132, or 136 characters (among others). Many teletypewriters, CRT terminals, and paper tape devices handle data one character at a time, with line lengths of 70, 72, 80, 120, 132, or 136 characters. In this text we will consider only the standard MIX input/output devices. If your installation has nonstandard peripherals, special attention may be necessary on your part in their programming, but the concepts presented here will still be applicable.

Since an IN or OUT instruction only starts an operation, at any time each device may be in either of two states: *ready* for a new command, or *busy* with a previous one. Each device alternates between these two states. Initially, the state of the device is ready; it is waiting for a command to do something. When the CPU executes an I/O instruction which selects this device, the device begins work on the task which it is assigned, becoming busy. After as long a time as needed to perform the task requested of it by the CPU, it finishes and becomes ready again, able to perform another I/O command. One bit for each device records the state of the device, as ready or busy. The setting and clearing of this bit are controlled completely by the device.

The ready/busy bit is used in several ways. First, it may be tested by the JRED and JBUS instructions which can be used to control the execution of the CPU. The JRED and JBUS instructions specify a device unit number in their F field, and will jump to the effective address if the device is ready (JRED) or busy (JBUS). The state of the device is not affected in any way.

The other use of the busy/ready bit is in controlling the IN, OUT, and IOC instructions. When an IN, OUT, or IOC instruction is decoded by the control unit, it will mean that a new I/O command is to be issued to the (controller of the) device specified by the unit number given in byte 4 of the instruction. If that device is ready, the new command can be issued and the CPU can continue to the next instruction. If the device is busy, however, the new command cannot be issued. I/O devices (and their controllers) are generally rather simple devices and so they can only do one thing at a time. Because of this, it is only possible to have one outstanding I/O request per device at a time. If the control unit decodes an I/O command (IN, OUT, IOC) for a busy device, it must wait until that device becomes ready before it can issue the new command.

Thus, if a device is ready when an I/O instruction is executed for that device, it only takes one time unit to execute. If, however, the device is busy, the execution time for that instruction can take an arbitrarily long and unpredictable length of time, however long it takes until the device finishes its last command and becomes ready (only to become busy again with the new command). This extra time is called *interlock* time.

We have discussed the IN, OUT, JRED, and JBUS instructions so far and have avoided mention of the IOC instruction. The IOC instruction is used to provide special-purpose control functions for some I/O devices; its use and meaning is entirely dependent upon the device with which it is used. It is the instruction which allows all of the special device-dependent functions we may need to do but do not really need a separate instruction for. We would like to be able to tell the tape units to rewind, but a rewind command would not make much sense for most other devices. (Rewind a line printer?) The IOC instruction has a different interpretation for each device, and allows us to skip to the top of a page on the line printer, position magnetic tapes forward or backward, move the read-write head of a moving head disk to a new track, or rewind a roll of paper tape. The specific coding of the IOC instruction for each device is covered below when we discuss the programming of each MIX I/O device.

5.2 PROGRAMMING MIX I/O DEVICES

The standard programming for MIX I/O devices varies from device to device. Because of this we give here a short description of the standard programming techniques used for each of the normal MIX I/O devices: card reader, card punch, line printer, magnetic tape, magnetic disk and drum, teletype, and paper tape reader/punch.

Input devices

These devices are the main source of input for a program. They are all character-oriented and transmit the six-bit MIX character code. The only difference in their programming is in their record lengths. For the card reader, the input record is one card, 80 characters, 16 words; for the teletype and paper tape reader, the input record is one line, 70 characters, 14 words. This affects only the size of the buffer which needs to be allocated and the values of indices used in loops to use the input data. For convenience of explanation, we discuss all of these devices in terms of the card reader. The changes for the other devices only involve changing the device numbers and record lengths.

Input is initiated by the IN instruction. If we have defined a 16-word buffer CARD (CARD ORIG *+16), then we can read a card into it by

```
IN    CARD(16)     BEGIN READING CARD
JBUS  *(16)        WAIT UNTIL READ
```

The card reader is device number 16. The IN instruction sends a command from the control unit through the I/O system to the controller of the card reader, telling it to read a card into memory beginning at location CARD. The controller of the card reader begins the action of reading a card while the computer continues with the next instruction. Notice that the IN instruction only began the input of a card. In order to use the card, we must wait until it has actually been read into memory. Since the card reader will be in a busy state until the card has been read, we need only wait until the device is not busy; then we will know that the card has been read and can be used. We program this by a very short loop (a *tight* loop) which does nothing but repetitively test the device state, waiting for it to become nonbusy (JBUS * (device)).

While the computer is executing the JBUS instruction, the card reader is reading characters off the card one at a time as they pass in front of the reading station in the card reader. These are sent, one at a time, to the card reader controller. When the controller has five characters, it packs them into one MIX word, sets the sign bit to "+" and stores this word in the next buffer location in MIX memory. The controller has an internal register which is used to remember the address of the next memory location into which the next word will be stored. After each new word is stored in memory, this register is incremented by one. Thus successive five character groups are packed together and stored in successive locations in memory as they are read. Each character may take from 100 to 600 MIX time units to be read. When the entire card is safely placed in memory, the controller sets its ready/busy bit back to ready and waits for a new command from the computer.

All this time the CPU is executing the JBUS *(16) instruction over and over again. When the controller finally sets its state to ready, the jump test fails and we drop out of the wait loop and can proceed to use the newly read card. When we want another card, we can repeat this code.

A programmer must always be very careful that the input device is done with an input operation before attempting to use the data being read in. For example if we were to write

```
IN    CARD(16)     READ A CARD
ENT1  0            INDEX INTO CARD 0..15
LDA   CARD,1       LOAD FIRST FIVE CHARACTERS
```

The contents of the A register would *not* be the contents of the first five columns of the card read by the IN. It will take 500 to 3000 time units before that new data is read and put in memory. In the meantime the previous contents of the buffer locations remain there, and so the LDA, coming only two time units after the card started to be read, will load these old values into the A register. However, this should not be depended upon either. Card readers, like all I/O devices, are asynchronous and have no concept of CPU time. Also, the design of the card reader may be such that its timing is almost unpredictable. Card reader controllers have been built which have little 80-character memories built into them. When the card reader is turned on, they automatically read the first card into this internal memory. When an IN instruction is issued, they immediately transfer this previously read card into memory and start to read the next into their private 80-character memory, trying to always keep one card ahead of the input requests. If a new IN instruction occurs before the next card is read, however (which is likely), the controller reverts to the old way of reading and storing into MIX memory as before. The important point is simply to *never* make any assumptions about the I/O speeds of I/O devices. Being off by only one time unit can ruin the entire program.

Output devices

The card reader, teletype keyboard, and paper tape reader are the standard input devices, while the line printer, card punch, teletype printer, and paper tape punch are the standard output devices. As with the input devices, the programming of these output devices varies only with respect to their record lengths and speeds. The record lengths (120 characters for the line printer, 80 characters for the card punch, 70 characters for the teletype printer and paper tape punch) only determine the amount of space needed for the buffers for these devices; thus, we will limit our discussion to the line printer. The concepts apply equally to the other devices.

Outputting to the line printer is essentially the same as reading from the card reader, with the exception that since we are outputting, the programming to create the output line must be programmed and executed before the line is output. Once this is done, and the appropriate character codes are stored in memory—for example, in a buffer called LINE—we simply write

```
OUT    LINE(18)      PRINT A LINE
JBUS   *(18)         LINE PRINTER IS DEVICE 18
```

The OUT will start the output and the JBUS will assure that it is complete before continuing. The controller for the output device loads five characters (one word) at a time from memory and prints or punches them. The sign bit of each word is ignored. When the entire record has been output, the state of the device is reset from busy to ready.

An IOC 0(18) will cause the line printer to skip to the top of a page. IOC 0(19) will rewind the paper tape. IOC has no effect on a card reader or card punch.

The main effort in I/O programming for these devices is not the actual I/O but rather in the conversion between numeric and character code representation of data, and *formatting* input and output. The format of our input and output is simply a statement of what it looks like.

For input, the format of the data is the form in which the data is expected to be by the program which is inputting the data. Examples: two decimal integer numbers, one in columns 4 and 5, the other in columns 9 and 10, with all other columns blank; or a 10-character name in columns 1 to 10, with a description of any kind (i.e., any sequence of characters) in columns 15 to 72, columns 11 to 14 should be blank. It is the problem of the programmer to interpret this input correctly. This generally becomes a problem of character manipulation. The only help that MIX offers is the NUM instruction. If a character code representation of a number (up to 10 characters long) is put into the A and X registers, the NUM instruction will convert this to numeric binary and put the result in the A register. The signs of both registers and the contents of the X register are unchanged. An example of the use of this instruction: Suppose we have a number punched in columns 11–20 of a card. To read it and use it, we write

```
IN     CARD(16)      READ CARD
JBUS   *(16)
LDA    CARD+2        COLUMNS 11–15
LDX    CARD+3        COLUMNS 16–20
NUM                  CONVERT CHARACTER TO NUMERIC
STA    NUMBER
```

This code will read a card, wait until it is read, then convert the character code representation of the number in columns 11 through 20 into a numeric representation and store in the memory location labelled NUMBER.

What happens if columns 11–20 have nonnumeric punches? The NUM instruction works anyway, by treating each character, numeric or not, as having a value equal to the units digit of its character code expressed in decimal. Thus the characters "A", "J", "1", comma, and ">" all have a value of 1 for the NUM instruction, while "B", "K", "S", "2", "(", and "@" have the value 2.

For output, the conversion is performed in the opposite direction, numeric to character code, by the CHAR instruction. If we have a number in the location NUMBER, we can convert it to character code and print it by

```
LDA    NUMBER
CHAR                      CONVERT NUMBER TO CHARACTERS
STA    LINE+2
STX    LINE+3             STORE IN OUTPUT COLUMNS 11-20
OUT    LINE(18)           START PRINT
JBUS   *(18)              WAIT UNTIL PRINT DONE
```

The CHAR instruction converts a numeric integer in the A register into a 10-byte decimal character code representation. This character representation can be stored into an output line image and printed. Note that the programmer has complete control over where in the output line the characters to be printed are put. The format of the output line is determined by the programmer. The preparation of the output line may involve some character manipulation.

Magnetic tape

The I/O devices which we have considered so far have been for the input and output of character representation of data. Magnetic tape, on the other hand, is basically a storage I/O device. Information can be written to tape and then read back into the computer, but it is very difficult for a human to either read or write magnetic tape. Because of this, programming of magnetic tape devices differs from the devices which we have already considered.

The writing of information to a tape is done by the OUT instruction as

```
⟨construct a buffer of information in TAPEBUF⟩
OUT    TAPEBUF(unit)
JBUS   *(unit)        WAIT UNTIL IT IS OUTPUT
```

where *unit* is the device number of the tape drive being used. This information can later be read back in with

```
IN     TAPEBUF(unit)
JBUS   *(unit)
```

The record for a magnetic tape is always 100 words long and the entire word, including sign, is transmitted.

The magnetic tape at any given time has a number of records on it. Each time a new record is read or written, the tape moves so that the read-write heads are positioned after the most recently read-written record and before the next one.

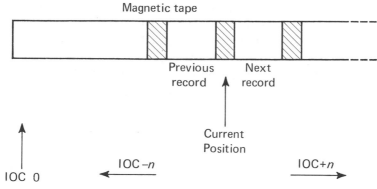

FIGURE 5.2   Magnetic tape usage on the MIX system.

Typical use of a tape is to write out successively a number of records. Then the tape is rewound and the records are read back in.

The IOC instruction is used to position the tape, relative to its current position. The effective address, M, is used to specify the direction the tape should be moved. If M is less than zero, the tape is moved backwards; if M is greater than zero, the tape is moved forward. The magnitude of M specifies the number of physical 100 word records to move. Thus, IOC −1(2) moves tape unit number 2 back one physical record, while IOC +3(1) moves tape unit 1 forward 3 records. IOC 0(n) would mean to not move the tape (forward or backward) and hence is meaningless, so this code (effective address = 0) is used to mean to rewind the tape. To position a tape just before the first record on the tape, we would simply IOC 0(n); if we wanted to position before the second record, we would IOC 0(n) and then IOC +1(n).

Since the effective address is used to determine the positioning it can be indexed. This allows code like the following to be used. Assume that index register 4 contains the number of the record before which we are currently positioned on tape unit 5 (after a rewind, register I4 would contain 1, and after each read I4 would be incremented by one). Index register 1 contains the record number of the record we want to read in next. Then we can execute the following code to position tape 5 correctly

```
        ENT2   0,1           INDEX 2 = INDEX 1
        DEC2   0,4           INDEX 2 = INDEX 1 - INDEX 4
        J2Z    *+2           IF ALREADY POSITIONED RIGHT
        IOC    0,2(5)        MOVE TAPE TO RIGHT SPOT
        IN     TAPEBUF(5)    READ IN DESIRED RECORD
        ENT4   1,1           NEW TAPE POSITION
```

The first two lines of code set index register 2 to the difference between the current position and the desired position. The J2Z instruction is included to prevent a rewind (effective address zero) when no repositioning is desired (index register 4 = index register 1).

Remember that, because of the nature of magnetic tape, a write (OUT) instruction destroys all information from the point of the write to the physical end of the tape. Hence, at any given time it is possible to read only as far as the last record written; the remainder of the tape is garbage. This constraint applies to positioning also. The tape cannot be positioned beyond the end of the most recently written record on the tape.

Magnetic disks and drums

Magnetic tape is by its nature a sequentially accessed device; records are accessed from the beginning to the end, one at a time. This is due to the physical nature of the device. Disk and drum storage devices have been constructed to allow any given record to be directly accessible, however, so these are called *direct access*, or sometimes *random access* devices, as opposed to the *sequentially accessed* magnetic tape devices.

The differences between disks and drums are mainly physical. A drum is constructed as a recording surface on the side of a cylinder, while a disk unit has perhaps several flat disc-shaped objects with recording being done on both the top and bottom surfaces of each disk. Each device has a number of tracks which are broken up into 100-word sectors. There are 4096 sectors per device. Each sector corresponds to a record for that device: 100 words (including sign).

The real difference between these two types of devices concerns how the read-write heads are used. Just as with magnetic tape, it is necessary to move the recording surface past a read-write head to convert between the magnetic form of information on the disk/drum and the electronic form of information used in the CPU. This is accomplished in two ways. In the one case, usually used for

FIGURE 5.3   Disk structure for the MIX system. Each disk has 64 tracks, with 64 sectors per track.

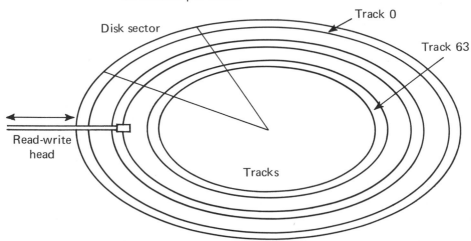

drums, each track has its own head. This is known as a *fixed-head* device. When a particular record is to be read or written, the head for that track is selected and the device controller waits until the sector for that record rotates beneath the heads, then the data is transferred (to the device for a write; to memory for a read). The time waiting for the device to rotate is called *latency time*; the time for the actual read or write is called *transfer time*.

This architecture can be very expensive. With one head per track, a drum with 200 tracks requires 200 read-write heads, and heads are not cheap. The most common solution to this is the *moving-head* device (generally a disk). In these devices, there is only one head per surface (for a single disk platter, this requires two heads: one for the top surface and the other for the bottom). The heads are attached to a movable arm. An I/O operation requires several steps. First the heads are moved to be over the desired track. This is called a *seek* operation, and the time to perform it is *seek time*. Once the head is positioned over the correct track, the controller waits until the correct sector rotates under the head (latency time) and then begins the requested I/O operation (transfer time).

For either fixed-head or moving-head devices, every I/O operation must supply the addresses of the locations involved in the transfer: the address of the memory buffer of 100 words in MIX memory, and the address of the sector to be used. The address in memory is the effective address given in the IN or OUT instruction; the address on the disk/drum is specified by bytes 4 and 5 of the X register. When the IN or OUT instruction is executed by the control unit for a disk or drum, the contents of the lower two bytes of the X register are copied into the disk/drum controller which then performs a seek operation (if the device is moving-head), waits for latency, and finally performs the transfer. This can be programmed by

```
        LDX   DISKADD      ADDRESS FOR SECTOR TO USE
        OUT   BUFFER(unit)
        JBUS  *(unit)      WAIT UNTIL OUTPUT COMPLETE
```

where *unit* is the device number of the disk or drum unit. If we have a loop which is outputting repeated records to the disk, this can look like

```
        STZ   DISKADD      INITIALIZE TO SECTOR 0
        ...
LOOP    ...
        LDX   DISKADD
        OUT   BUFFER(unit)  OUTPUT BUFFER TO DISK
        JBUS  *(unit)
        INCX  1
        STX   DISKADD      INCREASE X TO NEXT SECTOR
        ...
        JMP   LOOP
```

In this code, we output to each successive physical record on the disk. To read this information back into memory, we simply set DISKADD back to zero and read back in from the same disk addresses that we wrote out to, incrementing DISKADD after each read, of course.

Disk records need not be accessed strictly sequentially either. In an information storage system for names, we might store all names starting with "A" in records 0 to 9, all names starting with "B" in records 10 to 19, and so on. Then, to update a record for a given name, we can write

```
          LDA   NAME(1:1)   FIRST CHARACTER
          DECA  1           A=0,B=1,C=2,...
          MUL   =10=        A=0,B=10,C=20, ...
2H        IN    BUFFER(DISK) MUL LEAVES ANSWER IN X
          JBUS  *(DISK)
*

          ⟨search for NAME in this record⟩
*
NOTFOUND  INCX  1           TRY NEXT RECORD
          JMP   2B
*
FOUND     ⟨update information in BUFFER⟩
*
          OUT   BUFFER(DISK)
          JBUS  *(DISK)      PUT UPDATED INFO BACK ON DISK
```

We assume in this code that the search for the name and the updating do not change the X register, so that we simply leave in it the address of the sector we are using. If this was not the case, then we would simply need to STX TEMPX before changing X and then LDX TEMPX before our IN and OUT to the disk. Also, we are using a symbolic constant DISK for the specific unit we want, so earlier in the program we would have a DISK EQU 9, or DISK EQU 13, or whatever unit we wish to use.

An IOC for a disk or drum initiates a seek instruction. The seek time for a moving-head disk or drum can be quite long, on the order of 10 to 100 milliseconds, and much longer than either latency or transfer time. Because of this, it is sometimes possible, and advantageous, to seek ahead by moving the head to the track which contains the sector to be used next, so that the head will already be there before the actual IN or OUT is issued. The effective address of the IOC should be zero. The track to seek to is given by bytes 4:5 of the X register. An IOC for a fixed-head disk or drum is ignored, since no seek is needed. For example, to access records sequentially

```
          STZ   DISKADD     ZERO INITIAL VALUE
          ...
          LDX   DISKADD     SECTOR ADDRESS
```

```
IN    BUFF(DISK)
INCX  1
STX   DISKADD     ADDRESS OF NEXT SECTOR
IOC   0(DISK)     START SEEK TO NEXT RECORD
```

Notice that it is still necessary to load the disk address into the X register for any IN or OUT instructions (since we may have changed our minds about where we want to IN or OUT from). However, we no longer need a JBUS * (DISK) since the IOC automatically waits until the previous operation (the IN in this case) is complete before the IOC can be issued to the controller, and the control unit can continue to the next instruction.

5.3 A SIMPLE I/O PROGRAM

Consider a simple, but useful problem: we have a deck of cards and we wish to copy them from the card reader onto the line printer in order to get a listing of them. In order to do this, we must first read a card, then print it on the line printer, read the next card, print it, and so forth until the last card is read.

How do we tell when the last card is read? The MIX card reader has no way

FIGURE 5.4   Input/output structure—basic structure of a simple program to input data, process it, and output the results.

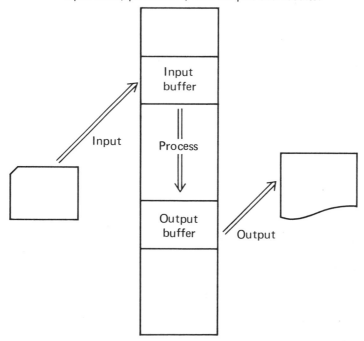

of telling the CPU that there are no more cards, so we must find some way to mark the end of our input. This will be done by an *end-of-file card*, a special card which marks the end of our deck. Since it is easy to compare an entire word at once, we will use a card with *EOF* in columns 1–5 to mark the end of a card deck. We could use any set of letters in any columns, but we want to avoid any end-of-file marker which might be expected to occur in the input. If the input to be listed were to accidentally contain the end-of-file marker as part of the normal deck, the listing would stop prematurely, which can be most frustrating. Thus we do not want to interpret a card which is blank in column 1 as the end-of-file, since this is very likely to happen in most decks.

Now that we have made this decision, we can begin to write our program. The general flow is:

1. Read a card.
2. Print the card.
3. If not the last card, go back to 1.

Notice that this program will print the *EOF* card so that we can easily see that the entire deck has been printed. Expanding this description of the program into code, we will need two buffers, one to read into and one to write from. Thus our declarations are

```
CARD          ORIG  *+16        INPUT BUFFER
LINE          ORIG  *+24        OUTPUT BUFFER
EOF           ALF   *EOF*       EOF MARKER
```

and our code is

```
COPY          IN    CARD(16)    READ CARD
              JBUS  *(16)       WAIT UNTIL READ
              ENT1  LINE
              MOVE  CARD(16)    MOVE INPUT TO OUTPUT
              OUT   LINE(18)    OUTPUT LINE
              JBUS  *(18)
              LDA   CARD        CHECK FOR EOF
              CMPA  EOF
              JNE   COPY        IF NOT EOF, REPEAT
              HLT
              END   COPY
```

This program shows the basics of reading from the card reader and writing on the line printer. To input from a device, first define an array as large as the record for that device as

```
X             ORIG  *+record length
```

Then, to read into that array

```
              IN    X(device number)
```

This initiates the input. To wait until the input is complete

```
JBUS  *(device number)
```

To output, the same procedure is followed, but OUT is used instead of IN.

A number of improvements of the above copy program are possible. First, notice that there is no need to move the input card from CARD to LINE; we can output directly from our input buffer (or input directly into our output buffer). Second, the *EOF* constant is used to compare against the first word of the input record, which requires loading one of them into the A register (or the X register). In the above, we chose to load the first word of the input. If we load *EOF* instead, it need never be reloaded, since the A register is not used for anything else. Third, notice that the above card-reader-to-line-printer copy program will work equally well for a card-reader-to-card-punch copy program if we simply change the unit numbers. In fact, the unit numbers are only an artifact of the standard unit numbers assigned by the factory; they may be changed for another MIX computer system. For these reasons, it is better to use symbolic constants for unit numbers rather than numeric unit numbers.

With these modifications, we can rewrite COPY as

```
CR        EQU   16            INPUT DEVICE NUMBER
LP        EQU   18            OUTPUT DEVICE NUMBER
BUFFER    ORIG  *+24          BUFFER FOR LARGEST RECORD SIZE
EOF       ALF   *EOF*
COPY      LDA   EOF           SET A REGISTER FOR COMPARE
LOOP      IN    BUFFER(CR)    START READ
          JBUS  *(CR)         WAIT UNTIL DONE
          OUT   BUFFER(LP)    NOW OUTPUT
          JBUS  *(LP)         WAIT UNTIL OUTPUT COMPLETE
          CMPA  BUFFER        CHECK FOR END
          JNE   LOOP
          HLT
          END   COPY
```

A slightly more complicated program will also give us line numbers for each line, to give us a count of the number of cards read. Noticing that (for a card-to-printer copy) each input record is 80 characters, while each output is 120, we have 40 columns of spacing and line numbers to use. Assuming that no more that 99,999 cards will be listed, we only need a five-character line number. Thus, we can format our output line as

```
Columns 1–5      blank
        6–10     line number
        11–15    blank
        16–95    input card image
```

This format has been chosen to be both convenient to program and pleasing to look at.

For this program, we must introduce a counter and instructions to convert the counter from binary to character code for output. We can still read our card directly into the locations used for the output buffer, and most of the above program remains the same.

```
CR          EQU   16          INPUT DEVICE NUMBER
LP          EQU   18          OUTPUT
BUFFER      ORIG  *+24        INPUT/OUTPUT BUFFER
COUNT       CON   0           COUNTER FOR LINES
*
BLANK       ORIG  *+24        BLANK LINE FOR SPACING
EOFLINE     ALF               LAST LINE FOR PRINTING
EOF         ALF   *EOF*       EOF MARKER
            ALF
            ALF   NUMBE
            ALF   R OF
            ALF   CARDS
            ALF   READ
            ALF   =
NCARDS      ALF
            ORIG  *+15        REST OF LAST LINE
*
COPY        STZ   COUNT       INITIALIZE COUNT
LOOP        IN    BUFFER+3(CR) READ A CARD
            JBUS  *(CR)
            LDA   BUFFER+3    CHECK FOR LAST CARD
            CMPA  EOF
            JE    EOFOUND     YES, LAST CARD
*
            LDA   COUNT       INCREASE CARD COUNT BY ONE
            INCA  1
            STA   COUNT
            CHAR              CONVERT COUNT TO CHARACTERS
            STX   BUFFER+1    CHARACTERS FOR COUNT
            OUT   BUFFER(LP)  WRITE BUFFER PLUS COUNT
            JBUS  *(LP)
            JMP   LOOP
*
EOFOUND     OUT   BLANK(LP)   PRINT ONE BLANK LINE
            LDA   COUNT       NUMBER OF CARDS READ
            CHAR              (EXCLUDING *EOF*)
            STX   NCARDS      STORE IN LAST OUTPUT LINE
            OUT   EOFLINE(LP)
            JBUS  *(LP)
            HLT
            END   COPY
```

In this program, we have done several things differently. In addition to numbering the cards, we have added special code to print the number of cards read (excluding the *EOF* card) after the listing, separated from it by one blank line. Notice that we are outputting from three different output buffers and that a JBUS is not needed after the OUT BLANK since the OUT EOFLINE(LP) will automatically wait for it to finish. Some local optimization can be done. The last CHAR sequence (in EOFOUND+1 and EOFOUND+2) is unnecessary, since the character code for COUNT is still in the X register from the previous output. The CHAR destroys both the A and X registers, which prevents keeping the EOF marker in a register for comparison, and since the index registers can only count to 4095, they cannot be used to store the counter (which can be as large as 99,999).

5.4 OVERLAPPED I/O

Local optimizations can only decrease the time to execute by microseconds or milliseconds, however. An entirely different form of optimization is needed to produce an effective speed-up in a program such as the above COPY routines. Consider our second, and shortest, COPY program. The loop which copied cards consists of IN, JBUS, OUT, CMPA, JNE. Thus the execution time for this program is the number of cards times (five time units for the IN, OUT, CMPA, and JNE plus however many times the JBUSs are executed). The time to execute the JBUSs is essentially the time to read a card and print a line.

If we assume that we have a fast card reader, we can read 1000 cards per minute, or one card every 60 milliseconds. If a MIX time unit is 1 microsecond, then it takes 60,000 time units to read a card. A slower card reader (like 300 cards per minute) will take longer (like 200,000 MIX time units). Line printer times are comparable. This is to emphasize that mechanical input/output operations are *extremely* slow, compared to electronic computing speeds. Programs such as the above COPY programs will spend only a very, very small fraction of their time doing any computation; the rest of the time is spent waiting on the I/O devices. These programs are known as *I/O-bound* programs. Many data processing and business application programs are I/O-bound. Many scientific programs, on the other hand, may input and output only a small amount of data, but may spend large amounts of time computing. These programs are *compute-bound* or *CPU-bound*. There are also programs which are neither I/O-bound nor CPU-bound, but so few that there is not even a special name for this kind of program.

Most programs do at least some I/O, and since I/O is so incredibly slow, it is necessary to try to take advantage of time spent waiting for I/O to perform other, more useful tasks. This results in I/O *overlap*. There are two kinds of overlap: I/O-I/O overlap, and CPU-I/O overlap. I/O-I/O overlap is the result of programming to try to keep several I/O devices busy at the same time, by overlapping the time to input or output on one device with the time to input or output on another device. CPU-I/O overlap tries to overlap the time to compute something with the time to perform input or output. An efficient program will often use both.

As an example of I/O-I/O overlap, consider the second COPY program

```
CR              EQU   16
LP              EQU   18
BUFFER          ORIG  *+24        INPUT/OUTPUT BUFFER
EOF             ALF   *EOF*       END OF DECK FLAG
COPY            LDA   EOF
LOOP            IN    BUFFER(CR)  READ A CARD
                JBUS  *(CR)
                OUT   BUFFER(LP)  PRINT A CARD
                JBUS  *(LP)
                CMPA  BUFFER      CHECK FOR EOF
                JNE   LOOP
                HLT
                END   COPY
```

In this program, only one I/O device is operating at any given time. A card is first read, then printed, then the next card is read. While a card is being read, the printer is idle; while a line is being printed, the card reader is idle. If we assume that the time to read a card is r time units and the time to print a line is p time units then this program takes

$$3 + n(5 + r + p)$$

time units to copy n cards from the card reader to the printer. Remember we are talking of r and p on the order of 50,000 to 200,000 time units. If we assume r is approximately equal to p, then this is roughly $2nr$ time units.

Now suppose we notice that while this program is executing both the card

FIGURE 5.5 A time chart of the execution of a simple program with no overlap of I/O with other I/O or processing.

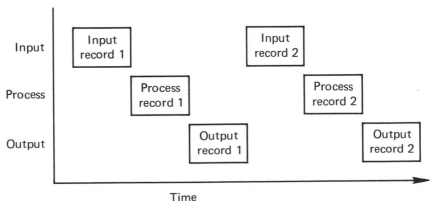

reader and the line printer are idle half the time. To read *n* cards takes only *nr* time units, so if the total program takes $2nr$ time units, the reader must be idle (i.e., ready, not busy) the other *nr* time units. Similarly for the line printer. Since these I/O devices are the slowest units in the system, they are the bottlenecks. Hence, we want to keep them busy as much as possible. Our approach is to keep both units busy all the time. This is done by a program which executes like

1.   Read first card.

2.   Next, read the second card, and print the first card at the same time.

3.   Read the third card and print the second card at the same time.

     . . .

n.   Read the *n*th card and print the $(n - 1)$st card at the same time.

n + 1.   Print the *n*th card.

The implementation of this idea can take many forms. First, we note that since we are reading and writing simultaneously, we must have two separate buffers, one for reading and the other for writing. This results in the necessity of moving our input card from the input buffer to the output buffer as

```
LP              EQU   18          OUTPUT UNIT
CR              EQU   16          INPUT UNIT
CARD            ORIG  *+24        INPUT CARD BUFFER
LINE            ORIG  *+24        OUTPUT LINE IMAGE
EOF             ALF   *EOF*       EOF MARKER
*
COPY            IN    CARD(CR)    READ FIRST CARD
                LDA   EOF         SET UP FOR EOF COMPARISON
*
*               THE FOLLOWING LOOP PRINTS THE ITH CARD AND
*               READS THE (I+1)ST CARD, SIMULTANEOUSLY.
*
LOOP            JBUS  *(CR)       WAIT UNTIL READ COMPLETE
                CMPA  CARD        CHECK FOR LAST CARD
                JE    QUIT
                ENT1  LINE        FOR MOVE
                JBUS  *(LP)       WAIT UNTIL PREVIOUS WRITE DONE
                MOVE  CARD(16)    MOVE CARD I TO OUTPUT
                IN    CARD(CR)    READ NEXT CARD
                OUT   LINE(LP)    AND OUTPUT PREVIOUS
                JMP   LOOP
*
*               LAST CARD READ. PRINT FROM INPUT BUFFER.
```

```
*
QUIT              OUT   CARD(LP)    PRINT LAST CARD
                  JBUS  *(LP)       WAIT
                  HLT   END         COPY
```

In this program, we move the input out of the input buffer as soon as possible (as soon as it is read and the previous one is printed), and begin the input of the next card immediately. Similarly, as soon as the previous output is complete, we move the next line into the output buffer and start to print it. This keeps both units busy almost all the time.

What does this do to our execution time? Well, the first card is read by itself and the last card is printed by itself. However, the reading of the last $n - 1$ cards and the printing of the first $n - 1$ lines overlap almost completely (the input actually starts one instruction ahead of the output). Thus, rather than taking $2nr$ time units, the program now takes only $r + (n - 1) \times (max(r,p) + m) + p$, where m is the amount of time it takes to move the record from the input buffer to the output buffer (33 units in this case). If p is approximately equal to r and m is very small, compared to r, then this is approximately $(n + 1)r$ and for n greater than just a few cards, we have effectively cut the execution time for the copy approximately in half. Not completely half, but almost.

There are other techniques for the same basic idea. Notice that the time it takes to move the data from one buffer to another cannot be overlapped. As with some of the previous programs, it is faster if we just read directly into the locations where we wish the data to be rather than reading into a buffer and then moving it. Rather than moving the data to (or from) the buffer, we simply use a different buffer. For this simple COPY, we need two buffers, one for input and one

FIGURE 5.6   A time chart of the execution of a program with overlap of I/O with other I/O and processing. Note that each record must still be input, processed, and output, in that order; but at any given time we can work with three different records, simultaneously.

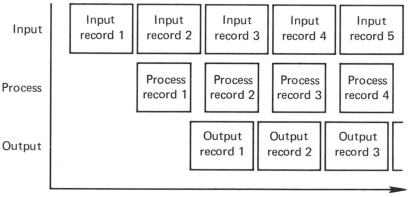

for output, but now when input is complete for one buffer, we immediately start to output from that buffer and then input into another buffer. When this second input is complete, we can output it and begin to input back into our first buffer again, and so on. This can be coded as

```
CR              EQU   16
LP              EQU   18
BUF1            ORIG  *+24
BUF2            ORIG  *+24
EOF             ALF   *EOF*        END OF FILE FLAG
*
*                     THIS PROGRAM COPIES CARDS TO THE PRINTER BY
*                     USING TWO BUFFERS AND SWITCHING INPUT AND
*                     OUTPUT BETWEEN THEM.
*
COPY            LDA   EOF          FOR COMPARISON
*
LOOP            IN    BUF1(CR)     READ CARD INTO BUF1
                JBUS  *(CR)
                CMPA  BUF1         CHECK END OF FILE
                JE    QUIT1
                OUT   BUF1(LP)     OUTPUT FROM BUF1
*                                  NOW SWITCH BUFFERS
                IN    BUF2(CR)     INPUT INTO BUF2
                JBUS  *(CR)
                CMPA  BUF2         CHECK END IN BUF2
                JE    QUIT2
                OUT   BUF2(LP)     OUTPUT FROM BUF2
*                                  NOW SWITCH BUFFERS
                JMP   LOOP         AND INPUT INTO BUF1
*
QUIT1           OUT   BUF1(LP)     FINISH LAST
                JBUS  *(LP)
                HLT
*
QUIT2           OUT   BUF2(LP)     LAST ONE IN BUF2
                JBUS  *(LP)
                HLT
*
                END   COPY
```

Notice that in this program we have taken advantage of the way that an OUT automatically waits for a previous OUT to be complete so that we may begin the next output and, as a side benefit, reuse the old output buffer as the new input buffer.

An advantage of this approach is that the MOVE is no longer necessary, and so the total time to copy a deck is less than for the previous versions with the MOVE. A disadvantage is the necessity of writing almost two complete sets of code, one for when we are inputting into BUF1 and outputting from BUF2, and almost the same code for when we are inputting into BUF2 and outputting from BUF1.

This latter disadvantage can be overcome by taking advantage of the effective address calculation of the MIX computer. The only real difference between the two sets of code written above is in the addresses, which differ. We define two variables INBUFADD and OUTBUFADD which will contain, in bytes 1:2, the address of the buffer which is being used for input (for INBUFADD) and for output (for OUTBUFADD). When we want to input, we use indirection to indicate where the next card should be read

```
          IN    INBUFADD,7(CR)
```

Similarly, for output

```
          OUT   OUTBUFADD,7(LP)
```

To switch buffers, we simply

```
          LDA   INBUFADD
          LDX   OUTBUFADD
          STA   OUTBUFADD
          STX   INBUFADD
```

Our entire copy routine is now

```
CR          EQU   16
LP          EQU   18              UNIT NUMBERS
BUF1        ORIG  *+24
BUF2        ORIG  *+24            BUFFERS
INBUFADD    CON   BUF1(0:2)
OUTBUFADD   CON   BUF2(0:2)       POINTERS TO BUFFERS
EOF         ALF   *EOF*           END-OF-FILE FLAG
*
COPY        IN    INBUFADD,7(CR)  READ CARD
            JBUS  *(CR)
*
            LDA   INBUFADD
            LDX   OUTBUFADD       SWITCH
            STA   OUTBUFADD       BUFFERS
            STX   INBUFADD
*
            OUT   OUTBUFADD,7(LP)
            LDA   OUTBUFADD,7     CHECK EOF
```

```
            CMPA  EOF
            JNE   COPY          IF NOT CONTINUE
*
            JBUS  *(LP)         WAIT FOR LAST CARD TO PRINT
            HLT
            END   COPY
```

An alternative implementation of the same method is to use indexing instead of indirection. In this version, we use index register 5 to point to the input buffer and index register 6 to point to the output buffer.

```
            . . .
COPY        ENT5  BUF1          INITIALIZE REGISTERS
            ENT6  BUF2
            LDA   EOF
*
LOOP        IN    0,5(CR)       READ CARD INTO INPUT BUFFER
            JBUS  *(CR)
*
            ENT4  0,5           SWITCH
            ENT5  0,6              BUFFER
            ENT6  0,4                 POINTERS
            OUT   0,6(LP)       OUTPUT FROM NEW OUTPUT BUFFER
*
            CMPA  0,6           CHECK FOR END-OF-FILE
            JNE   LOOP
*
            JBUS  *(LP)         WAIT FOR LAST PRINT
            HLT
            END   COPY
```

This code is a little shorter, since an index register swap is somewhat easier than a memory-to-memory swap and somewhat faster, since indexing is faster than indirection, but it ties up more registers, leaving them unavailable for other uses.

The COPY program we have been studying is a very special case demonstrating I/O-I/O overlap. More generally, some computation will need to be done on the input before it can be used as output. Thus, in addition to trying to do input and output simultaneously, we will also try to do computing at the same time. If we consider the time involved, let I be the time to do the input, C the time to do the computing, and O the time to do output. If we input a card, compute on it, and then output the card before going back to read another card (no overlap), then the total execution time will be on the order of $I + C + O$ for each card. If, on the other hand, we read a card and, while computing on that card, we also read the next card, and while printing the first card, are computing on the second and reading the third, then the total time will be more like $max(I,C,O)$ per card.

This will require at least three buffers, one for input, one for computing, and one for output. The data can be moved between buffers, or the buffers can be swapped, using index registers or indirection to point to the appropriate buffer for each activity. An example is the following program, which counts the number of blank spaces on a card, stopping when an *EOF* card is read.

```
*                   THIS PROGRAM INPUTS A DECK OF CARDS FROM THE
*                   CARD READER AND PRINTS EACH CARD WITH THE
*                   NUMBER OF BLANK SPACES WHICH OCCUR ON THAT
*                   CARD. I/O BUFFERING IS USED TO OVERLAP THE
*                   READING OF THE CARDS, THE COUNTING OF BLANKS,
*                   AND THE PRINTING OF THE OUTPUT LINES. LEADING
*                   ZEROS IN THE NUMBER OF BLANKS ARE SUPPRESSED
*                   BY CONVERTING THEM INTO BLANKS (LEADING-ZERO-
*                   SUPPRESSION).
*
CR          EQU  16            CARD READER UNIT
LP          EQU  18            LINE PRINTER UNIT
*
BUF1        ORIG *+24
BUF2        ORIG *+24
BUF3        ORIG *+24          SET OF I/O BUFFERS
*
BLANK       CON  00(1:1)       FOR LEADING ZERO SUPPRESSION
ZERO        CON  30(1:1)       FOR COMPARISON
EOF         ALF  *EOF*         EOF MARKER
*
*                   START FIRST INPUT. THEN SET UP REGISTERS
*                   I4, I5, AND I6 TO POINT TO BUFFERS FOR
*                   INPUT, COMPUTE, AND OUTPUT, RESPECTIVELY.
*
START       IN   BUF1+8(CR)    INPUT INTO BUFFER
            ENT4 BUF1
            ENT5 BUF2
            ENT6 BUF3          POINTERS TO BUFFERS
*
NEXTCARD    ENT3 0,6           SWITCH
            ENT6 0,5             BUFFER
            ENT5 0,4               POINTERS
            ENT4 0,3
            IN   8,4(CR)       INPUT NEXT CARD
*
*                   COUNT THE NUMBER OF CHARACTERS THAT ARE BLANK
*                   LINES ARE EXAMINED BACKWARDS TO SPEED END OF
```

```
*                 LOOP CHECKS. X COUNTS THE NUMBER OF BLANKS.
*                 A HAS THE NEXT WORD, INDEX 1 INDEXES THE WORDS
*                 AND RUNS FROM 16..0, INDEX 2 COUNTS THE BYTES
*                 IN EACH WORD (IN A) AND RUNS 5..0, INDEX 5
*                 POINTS TO THE BUFFER TO WORK ON (COMPUTE).
*
                  ENTX  0             BLANK COUNTER
                  ENT1  16            WORD INDEX
NEXTWORD          LDA   7,1:5         LOAD WORD FROM BUFFER+8-1+I1
                  ENT2  5             BYTE COUNTER
*
NEXTBYTE          CMPA  BLANK(1:1)    CHECK IF NEXT BLANK
                  JNE   *+2
                  INCX  1             FOUND A BLANK, INCREASE COUNT
                  SLA   1             SHIFT TO NEXT CHARACTER
                  DEC2  1
                  J2P   NEXTBYTE      STILL MORE BYTES?
*
                  DEC1  1             FINISHED WORD
                  J1P   NEXTWORD      STILL MORE WORDS?
*
*                 NUMBER OF BLANKS IN X, CONVERT TO CHARACTERS.
*
                  SLAX  5             MOVE X TO A FOR CHAR
                  CHAR
*
                  SUPPRESS LEADING ZEROS. I1 HAS BYTE COUNT
*
                  ENT1  9             ONLY CHECK LEADING 9 DIGITS
1H                CMPA  ZERO(1:1)     CHECK FOR LEADING ZERO
                  JNE   NONZERO
                  SLAX  1             SHIFT OFF LEADING ZERO
                  DEC1  1
                  J1P   1B            IF STILL MORE DIGITS
*
NONZERO           SLC   1,1           I1 HAS NUMBER NONZERO DIGITS
                  STA   1,5           STORE HIGH ORDER BYTES
                  STX   2,5           AND LOW ORDER BYTES
*
                  OUT   0,5(LP)       PRINT (AND WAIT IF NECESSARY)
                  JBUS  *(CR)         NEXT CARD
                  LDA   8,4           CHECK EOF
                  CMPA  EOF
                  JNE   NEXTCARD
```

```
                    *
                    JBUS  *(LP)        WAIT LAST PRINT
                    HLT   0
                    END   START
```

Computer programs are not restricted to just being of the form: "read a card, compute on that card, print a line of output," however. The program may read several cards before outputting anything or may output many lines while reading nothing. Still, we can attempt to overlap any required I/O as much as possible. All of the programs we have studied so far read into a buffer, and output from a buffer. For sequential devices, such as card readers, card punches, line printers, and magnetic tapes, we can use *buffering* to overlap our I/O time with computation time. Buffering is simply reading or writing with one buffer while other processing is being done with another buffer.

Double buffering is the simplest case of buffering. In double buffering, we have two buffers for each device. For input, we take our input out of one buffer while the other is being read into by the input device. When the one buffer is empty, we wait until the other buffer is filled (JBUS *) and then start the input of the next record into the empty buffer while we use the newly read one. This can be done either by moving from the one buffer into the other, or merely by switching pointers. For output, we place our output image in one buffer and when this is full, we begin its output (OUT) and immediately begin to place our new output into another buffer. When this new buffer is full we wait for the previous OUT to finish (JBUS *) and then OUT from the newly filled buffer while our program fills the newly emptied buffer with new material to be output. This results in programs such as

```
    BEGIN           IN    INBUF(CR)    INPUT FIRST CARD
                    ...
                    JBUS  *(CR)        WAIT FOR LAST INPUT
                    ENT1  OTHERBUF
                    MOVE  INBUF(16)    MOVE NEW DATA OUT OF INBUF
                    IN    INBUF(CR)
                    ...
```

Similarly, for output

```
                    ...
                    JBUS  *(LP)        WAIT UNTIL LAST PRINTED
                    ENT1  OUTBUF
                    MOVE  ONEBUF(24)   MOVE TO OUTPUT BUFFER
                    OUT   OUTBUF(LP)   AND START PRINT
                    ...
```

Both of these examples use the MOVE technique. The pointer approach (index registers or indirection) is also possible, and generally slightly faster (by milliseconds).

Note that buffering may not be possible for input from direct access devices like disk or drum, since accesses on these devices are not likely to be sequential. This means that it is not possible to buffer ahead on input by reading the next record (since we do not know what the next record will be). It is still possible to buffer behind on output, however, since we do know where the last record should be output.

5.5 BLOCKING

Another problem which arises from direct access devices is efficient storage utilization. Suppose we wished to copy a deck of cards from the card reader to the line printer, backwards. This requires storing the entire card deck in the computer until the last is read and then printing the entire deck. At 16 words per

FIGURE 5.7   No blocking—each logical record (in this case a card) is stored in one physical record (a disk or tape block).

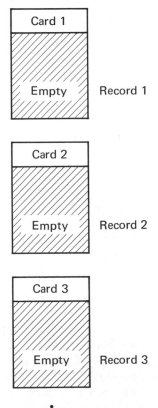

card, and only 4000 words of memory, we could only store $4000/16 = 250$ cards *if* we stored them in memory (and then we would have no room for the program). However, if we store them on disk, we could store 4096 cards by putting one card in each disk record. This would result in an input portion of the program such as

```
          IN    CARD(CR)
          ENTX  0              DISK ADDRESS
INLOOP    JBUS  *(CR)          WAIT UNTIL CARD READ
          LDA   CARD
          CMPA  EOF            CHECK EOF
          JE    OUTPUT
          ENT1  DISKBUF
          MOVE  CARD(16)       MOVE CARD TO DISK BUFFER
          IN    CARD(CR)
          OUT   DISKBUF(DISK)
          INCX  1
          JMP   INLOOP         CONTINUE WITH NEXT CARD
```

We are keeping our disk address in the X register, incrementing by one for each disk record written. Output is then

```
OUTPUT    ENT1  BUF1          POINTER TO OUTPUT BUFFER
          ENT2  BUF2
          DECX  1
          JXNP  QUIT           IF NO INPUT
  *
OUTLOOP   IN    0,1(DISK)      READ FROM DISK
          ENT3  0,1            SWITCH POINTERS
          ENT1  0,2
          ENT2  0,3
          DECX  1              DECREASE DISK ADDRESS
          JBUS  *(DISK)
          OUT   0,2(LP)        OUTPUT NEW DISK RECORD
          JXNN  OUTLOOP        CONTINUE IF MORE
  *
QUIT      JBUS  *(LP)          WAIT ON LAST
          HLT
          END
```

However, even this approach limits us to only 4096 cards (only about 2 boxes). Notice that the physical record size for a disk record is 100 words, while a card takes up only 16 words. Thus 84 words of each record are being wasted. We can avoid this waste by packing several card images into one disk record. This is called *blocking*, since we are then treating several cards as a block. For the situation mentioned above, we can block six cards per disk record easily and

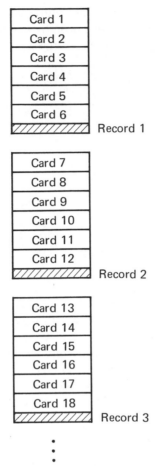

FIGURE 5.8 Loose blocking-multiple logical records are blocked into each physical record, but no logical records are split between physical records.

increase the number of cards which can be stored to 6 × 4096 = 24,576. The *blocking factor* is the number of cards per disk record, and in this case is 6.

A blocking factor of 6, for card images, still leaves 4 words per disk physical record being wasted. Things could be worse if the size of the information block we wish to store (a *logical record*) were some other number which does not divide evenly into the size of the physical record. For a 17-word logical record, and a blocking factor of 5, we would use only 85 words, leaving 15 words per physical record wasted. For a 51-word logical record, 49 words would be wasted.

These considerations rapidly lead to the conclusion that it is not always desirable to limit ourselves to only putting an integral number of logical records per physical record (*loose blocking*), but rather that it is to our advantage, at times, to split a logical record between two physical records. Thus, for 17-word logical records, we put logical records in physical records as

logical record number	physical record number	words
1	1	0–16
2	1	17–33
3	1	34–50
4	1	51–67
5	1	68–84
6	1	85–99
	and 2	0–1
7	2	2–18
. . .	. . .	. . .

Notice that the first 15 words of logical record 6 are in physical record 1, the last 2 words are the first 2 words of the next physical record. Retrieving a logical record may thus require the reading of two physical records.

Where is a given logical record? Each logical record is 17 words long, so the kth logical record follows the first $k - 1$ logical records and is words $17 \times (k - 1)$ through $17 \times (k - 1) + 16 = 17 \times k - 1$. Since there are 100 words per physical record, the physical record which holds the first word of the kth logical record is physical record number (starting at zero) $17 \times (k - 1)/100$. The remainder of this division is the word number within the physical record of the first word of the logical record. Thus, it is possible to access a given logical record directly even if we block logical records as tightly as possible.

For sequential access, the problem is much easier to solve. To extract the next logical record from a physical record buffer, we need a pointer which indicates the index of the last word which we have returned (the end of the last record). Putting this in a register, we transfer from the physical record buffer to the logical record buffer, one word at a time, the next 17 words. If the index into the physical record buffer at any time exceeds 100, this means that the physical record buffer is empty and a new record must be read and our index reset to zero before transferring the next word. The MIX code for this is

```
DISK        EQU   9
LOGSIZE     EQU   17          LOGICAL RECORD SIZE
PHYSIZE     EQU   100         PHYSICAL RECORD SIZE
LOGBUF      ORIG  *+LOGSIZE
PHYBUF      ORIG  *+PHYSIZE
PHYINDEX    CON   0           POINTER INTO PHYBUF
DISKADD     CON   0           DISK ADDRESS
*
```

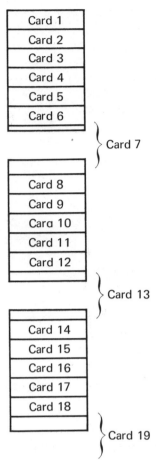

FIGURE 5.9 Tight blocking—multiple logical records are blocked into each physical record, and some logical records may be split between physical records.

```
   . . .
   STZ   PHYINDEX      SET INDEX TO ZERO
   ENTX  0
   IN    PHYBUF(DISK)  READ FIRST PHYSICAL BUF
   STZ   DISKADD
   JBUS  *(DISK)       WAIT UNTIL READ DONE
   . . .
*
*                TRANSFER NEXT LOGICAL RECORD FROM PHYSICAL
*                RECORD BUFFER TO LOGICAL RECORD BUFFER.
```

```
*                 INDEX 2 HOLDS THE INDEX INTO THE PHYSICAL
*                 BUFFER (0..99). INDEX 5 HOLDS THE INDEX
*                 INTO THE LOGICAL RECORD BUFFER (0..16).
*

        ENT5   0              LOGICAL INDEX
        LD2    PHYINDEX
2H      CMP2   =PHYSIZE=      CHECK IF END OF BUFFER
        JL     1F             NO
*                          .
        LDX    DISKADD
        INCX   1              READ NEXT PHYSICAL RECORD
        IN     PHYBUF(DISK)
        STX    DISKADD
        JBUS   *(DISK)        WAIT UNTIL READ COMPLETE
        ENT2   0              RESET INDEX TO ZERO
*
1H      LDA    PHYBUF,2
        STA    LOGBUF,5
        INC5   1
        INC2   1              INCREASE BOTH INDEXES
        CMP5   =LOGSIZE=      CHECK END OF LOGICAL RECORD
        JL     2B
*
        ST2    PHYINDEX       RESTORE UPDATED INDEX
*
```

We have purposely used a very simple I/O scheme without buffering here to illustrate how unblocking (or deblocking) is done. You should be able to easily modify this code to buffer ahead.

There are two other points which should be made. First, how do we know where the end of the data on the disk is (particularly since it may end in the middle of a physical record)? One method would be to use a special value for the logical record, such as the *EOF* marker we have used for card decks. As each logical record is used, we can check to see if it is the last one. A variant on this, for the case of alphanumeric character code information stored on the disk would be to use the sign bit (which is always set to "+" by the card reader) to signal the last logical record by setting the sign bit of the first word of a logical record to "+" for all logical records except the last one, for which the sign is set to "−".

A more general idea is to store at the beginning of the physical record a count of the number of information-bearing words in the physical record. If the value of this counter were 37 for a particular record, this would indicate that the first 37 words are valid and the other words (the last 62) are garbage. Notice that this reduces the effective size of the physical record by one word. Also, for most records, the value of this word will be constant (at 99); only the last physical record will have a different value.

The number stored in the first word could also be the number of valid logical records, the number of unused words, the beginning index of the last valid logical record, and so on.

5.6 SUMMARY

Input/output is a crucial part of most programs, since few programs operate in isolation from the outside world. At least the results of the program must be output, either to a person or for another program or computer. Input/output is basically asynchronous. Each device has a busy state and a ready state. The JBUS and JRED instructions allow this to be tested. The IN and OUT instructions start the transfer of information between the device and the memory of the MIX computer. Each device is programmed using its own techniques. Buffering is used to reduce the real time that it takes to execute a program by overlapping the execution of the CPU and input/output operations and to overlap the operation of different I/O devices. Blocking is a technique for making maximal use of disk, drum, or tape space by packing several logical records into a physical record.

Because I/O is so very slow relative to CPU operations, I/O programming must be very carefully done. Gear (1974), Stone and Siewiorek (1975), and Eckhouse (1976) all have a complete chapter on I/O programming. Knuth (1968) also devotes a section to I/O. These treatments are especially concerned with overlapped I/O.

A very important improvement over the ideas presented in this chapter is the technique of interrupts. Interrupts is a hardware feature which can help with I/O. MIX does not have an interrupt system, so we delay discussion of this topic until Chapter 10, where it will be presented in terms of other computer systems.

EXERCISES

a. What are the physical record sizes of the following MIX devices:
   1. card reader
   2. line printer
   3. disk
   4. drum
   5. tape
b. How is the track and sector address determined for an I/O instruction for a disk or drum?
c. What is a buffer?

d. What is I/O interlock time?

e. What is buffering and why is it used?

f. What is blocking and why is it used?

g. Define seek time, latency time, and transfer time for a moving head disk.

h. Why is the JBUS * (16) in the following code?

```
            IN     BUF(16)
            JBUS   *(16)
            LDX    BUF+5
```

i. Describe the results of the following program.

```
            ALF    DATA
BUF         ORIG   *+23
            ...
            IN     BUF(16)
            OUT    BUF-1(18)
```

j. Suppose you see the two lines

```
WAIT        JBUS   WAIT(16)
            IN     CARD(16)
```

in a MIXAL program. Can you always replace them with

```
WAIT               IN    CARD(16)
```

and still be assured of the same results?

k. If we wish to copy a card deck to drum, and reading a card takes 50 milliseconds, processing it takes 10 microseconds, and writing it to the drum, one card per drum record, takes 1 millisecond, and we do not overlap any processing or I/O, how long does it take to copy 1000 cards? What would be the effect on timing of overlapping the CPU processing and the drum and card I/O? What would be the effect of blocking multiple card images per drum record?

l. We want to copy a card deck to disk, and also make a listing of it. It takes 50 milliseconds to read or print a card and 1 millisecond to write a block to disk. In the best case, how much time would it take to process *n* cards?

m. What is the blocking factor (logical records per physical record) and the number of wasted words per physical disk block, if we store logical records of 7, 13, 18, 41, or 500 words on a MIX disk? Consider the cases of no blocking, loose blocking, and tight blocking.

n. Write a MIXAL program which reads cards and prints the card images after squeezing out multiple blanks. Any sequence of blanks should be replaced by one blank. Overlap I/O with I/O and CPU processing.

o. Write a program to read a file and print it backwards. How much I/O overlap can you do?

p. What is the difference between a sequential access device and a direct access device? Can we simulate one type of device on the other?

q. What are the differences between moving information between buffers and simply switching pointers to the buffers?

r. Can buffering be used for a direct access input device? For a direct access output device?

6

SUBROUTINES AND PARAMETERS

After a programmer has written a few assembly language programs, a number of things become obvious. One is the repetitive nature of assembly language programming. For almost every program, code must be written for inputting data and converting from character code, and code must be written for formatting and outputting results. This code is often very similar from program to program. It may be necessary to input or output at several points in the algorithm being programmed, so within the same program similar code must be written in several places.

This problem is compounded by the very low level of instructions available in assembly language. The operations performed by an assembly language statement are very simple, and to program even the simplest computations may take tens or hundreds of these simple instructions. To have to write the code necessary to effect some logically simple higher-level operation (such as summing the elements of an array, or counting the number of blanks in a line, or searching an array for the maximum element, and so on) more than once becomes tedious and boring.

For these reasons, *subroutines* are a standard programming technique of assembly language programmers (among others). A subroutine is a sequence of instructions which is a logical unit. Subroutines are also called *procedures* or *functions*. Their original and main purpose is to reduce the amount of code which must be repetitively written for a program. This makes assembly language programming easier and faster. Subroutines also allow code by another programmer to be used in a different program than it was originally written for.

Another effect of subroutines is to free the assembly language programmer from thinking only in terms of the instructions and data types provided by the hardware computer. Subroutines can provide the programmer with the opportunity to think and design a program in terms of abstract data types and instructions for these data types. For instance, MIX provides only the basic data types of integer numbers, floating point numbers, and characters (bytes). It does not provide arrays, or instructions to manipulate arrays. However, if we write a set of subroutines which add, subtract, compare, copy, input, and output arrays, then we can program in an extended instruction set, an instruction set which does have instructions to manipulate arrays. When it is necessary to actually operate on an array, the instruction is written as a call to the appropriate subroutine. Thus, subroutines free the programmer from some of the constraints of assembly language programming.

In this chapter, we consider many of the ideas, techniques and conventions which have developed regarding subroutines and their use. We are interested simply in the mechanics of how to write a subroutine and how to use it. Much of this information is applicable to both assembly language programming and higher-level language programming.

FIGURE 6.1   A main program and its set of subroutines (the main program calls two subroutines; each of these may then call other subroutines).

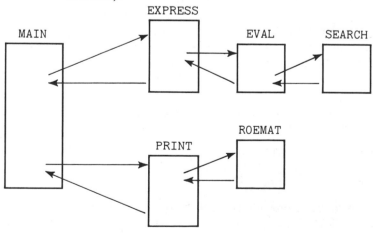

6.1 SUBROUTINE STRUCTURE

A subroutine is a closed piece of a program which has some logical function. It is executed by transferring control to its *entry point*. The subroutine executes, performing the task for which it was written and then returns to the program which called it. A subroutine may be completely self-contained and have the code to do everything itself, or it may call another subroutine.

A program is made up of a main program and subroutines. These subroutines are the subroutines which the main program calls, the subroutines which are called by the subroutines which are called by the main program, the subroutines which are called by the subroutines which are called by the subroutines which are called by the main program, and so on. Both the main program and the subroutines can be called *routines*. For each call, two routines are involved: the *calling routine* and the *called routine*.

Return addresses

A subroutine normally has a name. The name of the subroutine is often also the name of its entry point, the address where execution of the subroutine should begin. A subroutine is called by transferring control to the entry point of the subroutine. When the subroutine completes its execution, it will return control back to the calling routine. Normally, control is returned to the instruction immediately following the call in the calling routine. The address of this instruction is called the *return address*. Notice that if the subroutine is called from two different locations in the calling routine (or from two different calling routines) it will need to return control to two different addresses after it is through with its execution. This requires that every call of a subroutine not only transfer control to the entry point of the subroutine but also supply it with a return address where it should transfer control upon completion of its code.

On the MIX machine, subroutine calls are made by using the jump instructions to transfer control to a subroutine. The J register has been specifically designed to be used for supplying the return address to the called routine. When a JMP is executed to the entry point of a subroutine, the address of the instruction following the JMP is put into the J register. Thus the J register has the return address for the subroutine call.

The called routine must save the J register, and when the subroutine finishes its task, return to that address. This is done by

```
ENTRY           STJ   EXIT
                〈code for subroutine〉
EXIT            JMP   *
```

The STJ instruction stores the contents of the J register (the return address) into the address field (bytes 0:2) of the JMP instruction at EXIT. Thus, when the instruction at EXIT is executed, the address to which control is transferred will

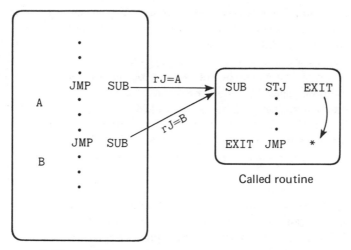

Calling routine

FIGURE 6.2 Illustration of the relationship between a calling routine and a called routine, and how the return address is passed.

be the return address for the call. Notice that this form of linkage is a self-modifying program.

As a simple example of a subroutine, consider a subroutine which computes the sum of the elements of an array INCOME of length 10. The subroutine could be

```
SUMMER          STJ    EXITSUM       SAVE RETURN ADDRESS
                ENTA   0             SUM = 0
                ENT1   9             I1 = 9, ..., 0
LOOP            ADD    INCOME,1       ADD INCOME(I1)
                DEC1   1
                J1NN   LOOP          CHECK FOR END OF LOOP
EXITSUM         JMP    *             THIS INSTRUCTION MODIFIED
```

This subroutine can be called by the simple instruction

```
                JMP    SUMMER        SUM INCOME ARRAY
```

and returns with the A register being the sum of the elements in the array INCOME.

Register saving and restoring

The subroutine given above (SUMMER) used the A register and index register 1 in the computation of the sum. It is possible that the calling routine was also using these registers to store important values for its own computations. When the subroutine is called, it is necessary to save these registers and restore them before the calling routine is resumed. If we let P be the set of registers used by the calling routine which need to be saved and Q be the set of registers used by the called routine, then the intersection of P and Q, those registers used by both the calling and called routines, are the only registers which need to be saved. Any register which is not used by the calling program, or is not used by the called program, or is not used by either, need not be saved.

There are two places that the saving and restoring of registers can be done. The registers can be saved in the calling program before the subroutine is called and restored after the subroutine returns. Alternatively, they can be saved in the subroutine before it modifies anything, and restored right before the subroutine returns to the calling routine. Notice that only the intersection of the set of registers used by calling and called routines need be saved. However neither routine may know what the other routine uses. Often different routines are programmed by different programmers, or at different times. It is considered poor programming practice to make assumptions about how a subroutine works internally. Thus, since neither routine knows the registers used by the other, they are forced to save all the registers they use. If the calling routine saves and restores registers, then it should save all of the registers that it uses. If the called routine saves and restores registers, then it should save all of the registers it may need to use.

The question as to which routine, called or calling, saves registers can be decided either way. If the calling routine generally needs only a few registers saved, then it may save them. On the other hand, if the called routine only uses a few registers, it may save them itself. Different routines may save registers or assume that they are saved by someone else as long as the decisions are consistent. It is even acceptable (although wasteful) for both the calling and called routine to save the registers. What must be avoided is a situation where the calling routine assumes that the called routine will save registers, and vice versa, resulting in neither routine saving them.

To prevent any possible problem of forgetting to save and restore a register, many programmers adopt a personal rule to always save all registers used in a called routine, in that called routine. This convention means that the calling program need not worry about the value of the registers when it calls a subroutine, and eliminates a major source of errors in assembly language programming.

Using this rule, we would rewrite our subroutine SUMMER given above as follows

```
SUMMER       STJ   EXITSUM    SAVE RETURN ADDRESS
             ST1   SUMTEMP1
             ENTA  0
             ENT1  9
LOOP         ADD   INCOME,1
             DEC1  1
             J1NN  LOOP
```

```
                 LD1   SUMTEMP1    RESTORE I1
EXITSUM          JMP   *
SUMTEMP1         ORIG  *+1
```

Notice that we still did not save and restore the A register. This is because the A register is being used to pass the result of executing the subroutine back to the calling routine. This is typically the case for a *function*. A function is a subroutine which returns a value, generally in a register. A subroutine which does not return a value is called a *procedure*, or simply a subroutine.

In the above code, we stored the value of index register 1 in the temporary variable SUMTEMP1. This extra temporary variable could have been eliminated by saving and restoring the index register as follows.

```
SUMMER           STJ   EXITSUM
                 ST1   SUMT1(0:2)
                 ENTA  0
                 ENT1  9
1H               ADD   INCOME,1
                 DEC1  1
                 J1NN  1B
SUMT1            ENT1  *           MODIFIED BY ST1
EXITSUM          JMP   *           MODIFIED BY STJ
```

The extra code which has been added to the beginning of the subroutine which is only necessary because the code is a subroutine is called the *prologue* of the subroutine; the code at the end is the *epilogue*. The prologue typically consists of instructions to store the return address and save registers. The epilogue consists of code to restore the registers and transfer control back to the calling program.

Variables

If the registers are to be saved and/or if the computation is long enough or complicated enough, the subroutine may very well need to store values in memory for its own private use. At the same time, it may be necessary for the subroutine to access some variables in the main program. Variables which are meant solely for the internal coding of the subroutine and are never used by any other routine are *local* to that routine. Variables which may be accessed by many routines are called *global variables*. Global variables are *external* to the routines which access them.

In the writing of a program of many subroutines, global variables are often declared first. Then the code for subroutines is included, followed by the main program. The code for each subroutine would consist of first the declarations of its local variables, and then its prologue, code, and epilogue. Variations from this basic scheme are not uncommon. Each subroutine should be written as a

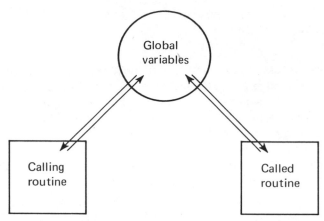

FIGURE 6.3   Global variables (global variables are shared by several routines in a program; many routines may load and store from these global locations).

separate package and should be well commented. A short paragraph at the beginning of the subroutine should explain what the subroutine does, what it assumes, what registers it affects, and what other subroutines are called.

Following this format, would require rewriting subroutine SUMMER.

```
*  *  *  *  *  *  *  *  *  FUNCTION SUMMER  *  *  *  *  *  *  *
*              THIS SUBROUTINE SUMS THE VALUES OF TEN
*              ELEMENTS OF THE ARRAY, INCOME. THE SUM IS
*              RETURNED IN THE A REGISTER.
*
*              REGISTERS:   A - RETURNS SUM OF ARRAY;
*                                PREVIOUS VALUE LOST.
*                          OT - MAY BE SET IF OVERFLOW.
*
*              SUBROUTINES CALLED: NONE
*
*              INDEX I1 IS USED TO INDEX THROUGH THE ARRAY.
*              IT IS SAVED AND RESTORED. ARRAY IS SUMMED
*              BACKWARDS FROM 9 DOWN TO 0.
*
SUMMER         STJ   EXITSUM       SAVE RETURN ADDRESS
               ST1   TEMP1SUM(0:2) AND REGISTER I1
*
               ENTA  0             SUM = 0
               ENT1  9             INDEX FROM 9 TO 0
*
1H             ADD   INCOME,1      SUM = SUM + INCOME(I)
```

```
                     DEC1  1
                     J1NN  1B              LOOP TEN TIMES
        *
        TEMP1SUM     ENT1  *               RESTORE INDEX 1
        EXITSUM      JMP   *               AND EXIT.
        *
```

6.2 PARAMETERS

The subroutine SUMMER used as an example in the last section is indeed a bona fide subroutine, but it is a very special purpose one. It always sums exactly 10 elements of the array INCOME. If we wanted to sum only the first five elements of INCOME, we would have to write another subroutine. If we wanted to sum the first 10 elements of some other array, we would again have to write another subroutine.

Rather than write separate subroutines for all of these basically similar functions, we write one general purpose subroutine. *Parameters* are used to specify those parts of the subroutine which may vary. For the SUMMER function, it is reasonable to assume that the array being summed and the length of the array may differ from one call of the subroutine to another. Thus, we define a function, called SUM, with two parameters. Parameters are also called *arguments*.

To refer to the parameters, we give them names. There are two types of parameter names. When we discuss the general subroutine, we use *formal parameters*, which are simply the names of the parameters. For any particular call of the subroutine, it is necessary to specify the specific variables to be used with the subroutine for this call. These specific variables are the *actual parameters*.

One of the major problems with subroutines is how to pass parameters. The calling routine knows, for each call, what the actual parameters are. It is necessary to transmit this information from the calling routine to the called routine somehow. The problem is, how? As with many problems in programming, many different solutions to the problem have been proposed. Each method may require a small amount of code in the calling routine to set up the parameters. This is called the *calling sequence* of the subroutine.

Passing parameters in registers

One of the most common solutions for assembly language programs is to pass parameters in the programmable registers of the central processor. In MIX, the A and X registers can be used to pass two five-byte-plus-sign numbers, or up to 10 characters. The index registers can pass small numbers or addresses. The return address can be considered as just another parameter which, for the MIX computer, is always passed in the J register. A function value is a parameter which is passed back from the function to the calling routine through the registers.

If values are passed into or out of a subroutine in the A and X registers, they can be accessed directly and used in the subroutine immediately. Often, however, a parameter may not fit into the A or X register. For example, for a subroutine which adds the elements of an array, we need the length of the array (a number easily passed in a register) and the array elements. However, the array cannot be put in the registers (unless it was a very small array), so a pointer to the array, its address in memory, is passed instead. This requires the elements of the array to be accessed indirectly, generally by using indexed or indirect addressing.

If registers are used to pass the address and length of the array to be summed, we can write a SUM subroutine which will add the elements of the array and return the value in the A register as follows.

```
*
*                  SUM: FUNCTION TO ADD THE ELEMENTS OF AN ARRAY
*                       AND RETURN THE VALUE IN THE A REGISTER.
*
*                  ON INPUT, I1 = ADDRESS OF THE ARRAY
*                            I2 = LENGTH OF THE ARRAY
*
SUM           STJ    SUMEXIT      SAVE RETURN ADDRESS
              ST2    TEMP2(0:2)   AND REGISTER
              ENTA   0
*
1H            ADD    -1,1:2       ADD ELEMENT OF ARRAY
              DEC2   1
              J2P    1B
*
TEMP2         ENT2   *            RESTORE INDEX 2
SUMEXIT       JMP    *            EXIT
```

An alternative subroutine which does not use double indexing is

```
SUM           STJ    SUMEXIT      SAVE RETURN ADDRESS
              ST2    TEMP2(0:2)   AND REGISTER
              ENTA   0
*
1H            ADD    0,1
              INC1   1            NEXT ELEMENT OF ARRAY
              DEC2   1
              J2P    1B           ADD FOR EACH ELEMENT OF ARRAY
*
TEMP2         ENT2   *            RESTORE REGISTER
SUMEXIT       JMP    *            AND EXIT
```

If desired, index register I1 could also be saved and restored.

The calling sequence for passing parameters in registers requires that the registers be properly loaded before the JMP to the subroutine is executed. For the SUM function above, we could sum the two arrays P and Q, whose lengths are equal and equal to the contents of location N, by

```
        ENT1  P              ADDRESS OF ARRAY
        LD2   N              LENGTH OF ARRAY
        JMP   SUM
        STA   SUMP           SAVE SUM
*
        ENT1  Q              ADDRESS OF ARRAY Q
*       LD2   N              INDEX 2 STILL HAS N IN IT
        JMP   SUM
        STA   SUMQ           SAVE SUM OF Q
```

The calling routine has the responsibility of making sure that any values which are in the registers used for parameter passing are correct when the subroutine is called. This may mean that the calling routine will need to save some registers.

Global variables

Another way to pass parameters is to use global variables. In this method, special global variables are declared which serve as the parameters for the subroutine. When a routine wishes to call the subroutine, it copies the actual parameters into the special global variables and then simply jumps to the subroutine. The subroutine accesses the parameters through the global variables.

For our array summing subroutine, we could declare two global variables, ARRAYADD and LENGTH.

```
*
*              GLOBAL PARAMETERS FOR SUM SUBROUTINE
*
ARRAYADD       ORIG  *+1
LENGTH         ORIG  *+1
```

The calling sequence becomes

```
        ENTA  P              ADDRESS OF P
        STA   ARRAYADD(0:2)
        LDA   N              VALUE OF N
        STA   LENGTH
        JMP   SUM
```

The subroutine itself is then

```
SUM            STJ   SUMEXIT
               ST2   TEMP2(0:2)
               ENTA  0
```

```
                    LD2    LENGTH
        *
        1H          DEC2   1
                    ADD    ARRAYADD,7:2
                    J2P    1B
        TEMP2       ENT2   *
        SUMEXIT     JMP    *
```

This version requires indirect addressing, and specifically post-indexed indirection. This could be eliminated, as the double indexing was above, by loading from ARRAYADD into I1 and then incrementing register I1 in the loop. Or the program can modify itself by substituting the actual parameter into the code before executing it. In this case, SUM would be written as

```
        SUM         STJ    SUMEXIT
                    ST2    TEMP2(0:2)
                    LD2    ARRAYADD(0:2)
                    ST2    2F(0:2)
                    LD2    LENGTH
                    ENTA   0
        1H          DEC2   1
        2H          ADD    *,2          ADDRESS OF ARRAY SUBSTITUTED
                    J2P    1B
        TEMP2       ENT2   *
        SUMEXIT     JMP    *
```

Substituting the parameter directly into the code may be acceptable if the parameter is used in only a few instructions in the subroutine, but generally indexing or indirection is a better method of accessing a parameter.

The use of global variables to pass parameters is similar to the use of registers to pass parameters, since registers are essentially just global variables with certain special properties and faster access times. However, use of global variables means that the number and size of parameters are not limited by the number and size of the registers. If a subroutine in MIX had 10 parameters, we could not pass the parameters in the registers, since there are only 8 registers. We would not be able to pass even three parameters if these parameters were each a full five bytes plus sign, since index registers are too small for such parameters. Only the A and X registers can be used to pass full-size parameters. Thus the use of global variables has certain advantages over the use of registers.

Passing parameters in the called routine

There are some problems with the use of global variables, however. Sometimes it is difficult, or inconvenient, to have to allocate global variables. Both the calling and called routines (which may be written by different programmers) must agree upon the location and names of these global parameters. Thus it is not possible to simply pick up a subroutine and use it; it is necessary to also allocate the appropriate global variables.

An alternative method of passing the parameters is to have the space for them be allocated in the subroutine to be called. This means that the subroutine is self-contained and need not reference, nor have allocated, global variables. Notice that the same amount of space is needed, and the parameters would still be accessed in the same manner; the question is simply where to put the parameters. One possibility is in global memory space, another is local to the called routine.

But if the parameters are to be put in the called routine, how is the calling routine to refer to the memory locations where the parameters are to be put? A subroutine should be treated as a black box. No other routine should make any assumptions about how it is internally structured. To do so invites possible errors in the program if the subroutine must be rewritten. The only information about a subroutine which should be necessary outside that subroutine is the location of the entry point, the parameters needed, and the function of the subroutine. It would be possible to require the definition of two entry points for each subroutine: one as the address of the code to which control should be passed to start execution of the subroutine, and the other the beginning address of a block of memory where the parameters should be put.

More often, however, these two addresses are combined, so that only one address need be defined to use a subroutine. To execute the subroutine, control is transferred to the entry point. This same address is also the address of the first location after the locations where the parameters are to be put. Thus the block of memory locations for passing parameters is just before the entry point to the

FIGURE 6.4   Parameters passed before the entry point (parameters are passed by placing them in the memory location before the entry point).

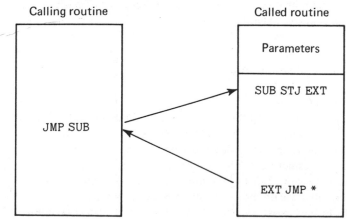

Calling routine   Called routine

Parameters

SUB STJ EXT

JMP SUB

EXT JMP *

subroutine. For a subroutine with an entry point SUB, for example, control is transferred to the subroutine by a JMP SUB. The first parameter is passed in SUB−1, the second parameter in SUB−2, the third in SUB−3, and so forth.

For our array summing routine, SUM, the code would look like

```
            ORIG  *+1          SAVE SPACE FOR ARRAY LENGTH
            ORIG  *+1          SAVE SPACE FOR ARRAY ADDRESS
*
SUM         STJ   SUMEXIT
            ST2   TEM2(0:2)
            ENTA  0
            LD2   SUM-2        LENGTH
1H          DEC2  1
            ADD   SUM-1,7:2    INDIRECT ACCESS OF ARRAY
            J2P   1B
TEM2        ENT2  *
SUMEXIT     JMP   *
```

The calling sequence is

```
            ENTA  P
            STA   SUM-1(0:2)   STORE IN ADDRESS FIELD
            LDA   N
            STA   SUM-2
            JMP   SUM
```

Parameter passing in the calling routine

For a system like the MIX computer, however, passing the parameters just before the entry point can cause definite problems. Specifically, if the subroutine is a forward reference then we cannot use expressions like SUB−1, SUB−2 in our program. Also (as we will see later in Chapter 7), some loaders do not allow expressions which involve entry points. Thus there may be problems with passing parameters in the calling routine.

Still the parameters must be passed from calling routine to called routine in some locations which are mutually accessible by both routines. If the parameters are not passed globally, or in the called routine, the natural place is the calling routine.

If the parameters are passed in the calling routine, the calling routine will have no difficulty accessing them. How does the called routine find them, however? What information does the called routine typically have about the calling routine? Only one thing: the return address. How can the return address be used to locate the parameters? The parameters cannot be put before the return address (as they were put before the entry point when passed in the called routine), since this will be the code which is executed just before the subroutine is called. Thus they must be placed *after* the call to the subroutine.

Calling routine   Called routine

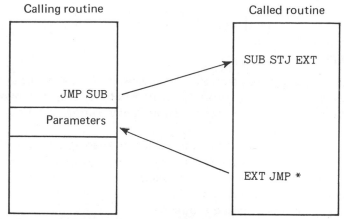

FIGURE 6.5 Parameters passed after the subroutine call (either the main program or the subroutine must remember to jump around the parameters).

This causes one minor problem: how does the subroutine return control to the calling routine without executing its parameters as instructions, by mistake? There are two standard solutions. One is to place a jump around the parameters immediately after the call to the subroutine. In this case, our calling sequence is

```
        LDA     LENGTH
        STA     *+4             SAVE LENGTH PARAMETER
        JMP     SUM
        JMP     *+3             JUMP AROUND PARAMETERS
        CON     P(0:2)          ADDRESS OF ARRAY
        ORIG    *+1             LENGTH OF ARRAY
```

To access parameters, we must fetch them indirectly through the return address. Often the return address is loaded into a register to facilitate this. For example, our SUM subroutine (for the calling sequence above) might be

```
SUM             STJ     SUMEXIT
                ST1     TEM1(0:2)
                ST2     TEM2(0:2)
                LD1     SUMEXIT(0:2)    RETURN ADDRESS
                LD2     2,1             LENGTH OF ARRAY
                LD1     1,1             ADDRESS OF ARRAY
*
                ENTA    0
1H              DEC2    1
                ADD     0,1
                INC1    1
                J2P     1B
```

```
*
TEM1            ENT1  *              RESTORE REGISTERS
TEM2            ENT2  *
SUMEXIT         JMP   *
```

Notice that accessing the parameters is somewhat more complicated than in previous versions of SUM. To access an element of the array, it is necessary to first use the return address to fetch the address of the array, and then index with this address.

The other standard solution to the problem of keeping the parameters from being executed is to require a subroutine with n parameters to return, not to the address R which is passed as the return address (in the J register) but to return to the address $R + n$. In this way, the parameters are skipped over by the subroutine. This allows a calling sequence like

```
            LDA   LENGTH
            STA   *+3           LENGTH OF ARRAY
            JMP   SUM
            CON   P             ARRAY ADDRESS
            ORIG  *+1           SPACE FOR LENGTH
```

Control from the subroutine will return to the instruction after the ORIG, rather than the instruction after the JMP. The subroutine SUM could be

```
SUM             STJ   SUMEXIT
                ST1   TEM1(0:2)
                ST2   TEM2(0:2)
*
                LD1   SUMEXIT(0:2) RETURN ADDRESS
                INC1  2            IS 2 BEYOND J REGISTER
                ST1   SUMEXIT(0:2) RESTORE FOR EXIT
*
                LD2   -1,1         LENGTH OF ARRAY
                LD1   -2,1         ADDRESS OF ARRAY
*
                ENTA  0
1H              DEC2  1
                ADD   0,1
                INC1  1
                J2P   1B
*
TEM1            ENT1  *
TEM2            ENT2  *
SUMEXIT         JMP   *
```

Again, it is necessary to be very careful when accessing the parameters to be sure when you have the value of the parameter and when you have the address of the parameter or the address of the address of the parameter.

Passing parameters in a table

The technique of passing parameters in the calling routine, as described in the last section, is widely used. In addition to a number of other advantages, the calling sequence is shorter than many of the other techniques. Since the parameter list is known at the time that the subroutine call is written, and is constant for that call, it can often be written directly after the call, eliminating the need to move the parameters into registers, global variables, or the called routine.

For many programs, an examination of the subroutine calls shows that the same parameter list is being used over and over again for different calls, sometimes even to different subroutines. Consider a program which manipulates vectors. We may have the following subroutines (among others),

ADD(*p*,*q*,*n*)   Add the vector *p* to the vector *q*.
SUB(*p*,*q*,*n*)   Subtract the vector *p* from the vector *q*.
COMP(*p*,*q*,*n*)   Compare the vector *p* to the vector *q*. Set the condition indicator.

If there were a program with 14 calls to these routines, all with actual parameters X0 and Y0, of length 27, then using the calling sequence

```
JMP   ADD, SUB, or COMP
CON   X0
CON   Y0
CON   27
```

there would be 14 sets of identical parameter lists in memory, one for each call. This seems somewhat wasteful of space.

To prevent this waste of memory, another parameter passing technique is to pass the parameters in a table. One table is allocated for every different set of actual parameters, thus there are never more tables than subroutine calls. The

FIGURE 6.6 Parameters passed in a table (the address of the table is placed in a register—typically, an index register).

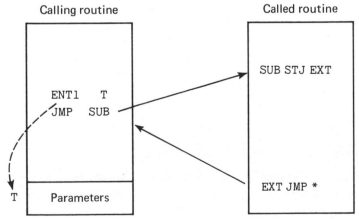

table is simply a list of the actual parameters of the subroutine call. The address of this table is put in one of the index registers before control is transferred to the subroutine. Thus, the calling sequence is

```
ENT1  ⟨address of parameter table⟩
JMP   ⟨subroutine entry point⟩
```

For the example above, the calling sequence would be

```
TABLE7        CON   XO        TABLE OF PARAMETERS
              CON   YO
              CON   27

              . . .
              ENT1  TABLE7
              JMP   ADD

              . . .
              ENT1  TABLE7
              JMP   COMP
              JLE   SMALL

              . . .
```

The subroutine accesses the parameters by indexing, through the register pointing at the table, to get the specific parameter desired. Notice that passing parameters immediately after the call in the calling routine is basically the same idea, except that the two addresses passed in the table method, the address of the table and the return address, are combined into simply the return address, which is passed in the J register.

Passing parameters on a stack

On machines or systems which facilitate the use of stacks, parameters are generally passed on a stack. A little thought shows that the last-in-first-out (LIFO) nature of the stack structure matches the last-called-first-returned nature of subroutine calls.

A stack calling sequence consists of the calling routine pushing onto the stack all parameters. The called routine pops these parameters off the stack and uses them. The return address can also be passed on the stack.

The real advantage with using stacks for passing parameters is when subroutines are nested. Since parameters are always added to the top of the stack, a subroutine need not consider which subroutines call it, nor what subroutines it calls, as long as each subroutine removes from the stack everything that it puts on the stack.

Other methods of passing parameters

Each of the methods of passing parameters which we have explained has been used by assembly language programmers, and each one has its advan-

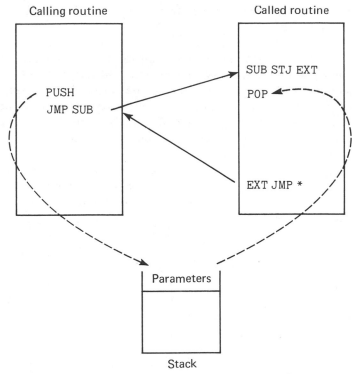

Calling routine   Called routine

PUSH
JMP SUB

SUB STJ EXT
POP

EXT JMP *

Parameters

Stack

FIGURE 6.7 Parameters passed on a stack (parameters are passed to the called routine by pushing them onto a stack; the called routine accesses them by popping the stack).

tages and disadvantages. But assembly language programmers are not restricted to only these techniques; they have the freedom to use any logically consistent method of passing parameters. Often programmers use a mixture of these techniques, passing several parameters through the registers while passing others as global variables or in the calling or called routine. The only important thing is that both the calling and called routine agree on how the parameters are to be passed. An assembly language programmer has the freedom to choose an appropriate method for each different subroutine.

This also calls for the responsibility to check that parameters are passed correctly in all cases. If each different subroutine has a different method of passing parameters, then this can become a major source of errors. To avoid this, programmers often adopt one standard calling sequence for the entire program. This eliminates a number of potential problems for the programmer, and hence means the program is more likely to be finished sooner.

Another source of standard calling sequences are subroutine libraries and compilers for higher-level languages. In the first case, a standard calling sequence increases the usability of the set of subroutines in the library. If you wish to use one of the subroutines in the library, you need only use the standard calling sequence to access it.

For compilers, when a higher-level language instruction calls a subroutine, the correct calling sequence must be generated, and when a subroutine accesses a parameter, the code which is generated must be consistent with the calling sequence. Thus, for most compilers, one standard calling sequence is used for all subroutines and functions. Often these calling sequences are published and available to any programmer who is interested. This allows the assembly language programmer to combine routines written in the higher-level language and assembly language.

A typical situation in which this is done is when a central computation is crucial to the speed of a program and must be carefully programmed to take an absolute minimal amount of time. In these cases, the central computation may be written as an assembly language subroutine which is called by a higher-level language main program. This allows the most important code to be written in assembly language without making it necessary to code the entire program (which might be quite large) in assembly language.

Another situation may involve I/O. I/O is often difficult in assembly language, since it requires considerable code to properly format, block, and buffer data for input or output. In this case it is often convenient to have an assembly language main program call subroutines written in a higher-level language to perform the I/O.

Notice that when combining routines in different languages, the higher-level language compiler normally has a fixed method of passing parameters, whichever method seemed best at the time that the compiler was written. Thus, such routines can be combined with assembly language routines only because the assembly language routine can be written to match the higher-level language calling sequence. This means that it is generally not possible to combine routines written in different higher-level languages or even compiled by different compilers for the same language. For example, the RUN Fortran compiler for the CDC 6600 computer passes parameters in its registers, unless there are more than six, when the extra parameters are passed before the entry point in the called routine. The FTN Fortran compiler for the same computer, on the other hand, uses a table. Thus routines compiled by these two compilers cannot be combined, because they use different standard calling sequences.

6.3 CALL BY VALUE, REFERENCE, OR NAME

In the previous section, we considered *how* information could be passed to a subroutine. In this section, we consider *what* information should be passed. The decision as to what information should be passed to a subroutine about a parameter often helps to determine how that parameter is passed. For example, the two most common kinds of information about a parameter are its address and its value. If its value is passed, then it may be necessary to utilize the A and X registers to pass the parameters. If more than two parameters are passed, this may mean that the parameters cannot be passed in the registers. On the other hand, if addresses are passed, then they can easily be passed in the index registers, allowing six or eight (if the A and X registers are used also) parameters to be passed in the registers.

Notice that although we are discussing what information should be passed to a subroutine, we do not address here the problem of what the parameters of a subroutine should be. That is a creative decision which is part of the programming problem. Here we are concerned only with how to *code* a problem once the program has been defined.

Input and output parameters

Parameters can be defined to have one of three kinds of effects on a subroutine. They can be input parameters, output parameters, or both input and output parameters. An *input parameter* is a parameter whose initial value (the value of the parameter at the time of the subroutine call) is used in the program. Both the array parameters and the length of the *array parameter in the* SUM subroutine used as an example in Section 6.2 were input parameters. An *output parameter* is a parameter whose value is defined by the called routine and returned to the calling routine. The sum of the elements of the array was an output parameter of the SUM subroutine. Some parameters may be both input and output parameters. Notice that if a parameter is neither an input parameter nor an output parameter, it need not be a parameter.

These different types of parameters result in different types of information being passed between routines.

Call by value

One type of information about a parameter which can be passed is its value. If the parameter is a simple variable or an element of an array, its value is loaded from memory and passed to the subroutine. Often the value is passed in a register.

Notice that this type of subroutine call, a *call by value*, is most suitable for input parameters. If a value of a parameter is passed into a subroutine for an output parameter, we have wasted our efforts to pass it in, since it will not be used. Furthermore, the subroutine lacks the ability to change the value of the parameter. At best, it can change the copy of the value of the variable which is passed in, but it cannot change the value of the actual parameter, which is in memory. The subroutine does not know where in memory the parameter is; it knows only the value that the parameter had when the subroutine was called.

To allow for output parameters, a variation on call by value is used. In this variation, *call by value/result*, the values of input parameters are passed into the subroutine, and the subroutine passes out the values of the output parameters which may then be used or stored by the calling routine. This allows both input, output, and input/output parameters. It is typically used by assembly language programmers.

Still there are some problems with call by value. Specifically, it is difficult to use call by value, or call by value/result when the parameter is an array or table. To pass an array by value would require copying the entire array and passing each element into the subroutine. This would be prohibitively expensive, in both time and space, for most situations.

Call by reference

A second type of information about a parameter which can be passed is its address. This form of passing parameters is *call by reference*, or *call by address*. The address of the parameter is passed to the subroutine. If this parameter is an input parameter, its value can be determined by loading indirectly through this address; if it is an output parameter, its new value can be stored indirectly through the passed address.

Call by reference is typically used whenever arrays or tables are passed as parameters. In this case, the base address of the array is passed into the subroutine. The subroutine can then index into the array and reference individual elements of the array without the entire array needing to be copied.

Call by reference can be easily used with any of the parameter passing mechanisms considered in Section 6.2, and so is often used as a standard calling technique. It is particularly common for compilers, like Fortran and PL/I compilers, to use call by reference. For a Fortran compiler, the code for a subroutine call such as CALL SUB(A,B,C,D,5), which uses call by reference and a calling sequence which lists the parameters in the calling routine, becomes simply

```
JMP    SUB
CON    A              ADDRESS OF FIRST PARAMETER
CON    B
CON    C
CON    D
CON    =5=            ADDRESS OF LITERAL FOR CONSTANT
```

Some problems with this approach do occur however. Since parameters in Fortran are allowed to be array elements, the call might be CALL SUB2(A,B(J)) where B is an array, and J an integer index. For call by reference, the address of B(J) is computed at the time of the call, and stored in the parameter list. Thus the code for this, using a parameter list in the calling routine as above, is

```
ENTA   B-1            BASE ADDRESS OF B
ADD    J              B(1) IS B, B(2) IS B+1, ETC
STA    *+3
```

```
JMP    SUB2
CON    A
CON    *              TO BE SET AT TIME OF CALL
```

A similar problem is caused by expressions. If the call is CALL POLY (P+Q*2, RESULT), the value of the expression P+Q*2 is quite easily calculated, so a call by value approach is straightforward. For call by reference, we must pass an address, and an expression has no obvious address associated with it. This problem is resolved by computing the value of the expression and storing that value in a temporary variable. Then the address of the temporary variable is passed to the subroutine. Thus, for the above call to POLY, a calling sequence is

```
LDA    Q              A = Q
MUL    =2=            PRODUCT IN X
SLAX   5              MOVE PRODUCT TO A
ADD    P              P + 2*Q
STA    TEMP
JMP    POLY
CON    TEMP           ADDRESS OF EXPRESSION VALUE
CON    RESULT
```

With this approach, the subroutine need not worry about what the parameter is that is being passed in (variable, constant, array element, or expression). In all cases, call by reference supplies an address.

In some subtle cases, call by reference and the lack of concern in the subroutine for what kind of parameter is being passed in can cause rather obscure bugs in a program. One of the problems with call by value is that it has no provision for output parameters, parameters whose value should be set by the subroutine. Call by value/result has provision for output parameters, but may result in a lot of unnecessary copying. By passing an address to the subroutine, as in call by reference, the subroutine can easily load and store in any parameter. And that is the problem. The subroutine can load and store in *any* parameter, including those in which it is not intended that it should store by the calling routine.

The classic example of this is as follows. Consider the subroutine,

```
SUBROUTINE ZERO (N)
N=0
RETURN
END
```

When call by reference is used, the MIX code for this subroutine would be (assuming the address of the parameter were passed in index register 1),

```
ZERO        STJ    ZEROEXIT
            STZ    0,1            ZERO PARAMETER
ZEROEXIT    JMP    *              AND RETURN
```

And the call for CALL ZERO(J) would be

```
ENT1  J           PUT ADDRESS OF J IN I1
JMP   ZERO        AND CALL SUBROUTINE
```

Follow through the execution of the call and the subroutine for the above. Notice that it works exactly as it should. The address of the parameter is passed in index register 1, and the contents of the parameter are set to zero by the indexed STZ.

Now consider the same subroutine for a CALL ZERO(5). The calling sequence is

```
ENT1  =5=         ADDRESS OF LITERAL 5
JMP   ZERO
```

But what happens when this is executed? Our literal with a value of 5, now has a value of zero. If we later say P = 5*Q, this will result in

```
LDA   Q
MUL   =5=
STX   P
```

and the value of P will be zero, independent of the value of Q. This is known as *clobbering a constant*. It has been the source of unknown numbers of bugs in programs (and probably still is). The problem is that the calling routine has no knowledge or control over which of the parameters are input parameters and which are output parameters for the subroutine, and once a subroutine has an address, it can either load or store as it wishes. Even more disastrous results can occur when the address of a simple variable is supplied to a subroutine which treats that address as the base address of an output array.

The simple variable and constant clobbering problem can be solved by treating these values as expressions, and copying them to temporary variables whose addresses are passed to the subroutine. If these are clobbered, there is no problem, as these values are never used by the calling routine. This is similar to call by value/result, only with addresses instead of values.

Call by name

The problems of call by reference bring up a larger problem relating to subroutines in higher-level languages and how they are implemented. Given a definition of a subroutine, what does a call on that subroutine *mean*? This is a subtle question and not an easy one to understand or answer. But consider the subroutine ZERO defined above. The meaning of CALL ZERO (J) is obvious: set the variable J to zero. But what is the meaning of CALL ZERO (5) or CALL ZERO (P+Q)? Some programming languages never really worry about the problem, assuming that ''strange'' subroutine calls are errors, and hence, let the programmer beware! Others have carefully defined what a subroutine call should mean. Algol has one of the most commonly referred to definitions.

The rules of the Algol programming language state that when a subroutine is executed, the results of that execution should be identical to the execution of the body of the subroutine with all occurrences of the formal parameters replaced by the names of the actual parameters. This means that the effect of a subroutine call should be the same as if the subroutine call were removed and the text of the subroutine body were copied into the calling routine where the call was, substituting the strings of characters which define the actual parameters everywhere that the corresponding formal parameter occurs. This is called the *copy rule* or the *replacement rule*.

As an example, consider

```
SUBROUTINE SUB4(A,B,C)
A = A+1
C = B+A
RETURN
END
```

According to the copy rule, the following code

```
X = 0
CALL SUB4 (X, G(J), G(J+1))
J = J+1
```

is equivalent to

```
X = 0
X = X + 1
G(J+1) = G(J) + X
J = J + 1
```

where we have copied the text of the subroutine into the calling routine, substituting "X", "G(J)", and "G(J+1)" for all occurrences of the formal parameters A, B, and C, respectively, in the subroutine.

This is a simple and seemingly reasonable definition of what a subroutine call should mean. It corresponds to what most people think subroutines should mean. However, there are some subtle complexities which are often overlooked.

Consider the subroutine SWAP(A,B) defined by

```
SUBROUTINE SWAP(A,B)
TEMP = A
A = B
B = TEMP
RETURN
END
```

For a simple CALL SWAP (P,Q), this would result in, according to the copy rule

```
TEMP = P
P = Q
Q = TEMP
```

which is what was expected. But consider a case where we wish to swap J and G(J), so that G(J) = J and J will have the old value of G(J). If we say SWAP(G(J),J), this is

```
TEMP = G(J)
G(J) = J
J = TEMP
```

which is what we wanted. But SWAP(A,B) should be the same as SWAP(B,A), so consider SWAP(J,G(J)).

```
TEMP = J
J = G(J)
G(J) = TEMP
```

Notice that the value of J (initially *j*) has changed and so we are swapping not J and G(*j*), but setting J to G(*j*) and G(G(*j*)) to *j*. (Let G be the array (4,3,2,1) and J = 1, and try it.)

This simple example should illustrate not only that the copy rule may result in unexpected results, but also that it cannot be implemented by call by value or call by reference. For either call by value or call by reference, the values or addresses of the parameters are calculated and fixed at the time of call. To properly implement the copy rule, a new parameter passing technique, *call by name*, is used. For call by name the values or addresses of parameters may change during the execution of the subroutine. This means that it is necessary to recalculate the value or address of each parameter each time it is used in the subroutine. This is done by creating a small subroutine with no parameters for each parameter. This subroutine is called a *thunk*. The thunk for a parameter is called by the subroutine whenever the parameter is about to be used. The thunk calculates the current address of the parameter and returns it to the subroutine. The subroutine then uses this address to access the parameter.

As an example, consider the above SWAP routine. Assume that each thunk for a parameter will leave the current address of that parameter in index register 6, and that the calling sequence is to put the addresses of the thunks of the parameters immediately after the call in the calling routine. Then the calling sequence for CALL SWAP(J,G(J)) is

```
          JMP   SWAP
          CON   THUNK1        THUNK FOR J
          CON   THUNK2        THUNK FOR G(J)
```

The code for the thunks is

```
THUNK1        STJ   EXITTHK1
              ENT6  J              ADDRESS OF J
EXITTHK1      JMP   *
*
THUNK2        STJ   EXITTHK2
```

```
                 LD6    J                VALUE OF J
                 INC6   G-1              ADDRESS OF G
EXITTHK2         JMP    *
```

and the code for SWAP is

```
TEMPA            CON    0
TEMP             CON    0                TEMPORARY VARIABLE
*
SWAP             STJ    EXITSWAP
                 STA    TEMPA
                 ST1    TEMP1(0:2)
                 ST2    TEMP2(0:2)
                 ST6    TEMP6(0:2)   SAVE REGISTERS TO BE USED
*
                 LD1    EXITSWAP(0:2)  RETURN ADDRESS
                 INC1   2               REAL RETURN ADDRESS
                 ST1    EXITSWAP(0:2)
                 LD2    -1,1            ADDRESS OF THUNK2
                 LD1    -2,1            ADDRESS OF THUNK1
*
                 JMP    0,1             CALL THUNK1
                 LDA    0,6             VALUE OF FIRST PARAMETER
                 STA    TEMP            (TEMP = FIRST)
*
                 JMP    0,2             CALL THUNK2
                 LDA    0,6             VALUE OF SECOND
                 JMP    0,1             CALL THUNK1
                 STA    0,6             (FIRST = SECOND)
*
                 LDA    TEMP
                 JMP    0,2             ADDRESS OF SECOND
                 STA    0,6             (SECOND = TEMP)
*
                 LDA    TEMPA           RESTORE REGISTERS
TEMP6            ENT6   *
TEMP2            ENT2   *
TEMP1            ENT1   *
EXITSWAP         JMP    *
```

This code is admittedly longer and more complex than call by reference or call by value. But this is what is necessary to implement call by name and the copy rule.

Some improvements can be made. Indirect addressing (with preindexing) can eliminate the need for index register 2. But the overhead of the code and calls for the thunks is fundamental to call by name, so minor improvements cannot really help much. Also, some systems require two subroutines per parameter, one to return the value of the parameter and the other to store a new value into the parameter. This seeks to prevent undesired storing into parameters in the way that call by value prevents illegal stores which are possible in call by reference.

Given the desire to implement the copy rule, the use of thunks is necessary. However, thunks are a very expensive way to access parameters. Thus call by name is seldom used. Call by reference is the most common technique with call by value or call by value/result also enjoying reasonable popularity. As always, an assembly language programmer has the freedom to pick and choose as appropriate. The techniques can even be mixed in assembly language so that of three parameters, one may be call by name, another call by reference, and the third call by value/result. Typically, expressions and simple variables are passed by value, where possible, while arrays and tables are passed by reference.

6.4 THE COST OF SUBROUTINES

The cost of a particular programming technique is generally measured in two ways: space and time. We have said that call by name is a very expensive method of passing parameters. Can we formalize that statement to some degree by showing just how expensive the use of call by name is, relative to call by reference or some other scheme? Yes, we can, but let us first consider the cost of using subroutines at all, versus not using them.

Consider a program which uses a subroutine to perform some task. Looking first at space, suppose that the subroutine is called from m different places in the text of the program, and that the body of the subroutine is k words long. The body of the subroutine does not include the prologue or epilogue of the subroutine. Now, if the subroutine were to be bodily written out in each of the m different places where it is called, then mk words would be needed for the subroutine part of the program. By using a subroutine, however, we reduce the code for each of the m calls to 1 word each, plus the body of the subroutine (k words) plus the prologue and epilogue. The prologue saves the return address (STJ) and the epilogue returns to the calling program (JMP). So with the subroutine, the number of words needed is $m + k + 2$. For the cases where $m + k + 2$ is less than mk, using a subroutine takes less space. Obviously, for $m = 1$ (subroutine only called from one place) or $k = 1$ (subroutine only one word long), we should not use a subroutine, *if* we are worried about space.

These equations are, in fact, too simple. The subroutine probably has parameters (p of them) and needs to save and restore registers (r of them). The prologue is at least $1 + r$ words, the epilogue is $1 + r$ words, and the calling sequence is $p + 1$. In addition, if call by name is used we must consider the space needed for the thunks (at least three words per parameter) and the additional code that is needed to access the parameters (if any). Thus the actual space used by a subroutine is relatively complex. In general, however, as long as your subroutine is longer than your calling sequence ($k > p + 1$) and your subroutine is called in more places than the number of words in the prologue and epilogue ($m > 2r + 2$), then using a subroutine probably saves space.

Another major consideration is time, and it may be more important than space. More computer systems charge for time than space, so as long as your program can fit in core, time is often of crucial importance. To calculate the amount of time needed for a subroutine, we need to know the number of times it is called, n. Notice that the number of times it is called is different from the number of places where it is called. Given that there are m different calls to the subroutine, some of these may be skipped due to conditional branching, and others may be in loops so that the subroutine is called over and over again although it is called from only one place. Thus we may have $m > n$, $m = n$, or $m < n$.

Now for each call of the subroutine, the subroutine will take some average execution time, t, to execute the body of the subroutine. Thus if no subroutine is used, the program will take nt time units to execute the function of the subroutine. If a subroutine is used, each call now takes 1 time unit for the JMP to the subroutine, 2 time units for the STJ, t time units for the subroutine body, and 1 time unit for the return jump. Thus, if a subroutine is used, our time is $n(t + 4)$, and in all cases, the use of a subroutine takes *more* execution time. The times become even worse when you add the additional time to set up the calling sequence, save and restore the registers, and fetch parameters.

If using subroutines always takes longer, why are they used? First, consider that if t is on the order of 1000 or 1000000 time units, the extra 4 or so time units per call are of minimal importance. Second, we have considered only execution time in this analysis. For a complete view of the cost of not using subroutines, the extra cost of programming time, keypunching time, assembly time, load time, and debug time, all of which tend to be larger for larger programs, must be considered. Except for trivial subroutines, the relative cost of using subroutines is generally far outweighed by the convenience of using subroutines. Subroutines make programs easier to read, to write, and to understand (hence debug) when used properly. Although one must be careful as to how to write subroutines and how to pass parameters, subroutines are considered good programming practice.

6.5 OTHER TOPICS ABOUT SUBROUTINES

There are several other aspects of subroutines which a good programmer should be aware of, although the use of these techniques is relatively rare. We discuss them briefly here simply to acquaint you with the ideas.

Multiple entry points

It is sometimes convenient to write the body of one subroutine which is used by several entry points. This saves unnecessary duplication of code. For example, consider a pair of subroutines to calculate the *sine* and *cosine* of an angle in radians. These routines could be written as two separate subroutines. However, it is well known that *sine(x) = cosine(x + pi/2)*. This can be exploited by writing one subroutine with two entry points. The *cosine* entry point adds *pi/2* to its parameter and then jumps directly to the code for the sine calculation. The basic structure for this in MIX might be, assuming that the parameter is passed by value in the A register.

```
COSINE          FADD  PIOVER2
SINE            STJ   EXIT
                ⟨calculate sine of A register⟩
EXIT            JMP   *
```

Multiple entry points can also be written as separate routines which call a common subroutine to do the common calculations. The JSJ instruction in MIX is sometimes used with multiple entry points,

Multiple exits

Some subroutines function as decision makers, testing some condition. The result of the test requires the execution of different code in the calling routine for each outcome. On the MIX machine, it is possible to effect this by having the subroutine set the condition indicator before it exits. The condition indicator can then be tested in the calling routine after the call. For example, to compare two vectors, P and Q, of length N, we could use a calling sequence

```
JMP   CMPV
CON   P
CON   Q
CON   N
JL    PLTQ          P LESS THAN Q
JG    PGTQ          P GREATER THAN Q
JE    PEQQ          P EQUAL TO Q
```

An alternative to this approach is to pass the addresses of the branches to the subroutine as parameters, and allow it to transfer control directly to the appropriate code. In this case the subroutine does not always transfer to the location following the call, but has multiple exits.

A combination of multiple entry points and multiple exit points can also be used. Suppose we wish to write a generalized search subroutine. The subroutine will search a table for a particular value (passed in the A register) and, if found, return its index in index register 1. An error condition exists if the value is not found. We construct a subroutine with two entry points. One entry point is used for performing a search. The other entry point is used to define where control should transfer to if the value is not found. It requires one parameter, the error address. This entry point sets internal variables so that if the other entry point is called later and the value is not found, the search subroutine will not return to the location after the entry point, but rather return to the error address defined by the call to the other entry point. This routine would have multiple entry points and multiple exits.

Variable number of parameters

Another variation on subroutine calling sequences is to allow a variable number of parameters. For some subroutines this may be very useful, as in a subroutine to calculate the maximum value of its parameters. It would be ridiculous to have to write separate subroutines for finding the maximum of 2, 3, 4, 5, 6, or more parameters. What is needed is one subroutine which allows a variable number of parameters.

Another use for this feature is with subroutines which have a long parameter list, most of which will not change from call to call. In these cases, the parameters are ordered so that the least frequently changing (or those assumed to be the least frequently changing) occur last in the list. Then if the last k parameters are the same as the previous call, they are simply not listed.

To properly effect this, two things are needed. First, the subroutine must keep copies of the previous parameters for possible use in subsequent calls. Second, there must be some way of determining the number of parameters. The first problem is simply a problem for the programmer of the subroutine to look after by storing copies of all parameters in local variables. The second may require the changing of the calling sequence.

Basically, what is done is to add another parameter which indicates the number of parameters in the parameter list. One technique places a special value after the last parameter in the parameter list. For example, in call by reference, all parameters are addresses. On the MIX machine, all addresses must be in the range 0 to 3999. Thus, we can use either a negative number, or a number larger than 3999 to indicate the end of the parameter list. For this approach, a call to a MAX function with parameters 0, X, and Z might be

```
JMP   MAX
CON   =0=              ADDRESS OF LITERAL 0
CON   X
CON   Z
CON   -1               END OF PARAMETER LIST
```

Another approach is to make the first parameter the number of parameters in the list. This has the advantage of being usable for either call by name, call by reference or call by value and careful coding can mean that no extra space is needed for a flag at the end of the list. In the simple case, the calling sequence is simply

```
        JMP   MAX
        CON   3               NUMBER OF PARAMETERS
        CON   =0=
        CON   X
        CON   Z
```

Special coding techniques can be used for the calling sequence which requires the calling routine to jump around the parameters (as opposed to the above where the called routine must calculate the correct return address). In this case the calling sequence is

```
        JMP   MAX
L       JMP   *+4
        CON   =0=
        CON   X
        CON   Z
```

The jump around the parameters has been labeled L to allow us to refer to it easily. The return address, supplied to MAX in the J register, is L. At L we have a JMP to L+4. Thus the number of parameters is the address field (bytes 0:2) of location L minus the address L (minus one). This can be easily computed by the subroutine by

```
MAX         STJ   EXITMAX
            ST1   TEMP1(0:2)
            ST2   TEMP2(0:2)
            LD1   EXITMAX(0:2)  GET L
            LD2   0,1(0:2)      GET ADDRESS OF JUMP
            DEC2  1,1           COMPUTE P = L+P+1 - 1 - L
   *                           I2 HAS NUMBER OF PARAMETERS
```

Subroutines or functions as parameters

In some situations, the variable part of a subroutine is not a variable or constant that is used, but a subroutine or function which is called. This would seem to rule out the use of a subroutine, but in fact a subroutine or function can be passed as a parameter to a subroutine quite easily. Call by reference or call by name are almost always used since what is needed is the address of the function parameter so that it may be called. (Thunks are simply special functions which are passed, by reference, to another subroutine.)

The major problem which arises is in the calling sequence of a function which is passed as a parameter. Since the function is not known by name when it is called, the calling sequences for all functions which may be the actual parameter for the formal parameter must be the same. Often a thunk is created for each function, so that the calling sequence for the function in the subroutine is the simplest possible, with at most one parameter, or more commonly with none. Passing a function as a parameter is a technique sometimes used in programs for numerical analysis.

Reentrant and recursive subroutines

In addition to the different types of parameters (call by value, call by reference, call by name) and different ways of passing them (in registers, globally, in called routine, in calling routine, in a table), there are different types of subroutines. These classifications are made on the basis of the programming techniques which are used, rather than on the subject matter of the subroutine.

One of the easiest to define but sometimes most difficult to implement is the *reentrant* subroutine. A subroutine is reentrant if it is non-self-modifying. Non-self-modifying means that the subroutine never changes. This is also called *pure code*, and requires quite simply that there be no store instructions whose operand is an instruction of the subroutine.

On the MIX computer, reentrant programs are quite difficult to write, since the standard subroutine call mechanism generally involves a STJ instruction to save the return address. Also, the saving and restoring of registers often involves storing index register values directly into the instructions which restore them. Both of these coding practices are invalid for reentrant programming.

How can subroutines be written which never store? They probably cannot be written, but luckily this is not quite the restriction. The restriction is that a subroutine cannot store *in* the subroutine, but it can store *outside* the subroutine. Typically, what is done is that the calling routine is required to pass, as a parameter, by reference, in one of the index registers, a large array which can be used by the reentrant subroutine for the temporary storage of data, return addresses and old register values. This allows the storage of variables outside the subroutine itself, meaning that the subroutine itself can be pure code.

Reentrant routines are useful in relatively rare circumstances. One situation where they are useful is in a computer system with multiple CPUs. Each CPU would have its own ALU, control unit, and registers, but they may share memory. To avoid having two copies of the same program, that program can be written as a reentrant program. Each CPU can execute the same code, at the same time, but with different work areas pointed at by their different register sets.

By analogy, consider a program to be like a cookbook. When a cook uses a recipe, he may need to take notes about what is done and at what time (local variables). If he writes these in the margins of the book, then his notes may confuse another cook trying to use the same recipe at the same time, especially if that cook is taking her own notes by erasing the first cooks notes and writing her own in the same place. For the cooks to be able to share the cookbook, the cookbook must be reentrant, with all notes being kept on a separate piece of paper for each cook.

Similarly, each CPU can execute the same subroutine or program only if all variables are kept in separate work areas and the code is pure and reentrant.

A less stringent requirement for a subroutine is *serial reentrancy*. A subroutine is serially reentrant if it works correctly whenever it is executed, perhaps by multiple processors, so that each processor executes the subroutine completely before the next processor starts executing it. That is, as long as only one processor at a time is executing the code, it works correctly. In terms of our cook/cookbook analogy, this means that several cooks can use the same cookbook but only one can use it at a time. Obviously, a cook can make notes in the cookbook, as long as either they are erased before she finishes with the cookbook and gives it to another cook, or the next cook erases them before he starts.

A serially reentrant subroutine can store information in local variables in a subroutine, as long as these local variables are properly initialized before the subroutine is executed again. Thus the STJ method of using the return address is acceptable, since the next time the subroutine is called that location will be reset properly for the call.

A simple example of a nonserially reentrant program is the following routine to return the A register as the sum of the array whose base address is in index register I1 and whose length is in index register I2.

```
TOTAL           CON    0
SUM             STJ    EXITSUM
LOOP            LDA    TOTAL
                ADD    -1,1:2
                STA    TOTAL
                DEC2   1
                J2P    LOOP
                LDA    TOTAL
EXITSUM         JMP    *
```

Ignore for the moment that this is rather inefficient code. This subroutine will work correctly the first time. But notice that the second time, the value returned will be the sum of the array plus the sum of the first array; the third time, the sum will be the sum of all three, and so on. The variable TOTAL is not being reset back to zero before the subroutine is executed again. Thus this subroutine is not serially reentrant. It can be made serially reentrant by including STZ TOTAL either after the STJ or before the JMP *.

Another type of subroutine is the *recursive* subroutine. A recursive subroutine is a subroutine which may call itself. Recursive subroutines are almost never written in assembly language and cannot be written even in some higher-level languages, such as Fortran. The problem is of course that the second call on the subroutine may clobber the return address passed to the subroutine by the first call, and hence the subroutine will never know how to return to the first call. Recursive subroutines are often written as reentrant subroutines and use a stack to hold return addresses and local variables.

Coroutines

Coroutines are another special type of subroutine, or rather a subroutine is a special type of coroutine. A called and calling routine exist in a specific relationship. The calling routine calls the called routine and the called routine returns control to the calling routine. The called routine is, in some sense, subservient to the calling routine. Hence the name *sub*routine.

A coroutine or a set of coroutines do not restrict themselves to a calling-called relationship but rather work more as equals. A coroutine does not simply call another coroutine, but also supplies a return address to which the called coroutine should return. When the called coroutine returns, it also passes an address which is where it should be resumed next. Thus each coroutine is equal, calling the other where it left off and specifying the address where it should be resumed.

For MIX, coroutines are quite easy to implement. A restart address is associated with each coroutine. A coroutine call involves resetting the coroutine restart address for the current coroutine and then jumping, indirectly through the restart address, to the next coroutine.

Although coroutines have their advantages, they seem not to have been adopted by assembly language programmers.

6.6 SUMMARY

Subroutines are a very important programming technique, especially for assembly language programmers. Subroutines allow redundant code to be grouped together and written only once, saving computer memory and programming time. Most subroutines require parameters to be passed to them, and many methods are used to do so. Parameters can be passed in registers, in global variables, in special parameter areas before the entry point or after the call, or in a table. The parameters themselves may be call by value, call by reference, or call by name, requiring that the value of, the address of, or the address of a thunk for, respectively, the parameter be passed.

Subroutines can save space but always require more time to execute than simply writing out the code repetitively. Subroutines may have multiple entry points or multiple exit points or both. The address of a subroutine or function can even be passed as a parameter to another subroutine.

Subroutines can be reentrant, serially reentrant, recursive, or none of these. Coroutines are programming structures related to subroutines.

Subroutine programming techniques have developed over the years and are part of the common knowledge of programmers. Knuth (1968) has a treatment of subroutines and coroutines, as do the books by Gear (1974) and Stone and Siewiorek (1975). The definition of thunks is due to Ingermann (1961), while coroutines are generally credited to Conway (1963).

EXERCISES

a. Give two reasons for writing subroutines.

b. What is a calling sequence?

c. Give one reason to save registers in the calling routine and one reason to save registers in the called routine.

d. Why does the J register exist?

e. List five methods of passing parameters for call by reference parameters.

f. The following code has been proposed as a simple subroutine in MIXAL. Comment on its probable usefulness, with reasons.

```
        ...                 SUB     LDA   0,1
        ENT1   X                   ...
        ENT2   Y                   STA   0,2
        JMP    SUB                 JMP   RTN
RTN     ...
```

g. Write a subroutine which will input the address of an array in I1 and the length of the array in I2, and produce in the A register, the minimum value of the array, and in I1 the address of that element.

h. Define call by value, call by reference, and call by name.

i. Suppose that the only parameters which are allowed to be passed to a subroutine are simple variables; no expressions, constants, arrays, array elements, and so on. It is desired to use the copy rule. Which of the calling methods can be used to implement the copy rule correctly?

j. In a Fortran-like language, suppose we had the program segment

```
I = 1
J = 2
A(1) = 100
A(2) = 0
CALL SUB (I,J,A(I), A(J))
```

and subroutine SUB is defined as

```
SUBROUTINE SUB (A,B,C,D)
A = B
C = D
RETURN
END
```

What is the value of I, J, A(1), and A(2) after the subroutine has been executed, assuming that parameters were passed by call by value, call by reference, and call by name?

k. Why are there thunks?

l. Explain briefly, but clearly, the terms: self-modifying code, serially reentrant, recursive, coroutines, pure code, reentrant.

m. A recursive subroutine normally needs what kind of a data structure?

n. Is a reentrant subroutine always serially reentrant? Is it always pure code? Is it position independent? Must it be recursive?

o. Draw a Venn diagram showing the relationships between the sets of subroutines which are recursive, serially reentrant, self-modifying, position independent, coroutines, reentrant, and pure.

p. What is the advantage of using pure procedures on a computer that is used by many people at the same time?

7

LOADERS
AND LINKERS

With the programming techniques which have been presented in Chapters 4, 5, and 6 fully understood, you have the basic information needed to program the MIX computer. In the next few chapters, we change our focus somewhat to consider not how to program the MIX machine, but rather its operation in normal use. The MIX computer, like all computers, is merely a simple electronic machine which can do no more than execute the simple instructions in its instruction set, although at very high speed. To make the computer useful, however, requires software. It is the software, the programs, which allows the computer to perform its many and varied functions.

Remember that all programs must be in the main memory of the computer, in machine language, in order for them to be executed. It is difficult to program in machine language, and so a number of programs have been written to ease the programming problem by allowing programs to be written in assembly or higher-level language, and then translated by the computer into the machine language required for execution.

We examine two of these programs in great detail: loaders and assemblers. These are considered for two reasons: first, they are widely used as tools for programming, and second, the techniques used in them are illustrative of the approaches taken in the writing of other system programs. We consider loaders here, and assemblers in Chapter 8. This order is used because loaders are much simpler than assemblers, although in typical usage the assembler is used first.

Let us briefly review the process of programming a computer. The programmer first conceives of a solution to the problem at hand and defines his solution in some English-like procedural manner. This may be in written form or strictly mental notes. Then the program is written. Let us assume the program is written in MIXAL. Now at this point the program exists in a well-defined representation. However, it cannot be executed by the computer because it is in the wrong representation. To be executed it must be in machine language in memory, not on cards in assembly language. Thus it must be translated into the correct form. A part of this translation is done by the assembler. The assembler could translate the assembly language into machine language and put it in memory for execution except for one problem: the assembler.

The assembler is a program. Like any other program, when it is being executed it resides in machine language in memory. The assembler is also a very large program. While assembling, it takes up almost all of available memory. The problem that this causes is that it leaves no place in memory into which the assembled program can be put. Hence, the assembler cannot both translate from assembly language to machine language and put the resulting program in memory.

The solution to this problem is quite simple. The assembler translates the assembly language into machine language and puts the resulting program on a secondary storage device, like a tape, drum, or disk. Then, when the assembler is finished with the assembly task, a separate program is called which does nothing but read the program into memory. This second program is called a *loader*. A loader reads (loads) a program from an input device into memory for execution.

There are several advantages to this scheme (in addition to the fact that it is

FIGURE 7.1   An input program is translated by the assembler from a source program into an object program (on tape), which is loaded into memory by the loader for execution.

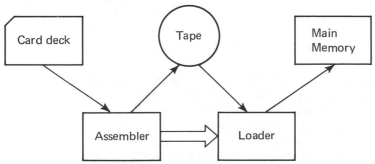

necessary). The main advantage is that to execute a program it is no longer necessary to have an assembly language version of the program and reassemble it every time it is to be executed. Instead, it is only necessary to save the output of the assembler and execute the loader to load it into memory for execution. Thus, if for example the assembler writes the machine language out on magnetic tape, the reel of tape can be dismounted and stored for an indefinite period of time before execution. It can also be executed repetitively by simply mounting the tape and executing the loader to reload the same program. For programs which are run over and over, this can result in substantial savings in computer time. Most computers have methods of loading from punched cards or punched paper tape in addition to magnetic tape, drum, or disk.

There are several different types of loaders. The simplest is an *absolute loader*. By making the loader more sophisticated, more complex functions can be done by the loader, resulting in even better utilization of the computer. We consider the absolute loader first, and then based on some problems in the use of the absolute loader, discuss more sophisticated loaders.

7.1 ABSOLUTE LOADERS

An absolute loader is the simplest of loaders. Its function is simply to take the output of the assembler and load it into memory. The output of the assembler can be stored on any machine-readable form of storage, but most commonly it is stored on punched cards or magnetic tape, disk, or drum.

Absolute load format

The input to an absolute loader is generally not quite in machine language. Machine language is really defined only in terms of a program in memory. The input is in *loader format*, a form of representation for a program which is so close to machine language that the loader need do nothing more than store the program in the appropriate memory locations.

How does the loader know which addresses the instructions (and data) should be loaded into? The assembler is told by ORIG statements written by the programmer, and this information must be passed on to the loader by the assembler. Thus the input to the loader must consist of two pieces of information: the instruction or data to be loaded, and the address where it should be loaded.

In addition, the loader will need to know when to stop loading, so we need some kind of an end-of-file marker at the end of the loader input. When the loader stops, it should transfer control to the newly loaded program. This means that a starting address is also needed.

All of these considerations lead to the following statement of the input to an absolute loader: a sequence of pairs of addresses and the values to be loaded

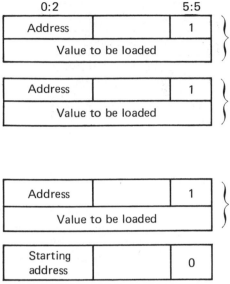

FIGURE 7.2 A simple format for the output of a translator for input to the loader. Each word in memory requires two words, one for the address and one for the value to be loaded.

into those addresses, followed by a starting address. The loader loads the values into the addresses until the starting address is reached, at which point it jumps to the starting address. This defines the basic structure of the loader program, and indicates what format the loader input should be in.

One approach would be to use two words for each word to be loaded by the loader. The first word contains the address where the value is to be loaded and the second contains the value to be loaded. Thus loader input would be a sequence of these pairs. A flag is needed to signal the end. We could use the sign bit to signal the end by setting it to "+" for the address/value pairs and "−" for the starting address (which comes at the end). However, if the address were zero, it would be difficult to distinguish a positive sign from a negative sign, so instead let us put the address in bytes 0:2 and use byte 5 to signal an address/ value pair (byte 5 = 1) or the starting address (byte 5 = 0). Notice that by putting the address in bytes 0:2, it may be possible to use indirect addressing to use the address.

Our load format can thus be as diagrammed in Figure 7.2. This load format certainly supplies the loader with all the information it needs to load. However, it is probably not very efficient about it. Consider the sequence of addresses where words should be loaded. Suppose the loader has just finished loading a word into location 1000. What is the most likely address for the next load? Probably 1001. And after 1001? Probably 1002. And so on. Most of the code and data to be loaded will be placed in sequential locations in memory. The only reason why this

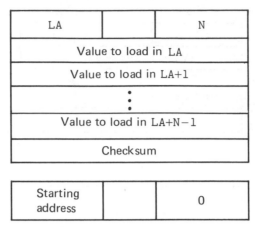

FIGURE 7.3   An alternative format for loader input which has better utilization of memory. Many values can be loaded in sequential memory locations with only one header word.

would not occur would be due to ORIG statements in the assembly language program, or the end of the program.

We can take advantage of this to reduce the size of our loader format for a given program. Instead of giving one load address, LA, and one value to be stored at location LA, we give one load address, LA, a number, N, and N values to be loaded into locations LA, LA+1, LA+2, . . . , LA+N−1. Each of these will be called a *loader record*. The load address and number of words will be the first word of the loader record, and will be followed by the values to be stored, one per word for the next N words. The starting address will still be the last value and will be indicated by an N of 0.

This revised format reduces the size of our loader image considerably. In the old loader format, we had one word of overhead for every value to be loaded. With our new format, we have only one word of overhead per loader record. If loader records average 100 words, then out of 100 words of loader format we have 99 words to load, while with the old format we have only 50 words.

The amount of memory needed to store a program in loader format is very important for two reasons. One is that the less efficient loader formats will take more space on the storage media. The other is that loading is a very I/O-bound process; virtually no computation is needed. Thus, reducing the size of the input reduces the amount which the loader must read, and hence the amount of time to load.

Error checking

All programs should be correct, and this is especially true for systems programs. Systems programs are used by many computer users, not just by the programmer who writes them. Thus errors in systems programs may result in expensive malfunctions of the computer which cost dearly in both time and money (and sometimes life). It is therefore wise to take a very conservative approach to writing systems programs.

Absolute loaders are relatively simple programs and hence most of the errors which may occur are limited to errors in the input to the loader. The input to the loader is normally produced as the output of an assembler, compiler, or other program, but even so, it may have errors. These errors must be checked for and appropriate steps taken if they are discovered.

What are appropriate steps? Almost all loader errors will result in being unable to correctly load the program. Hence in the case of loader errors, it would seem most reasonable to halt the loading process, after printing an appropriate error message.

There are two types of errors which can occur in loader input. One is the result of incorrect generation by the program which produces the loader input, and the other is the result of incorrect storage or transmission by the I/O devices involved. The errors of the first type which could occur would consist mainly of illegal load addresses or illegal values of N. The load address, LA, being an address, should obviously be greater than or equal to zero and less than 4000. Similarly, the number of values to be loaded, N, should be greater than or equal to zero, and less than or equal to 4000. In addition, since the last value loaded will be loaded at address $LA+N-1$, this address must be less than 4000 also. Thus we have the following requirements:

$$0 \leq LA < 4000,$$
$$0 \leq N \leq 4000,$$
$$LA+N-1 < 4000$$

Notice that if $N = 0$, then LA is the starting address and the above restrictions still hold. It is possible for the starting address to be zero, so that $LA+N-1$ would be -1, but no value is loaded in this case anyway.

In fact, the restrictions on addresses must be even stronger. Certainly it is the case that each address must be a legitimate machine address, but in addition, we cannot allow a load address or start address which would be an address in the loader either. The loader is a program and resides in memory. Since its code must remain correct in order for its function to be correctly carried out, we must prevent user code from being loaded into those locations which the loader occupies.

This may cause a problem, since this limits the size of user programs. The limitation is in fact quite reasonable. An absolute loader is quite small, occupying less than several hundred words. Thus most of memory is available for user programs. If all of memory is needed by a program, then it may be possible to overlay the loader with a large array, table, or I/O buffer whose initial value is unimportant. There are few programs that consist of 4000 words of solid code.

To allow the loader to stay out of the way of most user programs, it is generally written to occupy the last locations of memory. Most programmers write their programs to start at location 0. Thus placing the loader in high core means that it will seldom interfere with the user program. This effectively changes the limit 4000 in the above inequalities to 4000 − (size of the loader).

The second kind of error which can occur is an error by the I/O devices involved in the output, storage, and input of the loader input. It is not unknown for paper tape readers, or card readers, to misread a hole as a nonhole or vice versa, or to shift the position of a hole. Magnetic tape is generally more immune to this sort of problem due to parity checks, but still failures are known to have occurred. The errors may even occur in the CPU rather than in the I/O devices or in the electronics between the two devices.

Errors caused by storage or transmission of the loader input may cause illegal addresses or counts to be used, and hence would be detected by the above checks. However, it is more likely that they will occur in the values to be stored in memory, and hence be unnoticed, until the loaded program executes the incorrect instruction. Any possible number is permissible for the values to be loaded, and so no simple check (such as a range check) can be put on them to catch I/O errors.

The method most commonly used to detect I/O errors in loader input is a *checksum*. The idea of a checksum is similar to the idea of parity. A checksum is computed and stored by the assembler with each block of loader input. The computation of a checksum is quite easy: the sum of the entire block is computed (ignoring overflows). This sum (the checksum) is generally stored as the last word of the loader record. When the block is read back in, the checksum is computed on the input and compared with the stored checksum. If they match, no error has occurred; if they do not match, a *checksum error* has occurred.

To show that a checksum helps to prevent errors, assume that any one value changes. Then the sum of the values changes and so the stored checksum will not match a checksum which is computed when the block is read back in. Thus the error is detected. For an error to be undetected, multiple changes will need to occur in such a way that the arithmetic sum is unchanged; this is very unlikely.

A checksum is strictly an error detection technique. If a checksum error occurs, it is not possible to know which word (or words) have changed, or from what. In order to correct the error, it is necessary to go back to the original assembly language source and reassemble, producing new (and hopefully correct) input values for the loader.

An absolute loader

With all of the considerations of the above sections on loader formats and error checking, we can now turn to writing the code for an absolute loader. Our general algorithm is

1. Fetch the first word of a block and define N, the number of words in the block, as the value in bytes 4:5, and LA, the load address, as the value in bytes 0:2. Check for correct values of N and LA.

2. If N = 0, then go to 3. Otherwise, initialize the checksum value, and move the next N words to LA, LA+1, . . . , LA+N−1. As each word is moved, add it to the checksum value. When the entire block of N words has been loaded, compare the computed checksum with the stored checksum. Then return to step 1 for another block.

3. Since N = 0, LA is the starting address. Begin execution by jumping to the starting address.

If any errors are detected, an appropriate error message should be printed and the loader halted.

An absolute loader is heavily I/O-bound and so double buffering should be used. Also, the loader format is device independent and can be used with any device which can store words. Thus, for modularity we use a subroutine to properly handle all I/O. The subroutine, whenever it is called, returns the next word of the loader input. Thus, if a different I/O device is used, only this one subroutine need be changed. The subroutine will return the next word in the A register.

For example, if input were from magnetic tape, the input subroutine could be

```
*
*               DATA FOR INPUT SUBROUTINE
*
TAPE        EQU   0           DEVICE NUMBER
ADDR        ORIG  *+1         ADDRESS OF NEXT WORD TO RETURN
COUNT       CON   0           COUNT OF NUMBER OF WORDS
BUF1        ORIG  *+100          BUFFERS FOR
BUF2        ORIG  *+100              DOUBLE BUFFERING
INPUTBUF    CON   BUF1        BUFFER TO READ INTO
USINGBUF    CON   BUF2        BUFFER TO USE
*
*
*               INPUT SUBROUTINE FOR MAGNETIC TAPE.
*               100 WORD PHYSICAL RECORDS ARE READ FROM
*               TAPE AND RETURNED TO THE LOADER ONE WORD
*               AT A TIME, IN A REGISTER. DOUBLE BUFFERING
*               IS USED. NO REGISTERS, OTHER THAN A, ARE
*               CHANGED.
*
*               FIRST IN BUF1(TAPE) SHOULD BE EXECUTED IN MAIN
*               PROGRAM TO START DOUBLE BUFFERING.
*
*
```

```
INPUT           STJ   EXITINPUT
                ST1   TEMP1(0:2)
                ST2   TEMP2(0:2)   SAVE REGISTERS
*
                LD1   COUNT        CHECK IF WORDS LEFT IN BUFFER
                J1P   RETURNWORD
*
*               WORDS IN USINGBUF ALL GONE. INPUT MORE INTO
*               THAT BUFFER, AND SWITCH BUFFER POINTERS.
*               ALSO RESET COUNT AND ADDRESS FOR RETURN WORDS.
*
                LD1   USINGBUF
                IN    0,1(TAPE)    READ NEW BLOCK
                LD2   INPUTBUF
                ST2   USINGBUF     SWITCH BUFFER POINTERS
                ST2   ADDR
                ST1   INPUTBUF     BUFFER BEING INPUT TO
                ENT1  100          COUNTER
*
*               RETURN THE NEXT WORD.
*               ADDRESS IN I2, COUNT IN I1
*
RETURNWORD      LD2   ADDR         ADDRESS POINTER FOR NEXT WORD
                LDA   0,2
                INC2  1            SET FOR NEXT WORD
                ST2   ADDR
                DEC1  1            AND DECREMENT COUNTER
                ST1   COUNT
*
TEMP2           ENT2  *
TEMP1           ENT1  *
EXITINPUT       JMP   *
```

This should be easily written following the techniques of Chapter 5.

The loader itself is now very straightforward coding. The major coding is actually error checking and messages.

```
LP              EQU   18
*
                ORIG  3700
FIRST           CON   *
*
*
```

```
*                 DATA AND VARIABLES FOR LOADER
*
CHKSUM            ORIG *+1          FOR CHECKSUM COMPUTATION
HEADER            ORIG *+1          HEADER FOR ERRORS
*
*                 ERROR MESSAGE PRINTING
*
CHKMSG            ALF   CHECK
                  ALF   SUM E
                  ALF   RROR
HDRMSG            ALF   ERROR
                  ALF    IN H
                  ALF   EADER
*
*
ERRORLINE         ALF   ***
ERRORMSG          ORIG *+3          SPACE FOR MESSAGE
                  ALF
                  ALF     BLO
                  ALF   CK =
ERRORBLK          ORIG *+1
                  ALF
                  ALF    HEAD
                  ALF   ER =
ERRORLA           ORIG *+1          LOAD ADDRESS
                  ALF   (LA),
                  ALF
ERRORN            ORIG *+1          NUMBER OF WORDS
                  ALF   (N)
                  ORIG *+8
*
*
*                 AN ABSOLUTE LOADER FOR A MIX MACHINE
*
*                 LOADER INPUT IS ASSUMED TO BE ON TAPE 0 AS A
*                 SEQUENCE OF BLOCKS. THE FIRST WORD OF EACH
*                 BLOCK IS A HEADER, CONTAINING THE NUMBER OF
*                 WORDS TO BE LOADED (N), AND THEIR LOAD
*                 ADDRESS (LA), FOLLOWED BY THE WORDS TO
*                 BE LOADED AND A CHECKSUM. AN EMPTY BLOCK
*                 (N = 0) MEANS THAT LA IS THE STARTING ADDRESS.
*
*
```

```
*               INITIALIZATION
*
LOADER          IN    BUF1(TAPE)   START DOUBLE BUFFERING
                ENT3  0            BLOCK COUNTER
*
*               START NEXT BLOCK. INPUT LOAD ADDRESS AND
*               NUMBER OF WORDS. INITIALIZE CHECKSUM.
*               INCREMENT BLOCK NUMBER STORED IN I3.
*
NEXTBLOCK       JMP   INPUT
                STA   CHKSUM       INITIAL CHECKSUM VALUE
                STA   HEADER       SAVE HEADER FOR POSSIBLE ERROR
                INC3  1
*
*               USE I1 FOR LOAD ADDRESS
*               AND I2 FOR NUMBER OF WORDS
*
                LD1   HEADER(0:2)
                LD2   HEADER(4:5)
                J1N   HDRERROR     CHECK FOR 0 ≤ LA
                CMP1  FIRST        AND LA < LOADER
                JGE   HDRERROR
*
                ENTA  -1,2         N-1
                INCA  0,1          LA+N-1
                CMPA  FIRST
                JGE   HDRERROR
*
                J2Z   0,1          IF N=0, I1 IS START ADDRESS
*
*               LOAD THE NEXT N WORDS INTO LA, LA+1, ...
*               COMPUTE THE CHECKSUM AS WE GO.
*
LOADLOOP        JMP   INPUT        GET WORD
                STA   0,1          LOAD INTO MEMORY
                INC1  1
                ADD   CHKSUM
                STA   CHKSUM
                DEC2  1
                J2P   LOADLOOP     CONTINUE FOR MORE WORDS
*
*               BLOCK IS LOADED. GET CHECKSUM AND COMPARE
*
                JMP   INPUT
```

```
                CMPA   CHKSUM
                JE     NEXTBLOCK
*
*               ERROR HANDLING. PRINT MESSAGE AND HALT
*
CHKSUMERR       ENT2   CHKMSG      CHECKSUM ERROR
                JMP    ERROR       PRINT AND HALT ROUTINE
*
HDRERROR        ENT2   HDRMSG      HEADER ERROR
*
                JMP    ERROR       FALL THROUGH TO ERROR ROUTINE
*
*               ERROR ROUTINE. FORMAT ERROR MESSAGE WITH
*               MESSAGE (ADDRESS IN I2), BLOCK NUMBER (IN I3),
*               LA AND N (FROM HEADER). PRINT AND HALT.
*
ERROR           ENT1   ERRORMSG
                MOVE   0,2(3)      MESSAGES OF 3 WORDS
                ENTA   0,3         BLOCK NUMBER
                CHAR
                STX    ERRORBLK
                LDA    HEADER(0:2)
                CHAR
                STX    ERRORLA(2:5)
                LDA    HEADER(4:5) NUMBER N
                CHAR
                STX    ERRORN(2:5)
                OUT    ERRORLINE(LP) PRINT LINE
                HLT
*
                END    LOADER
```

   Some minor points still need to be considered for the assembly of the loader. The loader should be ORIGed to the end of memory, but where is that? There are two ways to tell. One is to count the number of words used by the loader, by hand. The other is to submit the program to the assembler and then look at the output listing. Either way, we can then compute the length of the loader and the proper ORIG address.

   A more important problem is testing the loader. The loader is one of the most often used programs in the system and because of this should be very carefully coded. It is wise to both examine the written code by hand for possible errors and also to carefully test the code. A special driver program should be written to produce tapes for testing the loader. These test tapes should include both legitimate loader input and all possible error cases. The performance of the loader should be checked for both correctness, speed, and usefulness of error messages.

7.2 RELOCATABLE LOADERS

Absolute loaders have a number of advantages: they are small, fast and simple. But they have a number of disadvantages, too. The major problem deals with the need to assemble an entire program all at once. Since the addresses for the program are determined at assembly time, the entire program must be assembled at one time in order for proper addresses to be assigned to the different parts. This means that a small change to one subroutine requires reassembly of the entire program. Also, standard subroutines, which might be kept in a library of useful subroutines and functions, must be physically copied and added to each program which uses them.

There is one possible alternative to constant reassembly of unchanged subroutines. Given an estimate of the lengths of the subroutines involved, we can ORIG each subroutine separately, and assemble each one individually. Then we can load the subroutines into their predefined locations by feeding the separate loader files into the loader. A change in a single subroutine requires reassembly of only that subroutine and a new loader file to be loaded with the others which need not be reassembled.

The approach can work, but only with care, foresight, and a lot of luck. The problem is in knowing how big each subroutine will be. Since the subroutines cannot be allowed to overlap, we must not estimate too little, so to be safe, we must overestimate. This results in wasted, unused space between the subroutines. Also, if a subroutine needs changing it may grow in size. This may result in it overlapping the subroutine which follows it in memory, which would require reassembly of that routine with a different ORIG statement, but this might cause that subroutine to overlap the subroutine following it, and so forth.

For library subroutines, this can be even a greater problem. At the time that the library routines are written, it is nearly impossible to decide where they should go in memory. The subroutine should be placed in memory so that it does not overlap any other subroutine, user-written or library, which may be in memory at the same time, and so that little memory is wasted between routines. For any sizable collection of subroutines, this is a nearly impossible task.

The problem here is one of *binding time*. Remember that one of the purposes of assembly language is to allow symbolic addresses to be used. These symbolic addresses are being *bound* to physical addresses at assembly time. To bind an address is simply to associate it with a physical memory location. The assembler is, using ORIG statements and its symbol table, assigning physical addresses to symbolic addresses. But this negates one of the possible benefits of assembly language, the ability of the assembly language programmer to ignore physical machine addresses. The binding of symbolic addresses to physical addresses is really important only when the program is actually loaded into memory. Thus, we would like to delay address binding until load time.

A *relocatable loader* is a loader which allows this delay of binding time. A relocatable loader accepts as input a sequence of segments, each in a special relocatable load format, and loads these segments into memory. The addresses into which segments are loaded are determined by the relocatable loader, not by the assembler or the programmer.

Each segment is a subroutine, function, main program, block of global data, or some similar set of memory locations which the programmer wishes to group together. Segments are loaded into memory one after the other, to use as little space as possible. The relocatable load format is defined so that separate segments can be assembled or compiled separately and combined at load time.

Relocation

The relocation implied in the name "relocatable loader" refers to the fact that on two separate loads, the same segment can be loaded into two different locations in memory. If any of the segments which are loaded into memory before a segment change in size due to recoding and reassembly between the two loads, then the addresses in memory into which the segment is loaded will change by the same amount.

FIGURE 7.4 An example of the use of a relocatable loader to load three separately assembled segments into memory.

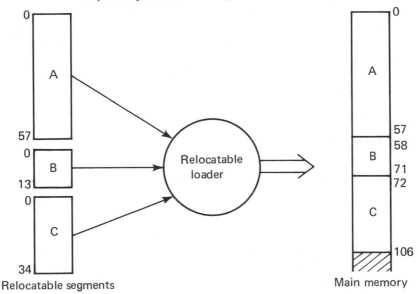

Relocatable segments

Main memory

How can this be done? Consider the following simple program

```
BEGIN       LD2    LENGTH
LOOP        IN     BUFFER(16)
            OUT    BUFFER(18)
            DEC2   1
            J2P    LOOP
            HLT
LENGTH      CON    10
BUFFER      ORIG   *+24
            END    BEGIN
```

This program has four symbols, BEGIN, LOOP, LENGTH, and BUFFER. If the program were to be loaded into memory starting at location 0, then the values of these symbols would be 0, 1, 6, and 7, respectively. If the starting address were 1000, the values of the symbols would be 1000, 1001, 1006, and 1007; if the base address were 1976, the values would be 1976, 1977, 1982, and 1983. In all cases, the addresses, for a base BASE, would be BASE+0, BASE+1, BASE+6, and BASE+7. Thus, to relocate the program from starting at an address BASE to starting at an address NEWBASE merely involves adding NEWBASE − BASE to the values of all of the symbols. If the assembler would produce all code as if it had a base of 0, then relocating this code would involve only adding the correct base.

Knowing this, how does a change in the values of the symbols affect the code generated by the assembler? The symbols which refer to addresses are used in the address field of an instruction. Thus, changing the value of a symbol, as a result of changing the base address for the program, means changing the address field of any instruction which refers to an address in the program.

For our sample program above, the addresses generated, assuming that the program starts at zero, would be

		code	*address generated*
BEGIN	LD2	LENGTH	6
LOOP	IN	BUFFER(16)	7
	OUT	BUFFER(18)	7
	DEC2	1	1
	J2P	LOOP	1
	HLT		0
LENGTH	CON	10	10
BUFFER	ORIG	*+24	
	END	BEGIN	0

If we were to start the program at 1000, the addresses would be

	code	address generated
	code	*address generated*
BEGIN	LD2 LENGTH	1006
LOOP	IN BUFFER(16)	1007
	OUT BUFFER(18)	1007
	DEC2 1	1
	J2P LOOP	1001
	HLT	0
LENGTH	CON 10	10
BUFFER	ORIG *+24	
	END BEGIN	1000

Notice that not all of the address fields changed. Only those address fields whose contents were defined in terms of relocatable symbols changed. Not all symbols are relocatable. For example, if we had included some symbolic constants such as

```
CR          EQU   16
LP          EQU   18
N           EQU   10
```

and used them as

```
            IN    BUFFER(CR)
            OUT   BUFFER(LP)
LENGTH      CON   N
```

the values of the fields defined by these absolute symbols would not change. Thus, we see that in a relocatable program, there are two types of symbols, relocatable and absolute. Later a third type, external symbols, will be added to this list.

The dichotomy between absolute and relocatable symbols means that when a program is loaded into memory with a base other than zero, some, but not all, of the address fields must be changed by addition of the correct base address. These addresses must be distinguished in some manner, so that the loader can correctly modify them during loading. Various techniques for this are used, and we discuss them shortly. The addresses used in the program when assembled are relocatable or *relative* addresses, since they are only the addresses relative to the base address.

The general flow of a relocatable loader can now be defined. A variable, LOADBASE, stores the value of the base address for the segment currently being loaded. As that segment is loaded, all relative addresses are modified by the addition of the base address. When the segment is loaded, LOADBASE is increased by the length of the segment to be ready for use as the base address of the next segment. Thus segments are loaded into memory one after another, with no overlap and no wasted space, just as desired.

Linking

At this point we might pause a moment to consider the usefulness of a relocatable loader. The objective is to allow separate subroutines and functions to be prepared and assembled separately and loaded together. The relocatable loader does this, but it provides no means for one subroutine to call another. Consider the three assembly statements for calling a subroutine SUM with two parameters

```
ENT1   ARRAY
ENT2   10
JMP    SUM
```

where ARRAY ORIG *+10 occurs elsewhere in the routine with the above code. The address of the ENT1 ARRAY instruction is relative and the assembler can produce the offset from the base of the routine for the loader. The loader can add the correct base address for this routine to correctly modify it. The ENT2 10 instruction has an absolute address field which requires no modification. But what about the JMP SUM instruction? Its address is not absolute; neither is it relative to the calling routine. It is *external* to that segment; it is in another segment somewhere.

Thus there are three types of addresses in a relocatable program: absolute, relative, and external. The treatment of absolute and relative addresses has already been discussed. Let us now consider externals. An external symbol in one segment must be an *entry point* in some other segment. For example, the subroutine name SUM used above as an external is an entry point in a separate segment. The loader must link up the reference to the external symbol SUM with the definition of the entry point SUM in a separate segment. The linking means that the address of SUM, in its segment, must be stored in the address field of the instruction which referenced SUM as an external, in its segment. This linking function is performed by a *linking loader*, or simply, a *linker*. Since it makes no sense to relocate programs in memory unless they have the ability to reference each other (which is what linking allows), most relocatable loaders are *relocatable linking loaders*. We follow standard practice by referring to a relocatable linking loader as a relocatable loader.

Relocatable assembly language

The changes that are necessary for use of a relocatable loader have implications for the assembly language which produces the input for the loader. The MIXAL language which is used on the MIX computer is an absolute assembly language; it is used in connection with an assembler which produces loader input for an absolute loader. It has no provisions for generating relocatable loader code. A relocatable MIXAL would vary in several respects.

One variation would be in the ORIG statement; it would be allowed in only limited ways, if at all. A programmer would no longer be able to ORIG her code to an arbitrary absolute address. The only uses which would be permitted would be relative ORIGs, like ORIG *+10, ORIG N*2+*, and so forth. Many assemblers thus replace the ORIG statement with a BSS statement. The BSS statement stands for "Block Storage Save" and takes one expression in its operand field. A BSS 10 is identical to an ORIG 10+*, a BSS N*2 to an ORIG N*2+*, and so on.

Another change is in allowed address expressions. Each symbol is either absolute or relocatable. Expressions can also be typed as absolute or relocatable. An absolute symbol is an absolute expression, and a relocatable symbol is a relocatable expression. The sum, difference, product, and quotient of absolute expressions are absolute expressions. Relocatable expressions are more difficult to define. A relocatable expression is one whose final value depends upon the base address in the same way as a relocatable symbol. The binding from relocatable to absolute should be a simple addition of a base. Let R be a relocatable symbol or expression, and let A be an absolute symbol, constant, or expression. Then the expressions, R+A, R−A, and A+R are relocatable. An expression like R−R is absolute. Expressions like R+R, R*R, R/R, A*R, or R/A are neither relocatable nor absolute and hence are not allowed.

Notice that either R or A can be an expression, and so expressions like R−R−A+R+A−R+R are allowed (and are relocatable). To determine if an expression is either relocatable or absolute, replace all relocatable symbols by R and all absolute symbols by A. Then check that no relocatable symbols are involved in multiplications or divisions. Finally combine subexpressions such as R+A, A+R, R−A and substitute with R, and A+A, A−A, A/A, A*A, and R−R, substituting with an A until the entire expression is reduced as far as possible. If the result is either R or A, the expression is valid and of the indicated type; otherwise it is illegal.

One other change is concerned with externals and entry points. To the assembler of a segment, any reference to an external will appear to be a reference to an undefined symbol, which is not what is meant. One possible approach to this would be to treat all undefined symbols as externals, but this would result in truly undefined symbols being treated incorrectly. Thus a new pseudo-instruction is introduced which is used to notify the assembler that a symbol is meant to be an external symbol, not an undefined one. This new pseudo-instruction, EXT, could be of the form

        EXT   ⟨list of external symbols⟩

or alternatively

    ⟨symbol⟩   EXT   ⟨operand field ignored⟩

Many assemblers require external symbols to be declared as such before their first use in the segment and often place restrictions on the use of externals in address expressions, allowing only an external by itself, or plus or minus an absolute expression.

Corresponding to the externals are entry points and they are treated in much the same way. In order for the loader to correctly link externals with the corresponding entry point, the loader must know where the entry points are. Thus assembly languages often include an entry point declaration pseudo-instruction ENT. The form of this pseudo instruction is often

ENT   ⟨list of entry point symbols⟩

Any symbol listed in an ENT pseudo-instruction must be defined as a relocatable symbol elsewhere in the segment, and can then be used by the loader for linking.

In addition to these programmer-visible changes in assembly language programs, the assembler itself must also produce relocatable, not absolute, loader code.

Relocatable load format

Many different formats can be used for relocatable loader input and each of the formats may have its own advantages and disadvantages. The basic information which must be provided by the assembler to the loader is,

1.   For each segment, its length, its block of instructions and data, and an indication of the end of the segment.
2.   For each code word, an indication of whether its address field is absolute, relative, or external, and if external, which external symbol.
3.   The names and locations of all entry points.
4.   The end of loader input.
5.   The starting address.

As a simple approach to the problem, we can use a loader format very similar to the absolute loader format of Figure 7.2 above. All input to the relocatable loader will consist of a sequence of codes which identify what information follows it. The codes will be stored in byte 3 of a header word, and are,

Code	Meaning
0	Start of a segment
1	Absolute address (no relocation needed)
2	Relocatable address (needs BASE added)
3	Entry point symbol
4	External symbol
5	Starting address
6	End of segment
7	End of loader input.

The remainder of the header word will contain various information depending upon the code. Specifically,

Code	Meaning
0	Start of segment. A segment name of up to 10 characters follows in the next two words.

1   Absolute. Bytes 0:2 of the header contain a relative address. The following word is an absolute value which should be loaded into memory at the relative address.

2   Relocatable. Bytes 0:2 of the header contain a relative address. The following word should be loaded into that location and the address field of the loaded value should be modified by the addition of the base address of the current segment.

3   Entry point. The next two words contain the 10-character symbolic name of an entry point. Its relative address is in bytes 0:2 of the header word.

4   External. The next two words contain the 10-character symbolic name of an external. The instruction (which must already have been loaded) which is at the relative address given in bytes 0:2 of the header uses this external.

5   Starting address. Bytes 0:2 contain the relative address in the current segment where execution should begin.

6   End of segment. Bytes 0:2 contain the length of the segment.

7   End of loader input. Control can now be transferred to the starting address.

As before, with our absolute loader input, we should consider the efficiency of this representation. Each instruction to be loaded here takes two words, at the least, plus additional words for segment definitions, entry points, and externals. This needs to be reduced if possible. There will probably be few entry points, externals, starting addresses or segments, so we can ignore those codes for now and concentrate on the representation of codes 1 and 2; these will be the bulk of our loader input.

With the input to the absolute loader, it was reasonable to assume that there would be a large number of contiguous locations to be loaded, and that one header word could serve a block of contiguous words as well as one word. For relocatable input, that is not strictly true, however. While it is reasonable to assume that blocks of contiguous words will need to be loaded, it is not reasonable to assume that blocks of contiguous absolute words or blocks of contiguous relocatable words will be loaded. Rather, it is more likely that relocatable and absolute words will be intermixed.

With the exception of adding the base address to the address field of a relocatable instruction, however, relocatable and absolute instructions can be treated the same. Thus, rather than an entire header word, only one extra bit per instruction is needed to distinguish between relocatable and absolute instructions. If that bit were supplied separately, then the loader could accept blocks of input instructions, loading them as if they were absolute, and then later returning to convert the address fields of some instructions from relative to absolute by the addition of the base address. This is the approach we take here. To reduce the size of the loader input, and consequently the amount of I/O time needed to load it, we allow each header word to prefix a block of words. The number of words is given in bytes 4:5 of the header word. Thus, we redefine the code 1 input as

1   Absolute. Bytes 0:2 of the header contain a relative address; bytes 4:5 contain a number of words (N). Load the N following words into memory at the relative address given in 0:2. Some of these words may be later modified as external or relocatable references.

Code 2 input must be redefined in light of this approach. What is needed is simply the (relative) addresses of all instructions which need relocation. One approach would be to simply list the addresses of the relocatable instructions, one after another, with bytes 4:5 specifying the number of such addresses. The addresses could also be packed two to a word, to reduce the amount of space needed.

A slightly different approach is more commonly used on binary computers. From examinations of typical programs, you notice that most instructions use an address and most of these are relocatable. Thus, many instructions are relocatable and contiguous to other relocatable instructions. Hence a list of addresses of relocatable instructions would be a list of addresses which could typically differ only by one or two locations. Thus rather than an address for each, we need only the address of the first (which can be stored in bytes 0:2 of the header) and an indicator, for each of the following words, whether it is or is not relocatable. This requires only one bit per word, so that the need for relocation of 30 words can be packed into one 5-byte word on a binary MIX machine. Consider the binary word

$$b_{29}b_{28}b_{27} \ldots b_1b_0$$

and a header word with an address of 1000 in bytes 0:2. If bit zero were 1, then the address field of location 1000 would need relocation, if bit 1 were 1, then the address field of location 1001 would need relocation, . . ., if bit i were 1, then the address field of location $1000+i$ would need relocation. This relocation could be done in a simple loop similar to the following (assuming index register 1 has the address of the first of the 30 words, the A register has the relocation bits, and index register 6 has the relocation base)

```
1H          JAE    2F           LOW ORDER BIT IS ZERO IF A EVEN
            LD3    0,1(0:2)     ADDRESS FIELD FOR
            INC3   0,6          RELOCATIONS
            ST3    0,1(0:2)
2H          SRB    1            SHIFT A RIGHT ONE BIT
            INC1   1            INCREMENT ADDRESS
            JANZ   1B           A NONZERO MEANS STILL 1 BIT
```

Notice that this technique requires the ability to test and shift bits and so is only really suitable for binary machines. For a decimal machine, or a binary machine without the extended instruction set, it would be necessary to divide by 2 to shift right one bit and examine the remainder to determine whether the low-order bit was zero or one.

Whichever representation is used for the code 2 information on relocation addresses, it should be clear how to write the code for relocating addresses in a program to be loaded. If we assume the list of addresses approach, then the loader code for the subroutine

```
                NAME  SUM10
                ENT   SUM10        ENTRY POINT DEFINITION
                EXT   ARRAY        EXTERNAL
TEM1            BSS   1
*
SUM10           STJ   EXITSUM
                ST1   TEM1
                ENT1  10
                ENTA  0
LOOP            ADD   ARRAY-1,1
                DEC1  1
                J1P   LOOP
                LD1   TEM1
EXITSUM         JMP   *
                END
```

would be

```
+0000 00 0002    CODE 0: START OF SEGMENT
+2630163736              NAME OF SEGMENT: SUM10
+0000000000

+0001 01 0011    CODE 1: 9 ABSOLUTE WORDS
+0011 00 0240            TO BE LOADED AT RELATIVE +0001
+0000 00 0231
+0012 00 0261
+0000 00 0260
-0001 01 0501
+0001 00 0161
+0005 00 0251
+0000 00 0211
+0011 00 0047

+0000 02 0005    CODE 2: LIST OF 5 ADDRESSES TO
+0000 00 0001            BE RELOCATED
+0000 00 0002
+0000 00 0007
+0000 00 0010
+0000 00 0011
```

```
+0001 03 0002    CODE 3: ENTRY POINT AT RELATIVE +0001
+2630163736              NAME OF ENTRY POINT SUM10
+0000000000

+0005 04 0002    CODE 4: EXTERNAL USED AT RELATIVE +0005
+0123230134              NAME OF EXTERNAL ARRAY
+0000000000

+0012 06 0000    CODE 6: END OF SEGMENT OF LENGTH 10 WORDS
```

Techniques for linking

The programming techniques which are used for linking entry points to externals are similar to techniques used in other system programs, particularly assemblers and compilers. Both entry points and externals are defined by their symbolic names. The problem is to match the definitions of these symbols, as entry points, to their uses, as externals.

This matching is performed by the use of a data structure called a *symbol table*, or in this case, an *entry point table*. This table is a list of the known entry points, both their symbolic name and their address in memory. This table is defined by the collection of all code 3 entry point definitions in the input. As each entry point definition is found, the name of the new entry point and its absolute address are entered into the entry point table. When a reference to an external (code 4) is found, the entry point table is searched for the correspondingly named entry point, and the address of that entry point is then used to modify the address field of the instruction which used that external/entry point.

This solution to the linking problem works very well, except for one problem: forward references. If an external reference to an entry point is encountered before the definition of that entry point is encountered, then the search of the entry point table will not find an address for the external. Since an entry point can be declared after it is used as an external, it cannot be known for certain if an external reference which finds no corresponding entry point is a reference to an undefined entry point (an error) or simply a reference to an entry point which is yet to be defined (a forward reference). This can be known only when the end of loader input (code 7) is encountered. At that point, any undefined externals are errors.

As always, there are many techniques for solving the problem of forward references. The simplest is to use a *two-pass* loader. After inputting all of the loader input once, all entry points are defined. On the first pass through the loader input, we can ignore all loader input except the entry point definitions and the length of the segments (so we can convert the relative addresses of the entry point definitions to absolute addresses). When the end of loader input is encountered, the loader input is read a second time (pass two). This time the segments are loaded into memory, and all external references are resolved. Forward references will not be a problem, since all entry points were defined and

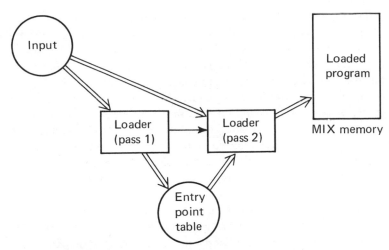

FIGURE 7.5   A two-pass loader; pass 1 creates the entry point table which is used by the second pass to properly link segments together.

entered into the symbol table during pass one. Any forward reference during pass two is a reference to an undefined external, and is an error.

The mechanics of a two-pass loader depend upon the I/O devices involved. If the loader input is on a mass storage device (magnetic tape, disk, or drum), then the loader can reread the input by rewinding or repositioning the input to the beginning for the second pass. If input is on cards or paper tape, it is often copied to a mass storage device during pass one, and then read back from this device during pass 2. If no mass storage is available, the loader input must simply be read into the computer twice.

A two-pass solution to forward references is conceptually simple, and hence easy to write. However, it requires twice as much I/O as might be desired, and since loading is an I/O-bound process anyway, will produce a slow loader. This is quite unfortunate, since the loader is so frequently used. Thus, other approaches have been tried to reduce the amount of I/O which is necessary.

One variant is to notice that all of the loading functions (storing in memory, relocation, entry point table definition) can be accomplished in one pass, except external reference resolution. Even this can be done except for forward references. Thus, instead of inputting the entire loader input twice, on pass one we do all possible loading. If forward external references are encountered, then the (absolute) address of the reference and the name of the referenced external are written to mass storage. Pass two consists of nothing more than rewinding this device and rereading it. The amount of I/O during pass two is reduced considerably.

A more radical approach is to eliminate the second pass entirely, rather than simply trying to reduce it in size. In this case, rather than storing the external references on a mass storage device, they are stored in memory. Two tables are constructed during pass one, an entry point table, and an *external reference table* (often call a *use table*). The external reference table stores, for each (forward) external reference, the name of the external and the (absolute) address where it is used. Pass two now no longer need do any I/O, and need not even be a separate pass. During pass one, if a forward external reference is found, then it is entered into the external reference table. When an entry point is defined, the external reference table is searched, and any references to this newly defined entry point are resolved (i.e., the address of the entry point is used to modify the address field of the referencing instruction). The entry in the external reference table is then deleted. When pass one is completed, the external reference table should be empty. Any remaining entries are references to externals which were never defined as entry points.

The problem is now reduced to the construction and maintenance of the two tables, the entry point table and the external reference table. The entry point table is an easier table to construct and maintain since deletions are never made

FIGURE 7.6 The entry point table and external reference table of a one-pass loader. The entry point table records where entry points are defined to be; the external reference table records where they are used.

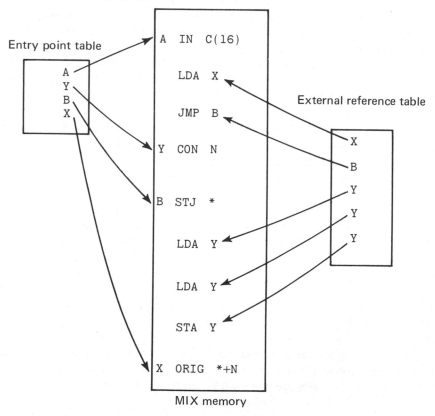

from it. Thus only search and enter subroutines are needed. The external reference table is much more difficult. The table must be able to add entries, search for entries, and delete entries. This requires care that deleted entries are not used after they are deleted. Also, the memory space they occupied should be reused if possible to reduce the total amount of memory needed. This requires very careful design of an appropriate data structure.

Some loaders have merged the entry point table and the external reference table into one table. Each entry in this table consists of several fields. One field is a name, another is a bit. If the bit is 0, then the name is the name of an external reference which has not yet been defined as an entry point (a forward external reference). If the bit is 1, the name is the name of an entry point. For an entry point, we need an absolute address for that entry point. For an external reference, we need a list of all the addresses which reference that external. The problem is that the length of this list is variable and unbounded. How much space should be allocated for the list?

Since the list is of variable length, the standard approach is to use a *linked list*. In the table entry itself, we do not store the list, but only a *pointer* to the list. This means that each table entry is a name, an address, and a bit. The bit distinguishes between forward external references and entry point table entries. For forward external references, the word is the external name and the address is the address of a list of addresses which reference the external; for entry points, the word is the entry point name and the address is the address of the entry point in memory.

Where should the list be stored? One approach is to store the list in a large array of available memory. Another is to restrict the assembly language, so that external references cannot be used in expressions, but only by themselves. Thus LDA EXTERNAL is acceptable, but LDA EXTERNAL+1 is not. In this case, resolving an external reference consists in simply storing the address of the entry point in the address field of the instruction. That means that the address field has no necessary information and hence can be used as temporary storage until the external reference is resolved. This allows the list of external references to be stored in the address fields of the instructions which reference the externals. This technique is known as *chaining*.

In chaining, the first reference to a forwardly referenced external stores in its address field a special value (like 4095 or −1 or any other value which cannot be interpreted as a legal address). The entry point/external table entry points to this by saving the address of this instruction. When the loader finds the next reference, it sets the address field of the second reference to point to the first reference, and the address of the second reference is stored in the table. The third reference would point to the second reference, and so on. Thus, when the entry point is finally defined, the table entry points to the last reference, which points to the previous reference, . . ., which points to the first reference, which has a special easily recognizable pointer. The loader must follow down this chain of addresses, replacing them all with the address of the entry point.

Another technique is to set all external reference addresses to refer indi-

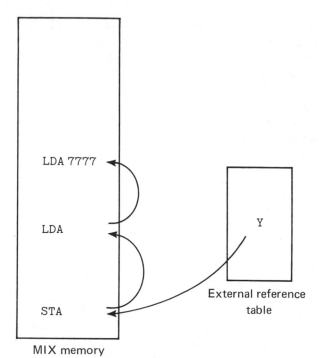

MIX memory

FIGURE 7.7   Chaining (rather than storing the addresses of the uses of an external symbol in the external reference table, the uses are chained together by a linked list).

rectly through the entry point table entry. The address of the entry point table entry can be defined as soon as the name of the symbol is known. Since at execution time the addresses of all entry points will have been put into the entry point table, every access to an external can simply be made indirectly through the entry point table. In this case the entry point table is an example of a *transfer vector*.

All of these linking techniques have their advantages and disadvantages. A two-pass loader is relatively simple, but takes more time than a one-pass loader. The transfer vector approach is straightforward, but requires additional memory at execution time for the transfer vector and additional time due to the indirect references. Indexing or indirection on externals may not occur correctly with the transfer vector approach. Chaining can be done in one pass without additional memory, but the coding for resolving the chain must be carefully written to avoid errors, and the use of external references must be restricted. The use of an external reference table may require considerable memory for the table, but allows the loader to produce a *cross reference table* for entry points and externals, showing where every entry point is and the addresses of all of its uses.

An entry point cross reference listing generally accompanies a *memory map*. A memory map lists the names, lengths, and load address of all segments and entry points. A memory map and cross reference listing can be very valuable aids in debugging a program.

Relocatable load errors

As with the absolute loader, a relocatable loader must check carefully for possible errors in loading. The errors which an absolute loader checked for were relatively obvious, while the errors of a relocatable loader are more complex. Certainly the relocatable loader must insure that all absolute addresses are legal and do not overlap the relocatable loader. To assure this, the relocatable loader is again generally placed in high memory, while user programs are loaded into low memory. The tables for the loader are of variable size and so generally start just below the loader and grow towards the user's programs. Thus a large program with few symbols or a small program with many symbols will have no problem being loaded.

In addition, some other errors which may be detected by a relocatable loader include,

1. Multiply defined segments. Two or more segments may have the same name.
2. Multiply defined entry points. Two different segments may have entry points with the same name.
3. Undefined external. An external reference is made to a symbol which is never declared as an entry point.
4. Load attempt out of segment. A relative load address may exceed the segment length. If a segment is of length L, then all (relative) load addresses should be in the range 0 to L−1.
5. No starting address or multiple starting addresses. There should be one and only one starting address per program.
6. Incorrect loader input. Loader blocks may come out of order. For example, following the end of a segment (code 6), the next code should be either a code 0 (start of next segment) or a code 7 (end of loader input). Any other code would be in error.

Other strange conditions may or may not be errors depending upon your philosophy. Should one segment be allowed to declare the same symbol both external and an entry point?

7.3 VARIATIONS OF LOADERS

Linkage editors

A variation on the idea of a relocatable linking loader is a *linkage editor*. A linkage editor can be thought of as a relocatable linking nonloading loader. Its purpose is to input a number of segments in a relocatable load format, and to

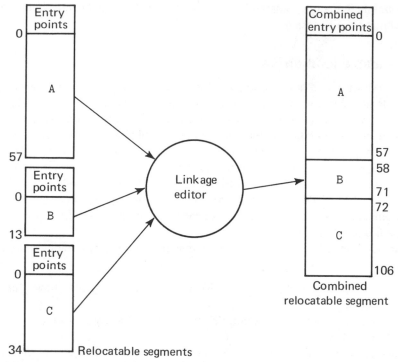

FIGURE 7.8 A linkage editor inputs several relocatable segments and outputs one relocatable segment which combines the code and entry points of all its inputs.

output a new segment which is the combination of the input segments. In so doing, some relocation is done, and some linkage.

As an example, consider two segments, MAIN and ZERO. MAIN is 43 words long, has one entry point, START, and references the externals ONE and TWO. ZERO is 15 words long, has two entry points, TWO and ZERO, and references the externals START and STOP. A linkage editor which receives as input MAIN and ZERO would produce as output a new segment which would consist of both segments MAIN and ZERO, so it would be 58 words long. In addition, all addresses in ZERO would be relocated by 43 words, so that they would be correct for following MAIN. Any externals in one segment which are entry points in the other would be resolved and would no longer appear as externals, while all the entry points of both segments would appear as entry points of the new segment. Thus, the new segment would have three entry points, START, TWO and ZERO. It would reference two externals, ONE and STOP. The references to TWO in MAIN would be linked to the entry point in ZERO, the references to START in ZERO would be linked to the entry point in MAIN. These references would now appear like any other relocatable memory references.

The reasons for wanting a linkage editor vary. From a user point of view, the repetitive linking of many routines can be quite expensive. If these routines are not changing, then they could be linked together, once and for all, by the linkage editor, while the remainder of the program is modified, reassembled, relinked, and debugged as needed. Thus a linkage editor may save valuable time.

From a system point of view the use of a linkage editor can separate the linking function from the loading function. That is, a user may need to run his entire program first through the linkage editor, until no externals remain to be linked. Then, although the program remains in relocatable format, the relocation for it for loading is zero. Thus it can be loaded by what is essentially an absolute loader. This means the loader can be considerably smaller and faster than a relocating linking loader, since it need do no linking (and generally no relocation).

A linkage editor is normally a two-pass linker. Since the program is not being loaded into memory, we cannot use chaining or an in core fix-up for externals. We must make one pass first to define the entry point table and then another pass to link and relocate the segments together.

Overlays

Sometimes a program is too large to fit in memory. There is only a fixed amount of memory on a MIX machine and some problems can only be solved by programs which require more than 4000 words of memory. However, often it is the case that the program can easily be partitioned into separate sections which are never needed at the same time. In this case, if a mass storage device is available, the program may still be able to be written and executed.

The idea of overlaying is to store the entire program only on the mass storage device. In memory is kept only the common (global) data that the sections use and any heavily used subroutines. At any given time, only one of the sections will be in main memory. When control needs to transfer from one section to another, a jump is made to a small special subroutine called an overlay monitor. The overlay monitor loads the next section from the mass storage device into memory in the same memory locations as the previous section. The sections are called *overlays*.

On the MIX machine, for example, assume that the common data and overlay monitor took 2000 words of memory and each of three overlays took 2000 words of memory. Although only 4000 words of memory are available, an overlay system could run this program, although it would take 8000 words to run without overlays. (What we gain in space, we lose in time, since bringing in overlays requires considerable input/output time.)

Loaders are involved with overlays in two ways. First, the overlay monitor is obviously a loader of sorts, prepared to load any of several overlay sections as directed. Second, a linkage-editor-type loader is generally used to link and relocate the program into the form needed for the overlay monitor on the direct access device.

Bootstrap loaders

Suppose the computer is executing your program. You now know how that program got into memory. It was loaded by the relocatable linking loader. You also know (or can guess) that the relocatable loader was loaded into memory by an absolute loader. How did the absolute loader get into memory? It was obviously loaded, but by what?

On most machines someone has written a small special purpose loader program which is meant only for loading the absolute loader. This program is used to load the absolute loader. But, you continue, how did this program get into memory? Answer: it loaded itself into memory (with a little help from its friends).

The bottom line in loaders is a special program called a *bootstrap loader*. A bootstrap loader loads itself into memory. Obviously, however, it cannot do this all by itself. The first few instructions of a bootstrap loader are I/O instructions which read into memory from a specific I/O device. The I/O is done into the memory locations which directly follow these few instructions. The information read in by these few instructions is the remainder of the bootstrap loader. For example, if the bootstrap loader is written on a magnetic tape on tape drive 1, then the following instructions are enough to get the bootstrap loader started.

```
IN    *+2(1)
JBUS  *(1)
```

When the I/O is complete, control will drop through the JBUS to the newly read in bootstrap loader.

These first few instructions were loaded into the computer by hand. The computer operator, when a computer is first turned on, must enter these instructions, by hand, in binary, through the console of the computer. When these instructions are executed, they read in the remainder of the bootstrap loader, which then loads the absolute loader, which then loads the relocatable loader, which then loads your program.

Many computers now have special options which provide a bootstrap loader in special memory which can be read but not written (read-only memory), so that the loader cannot be clobbered, intentionally or unintentionally. This relieves the operator of needing to enter the bootstrap loader by hand.

Subroutine libraries

On most computer systems there exists a set of subroutines which have been written and are used by many programmers. Subroutines for common mathematical functions and for input/output are typical. This set of subroutines is often grouped into a *library*. A loader uses this library to try to satisfy any unsatisfied externals when the end of a relocatable load results in undefined externals.

A programmer can use any of these subroutines simply by declaring them to be external. When loading of user input is complete, the loader checks for any unsatisfied external references. If there are any, each reference causes the loader to search the library of subroutines, looking for an entry point for any of these subroutines which matches the unsatisfied external. If none is found, we have an error as before. If one is found, however, it is then loaded into memory and the external reference resolved.

Since blind searching of the entire library may be quite time consuming, the library is generally structured so that the searching can be more efficient. The names of all entry points and the name and location of their segments are stored in a directory which is at the front of the library. It is possible to then search for an entry point and load it very quickly.

A linkage editor uses a library in much the same manner.

7.4 SUMMARY

As you can tell, there are a number of different approaches to loading a program into memory. Typically, the standard loader is either an absolute loader or a relocatable loader. The absolute loader is very simple and may be all that is needed or can be afforded for small computers. A relocatable loader is more complicated but allows programs to be written as separate subroutines which may be assembled or compiled by different translators at different times.

The relocatable loader must combine the many different segments, relocating addresses and linking external references and entry points. There are many different possible input formats and the format produced by the assembler must be appropriate for the loader to be used. A relocatable loader may use many techniques for linking as either a two-pass or a one-pass loader. If the loader is one-pass, it may link through a transfer vector, chaining, or an external reference table.

A linkage editor links many small segments into one large segment, with the same output format as input format. Thus the output of a linkage editor may be input into a relocatable loader or back into itself for combination with other segments.

Bootstrap loaders and overlay loaders are special purpose loaders.

Several books include a chapter on loaders and linkers, including Donovan (1972), Graham (1975), and Ullman (1976). Barron (1969) gives a brief treatment of loaders, in general, while Presser and White (1972) concentrate on the loader and linkage editor for the IBM 360/370 systems. Knuth(1968) gives a bootstrap loader for MIX in Volume 1.

EXERCISES

a. Name four kinds of loaders or linkers.

b. Describe the information in each logical record given to an absolute loader.

c. What is the name for a location within a routine which is used by another routine? Could it be called anything else? What determines which name is used for a location?

d. What is the purpose of a checksum?

e. Suppose that one of the logical operations of AND, ORR or XOR were used, instead of addition, to compute the checksum for loader input. Comment on how useful you think each operation would be.

f. What is a bootstrap loader? Under what circumstances is a bootstrap loader needed? Is a bootstrap loader normally an absolute loader or a relocatable loader?

g. Name two techniques for handling forward references in a linking loader.

h. Indicate which of the following assembly language statements should be marked as relocatable by the assembler in order for this subroutine to be properly loaded by a relocatable loader. What would you think would be the entry points and externals?

```
I               CON   0
N               CON   43
*
SQRT            STJ   EXIT
                STZ   I
1H              LDA   I
                MUL   I
                CMPX  N
                JG    FOUND
                LDA   I
                INCA  1
                STA   I
                JMP   1B
FOUND           LDA   I
EXIT            JMP   *
```

i. Assume that the following three routines had the indicated entry points and externals.

```
                ENTRY POINTS    EXTERNALS
MAIN            BEGIN               N
                ARY                 CS
                                    FORE
```

```
FUN       N                   CS
          FOD                 TOD
          NIX
TURKEY    CS             (none)
```

What would be the entry points and externals of the combined module which would result from processing the above three routines with a linkage editor?

j. How many passes are there in each of the following types of loaders? Absolute loader. Relocatable loader. Linkage editor. Bootstrap loader.

k. Assume that the input to a MIX relocatable loader is of the form

   address   type   contents

   where the "contents" is a MIX word which should be loaded at "address." If type = ABS, then nothing needs to be done to "contents," but if type = REL, then the address field of the instruction needs to be relocated. The "address" field is always a relocatable address.

   If the input to the loader is

```
0000    ABS    +0000000000
0003    REL    +0000000510
0004    REL    +0001000530
0005    ABS    +0001000260
0006    REL    +0002003430
```

   and the program is to be relocated to start at location 0432, what is loaded and where?

l. What is the latest binding time possible for the symbols in relocatable, absolute, or machine language programs?

m. Can a loader be relocating without being linking? Would it make sense if it were possible?

n. How does a linkage editor differ from a linking loader?

o. Suppose that you have just been put in charge of loaders for the new improved XCD-12A computer. In what order would you write the following loaders/linkers?

   1. Linkage editor
   2. Bootstrap loader
   3. Absolute loader
   4. Linking loader
   5. Relocatable loader

p. Write a relocatable loader which loads relocatable MIXAL programs from tape unit 1.

q. What changes are needed in the assembly language for a relocatable loader, as compared with an absolute loader?

8

ASSEMBLERS

Assemblers are the simplest of a class of systems programs called *translators*. A translator is simply a program which translates from one (computer) language to another (computer) language. In the case of an assembler, the translation is from assembly language to object language (which is input to a loader). Notice that an assembler, like all translators, adds nothing to the program which it translates, but merely changes the program from one form to another. The use of a translator allows a program to be written in a form which is convenient for the programmer, and then the program is translated into a form convenient for the computer.

Assembly language is almost the same as machine language. The major difference is that assembly language allows the declaration and use of symbols to stand for the numeric values to be used for opcodes, fields, and addresses. An assembler inputs a program written in assembly language, and translates all of the symbols in the input into numeric values, creating an output object module, suitable for loading. The object module is output to a storage device which allows the assembled program to be read back into the computer by the loader.

This is an external view of an assembler. Now we turn our attention to an internal view, in order to see how the assembler is structured internally to translate assembly programs into object programs.

8.1 DATA STRUCTURES

Appropriate data structures can make a program much easier to understand, and the data structures for an assembler are crucial to its programming. An assembler must translate two different kinds of symbols: assembler-defined symbols and programmer-defined symbols. The assembler-defined symbols are mnemonics for the machine instructions and pseudo-instructions. Programmer-defined symbols are the symbols which the programmer defines in the label field of statements in his program. These two kinds of symbols are translated by two different tables: the opcode table, and the symbol table.

The opcode table

The opcode table contains one entry for each assembly language mnemonic. Each entry needs to contain several fields. One field is the character code of the symbolic opcode. In addition, for machine instructions, each entry would contain the numeric opcode and default field specification. These are the minimal pieces of information needed. With an opcode table like this, it is possible to search for a symbolic opcode and find the correct numeric opcode and field specification.

Pseudo instructions require a little more thought. There is no numeric opcode or field specification associated with a pseudo-instruction; rather, there is a function which must be performed for each pseudo-instruction. This can be encoded in several ways. One method is to include in the opcode table, a *type* field. The type field is used to separate pseudo-instructions from machine instructions and to separate the various pseudo-instructions. Different things need to be done for each of the different pseudo-instructions, and so each has its own type. All machine instructions can be handled the same, however, so only one type is needed for them. One possible type assignment is then,

type	*instruction class*
1	Machine instruction
2	ORIG pseudo-instruction
3	CON pseudo-instruction
4	ALF pseudo-instruction
5	EQU pseudo-instruction
6	END pseudo-instruction.

Other type assignments are also possible. For example, in the above assignment, all machine instructions have one type, and are treated equally. This allows both instructions such as

    LDA   X(0:3)

and

    ENTA X(0:3)

But the ENTA instruction is encoded as an opcode of 60 and a field of 02. Thus, it is not correct to specify a field with an ENTA. This reasoning can lead to separating memory reference instructions (which may have field specifications) from nonmemory reference instructions (which should not have field specifications). Even further classification could separate the I/O instructions (which use the F field for a device number) and the MOVE instruction. The idea of attaching a type to a table entry is quite general.

    Another approach to separating the pseudo-instructions in the opcode table is to consider how the type field of the above discussion would be used. It would be used in a jump table. In this case, rather than using the type to specify the code address through a jump table, we could store the address of the code directly in the opcode table. In each opcode table entry, we can store the address of the code to be executed for proper treatment of this instruction, whether it is a machine instruction or a pseudo-instruction. This is a commonly used technique for assemblers.

    Other opcode table structures are possible also. Some assemblers have separate tables for machine instructions and for pseudo-instructions. Others will use a type field of one bit to distinguish between machine instructions and pseudo-instructions, and then store a numeric opcode and field specification for the machine instructions or an address of code to execute for pseudo-instructions.

    For simplicity, let us assume that we store, for each entry, the symbolic mnemonic, numeric opcode, default field specification and a type, as defined above. For pseudo-instructions, the numeric opcode and default field specification of the entry will be ignored. How should we organize our opcode table entries? The opcode table should be organized to minimize both search time and table space. These two goals may not be achievable at the same time. The fastest access to table entries would require that each field of an entry be in the same

FIGURE 8.1   Opcode table entry (each opcode table entry contains the symbolic opcode, numeric opcode and field specification, and a type field).

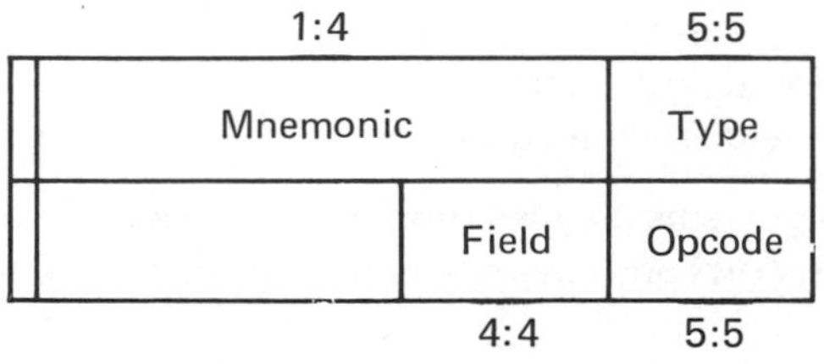

1:4		5:5
Mnemonic		Type
	Field	Opcode
	4:4	5:5

relative position of a memory word, such as in Figure 8.1. But notice that, in this case, three bytes of each entry are unused, so that the table includes a large amount of wasted space. (Actually, three bytes, two signs, and the upper three bits of the type byte are unused.) To save this space would require more code and longer execution times for packing and unpacking operations. Thus, to save time it seems wise to accept this wasted space in the opcode table.

To a great extent this wasted space is due to the design of the assembly language mnemonics. If the mnemonics had been defined as a maximum of three characters (instead of four), it would have been possible to store the mnemonic, field specifications, and opcode in one word. The sign bit would be "+"for machine instructions and "−" for pseudo-instructions. Pseudo instructions could have a type field or address in the lower bytes while machine instructions would store opcode and field specifications. On the other hand, once the decision is made that four character mnemonics are needed, then it is necessary to go to a multiword opcode table entry. In this case, we could allow mnemonics of up to seven characters, by using the currently unused three bytes of the opcode table entry. On the other hand, there may be no desire to have opcode mnemonics of more than four characters; mnemonics should be short.

Another consideration is the order of entries in the table. This relates to the expected search time to find a particular entry in the table. The simplest search is a linear search starting at one end of the table and working towards the other end until a match is found (or the end of the table is reached). In this case, one should organize the table so that the more common mnemonics will be compared first. If, as expected, the LDA mnemonic is the most common instruction, then it should be put at the end of the table which is searched first.

Rather than use a linear search, it can be noted that the opcode table is a static structure; it does not change. The opcode table is like a dictionary explaining the numeric meaning of symbolic opcodes. Like a dictionary, it can be usefully organized in an alphabetical order. By ordering the entries, the table can be searched with a *binary search*. A binary search is the method commonly used to look for an entry in a dictionary, telephone book, or encyclopedia. First the middle of the book is compared with the entry being searched for (the *search key*). If the search key is smaller than the middle entry, then the key must be in the first half of the book, if it is larger it must be in the latter half of the book. After this comparison, the same idea can be repeated on the half of the book which still needs to be searched. Each comparison splits the remaining section of the book in half.

In MIX, this might be coded as follows. Location KEY contains the value for which we are searching. LOW contains our low index, while HIGH contains our high index. Initially, LOW would point to the first entry of the table; HIGH would point to the last entry. The search loop would then be

```
SEARCHLOOP      LDA     LOW
                ADD     HIGH            A = LOW + HIGH
                SRAX    5
```

```
                    DIV    =2=             A = (LOW + HIGH)/2 = MIDDLE
                    STA    *+1(0:2)        MOVE TO INDEX 3
                    ENT3   0
                    LDA    TABLE,3         MIDDLE OF TABLE
                    CMPA   KEY
                    JE     FOUND           IF EQUAL, FOUND ENTRY
                    JL     1F
      *
                    DEC3   1               IF TABLE[MIDDLE] > KEY
                    ST3    HIGH            HIGH = MIDDLE - 1
                    JMP    2F
      *
      1H            INC3   1               IF TABLE[MIDDLE] < KEY
                    ST3    LOW             LOW = MIDDLE + 1
      2H            LDA    HIGH
                    CMPA   LOW             IF LOW > HIGH, STOP
                    JGE    SEARCHLOOP
NOTFOUND                   . . .
```

The search code has two exits. If the search key is found in the table, a jump is made to the label FOUND, with index register 3 being the index into the table of the search key entry. If the key is not in the table, control transfers to the label NOTFOUND.

A binary search is not always the best search method to use. Each time through, the search loop cuts the size of the table yet to be searched in half. In general, a table of size 2^n will take about n comparisons to find an entry. Thus, a table of size 32 will take only 5 comparisons, while for a linear search, it is normally assumed, that on the average, half of the table must be searched, resulting in 16 comparisons. Thus, the binary search almost always requires fewer executions of its search loop than a linear search. However, notice that the binary search requires considerably more computation per comparison than a linear search. The binary search loop requires about 35 time units per comparison while a linear search can require only 5 time units. Thus, for a table of size 32, the binary search takes 5 comparisons at 35 time units each, for 175 time units, while the linear search takes 16 comparisons at 5 time units each for 80 time units. This is not to say that a binary search should never be used. For a table of size 128, a binary search will take about 245 ($= 7 \times 35$) time units, while a linear search will take 320 ($= 64 \times 5$). Thus, for a large table a binary search is better. Also, if a shift (SRB) could be used instead of the divide, the time per loop could be cut by 11 time units, making the binary search better. Since there are around 150 MIX opcodes, we use a binary search for the opcode table.

The symbol table

The opcode table is used to translate the assembler-defined symbols into their numeric equivalents; the symbol table is used to translate programmer-defined symbols into their numeric equivalents. Thus, these two tables can be quite alike. A symbol table, like an opcode table, is a table of many entries, one entry for each programmer-defined symbol. Each entry is composed of several fields.

For the symbol table, only two fields are basically needed. It is necessary to store the symbol and the value of the symbol. A symbol in a MIXAL program can be up to 10 characters in length. This requires two MIX words. In addition, the value of the symbol can be up to five bytes plus sign, requiring another MIX word. Thus, each entry in the symbol table takes at least three words. Additional fields may be added for some assemblers. A bit may be needed to indicate if the symbol has been defined or is undefined (i.e., a forward reference). Another bit may specify whether the symbol is an absolute symbol or a relative symbol (depending on whether the output is to be used with a relocatable or absolute loader). Other fields may also be included in a symbol table entry, but for the moment let us use only the two fields, for the symbol and its value.

As with the opcode table, the organization of the symbol table is very important for proper use. But the symbol table differs from the opcode table in one important respect: it is *dynamic*. The opcode table was *static*; it is never changed, neither during nor between executions of the assembler. It is the same for each and every assembly program for the entire assembly process. The symbol table is dynamic; each program has its own set of symbols with their own values and new symbols are added to the symbol table as the assembly process proceeds. Initially the symbol table is empty; no symbols have been defined. By the time assembly is completed, however, all symbols in the program have been entered into the symbol table.

This requires the definition of two subroutines to manipulate the symbol table: a search routine and an enter routine. The search routine searches the symbol table for a symbol (its search key) and returns its value (or an index into the table to its value). The enter subroutine puts a new symbol and its value into the table.

These two subroutines need to be designed together, since both of them affect the symbol table. A binary search might be quite efficient, but it requires that the table be kept ordered. This means that the enter subroutine would have to adjust the table for each new entry, so that the table was always sorted into the correct order. Thus, although a binary search might be quick, the combination of a binary search plus an ordered enter might be very expensive.

Also consider that a linear search is more efficient than a binary search for small tables. Many assembly language programs have less than 200 different symbols, and so a linear search may be quite reasonable. A linear search allows the enter routine to simply put any new symbol and its value at the end of the table. Thus, both the search and enter routines are simple.

Many other table management techniques have been considered and are used. Some of these are quite complex and useful only for special cases. Others have wide applicability. One of the most commonly used techniques is *hashing*. The objective of hashing is quite simple. Rather than have to search for a symbol at all, we would prefer to be able to compute the location in the table of a symbol from the symbol itself. Then, to enter a symbol, we compute where it should go, and define that entry. For accessing, we compute the address of the entry and use the value stored in the table at that location.

As a simple example, assume that all of our symbols were one-letter symbols (A, B, C, . . . , Z). Then if we simply allocated a symbol table of 26 locations, we could index directly to a table entry for each symbol by using its character code for an index. No searching would be needed. If our symbols were any two-letter symbols, we could apply the same idea if we had a symbol table of 676 (= 26 × 26) entries, where our hash function would be to multiply the character code of the first letter by 26 and add the character code of the second (and subtract 26 to normalize). However, for three-letter symbols, we would need l7,576 spaces in our symbol table. This is clearly impossible. (Our MIX memory is only 4000 words long.) It also is not necessary, since we assume that at most only a few hundred symbols will be used in each different assembly program. What is needed is a function which produces an address for each different symbol, but maps them all into a table of several hundred words.

Many different hashing functions can be used. For example, we can add together the character codes for the different characters of the symbol, or multiply them, or shift some of them a few bits and exclusive-or them with the other characters, or whatever we wish. Then, after we have hashed up the input characters to get some weird number, we can divide by the length of the table and use the remainder. The remainder is guaranteed to be between 0 and the length of the table and hence can be used as an index into the table. For a binary machine and a table whose length is a power of two, the division can be done by simply masking the low-order bits.

The objective of all this calculation is to arrive at an address for a symbol which hopefully is unique for each symbol. But since there are millions of 10-character symbols, and only a few hundred table entries, it must be the case that two different symbols may hash into the same table entry. For example, if we use a hash function which adds together the character codes of the letters in the symbol, then both EVIL and LIVE will hash to the same location. This is called a *collision*. The simplest solution to this problem is to then search through successive entries in the table, until an empty table entry is found. (If the end of the table is found, start over at the beginning).

The search and enter routines are now straightforward. To enter a new symbol, compute its hash function, and find an empty entry in the table. Enter the new symbol in this entry. To search for a symbol, compute its hash function and search the table starting at that entry. If an empty entry is found, the symbol is not in the table. Otherwise, it will be found before the first empty location.

The problem with using hashing is defining a good hash function. A good hash function will result in very few collisions. This means that both the search and enter routines will be very fast. In the worst case, all symbols will hash to the same location and a linear search will result. Hashing is sometimes also used for opcode tables, where, since the opcode table is static and known, a hashing function can be constructed which guarantees no collisions.

More about hashing can be found in the paper by Morris (1968), or in Knuth (1973), Volume 3.

Other data structures

The opcode table and the symbol table are the major data structures for an assembler, but not the only ones. The other data structures differ from assembler to assembler, depending upon the design of the assembly language and the assembler.

A buffer is probably needed to hold each input assembly language statement, and another buffer is needed to hold the line image corresponding to that statement for the listing of the program. In addition buffers may be needed to create the object module output for the loader, and to perform double buffering in order to maximize CPU-I/O overlap. Various variables are needed to count the number of cards read, the number of symbols in the symbol table, and so on.

One variable in particular is important. This is the *location counter*. The location counter is a variable which stores the address of the location into which the current instruction is to be loaded. The value of the location counter is used whenever the symbol "*" is used, and this value can be set by the ORIG pseudo-instruction. Normally the value of the location counter is increased by one after each instruction is assembled, in order to load the next instruction into the next location in memory. The value of the location counter for each instruction is used to instruct the loader where to load the instruction.

8.2 GENERAL FLOW OF AN ASSEMBLER

With a familiarity with the basic data structures of an assembler (the opcode table, the symbol table, and the location counter), we can now describe the general flow of an assembler. Each input assembly statement, each card, is handled separately, so our most general flow would be simply, "Process each card until an END pseudo-instruction is found."

More specifically, consider what kind of processing is needed for each card:

1. Read in a card.
2. If the card is a comment (column 1 is an "*") then skip over processing to step 4 for printing.
3. For noncomment cards, get the opcode and search the opcode table for it. Using the type field of the opcode table entry, process this card.
4. After the card has been processed, print a line of listing for this card.
5. If the opcode was not an END pseudo-instruction, go back to step 1 to process the next card.

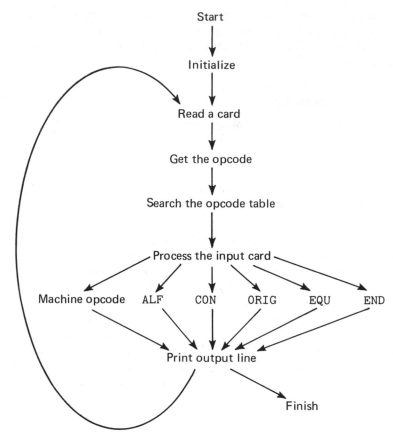

FIGURE 8.2 The general flow of an assembler (for MIXAL). Refinement of this general design resulted in the assembler described in Section 8.3.

This much of the assembly process is common to all of the input cards. The important processing is in step 3, where each card is processed according to its type. This level of the assembler provides an organizational framework for further development.

Machine language instructions

Continuing then, what processing needs to be done for each type of opcode? Consider a machine language instruction. For a machine language instruction, we need to determine the contents of each of the four fields of a machine language instruction. In addition, we must define any label which is in the label field. Let us define the label first. Defining a label is simply a matter of entering the label (if any) in the label field of the assembly language statement into the symbol table with a value which is the value of the current location counter.

Now we need to determine the fields of the machine language instruction. The opcode field (byte 5:5) and the field specification (byte 4:4) are available in the opcode table entry which has already been found. To find the other fields (address and index), let us assume that we have a subroutine which will evaluate an expression. This subroutine will be written later. Then, to define the address field, we call our expression evaluator. The value it returns is the contents of the address field (bytes 0:2). When it returns, we check the next character. If the next character is a comma ",", then an index part follows and we call the expression evaluator again to evaluate the index part. If the next character is not a comma, then the index part is zero (default). When the index has been processed, we check the next character. If it is a left parenthesis, then the expression which follows is a field specification, and we call the expression evaluator again. Otherwise, we use the default specification from the opcode table.

Basically, we have defined an assembly language statement to be of the form

```
LABEL          OP    EXPRESSION,EXPRESSION(EXPRESSION)
```

and have written one subroutine which will evaluate each expression. From this we can determine the value of each of the fields of the machine language instruction to be generated for this assembly language instruction. Now, we assemble the generated word

```
              LDA    OPCODE
              STA    MACHLANG(5:5)
              LDA    FIELD
              STA    MACHLANG(4:4)
              LDA    INDEX
              STA    MACHLANG(3:3)
              LDA    ADDRESS
              STA    MACHLANG(0:2)
```

and output it for the loader, to be loaded at the address indicated by the location counter. Then we advance the location counter and we are ready for the next input card.

Pseudo instruction processing

The processing for each pseudo-instruction is generally easy.

For an ORIG instruction, no code is generated. Rather, only two things need be done. First, if a label is present, it should be defined. Its value is the value of the location counter. Second, the expression in the operand field is evaluated and the value of the expression is stored as the new value of the location counter. We can use the same expression evaluator that is used for evaluation of the machine language operands.

The EQU pseudo-instruction is similarly straightforward. For an EQU instruction, we first evaluate the operand expression (using the expression evaluator as before), and then we enter the symbol in the label field into the symbol table with a value of the expression.

The ALF pseudo-instruction is even easier. In this case we first define the label of the instruction. Then we pick up the character code of the five characters of the ALF operand and issue them as a generated word, incrementing the location counter after we do so.

The most complicated pseudo-instruction is probably the CON instruction. The general form of this instruction is

$$\text{CON} \quad exp_1(fexp_1), exp_2(fexp_2), \ldots, exp_n(fexp_n)$$

Notice that again we can use our expression evaluation routine. With this subroutine, the assembler code to handle a CON instruction is simply,

1. Initialize the generated word to zero.
2. Evaluate the next expression.
3. If the next character is a left parenthesis, then evaluate the next expression to get a field specification; otherwise use a field specification of 0:5.
4. Store the expression from step 2 in the indicated field of the generated word.
5. If the next character is a comma, then go back to step 2, to repeat for the next part of the CON instruction.

Once the operand of the CON instruction has been generated, it can be output for loading and the location counter can be incremented.

The last pseudo-instruction the assembler will encounter is the END pseudo-instruction. For this pseudo-instruction, we first define the label. Then we evaluate the operand expression and output it to the loader as the starting address.

As you can see, each pseudo-instruction requires its own section of code for correct processing, and the pseudo-instruction processing for each is different. However, the processing for each individual pseudo-instruction, considered separately, is not overly complicated. The basic functions used in processing all assembly language instructions involve defining labels, evaluating expressions, and generating code. The first of these was discussed in Section 8.1, so now let us consider the evaluation of expressions.

Expression evaluation

An expression in MIXAL is composed of two basic elements: operands and operators. The operators are addition (+), subtraction (−), multiplication (*), division (/), and "multiplication by eight and addition" (:). The operands are of three types: numbers, symbols, and "*". Numbers have a value which is defined by the number itself, interpreted as a decimal number. Symbols are defined by the value field of their symbol table entry. The value of * is the value of the location counter.

The operators are applied to the operands strictly left to right, without precedence. This allows a very simple expression evaluation routine whose code is basically as follows.

1. Evaluate the first operand. Save its value in VALUE1.
2. If the next character is an operator, remember it and go on to step 3. Otherwise stop. VALUE1 is the value of the expression.
3. Evaluate the second operand. Save its value in VALUE2.
4. Apply the operator to VALUE1 and VALUE2, saving the result in VALUE1. Then go back to step 2.

And that is all that there is to it. Expressions for MIXAL have been defined in such a way that their evaluation is quite simple. Only one problem has been ignored. That problem is forward references.

Forward references

The forward referencing problem arises in a very simple way: the expression evaluator attempts to evaluate an operand which is a symbol by searching the symbol table, and finds that the symbol is not in the symbol table. The symbol is not defined, the expression cannot be evaluated, and the assembly language statement cannot be assembled. What can be done?

One solution is to disallow forward references. MIXAL uses this approach in several places. No pseudo-instruction can make a forward reference. Forward references are not allowed in the index or field specification fields of an instruction. However, a restriction to no forward references would be extremely inconvenient and so two other solutions are more commonly used for allowing some forward references. These two solutions result in two classes of assemblers: *one pass* assemblers and *two-pass* assemblers. Since two pass assemblers are conceptually simpler, we consider them first.

Two pass assemblers

A two-pass assembler makes two passes over the input program. That is, it reads the program twice. On the first pass, the assembler constructs the symbol table. On the second pass, the complete symbol table is used to allow expressions to be evaluated without problems due to forward references. If any symbol is not in the symbol table during an expression evaluation, it is an error, not a forward reference.

Briefly, for a two-pass assembler, the first pass constructs the symbol table; the second pass generates object code. This causes a major change in the basic flow of an assembler, and results in another important data structure: the intermediate text. Since two passes are being made over the input assembly lan-

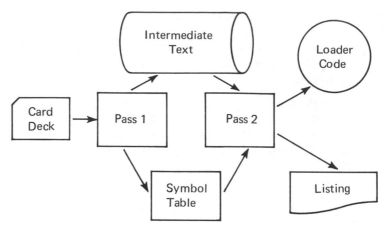

FIGURE 8.3 A block diagram of a two-pass assembler. Pass 1 produces a symbol table and a copy of the input source program for pass 2. Pass 2 produces loader code and a listing.

guage, it is necessary to save a copy of the program read for pass 1, to be used in pass two. Notice that since the assembly listing includes the generated machine language code, and the machine language code is not produced until pass 2, the assembly listing is not produced until pass 2. This requires storing the entire input program, including comments, and so forth, which are not needed by the assembler during pass 2.

The intermediate text can be stored in several ways. The best storage location would be in main memory. However, since MIX memory is so small, this technique is not possible on the MIX computer. On other machines, with more memory, this technique is sometimes used for very small programs. Another approach, used for very small machines, is to simply require the programmer to read his program into the computer twice, once for pass 1, and again for pass 2. A PDP-8 assembler has used this approach, even going so far as to require the program be read in a third time if a listing is desired.

A more common solution is to store the intermediate text on a secondary storage device, such as tape, drum, or disk. During pass 1, the original program is read in, and copied to secondary storage as the symbol table is constructed. Between passes, the device is repositioned (rewound for tapes, or the head moved back to the first track for moving head disk or drum). During pass 2, the program is read back from secondary storage for object code generation and printing a listing. (Notice that precautions should be taken that the same tape is not used for both storage of the intermediate text input for pass 2 and the storage of the object code produced as output from pass 2 for the loader.)

The general flow of a two-pass assembler differs from that given above, in that now each card must be processed twice, with different processing on each pass. It is also still necessary to process each type of card differently, depending upon its opcode type. This applies to both pass 1 and pass 2.

For machine instructions, pass 1 processing involves simply defining the label (if any) and incrementing the location counter by one. ALF and CON pseudo-instructions are handled in the same way. ORIG statements must be handled exactly as we described above, however, in order for the location counter to have the correct value for defining labels. Similarly, EQU statements must also be treated on pass 1. This means that no matter what approach is used, no forward references can be allowed in ORIG or EQU statements, since both are processed during pass 1. The END statement needs to have its label defined and then should jump to pass 2 for further processing.

During pass 2, EQU statements can be treated as comments. The label field can likewise be ignored. ALF, CON, and machine instructions will be processed as described above, as will the END statement.

The need to make two passes over the program can result in considerable duplication in code and computation during pass 1 and pass 2. For example, on both passes, we need to find the type of the opcode; on pass 1, to be able to treat ORIG, EQU, and END statements; on pass 2, for all types. This can result in having to search the opcode table twice for each assembly language statement. To prevent this, we need only save the index into the opcode table of the opcode (once it is found during pass 1) with each instruction. Also, consider that since the operand "*" may be used in the expressions evaluated during pass 2, it is necessary to duplicate during pass 2 the efforts of pass 1 to define the location counter, unless we can simply store with each assembly language statement the value of the location counter for that statement.

These considerations can result in extending the definition of the intermediate text to be more than simply the input to pass 1. Each input assembly language statement can be a record containing (at least) the following fields.

1. the input card image.
2. the index of the opcode into the opcode table.
3. the location counter value for this statement.

Additional fields may include error flags, a pointer to the column in which the operand starts (for free-format assemblers), a line number, and so on; whatever is conveniently computed on pass 1 and needed on pass 2.

Even more can be computed during pass 1. For example, ALF and CON statements can be completely processed during pass 1. The opcode field, field specification, and index field for a machine instruction can be easily computed during pass 1, and most of the time the address field, too, can be processed on pass 1. It is only the occasional forward reference which causes a second pass to be needed. Most two-pass assemblers store a partially digested form of the input source program as their intermediate text for pass 2.

Assemblers, like loaders, are almost always I/O-bound programs, since the time to read a card generally far exceeds the time to assemble it. Thus, requiring two passes means an assembler takes twice as long to execute as an assembler which only uses one pass.

One pass assemblers

It is these considerations which have given rise to one-pass assemblers. A one-pass assembler does everything in one pass through the program, much as described earlier. The only problem with a one-pass assembler is caused by forward references, of course. The solutions to this problem are the same as were presented earlier for one-pass relocatable linking loaders: use tables or chaining.

In either case, use table or chaining, it is not possible to completely generate the machine language statement which corresponds to an assembly language statement; the address field cannot always be defined. Thus, some later program must fix-up those instructions with forward reference. In a two-pass assembler, this program is pass 2. In a one-pass assembler, there is no second pass, and so the program which must fix-up the forward references is the *loader*. The loader resolves forward references for a one-pass assembler.

If use tables are used to solve the future reference problem, then the assembler keeps track of all forward references to each symbol. After the value of the symbol is defined, the assembler generates special loader instructions to tell the loader the addresses of all forward references to a symbol and its correct value. When the loader encounters these special instructions during loading, it will fix-up the address field of the forward reference instruction to have the correct value.

A variation of this same idea is to use chaining. With chaining, the entries in the use table are kept in the address fields of the instructions which forward reference symbols. Only the address of the most recent use must be kept. When a new forward reference is encountered, the address of the previous reference is used, and the address of the most recent reference is kept. When a symbol is defined which has been forward referenced (or at the end of the program), special instructions are again issued to the loader to fix-up the chains which have been produced.

Variations on this basic theme are possible also. For example, if the standard loader will not fix-up forward references, it would be possible for the assembler to generate some special instructions which would be executed first, after loading, but before the assembled program is executed to fix-up forward references. But the basic idea remains the same: a one-pass assembler generates its object code for the loader in such a way that the loader, or the loaded program itself, will fix-up forward references.

Other considerations

Listings

Throughout the discussion of the assembly process, so far, we have ignored many of the (relatively) minor points concerning the writing of an assembler. One of the most visible of these considerations is the assembly listing. The assembly listing gives, for each input assembly line, the correspondingly generated machine language code. Notice, however, that not all assembly language statements result in the generation of machine language code, and not all code is meant to be interpreted in the same way (some are instructions, others numbers or character code).

For a machine language statement, useful information which can be listed includes the card image, card number, location counter, and generated code, broken down by field. For an ORIG, EQU, or END statement, on the other hand, no code is generated, but the value of the operand expression would be of interest. A CON or ALF statement would need to list the generated word, but as a number, not broken down by fields, as an instruction. Forward references in a one-pass assembler might be specially marked, as might a relocatable address field in a relocatable assembly program.

In addition to the listing of the input assembly, some assemblers also print a copy of their symbol table after it is completed. This symbol table listing would include the defined symbols, their values, and perhaps the input card number where they were defined. Some assemblers will also produce a *cross reference listing*, which is a listing, for each symbol, of the card numbers or memory locations in the program of all references to that symbol. Most symbol table listings and cross reference listings are ordered alphabetically by symbol to aid in finding a particular symbol.

Errors

Another concern is the problem of errors. Many programs have assembler errors in them. These are errors not in what the program does, but in its form. These can be caused by mistakes in writing the program, or in the transcription of the program into a machine-readable form, like keypunching. The assembler must check for errors at all times. Typical errors include, multiply-defined symbols (using the same symbol in the label field twice), undefined symbols (using a symbol in the operand field of a statement, but never defining it in the label field), undefined opcodes (opcode cannot be found in the opcode table), illegal use of a forward reference, an illegal value for a field (index or field specification value not between 0 and 63, or address expression not between -4095 and $+4095$), and so on.

For each possible error, two things must be decided: (1) how to notify the programmer of the error, and (2) what to do next. The notification is often simplest. An error symbol or error number is associated with each type of error. The degree of specification of the exact error varies. One approach is to simply declare "error in assembly" or "error in *xxxx* part", where *xxxx* may be replaced by "label", "opcode", or "operand." However, these approaches may not give the programmer enough information to find and correct the error. The opposite approach is also sometimes taken, over-specifying the error to the extent that the user's manual lists thousands of errors, most of which are equivalent (from the point of view of the programmer), and with each error highly unlikely.

More typically, the major errors are classified and identified, while more obscure and unlikely errors are grouped into a category such as "syntax error in operand part." The listing line format may include a field in which errors are flagged, or a statement with an error may be followed by an error message.

In any case, the writer of the assembler must check for all possible errors in the input assembly program. If one is found, a decision must be made as to what to do next. This often may depend upon the type of error which is found, and the error handling code for each error is generally different. For a multiply-defined label, the second definition is often ignored, or the latest definition may always be used. An undefined opcode may be assumed to be a comment card, or treated like a HLT or NOP instruction. Illegal values for any of the fields of an instruction can result in default values being used.

Whatever the specific approach taken to a specific error, a general approach must also be taken. From the way in which an assembly language program is written, each input statement is basically a separate item to be translated. Thus, an error in one statement still allows the assembler to continue its assembly of the remaining program by simply ignoring the statement which is in error. This is in contrast to some systems which cease all operations whenever the first error is found. An assembler can always continue with the next card, after an error is found in the current card.

A more subtle point is whether or not an assembler should attempt to continue assembling the card in which the error occurs. If the opcode is undefined, the assembler may misinterpret the label field or operand field, causing it to appear that there are more (or fewer) errors than exist, once the incorrect opcode is corrected. (For example, a typing error on an ALF card may result in an undefined opcode. If the operand field of the incorrect ALF is treated as if the opcode were a machine instruction, then the character sequence for the ALF may result in an apparent reference to an undefined symbol.) On the other hand, attempting to continue assembling a card after an error may identify additional errors which would save the programmer several extra assemblies to find.

Relocatable versus absolute assembly

The discussion of loaders and linkers in Chapter 7 mentioned several differences between an assembly language which is used with a relocatable loader and an assembly language for an absolute loader. These differences show up in the assembly language in terms of the pseudo-instructions available and also in restrictions on the types of expressions (absolute or relocatable) which can be used.

It should be relatively obvious that the changes in the assembler for absolute and relocatable programs are not major changes, but consist mainly in the writing of some new code to handle the new pseudo-instructions and some changes in code generation format to match the input expected by a relocatable loader. Extra tables may be required for listing entry points and external symbols, and a type field will need to be added to the symbol table to distinguish between absolute symbols, relocatable symbols, entry points, and external symbols.

Load-and-go assemblers

Another type of assembler, in addition to relocatable versus absolute and one-pass versus two-pass, is the *load-and-go* assembler. These assemblers are typically used on large computers for small programs (like programs written by students just learning the assembly language). The idea of a load-and-go assembler is to both assemble and load a program at the same time. The major problem with this, on most machines, including the MIX computer, is the size of memory and the size of the assembler. There is simply not enough room for both a program and the assembler in memory at the same time.

However, for a simple assembly language, giving rise to a simple and small assembler, and with a large memory, it is possible to write an assembler which, rather than generating loader code, loads the program directly into memory as it is assembled. The assembler acts as both an assembler and a loader at the same time. These load-and-go systems often are one-pass, absolute assemblers, but can just as well be two-pass and/or relocatable assemblers.

Where they are possible, load-and-go systems are generally significantly faster than nonload-and-go systems, since they save on I/O.

8.3 AN EXAMPLE ASSEMBLER

To demonstrate the techniques which have been discussed in this Chapter, we present here the actual code for a one-pass absolute assembler for MIXAL. The assembler accepts a MIXAL program from the card reader. It produces a listing on the line printer, and object code similar to that accepted by the absolute loader of Section 7.1 (with modifications for fix-ups).

The assembler is presented from the bottom up. That is, the simpler routines, which do not call other routines, are written first. Then we write routines which may call these routines, and so forth until the main program is written. This order of writing the assembler is possible mainly because the discussion in Section 8.2 has shown which routines we need for the assembler and how they fit together.

Each routine is written to be an independent function, as much as possible. Registers should be saved and restored by each routine as needed, with the exception of registers I5 and I6. Register I6 is used as the location counter of the assembly program. Register I5 is a column indicator for the lexical scan portion of the assembler.

Tape output routines

Since the loader output is being written to tape, but is produced one word at a time by the assembler, several routines are needed to handle the tape output.

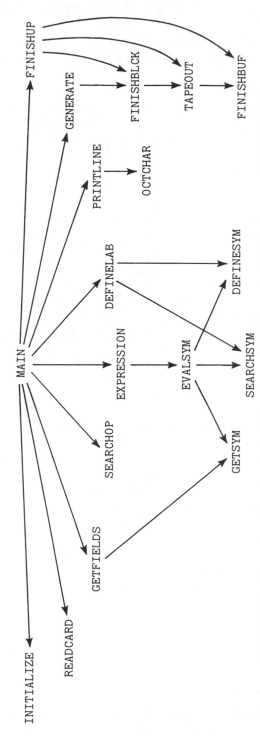

FIGURE 8.4 The subroutine structure of the example MIXAL assembler. Each name is the name of a subroutine, and an arrow from one subroutine to another indicates that one subroutine may call the other in the course of its program. For example EXPRESSION may call EVALSYM, which may call GETSYM SEARCHSYM, and DEFINESYM.

The first two routines TAPEOUT and FINISHBUF are standard blocking routines such as discussed in Chapter 5. TAPEOUT accepts as a parameter one word, in the A register. These words are stored into a buffer of 100 words (one physical record) until the buffer is full. When the buffer is full, TAPEOUT calls FINISHBUF, which simply outputs the current buffer and resets the buffer pointers to allow double buffering. FINISHBUF can also be called to empty the last, partially filled buffer before the assembler halts.

Variables for these routines would include the two buffers (BUF1 and BUF2), pointers to these two buffers for double buffering, and a counter of the number of words in the buffer.

```
*
*                 TAPE  BUFFER  VARIABLES
*
BUF1              ORIG  *+100    BUFFERS
BUF2              ORIG  *+100
STOREBUF          CON   BUF1     POINTER TO BUFFER FOR STORING
TAPEBUF           CON   BUF2     POINTER TO BUFFER FOR OUTPUT
TAPEBUFPTR        CON   BUF1     CURRENT WORD POINTER
TAPECNTR          CON   100      NUMBER OF WORDS LEFT
*
*
*
*                 SUBROUTINE FINISHBUF
*
*                 LOADER WORDS TO BE WRITTEN TO TAPE FOR
*                 LOADING ARE STORED IN A BUFFER UNTIL 100
*                 WORDS ARE ACCUMULATED. THEN THIS ROUTINE
*                 IS CALLED TO DUMP THE BUFFER TO TAPE. DOUBLE
*                 BUFFERING IS USED.
*
FINISHBUF         STJ   FIBEXIT
                  ST1   FIBSAVE1(0:2)  SAVE REGISTERS
                  ST2   FIBSAVE2(0:2)
*
                  LD1   STOREBUF       CURRENT BUFFER
                  OUT   0,1(TAPE)      WRITE BUFFER TO TAPE
                  LD2   TAPEBUF        SWITCH BUFFER POINTERS
                  ST2   STOREBUF
                  ST2   TAPEBUFPTR     AND RESET POINTER
                  ST1   TAPEBUF
*
FIBSAVE1          ENT1  *              RESTORE REGISTERS
FIBSAVE2          ENT2  *
```

```
FIBEXIT         JMP   *
*
*
*
*               SUBROUTINE TAPEOUT
*
*               THIS SUBROUTINE ACCEPTS ONE WORD TO BE
*               WRITTEN TO THE TAPE FOR THE LOADER AND
*               STORES IT IN THE BUFFER UNTIL THE BUFFER IS
*               FULL. THEN IT CALLS FINISHBUF TO EMPTY
*               THE BUFFER.
*
*               INPUT WORD IS IN THE A REGISTER
*
TAPEOUT         STJ   TOEXIT       SAVE REGISTERS
                ST1   TOSAVE1(0:2)
*
                LD1   TAPEBUFPTR   NEXT WORD POINTER
                STA   0,1          SAVE WORD
                INC1  1
                ST1   TAPEBUFPTR   UPDATE POINTER
*
                LD1   TAPECNTR     CHECK FOR FULL BUFFER
                DEC1  1
                J1P   STILLROOM
                JMP   FINISHBUF    BUFFER FULL
                ENT1  100          RESET COUNTER
*
STILLROOM       ST1   TAPECNTR     RESTORE COUNTER
*
TOSAVE1         ENT1  *
TOEXIT          JMP   *
*
```

Loader code generation routines

The TAPEOUT routine is called mainly by the routines which create the loader output. These routines are mainly concerned with formatting the output from the assembler. The loader output is a series of logical records, as described in Chapter 7. For a one-pass absolute loader, we need three types of loader records: (a) words to be stored in memory, (b) chain addresses for forward reference fix-up, and (c) the start address of the assembled program. Each block is identified by a header word of the format shown in Figure 8.5.

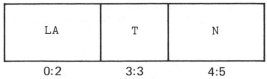

LA	T	N
0:2	3:3	4:5

FIGURE 8.5   The format of the header word for a loader record.

Byte 3 (T) is a type byte which is used to indicate the type of information in N (bytes 4:5) and LA (bytes 0:2). They can have only a value of 0, 1, or 2, as follows,

1. $T = 0$. The address LA is a load address. The next N words on the tape should be loaded into locations LA, LA+1, . . . , LA+N−1. A checksum follows these N words.
2. $T = 1$. The address LA is the first address of a chain of addresses of locations which were forward references. The value N should be used to fix-up this chain of forward references.
3. $T = 2$. The address LA is the starting address of the program. N should be zero.

Most of the output to the tape will be of type 0. These words are produced by the assembler one at a time and need to be blocked into N word groups with a header in front and a checksum following. Notice that the header cannot be output until the value of N is known. So words are stored in a buffer (LDRBLOCK) until a discontinuity in load addresses occurs, or the buffer is full. Then the

FIGURE 8.6   The three types of loader records. The type of record is determined by byte 3:3.

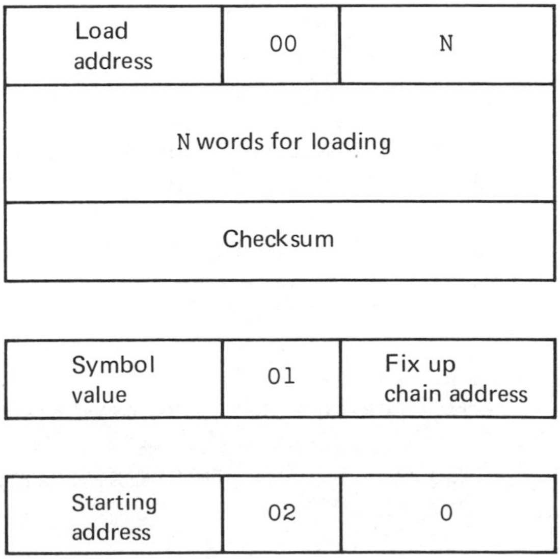

Load address	00	N
N words for loading		
Checksum		

Symbol value	01	Fix up chain address

Starting address	02	0

header and checksum are attached and the entire block written to tape by use of the routine `TAPEOUT`. The variables and code for this are

```
*
*                  LOADER BLOCK VARIABLES
*
BLCKLENGTH    CON  63              LENGTH OF LDRBLOCK
LDRBLOCK      ORIG *+64            BLOCK FOR LOADER RECORDS
NXTLOADLOC    CON  0              INDEX INTO LDRBLOCK
*
```

Two routines are used; one (`GENERATE`) puts the words into the loader record block (`LDRBLOCK`), while the other (`FINISHBLCK`) will empty the buffer, output it to tape, and compute the checksum.

```
*
*              GENERATE
*
*              GENERATE A WORD OF LOADER OUTPUT.
*              THE LOADER WORD IS IN VALUE. REGISTER I6 HAS
*              THE ADDRESS OF THE LOCATION WHERE IT SHOULD
*              BE LOADED. IF THIS WORD IS A CONTINUATION
*              OF THE CURRENT BUFFER, IT IS SIMPLY STORED.
*              IF THE WORD IS NONCONTIGUOUS OR FILLS THE
*              BUFFER, THE BUFFER IS EMPTIED.
*
GNSAVEA       ORIG *+1
*
GENERATE      STJ  GENEXIT
              STA  GNSAVEA
              ST1  GNSAVE1(0:2)
*
              CMP6 NXTLOADLOC      CHECK IF CONTIGUOUS
              JNE  FINISHBLCK      IF NOT, FINISH OLD BLOCK
*
              LD1  LDRBLOCK(4:5)   NUMBER OF WORDS
              INC1 1
              ST1  LDRBLOCK(4:5)
*
              LDA  VALUE
              STA  LDRBLOCK,1   STORE GENERATED WORD
*
              INC6 1              INCREASE LOCATION COUNTER
              ST6  NXTLOADLOC
*
```

```
                 CMP1 BLCKLENGTH  CHECK FOR END OF BLOCK
                 JGE  FINISHBLCK  IF SO, FINISH BLOCK
                 LDA  GNSAVEA
GNSAVE1          ENT1 *           RESTORE REGISTER
GENEXIT          JMP  *
*
*
*
*                SUBROUTINE FINISHBLCK
*
*                OUTPUT TO THE LOADER THE BLOCK IN LDRBLOCK.
*                NUMBER OF WORDS IS IN BYTE 4:5 OF FIRST WORD.
*                (MAY BE ZERO, IN WHICH CASE IGNORE CALL).
*                COMPUTE CHECKSUM AND OUTPUT IT TOO
*
CHECKSUM         ORIG *+1
FLBSAVEA         ORIG *+1
FINISHBLCK       STJ  FLBEXIT
                 STA  FLBSAVEA
                 ST1  FLBSAVE1(0:2)
*
                 LD1  LDRBLOCK(4:5)
                 J1Z  FLBQUIT     IF BLOCK IS EMPTY
*
                 STZ  CHECKSUM    INITIALIZE CHECKSUM
                 ENT1 0           INDEX AND COUNTER
*
BLOCKOUT         LDA  LDRBLOCK,1
                 JMP  TAPEOUT     OUTPUT EACH WORD
                 ADD  CHECKSUM(1:5)
                 STA  CHECKSUM(1:5) AND COMPUTE CHECKSUM
*
                 INC1 1
                 CMP1 LDRBLOCK(4:5)  CHECK ALL WORD OUT
                 JLE  BLOCKOUT
*
                 LDA  CHECKSUM(1:5)  OUTPUT CHECKSUM
                 JMP  TAPEOUT
*
                 JOV  *+1         TURN OVERFLOW OFF (IF ON)
*
FLBQUIT          STZ  LDRBLOCK    NEW HEADER WORD
                 ST6  LDRBLOCK(0:2)
*
```

```
                      LDA   FLBSAVEA      RESTORE REGISTERS
FLBSAVE1              ENT1  *
FLBEXIT              JMP   *
*
```

Input routines

Subroutine READCARD will read one card and unpack it into a one-character-per-word card image form. Double buffering is used.

```
*
INBUF                ORIG  *+16
CARD                 ORIG  *+80
CARDNUMBER           CON   0             NUMBER OF CARDS READ
*
*
*
*                    SUBROUTINE READCARD
*
*                    READ THE NEXT CARD FROM THE CARD READER AND
*                    UNPACK IT INTO THE CHARACTER ARRAY CARD. THE
*                    CARD IS READ INTO THE BUFFER INBUF AND WE
*                    TRY TO KEEP THE CARD READER BUSY BY THIS
*                    DOUBLE BUFFERING.
*
RCSAVEA              ORIG  *+1
*
READCARD             STJ   RCEXIT        SAVE REGISTERS
                     STA   RCSAVEA
                     ST1   RCSAVE1(0:2)
                     ST2   RCSAVE2(0:2)
                     ST3   RCSAVE3(0:2)
*
                     JBUS  *(CR)         WAIT TILL CARD READ
                     ENT1  79            79..0 CHARACTER COUNTER
                     ENT2  15            15..0 WORD COUNTER
*
*                    UNPACK CARD FROM RIGHT TO LEFT
*
NEXTWORD             LDA   INBUF,2
                     DEC2  1
                     ENT3  4                 4..0 NUMBER OF CHARACTERS
*
NEXTCHAR             STA   CARD,1(5:5)
```

```
                DEC1  1
                J1N   CARDDONE    IF ALL DONE
                DEC3  1
                J3N   NEXTWORD    OR NEW WORD NEEDED
                SRA   1
                JMP   NEXTCHAR    ELSE SHIFT AND CONTINUE
*
CARDDONE        IN    INBUF(CR)   START NEXT READ
                LDA   CARDNUMBER
                INCA  1           INCREMENT NUMBER OF CARDS
                STA   CARDNUMBER
*
                LDA   RCSAVEA     RESTORE REGISTERS
RCSAVE1         ENT1  *
RCSAVE2         ENT2  *
RCSAVE3         ENT3  *
RCEXIT          JMP   *
*
```

Lexical scan routines

GETSYM is the main lexical scan routine. Using index register I5 as a pointer to the card image in CARD, GETSYM packs the next symbol into SYM. SYM is 2 words, to allow up to 10 characters per symbol. A symbol is delimited by any nonalphabetic, nonnumeric character. If the current character is nonalphanumeric, then SYM will be blank. The variable LETTER is used to indicate if the symbol is strictly numeric (LETTER zero) or contains an alphabetic character (LETTER nonzero). Numeric symbols are right-justified (to allow NUMing), while symbols with letters are left-justified.

```
*
SYM             ORIG  *+2         SYMBOL
LETTER          ORIG  *+1         NUMERIC=ZERO
*
*
*
*                     SUBROUTINE GETSYM
*
*                     GET THE NEXT SYMBOL FROM CARD(I5) AND PACK
*                     IT INTO SYM UNTIL A DELIMITER. I5 WILL BE
*                     MOVED TO POINT TO THE DELIMITER. LETTER IS
*                     ZERO IF NO LETTER FOUND.
*
GSSAVEA         ORIG  *+1
```

```
GSSAVEX         ORIG  *+1
*
GETSYM          STJ   GSEXIT        SAVE REGISTERS
                STA   GSSAVEA
                STX   GSSAVEX
                ST1   GSSAVE1(0:2)
                ST2   GSSAVE2(0:2)
*
                ENT1  10            MAXIMUM NUMBER OF CHARACTERS
                STZ   LETTER
                ENTX  0
                ENTA  0             BLANK AX
*
SCANSYM         LD2   CARD,5
                CMP2  CHARA(5:5)    MUST BE AT LEAST A
                JL    ENDSYM
                CMP2  CHAR9(5:5)    AND NOT MORE THAN 9
                JG    ENDSYM
                CMP2  CHAR0(5:5)    ALSO CHECK IF 0..9
                JGE   *+2
                STJ   LETTER(4:5)   LETTER FOUND
*

                DEC1  1             DECREMENT NUMBER OF CHARACTERS
                J1N   *+3
                SLAX  1
                INCX  0,2           ADD NEW CHARACTER TO SYMBOL
                INC5  1             NEXT COLUMN
                JMP   SCANSYM
*
SYMERROR        JMP   BADSYM        BAD SYMBOL (TOO LONG)
                JMP   GSQUIT        NO JUSTIFICATION NEEDED
*
ENDSYM          J1N   SYMERROR      CHECK IF TOO LONG
                LD2   LETTER        CHECK IF NEED JUSTIFY
                J2Z   *+2
                SLAX  0,1           REGISTER 1 HAS COUNT
*
GSQUIT          STA   SYM           SAVE SYMBOL
                STX   SYM+1
*
                LDA   GSSAVEA
                LDX   GSSAVEX
GSSAVE1         ENT1  *
```

```
GSSAVE2         ENT2  *
GSEXIT          JMP   *
*
```

GETSYM is used by GETFIELDS (among others). GETFIELDS gets the label
and opcode fields of an assembly language program for later processing. This
MIXAL assembler accepts only fixed-format input, and GETFIELDS reflects this.
Notice that the change to a free-format assembler would require only that this
one subroutine need be changed.

```
*
LABEL           ORIG  *+2       SPACE FOR LABEL (IF ANY)
OP              ORIG  *+1       AND OPCODE
*
*
*                     SUBROUTINE GETFIELDS
*
*                     GET THE FIELDS FOR THE ASSEMBLY LANGUAGE.
*                     FIELDS ARE LABEL, OPCODE AND OPERAND. LABEL
*                     MAY BE MISSING. REGISTER I5 IS LEFT
*                     POINTING JUST BEFORE THE OPERAND.
*                     THE EXPRESSION ROUTINE WILL SKIP ONE COLUMN
*                     TO BEGIN EVALUATION, SO LEAVE I5 ONE BEFORE
*                     THE START OF THE OPERAND.
*
*                     FIXED FIELD
*
GFSAVEA         ORIG  *+1
*
GETFIELDS       STJ   GFEXIT       SAVE REGISTERS
                STA   GFSAVEA
                ST1   GFSAVE1(0:2)
*
                STZ   LABEL        DEFAULT IS BLANK LABEL
                LDA   CARD         CHECK COLUMN ONE
                JAZ   NOLABEL
                ENT5  0            COLUMN OF LABEL
                JMP   GETSYM
*
                LDA   LETTER       ERROR CHECKING
                JANZ  LEGALLABEL
                JMP   BADSYM       NUMERIC SYMBOL
                JMP   NOLABEL
*
LEGALLABEL      ENT1  LABEL        MOVE LABEL FROM SYM
```

```
                        MOVE  SYM(2)
        *
        NOLABEL         ENT5  11              OPCODE
                        JMP   GETSYM
                        LDA   SYM(1:4)      FOUR CHAR OPCODE
                        STA   OP
        *
                        ENT5  15              READY FOR OPERAND
        *                                     (COLUMN 17)
        *
                        LDA   GFSAVEA
        GFSAVE1         ENT1  *
        GFEXIT          JMP   *
        *
```

Table search and enter routines

Both the opcode table and symbol table need search routines, and the symbol table needs an enter routine.

Each entry of the opcode table is two words. The symbolic opcode is in bytes 1:4 of the first word. Byte 5:5 is a type field. For machine instructions, word 2 has the default field and the numeric opcode in bytes 4 and 5, while word 2 is ignored for pseudo-instructions.

```
        OPTAB           EQU   *
                        ALF   ADD
                        ADD
                        ALF   ALF C
                        CON   0
                        ALF   CHAR
                        CHAR
                        ALF   CMPA
                        CMPA
                        ALF   CMPX
                        CMPX
                        ALF   CMP1
                        CMP1
                        ALF   CMP2
                        CMP2
                        ...
                        ALF   ENT6
                        ENT6
                        ALF   EQU D
                        CON   0
```

```
HLTINDEX        EQU   *-OPTAB/2    INDEX OF HLT
                ALF   HLT
                HLT
                ALF   IN
                IN
                ALF   INCA
                INCA
                ...
                ALF   ST6
                ST6
                ALF   SUB
                SUB
*
NUMBEROPS       EQU   *-OPTAB/2    2 LOCATIONS PER ENTRY
*
OPTYPE          CON   0
*
VALUE           ORIG  *+1
```

Each entry of the symbol table takes four words. The name of the symbol is stored in the first two words, and the value in the third word. If there were any forward references to this symbol, the fourth word contains the address of the last forward reference in bytes 4:5. Forward references are chained through this address.

The sign bit of the first word (D) is used to indicate if the symbol has been defined (D = +) or undefined (D = −). A symbol is undefined only if there has been a (forward) reference to it but it has not yet appeared in the label field.

```
*
NSYMBOL         CON   0            NUMBER OF SYMBOLS (TIMES 4)
SYMINDEX        ORIG  *+1
```

FIGURE 8.7 A symbol table entry (each entry contains the 10-character symbol, value, and a fix-up address, along with a defined/forward reference bit, D).

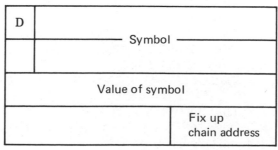

```
SYMTAB          ORIG  4*MAXSYMBOL+*  SYMBOL TABLE
*
```

The opcode table search routine uses a binary search on the ordered opcode table. If the opcode is not found, an error is flagged and a HLT instruction is assumed as the opcode. The division by two in the binary search could be replaced by a right shift by one bit if a binary MIX machine is used.

```
*
*               SUBROUTINE SEARCH OP
*
*               SEARCH THE OPCODE TABLE (OPTAB) FOR THE
*               OPCODE IN OP. A BINARY SEARCH IS USED. IF
*               THE OPCODE IS NOT FOUND, AN UNOP ERROR
*               OCCURS. A HLT IS USED FOR UNOP ERRORS. THE
*               VALUE OF THE SECOND WORD IS STORED IN
*               VALUE AND THE TYPE OF THE OPCODE IN
*               OPTYPE.
*
SOPSAVEA        ORIG  *+1
SOPSAVEX        ORIG  *+1
OPHIGH          ORIG  *+1
OPLOW           ORIG  *+1
OPMID           ORIG  *+1
*
SEARCHOP        STJ   SOPEXIT       SAVE REGISTERS
                STA   SOPSAVEA
                STX   SOPSAVEX
                ST1   SOPSAVE1(0:2)
*
                ENT1  NUMBEROPS-1
                ST1   OPHIGH
                STZ   OPLOW         INITIALIZE HIGH AND LOW
*
SOPLOOP         LDA   OPLOW
                ADD   OPHIGH
                SRAX  5
                DIV   TWO           COMPUTE OPMID = (HIGH+LOW)/2
                STA   OPMID
                LD1   OPMID
                INC1  0,1           2*OPMID (TWO WORDS PER ENTRY)
*
                LDA   OPTAB,1(1:4)
                CMPA  OP            COMPARE OPCODES
                JE    SOPFOUND
```

```
*
                JL    UPLOW
DOWNHIGH        LD1   OPMID        OP < OPTAB[OPMID]
                DEC1  1
                ST1   OPHIGH       SO HIGH = OPMID - 1
                JMP   SOPDONE
*
UPLOW           LD1   OPMID        OP > OPTAB[MID]
                INC1  1
                ST1   OPLOW        SO LOW = OPMID + 1
*
*               JMP   SOPDONE

SOPDONE         LDA   OPHIGH       CHECK FOR END
                CMPA  OPLOW
                JGE   SOPLOOP      CHECK FROM LOW TO HIGH
*
                JMP   UNOP         OPCODE NOT FOUND IN OPTAB
                ENT1  2*HLTINDEX   DEFAULT OPCODE
*
SOPFOUND        LDA   OPTAB+1,1    NUMERIC OPCODE
                STA   VALUE
                LD1   OPTAB,1(5:5) OPCODE TYPE
                ST1   OPTYPE
*
                LDA   SOPSAVEA     RESTORE REGISTERS
                LDX   SOPSAVEX
SOPSAVE1        ENT1  *
SOPEXIT         JMP   *
*
```

A linear search is used for the symbol table. This is not the best search possible, but it is relatively simple. Since the search is done only in this one routine, it can be changed later, if we find a linear search to be too slow. The symbol definition routine simply adds symbols to the end of the table.

```
*
*               SUBROUTINE DEFINESYM
*
*               DEFINE A SYMBOL. PUT IT IN THE SYMBOL
*               TABLE. THE A REGISTER HAS ITS VALUE. THE
*               FORWARD REFERENCE FIELD IS SET TO INDICATE
*               NO FORWARD REFERENCES (YET) BY SETTING IT
*               TO CHAINEND.
*
```

```
DEFINESYM      STJ   DSEXIT       SAVE REGISTERS
               ST1   DSSAVE1(0:2)
*
               LD1   NSYMBOL      NEXT SYMBOL TABLE SPACE
               STA   SYMTAB+2,1   SYMBOL VALUE
               LDA   SYM
               STA   SYMTAB,1     FIRST FIVE CHARS
               LDA   SYM+1
               STA   SYMTAB+1,1   SECOND FIVE
               LDA   CHAINEND
               STA   SYMTAB+3,1(4:5)  FORWARD REFERENCE
*
               ST1   SYMINDEX     SYMBOL INDEX
               INC1  4
               ST1   NSYMBOL      UPDATE NUMBER OF SYMBOLS
*
               LDA   SYMTAB-2,1   RESTORE A REGISTER
DSSAVE1        ENT1  *
DSEXIT         JMP   *
*
*
*
*              SUBROUTINE SEARCHSYM
*
*              SEARCH SYMBOL TABLE. SYMBOL TABLE
*              IS SEARCHED FROM THE BACK TO THE FRONT.
*              THE RESULT OF THE SEARCH IS RETURNED IN
*              SYMINDEX. SYMINDEX IS AN INDEX INTO SYMTAB
*              IF FOUND, OR NEGATIVE
*
SSSAVEA        ORIG  *+1
SSSAVEX        ORIG  *+1
*
SEARCHSYM      STJ   SSEXIT       SAVE REGISTERS
               STA   SSSAVEA
               STX   SSSAVEX
               ST1   SSSAVE1(0:2)
*
               LDA   SYM
               LDX   SYM+1        SYMBOL TO SEARCH FOR
               LD1   NSYMBOL      SYMTAB INDEX
*
SYMLOOP        DEC1  4
               J1N   SYMDONE      IF NEGATIVE, NOT FOUND
```

```
               CMPA  SYMTAB,1(1:5)  COMPARE
               JNE   SYMLOOP
               CMPX  SYMTAB+1,1(1:5)  AND COMPARE
               JNE   SYMLOOP
*
SYMDONE        ST1   SYMINDEX      EITHER FOUND OR NOT
*
SSSAVE1        ENT1  *
               LDA   SSSAVEA
               LDX   SSSAVEX
SSEXIT         JMP   *
*
```

Expression evaluation

Expression evaluation for the MIXAL language is relatively simple since it involves only three types of operands (symbols, numbers, and *) and evaluation of operators is strictly left to right. After checking first for a *, the EVALSYM routine uses GETSYM to get the next symbol from the input card. If the symbol has no letters (LETTER = 0), it is numeric and is converted from character code to a numeric value by the NUM instruction. If the symbol has letters, then the symbol table is searched and the value of the symbol in the symbol table is used.

The evaluation of a symbol is actually more complicated due to forward references. Two special cases may arise in the symbol table search. First, the symbol may not be there. In this case, it must be entered into the table (using DEFINESYM). Then it can be treated like the second case, which involves symbols in the table, but not defined. These are symbols which have previously appeared as forward references. They are distinguished by a "−" sign in the sign bit of the first word of the symbol table entry. In this case, the "value" of the symbol is the previous reference address and the reference address is updated to be this instruction. Since forward references are not always allowed, the undefined nature of the symbol is noted by setting the variable UNDEFSYM to nonzero.

EVALSYM is used by EXPRESSION to evaluate the components of an expression. EXPRESSION evaluates the first component (using EVALSYM) and then examines the next character. If it is a delimiter, the evaluation stops; if it is an operator, the evaluation continues. This decision is made by the use of an array (OPERATOR) which is indexed by the character code of the next character. If the value is zero, the character is a delimiter. If it is nonzero, then the character is an operator and the value is in the range 1 to 5, to be used in a jump table for interpreting that operator. Thus, since the character code for "+" is 44, OPERATOR+44 is 1, OPERATOR+45 is 2 ("−"), OPERATOR+46 is 3 ("*"), OPERATOR+47 is 4 ("/"), and OPERATOR+54 is 5 (":"). All other values are zero.

If the character following an evaluated symbol is an operator, EVALSYM is called again and the two values are combined according to the operator. This process of finding operators, calling EVALSYM to evaluate the symbol, and combining its value with the previously computed value, continues until a delimiter is found.

Several problems must be attended to. Forward references are only allowed when NOFORWARD is zero. UNDEFSYM is used to tell when a symbol is a forward reference. Overflow must also be checked and flagged as an error. This includes expressions which exceed the range which is appropriate for their intended use. (An expression for an index or field specification can only be in the range 0 to 63.) These upper and lower bounds are passed as a parameter to EXPRESSION. The address of the lower bound is passed in register I1; the upper bound follows at 1,1.

```
          *
UNDEFSYM      ORIG  *+1
NOFORWARD     CON   1              NONZERO, NO FORWARDS
          *
          *             UPPER AND LOWER BOUNDS FOR EXPRESSIONS
          *
HLBYTE        CON   0              INDEX, FIELD
              CON   63
HLADDR        CON   0              ADDRESSES (ORIG, END)
              CON   3999
HL2BYTE       CON   -4095          ADDRESS FIELD
              CON   +4095
HLWORD        CON   -1073741823 MIN AND MAX WORD
              CON   +1073741823
          *
          *
OPERATOR      ORIG  *+44           FIRST 44 ZEROS
              CON   1              ADD
              CON   2              SUBTRACT
              CON   3              MULTIPLY
              CON   4              DIVIDE
              ORIG  *+6
              CON   5              COLON OPERATOR
              ORIG  *+10
          *
          *
          *             SUBROUTINE EVALSYM
          *
          *             EVALUATE THE NEXT SYMBOL. VALUE RETURNED
          *             IN A. UNDEFSYM IS NONZERO IF VALUE IS
          *             UNDEFINED. SYMBOLS MAY BE *, NUMBER
```

```
*              OR SYMBOL. GETSYM IS USED TO GET NUMBERS
*              OR SYMBOLS.
*
ESSAVEX      ORIG  *+1
*
EVALSYM      STJ   ESEXIT      SAVE REGISTERS
             ST1   ESSAVE1(0:2)
             STX   ESSAVEX
*
             LDA   CARD,5      CARD(COLUMN)
             CMPA  CHARSTAR    CHECK FOR *
             JNE   NOTSTAR
*
ISSTAR       INC5  1           INCREASE COLUMN COUNTER
             ENTA  0,6         VALUE
             STZ   UNDEFSYM    DEFINED
             JMP   ESQUIT
*
NOTSTAR      JMP   GETSYM      GET SYMBOL
             LD1   LETTER
             J1NZ  ISSYMBOL    LETTER NONZERO MEANS SYMBOL
*
ISNUMBER     LDA   SYM
             LDX   SYM+1       CONVERT SYMBOL TO NUMERIC
             NUM
             JOV   EXPOV       IF OVERFLOW, ERROR
             STZ   UNDEFSYM    DEFINED
             JMP   ESQUIT
*
ISSYMBOL     JMP   SEARCHSYM   SEARCH FOR SYMBOL
             LD1   SYMINDEX
             J1N   ISNOTTHERE  NOT IN SYMBOL TABLE
             LDA   SYMTAB,1
             JAN   ISNOTDEF    IF IN TABLE, NOT DEFINED
*
ISDEFINED    LDA   SYMTAB+2,1
             STZ   UNDEFSYM    DEFINED
             JMP   ESQUIT
*
ISNOTTHERE   ENTA  -1          NOT IN SYMBOL TABLE, ENTER
             JMP   DEFINESYM   ARBITRARY VALUE)
             LD1   SYMINDEX
             STA   SYMTAB,1(0:0) MARK NEGATIVE: FORWARD REF
*
```

```
ISNOTDEF        LDA   SYMTAB+3,1   FORWARD REFERENCE
                STJ   UNDEFSYM(4:5) UNDEFINED VALUE
                ST6   SYMTAB+3,1   UPDATE CHAIN ADDRESS
*
ESQUIT          EQU   *
                LDX   ESSAVEX
ESSAVE1         ENT1  *
ESEXIT          JMP   *
*
*
*               SUBROUTINE EXPRESSION
*
*               EVALUATE THE NEXT EXPRESSION. EXPRESSION
*               STARTS AT COLUMN+1 (COLUMN IN I5). (THE
*               PLUS ONE IS TO SKIP OVER THE LAST DELIMITER)
*               OPERANDS ARE EVALUATED BY EVALSYM.
*               OPERATORS ARE + - * / :
*               AND ARE APPLIED LEFT TO RIGHT UNTIL A
*               DELIMITER IS FOUND.
*
VALUE1          ORIG  *+1
VALUE2          ORIG  *+1
EXPSAVEX        ORIG  *+1
*
EXPRESSION      STJ   EXPEXIT      SAVE REGISTERS
                ST1   EXPSAVE1(0:2)
                ST2   EXPSAVE2(0:2)
                STX   EXPSAVEX
*
                INC5  1
                JMP   EVALSYM      EVALUATE FIRST OPERAND
*
EXPLOOP         LD2   CARD,5       CHECK NEXT COLUMN
                LD2   OPERATOR,2   FOR OPERATOR
                J2NP  EXPOVER
*
                LD1   UNDEFSYM     NO UNDEFS AND OPERATORS
                J1NZ  FORERROR     FORWARD REFERENCE ERROR
*
                INC5  1            SKIP OPERATOR
                STA   VALUE1
                JMP   EVALSYM      SECOND OPERAND
                STA   VALUE2
                LDA   VALUE1
```

```
            JMP   *,2             APPROPRIATE OPERATOR
            JMP   OPADD
            JMP   OPSUB
            JMP   OPMUL
            JMP   OPDIV
            JMP   OP8ADD
*
OPADD       ADD   VALUE2          VALUE1 = VALUE1 + VALUE2
            JMP   NEXTOP
*
OPSUB       SUB   VALUE2          VALUE1 = VALUE1 - VALUE2
            JMP   NEXTOP
*
OPMUL       MUL   VALUE2          VALUE1 = VALUE1 * VALUE2
            JANZ  EXPOV           IF A NONZERO, OVERFLOW
            SLAX  5               PUT VALUE IN A
            JMP   NEXTOP
*
OPDIV       SRAX  5               VALUE1 = VALUE1 / VALUE2
            DIV   VALUE2
            JMP   NEXTOP
*
OP8ADD      MUL   EIGHT           VALUE1 = 8*VALUE1 + VALUE2
            JANZ  EXPOV
            SLAX  5
            ADD   VALUE2
            JMP   NEXTOP
*
NEXTOP      JOV   EXPOV           CHECK OVERFLOW
            JMP   EXPLOOP
*
EXPOVER     LD1   UNDEFSYM
            J1Z   EXPQUIT         CHECK IF UNDEFINED
            LD1   NOFORWARD       AND FORWARD REFERENCES
FORERROR    J1NZ  ILLFOR          NOT ALLOWED => ERROR
*
EXPQUIT     EQU   *
EXPSAVE1    ENT1  *               RESTORE INDEX 1
            CMPA  0,1             CHECK LOWER BOUND
            JGE   *+3
            JMP   EXPOV           LESS THAN LOWER
            LDA   0,1
            CMPA  1,1             CHECK UPPER
            JLE   *+3
```

```
                         JMP    EXPOV              EXCEEDS UPPER
                         LDA    1,1
        *
                         STJ    NOFORWARD(4:5)  FORWARDS NOT ALLOWED
        *
                         LDX    EXPSAVEX
EXPSAVE2                 ENT2   *
EXPEXIT                  JMP    *
*
```

Formatting print lines

The print routine is relatively straightforward, although lengthy. Each input statement generates an output line in the listing. The most common format is the format of a machine instruction, which is

Location counter	Generated instruction	Card image	Card number
+3516	+3514 00 05 30	STA ERRSAVEA	469

Since the individual fields for an instruction are of interest, these fields are separated by a blank.

For other types of assembly language statements, this format is not always appropriate. For the CON and ALF statements, the generated code is not normally interpreted as an instruction, so it could be better presented as a five-byte signed value. For the EQU statement, no code is generated, and no location counter can thus be meaningfully associated with the statement, but the operand expression should be printed. The ORIG and END statements likewise do not generate code, but their operand expressions, which are addresses (not five-byte values) should be printed. Thus, there are several different formats for output, depending upon the type of the opcode. These are encoded in the PRTFMT table.

The PRINTLINE routine formats the output line in LINE according to the entry in PRTFMT determined by OPTYPE. LINE is then packed into PRTBUF and printed. By positioning the CARD array in the LINE array, the copying from CARD to LINE is not needed for the card image. Since the location counter may have been changed by the time that the line is formatted and printed, a separate variable, PRINTLOC, is used to store the location to be printed on the output line.

```
     *
     *              PRINTER SELECTION FORMAT VARIABLES
     *
PRT             CON    0              PRINT FORMAT HOLDING VARIABLE
ADR             EQU    4:4            PRINT VALUE AS ADDRESS
VAL             EQU    3:3            PRINT VALUE AS WORD
INST            EQU    2:2            PRINT VALUE AS INSTRUCTION
```

```
LOC             EQU    1:1            PRINT LOCATION COUNTER
*
PRTFMT          CON    0              COMMENT PRINT
                CON    1(LOC),1(INST) MACHINE
                CON    1(LOC),1(ADR)  ORIG
                CON    1(LOC),1(VAL)  CON
                CON    1(LOC),1(VAL)  ALF
                CON    1(VAL)         EQU
                CON    1(LOC),1(ADR)  END
*
PRTBUF          ORIG   *+24           PRINTER BUFFER
LINE            ORIG   *+30           FIRST 30 COLUMNS
CARD            ORIG   *+80           CARD IMAGE
                ORIG   *+10           CARD NUMBER
*
PRINTLOC        ORIG   *+1            LOCATION COUNTER FOR PRT
*
```

On a binary machine, it is most useful to print the output in octal, not decimal. Since the CHAR instruction converts from numeric into decimal character code, a separate routine, OCTCHAR, is used to convert into octal character code. Notice that by simply changing the divide by 8 to a divide by 10, decimal output can be generated.

```
*
*               SUBROUTINE OCTCHAR
*
*               CONVERTS A NUMBER FROM A NUMERIC FORMAT INTO
*               AN OCTAL CHARACTER REPRESENTATION.
*               CHARACTERS ARE STORED ONE PER WORD., SIGN FIRST,
*               ZERO FILL. THE NUMBER IS IN THE A REGISTER,
*               THE NUMBER OF CHARACTERS TO BE USED IN I2
*               AND THE ADDRESS IN WHICH THEY SHOULD BE
*               STORED IN REGISTER I1.
*
OCSAVEX         ORIG   *+1
OCTEMPA         ORIG   *+1
*
OCTCHAR         STJ    OCEXIT         SAVE REGISTERS
                STX    OCSAVEX
*
                STA    OCTEMPA        SAVE VALUE
                STA    *+1(0:0)       SAVE SIGN FOR TESTING
                ENTA   1              PLUS OR MINUS
                ENTX   44             PLUS SIGN
```

```
                    JAP   STORESIGN
                    ENTX  45              MINUS SIGN
    STORESIGN       STX   0,1             FIRST CHARACTER IS SIGN
                    LDA   OCTEMPA(1:5) MAGNITUDE ONLY
    *
                    INC1  0,2             LOW ORDER CHARACTERS FIRST
    *
    NXTDIGIT        SRAX  5               SHIFT TO X FOR DIVIDE
                    DIV   EIGHT           OCTAL
                    INCX  30              X HAS DIGIT, CONVERT TO CHAR
                    STX   0,1             STORE CHARACTER
    *
                    DEC1  1
                    DEC2  1               NUMBER OF CHARACTERS
                    J2P   NXTDIGIT
    *
                    LDX   OCSAVEX         RESTORE REGISTERS
    OCEXIT          JMP   *
    *
    *
    *
    *               SUBROUTINE PRINTLINE
    *
    *               PRINT A LINE FOR THE OUTPUT LISTING.
    *               LINES CAN BE OF DIFFERENT TYPES.
    *               THE FORMAT OF EACH LINE IS
    *               DETERMINED BY PRTFMT(OPTYPE).
    *
    PLSAVEA         ORIG  *+1
    PLSAVEX         ORIG  *+1
    *
    PRINTLINE       STJ   PLEXIT          SAVE REGISTERS
                    STA   PLSAVEA
                    STX   PLSAVEX
                    ST1   PLSAVE1(0:2)
                    ST2   PLSAVE2(0:2)
                    ST3   PLSAVE3(0:2)
    *
                    LD1   OPTYPE
                    STZ   OPTYPE          LAST USE OF OPTYPE, RESET
                    LDA   PRTFMT,1        PRINT FORMAT FOR THIS TYPE
                    STA   PRT
    *
    *               CHECK IF LOCATION COUNTER TO BE PRINTED.
```

```
*                    IF SO PRINT IN COLUMNS 8 - 13.
*

                LDA   PRT(LOC)      LOCATION COUNTER
                JAZ   NOLOCPRT
                LDA   PRINTLOC      PRINT VALUE
                ENT1  LINE+7
                ENT2  4             FOUR CHARACTERS (PLUS SIGN)
                JMP   OCTCHAR
NOLOCPRT        EQU   *
*
*
*                    CHECK IF VALUE SHOULD BE PRINTED AS NUMBER
*

                LDA   PRT(VAL)      VALUE AS NUMBER
                JAZ   NOVALPRT
                LDA   VALUE         VALUE HAS VALUE
                ENT1  LINE+17       COLUMNS 18 - 27
                ENT2  10
                JMP   OCTCHAR
NOVALPRT        EQU   *
*
*                    PRINTVALUE AS AN ADDRESS FOR ORIG AND END
*

                LDA   PRT(ADR)
                JAZ   NOADRPRT
                LDA   VALUE         VALUE HAS ADDRESS
                ENT1  LINE+23       COLUMNS 24 - 28
                ENT2  4
                JMP   OCTCHAR
NOADRPRT        EQU   *
*
*                    CHECK IF VALUE SHOULD BE AN INSTRUCTION
*

                LDA   PRT(INST)
                JAZ   NOOPPRT
                LDA   VALUE(0:2)    ADDRESS FIELD
                ENT1  LINE+14       COLUMNS 15 - 19
                ENT2  4
                JMP   OCTCHAR
*

                LDA   VALUE(3:3)    INDEX FIELD
                ENT1  LINE+19       COLUMNS 20-22 BUT
                ENT2  2
                JMP   OCTCHAR
```

```
                    STZ   LINE+19      CLEAR SIGN
       *
                    LDA   VALUE(4:4)   FIELD SPECIFICATION
                    ENT1  LINE+22      COLUMNS 23-25 BUT
                    ENT2  2
                    JMP   OCTCHAR
                    STZ   LINE+22      CLEAR SIGN
       *
                    LDA   VALUE(5:5)   OPCODE FIELD
                    ENT1  LINE+25      COLUMNS 26-28 BUT
                    ENT2  2
                    JMP   OCTCHAR
                    STZ   LINE+25      CLEAR SIGN
       *
NOOPPRT             EQU   *
       *
       *            CARD IMAGE IS ALREADY IN LINE IMAGE IN CARD.
       *            NOW APPEND CARD NUMBER.  CARD NUMBER IS
       *            DECIMAL, SO WE USE CHAR, BUT THEN MUST
       *            SUPPRESS LEADING ZEROS.
       *
                    LDA   CARDNUMBER
                    CHAR
                    ENT1  LINE+110     COLUMNS 111-120
       *
LEADZERO            STZ   0,1          BLANK
                    INC1  1
                    ENTA  0
                    SLC   1
                    CMPA  CHARO(5:5)   CHECK FOR LEADING ZEROS
                    JE    LEADZERO
       *
STRCHR              STA   0,1          STORE NONZERO CHARACTER
                    JXZ   ENDCARDNUM
                    INC1  1
                    ENTA  0
                    SLC   1            NEXT CHARACTER
                    JMP   STRCHR
ENDCARDNUM          EQU   *
       *
                    JBUS  *(LP)
       *
       *            NOW OUTPUT LINE MUST BE PACKED INTO BUFFER
       *
                    ENT1  119          120 CHARACTERS
```

```
                   ENT2  24                NUMBER OF WORDS
*
PCKWORD            ENT3  5
                   ENTX  0                 PACK BACKWARDS
*
PCKCHAR            LDA   LINE,1            NEXT CHARACTER
                   STZ   LINE,1            BLANK FOR NEXT TIME
                   DEC1  1
                   SRC   1
                   DEC3  1
                   J3P   PCKCHAR           GET NEXT CHARACTER
                   DEC2  1
                   STX   PRTBUF,2
                   J2P   PCKWORD
*
                   OUT   PRTBUF(LP)
*
                   LDA   LINERROR          NUMBER OF ERRORS THIS LINE
                   ADD   NERROR            TOTAL NUMBER OF ERRORS
                   STA   NERROR
                   STZ   LINERROR
*
                   LDA   PLSAVEA
                   LDX   PLSAVEX
PLSAVE1            ENT1  *
PLSAVE2            ENT2  *
PLSAVE3            ENT3  *
PLEXIT             JMP   *
*
```

Error routines

Any system program must check its input carefully for possible errors, and an assembler has many opportunities for errors. Thus, errors must be checked for continuously, throughout the program.

When an error is detected, it should be signalled to the programmer somehow. For this assembler, we have elected to place flags in the first five characters to indicate any errors. If the first five characters of an output line are blank, no errors were found. If errors are found, the type of error can be identified by the character in the first five columns.

M   Multiply-defined label. This label has been previously defined.

L   Bad symbol or label. A symbol exceeds ten characters in length or the label is numeric.

U   Undefined opcode. The symbolic opcode in the opcode field cannot be found in the opcode table.

F   Illegal forward reference. A forward reference occurs in an expression or where it is not allowed (EQU, CON, ORIG or END, or in I or F field).

O   Expression overflow. The expression evaluation resulted in a value which exceeded one MIX word, or exceeded the allowable range of the expression.

S   Illegal syntax. The assembly language statement does not have correct syntax; it is not of the correct form.

```
*
LINERROR        CON   0                NUMBER OF ERRORS THIS LINE
*
*
*              SUBROUTINE ERROR
*
*              THIS SUBROUTINE PUTS AN ERROR FLAG INTO THE
*              OUTPUT LINE IMAGE AND COUNTS THE NUMBER OF
*              ERRORS PER LINE. UP TO 5 ERROR FLAGS WILL BE
*              SIGNALLED. THE ERROR FLAG IS THE CHARACTER IN
*              BYTE 1:1 OF THE WORD FOLLOWING THE CALL TO
*              ERROR.
*
ERRSAVA         ORIG  *+1
*
ERROR           STJ   *+3(0:2)    SAVE REGISTERS
                STA   ERRSAVA
                ST1   ERRSAVE1(0:2)
*
                ENT1  *              RETURN ADDRESS
                LDA   0,1(1:1)       ACTUALLY FLAG ADDRESS
                INC1  1              INCREASE ADDRESS
                ST1   ERREXIT(0:2) STORE REAL RETURN ADDRESS
*
                LD1   LINERROR     INCREASE NUMBER OF
                INC1  1
                ST1   LINERROR     ERRORS IN THIS LINE
*
                DEC1  5            CHECK IF MORE THAN 5
                J1P   *+2
                STA   LINE+5,1     STORE ERROR FLAG IN OUTPUT
*
```

```
                    LDA    ERRSAVEA       RESTORE REGISTERS
ERRSAVE1            ENT1   *
ERREXIT            JMP    *
*
*
*                   A SEPARATE ERROR ROUTINE FOR EACH TYPE.
*
MULDEF             STJ    *+3            MULTIPLY-DEFINED LABELS
                   JMP    ERROR
                   ALF    M
                   JMP    *
*
BADSYM             STJ    *+3            BAD SYMBOL (TOO LONG, NUMERIC)
                   JMP    ERROR
                   ALF    L              L FOR LABEL
                   JMP    *
*
UNOP               STJ    *+3            UNDEFINED OPCODE
                   JMP    ERROR
                   ALF    U
                   JMP    *
*
ILLFOR             STJ    *+3            ILLEGAL FORWARD REFERENCE
                   JMP    ERROR
                   ALF    F
                   JMP    *
*
EXPOV              STJ    *+3            OVERFLOW IN EXPRESSION
                   JMP    ERROR
                   ALF    O
                   JMP    *
*
ILLSYN             STJ    *+3            ILLEGAL SYNTAX
                   JMP    ERROR
                   ALF    S
                   JMP    *
*
*
```

Label definition

One additional routine which is useful is DEFINELAB. This routine uses DEFINESYM to define a label for an assembly language statement. It does not simply call DEFINESYM, however, but must first call SEARCHSYM to check for multiply-defined symbols, or symbols which have been forward referenced. The label is taken out of the variable LABEL, where it was put by GETFIELDS. The value of the label is in the A register.

```
      *
      *              SUBROUTINE DEFINELAB
      *
      *              DEFINE A LABEL IF THERE IS ONE. THE VALUE
      *              OF THE LABEL IS IN THE A REGISTER. FIRST
      *              SEARCH THE SYMBOL TABLE FOR MULTIPLY
      *              DEFINED LABELS OR FORWARD REFERENCES.
      *
DEFINELAB     STJ    DLEXIT       SAVE REGISTERS
              ST1    DLSAVE1(0:2)
              ST2    DLSAVE2(0:2)
      *
              LD1    LABEL(1:1)   CHECK IF THERE IS LABEL
              J1Z    DLSAVE1      NO LABEL
      *
              ENT1   SYM
              MOVE   LABEL(2)     MOVE LABEL TO SYM
      *
              JMP    SEARCHSYM    SEARCH TABLE FOR LABEL
      *
              LD1    SYMINDEX
              J1N    NEWLABDEFN   NOT FOUND
      *
              LD2    SYMTAB,1(0:1) CHECK SIGN FOR DEFINED/NOT
              J2P    MULDEF       MULTIPLY-DEFINED
      *
              STA    SYMTAB+2,1   SAVE VALUE OF FORWARD REF
              STZ    SYMTAB,1(0:0)
              JMP    DLSAVE1
      *
NEWLABDEFN    JMP    DEFINESYM    DEFINE NEW LABEL
      *
DLSAVE1       ENT1   *
DLSAVE2       ENT2   *
DLEXIT        JMP    *
      *
```

Main loop code

With these subroutines to perform most of the processing, the main assembler code is now quite simple. The main loop is

```
*
*              MAIN LOOP STARTS HERE
*
MAIN           JMP    INITIALIZE
*
MAINLOOP       JMP    READCARD
*
               LDA    CARD          CHECK FOR COMMENT
               CMPA   CHARSTAR(5:5)
               JE     PRTLINE       IF COMMENT JUST PRINT
*
               JMP    GETFIELDS     GET LABEL, OP, OPERAND
               JMP    SEARCHOP      SEARCH FOR OPCODE
*
               ST6    PRINTLOC      SAVE LOCATION COUNTER FOR PRT
*
               LD1    OPTYPE
               JMP    *+1,1         JUMP TABLE ON TYPE OF OPCODE
               JMP    PRTLINE       COMMENT
               JMP    MACHINEOP     MACHINE OPCODE
               JMP    ORIGOP        ORIG
               JMP    CONOP         CON
               JMP    ALFOP         ALF
               JMP    EQUOP         EQU
               JMP    ENDOP         END
*
*
ENDCASE        LDA    CARD,5        AFTER PROCESSING COLUMN SHOULD
               JANZ   ILLSYN        BE BLANK, IF NOT, ERROR
*
PRTLINE        JMP    PRINTLINE     PRINT
               LDA    ENDASSEM      CHECK FOR END
               JAZ    MAINLOOP
               JMP    FINISHUP      FINISH ASSEMBLY
               HLT
               END    MAIN
```

Machine instructions

Each opcode type has its own section of code to process each assembly language statement. For a machine opcode, this involves first defining the label (JMP DEFINELAB). Then the address expression is evaluated (JMP EXPRESSION) and saved in the 0:2 field of the word to be generated (VALUE). If the next character is a comma, an index field is evaluated; if the next character is a left parenthesis, a field specification is evaluated. Finally, the word is generated.

```
MACHINEOP       ENTA 0,6              VALUE OF LABEL IS *
                JMP  DEFINELAB
*
                ENT1 HL2BYTE
                STZ  NOFORWARD        FORWARDS ALLOWED
                JMP  EXPRESSION       GET ADDRESS PART
                STA  VALUE(0:2)
*
                LDA  CARD,5           CARD(COLUMN)
                CMPA CHARCOMMA        IS IT COMMA?
                JNE  NOIPART
*
IPART           ENT1 HLBYTE           I FIELD IS ONE BYTE
                JMP  EXPRESSION
                STA  VALUE(3:3)
NOIPART         EQU  *
*
                LDA  CARD,5
                CMPA CHARLEFTP        CHECK FOR ( FOR FIELD
                JNE  NOFPART
                ENT1 HLBYTE           F FIELD IS ONE BYTE
                JMP  EXPRESSION
                STA  VALUE(4:4)
*
                LDA  CARD,5           CHECK FOR TRAILING )
                CMPA CHARRIGHTP
                JNE  ILLSYN
                INC5 1                SKIP OVER )
NOFPART         EQU  *
*
                JMP  GENERATE
                JMP  ENDCASE
*
```

EQU *statements*

EQU statements are even simpler. The expression is evaluated, and the label
defined to have this value.

```
*
EQUOP           ENT1 HLWORD          EQU VALUE CAN BE ANY WORD
                JMP  EXPRESSION
                STA  VALUE
                JMP  DEFINELAB DEFINE LABEL
                JMP  ENDCASE
*
```

ORIG *statements*

ORIG statements are almost as simple as EQUs.

```
*
ORIGOP          ENTA  0,6           DEFINE LABEL FIRST
                JMP   DEFINELAB
*
                ENT1  HLADDR        ORIG VALUE IS ADDRESS
                JMP   EXPRESSION
*
                STA   VALUE         (FOR PRINT)
                LD6   VALUE         SET LOCATION COUNTER
*
                JMP   ENDCASE
*
```

ALF *statements*

ALF statements are processed by simply picking up the five characters in columns 17 through 21 and packing them into VALUE.

```
*
ALFOP           ENTA  0,6           DEFINE LABEL
                JMP   DEFINELAB
*
                ENT1  16            COLUMN 17
                LDA   CARD,1
                ENT2  4             FOUR MORE
*
NXTALFCHAR      INC1  1
                SLA   1             SHIFT OVER CHARACTERS
                ADD   CARD,1(5:5)   AND ADD IN NEXT
                DEC2  1             ONE LESS CHARACTER
                J2P   NXTALFCHAR
*
                STA   VALUE
                JMP   GENERATE      OUTPUT WORD
                JMP   ENDCASE
*
```

CON *statements*

The CON statement is perhaps the most complicated of the pseudo-instructions. It consists of evaluating the first expression, and checking for a field specification. If a field is given, the value is stored in that field. This repeats until no more expressions are found. The major complexity in the code comes from the necessity of checking that the field specification given is valid.

```
            *
CONTEMPVAL  ORIG  *+1
CONTEMP     ORIG  *+1             TEMPORARY VARIABLES
            *
CONOP       ENTA  0,6
            JMP   DEFINELAB       DEFINE LABEL FIRST
            *
            STZ   VALUE           DEFAULT VALUE
            *
NEXTCON     ENT1  HLWORD          EXPRESSION ARE ANY VALUE
            JMP   EXPRESSION
            *
            LDX   CARD,5          CHECK FOR (FIELD)
            CMPX  CHARLEFTP
            JE    CONF
            STA   VALUE           NO FIELD IS (0:5)
            JMP   NOF
            *
CONERROR    JMP   ILLSYN          ERROR IN CON
            JMP   NOFSTORE
            *
CONF        STA   CONTEMPVAL      SAVE EXPRESSION
            ENT1  HLBYTE          UNTIL FIELD EVALUATED
            JMP   EXPRESSION
            *
            STA   FMOD(4:4)       CHANGE FIELD OF STORE
            *
            SRAX  5               CHECK IF 0 ≤ L ≤ R ≤ 5
            DIV   EIGHT           L IN A, R IN X
            CMPX  FIVE
            JG    CONERROR        R > 5
            STA   CONTEMP
            CMPX  CONTEMP
            JL    CONERROR        L > R
            LDA   CONTEMPVAL      EXPRESSION
FMOD        STA   VALUE(0)        FIELD TO BE CHANGED
            *
NOFSTORE    LDA   CARD,5          CHECK FOR )
            CMPA  CHARRIGHTP
            JNE   ILLSYN          SYNTAX ERROR
            INC5  1
NOF         EQU   *
            *
            LDA   CARD,5          CHECK FOR COMMA
```

```
               CMPA   CHARCOMMA
               JE     NEXTCON      IF SO, DO NEXT PART
*
               JMP    GENERATE
               JMP    ENDCASE
*
```

END statements

The last pseudo-instruction processed will be an END statement. First, any label is defined. Then the starting address is evaluated and an end-of-assembly flag is set.

```
*
ENDASSEM       CON    0
STARTADD       CON    0            STARTING ADDRESS
*
*
ENDOP          ENTA   0,6
               JMP    DEFINELAB    DEFINE LABEL
*
               ENT1   HLADDR       STARTING ADDRESS IS ADDRESS
               JMP    EXPRESSION
               STA    VALUE        FOR PRINT
               STA    STARTADD     FOR LOADER
               STJ    ENDASSEM(4:5) SET NONZERO TO STOP
               JMP    ENDCASE
*
```

Initialization and termination

With most of the assembler written, we can easily see what needs to be initialized. The first card input should be started, the loader tape should be rewound, and the location counter set to zero. All other variables were initialized by CON statements when they were declared.

```
*
INITIALIZE     STJ    INITEXIT
               IN     INBUF(CR)    READ FIRST CARD
               IOC    0(TAPE)      REWIND TAPE
               ENT6   0            SET LOCATION COUNTER TO ZERO
INITEXIT       JMP    *
*
```

In addition, we need to define the following symbols and constants.

```
        *
TAPE            EQU     0               TAPE UNIT NUMBER FOR LOADER
CR              EQU     16              INPUT CARD READER
LP              EQU     18              OUTPUT LINE PRINTER
        *
MAXSYMBOL       EQU     250             MAXIMUM NUMBER OF SYMBOLS
        *
CHARA           ALF     AAAAA           CHARACTER CONSTANT
CHARO           ALF     00000
CHAR9           ALF     99999
CHARSTAR        ALF     *****
CHARLEFTP       ALF     (((((
CHARRIGHTP      ALF     )))))
CHARCOMMA       ALF     ,,,,,
TWO             CON     2
FIVE            CON     5
EIGHT           CON     8
CHAINEND        CON     4095
        *
```

Termination is more complicated. First, any unfinished loader block should be finished. Then the symbol table needs to be searched. Any undefined symbols are defined, and fix-up codes are output to the loader tape for symbols which were forward referenced. Finally, the start address is output and the last tape buffer written to tape.

```
        *
ASMDEF          ALF                     PRINT LINE FOR SYMBOLS
                ORIG    *+1             WHICH ARE DEFINED BY ASSEMBLER
                ALF
                ORIG    *+5
                ALF     ORIG
                ALF     *+1
                ORIG    *+3
                ALF     SYMBO
                ALF     L DEF
                ALF     INED
                ALF     BY AS
                ALF     SEMBL
                ALF     ER
                ORIG    *+5
        *
        *
        *               SUBROUTINE FINISH UP
        *
```

```
*                 WHEN AN END CARD IS READ, WE MUST FINISH
*                 LAST LOADER BLOCK, OUTPUT FORWARD REFERENCE
*                 FIX-UP COMMANDS, AND START ADDRESS.
*
FINTEMP           ORIG  *+5              FOR CHARACTERS FOR LOCATION
*
FINISHUP          STJ   FINEXIT
                  JMP   FINISHBLCK  FINISH LAST BLOCK
*
*                 CHECK FOR UNDEFINED SYMBOLS AND DEFINE THEM
*
                  ENTA  1
                  STA   VALUE(0:3)   TYPE FIELD FOR LOADER FIX-UPS
*
                  ENT3  0             COUNTER TO SYMBOL TABLE
NEXTSYM1          LDA   SYMTAB,3      LOAD DEFINED FLAG (SIGN)
                  JAP   DENFDSYM      IF DEFINED
*
                  STA   LABEL(1:5)
                  STA   ASMDEF+6(1:5)  FOR PRINT
                  LDA   SYMTAB+1,3   SECOND PART OF NAME
                  STA   LABEL+1
                  STA   ASMDEF+7
                  ENTA  0,6           VALUE FOR DEFINING SYMBOL
                  JMP   DEFINELAB
                  INC6  1             INCREASE * FOR NEXT
*
                  ENTA  -1,6
                  ENT1  FINTEMP       TEMPORARY FOR OCTAL CHARACTERS
                  ENT2  4
                  JMP   OCTCHAR       CONVERT * TO OCTAL FOR PRINT
*
                  LDA   FINTEMP
                  STA   ASMDEF+1(3:3)
                  LDA   FINTEMP+1
                  STA   ASMDEF+1(4:4)
                  LDA   FINTEMP+2
                  STA   ASMDEF+1(5:5)
                  LDA   FINTEMP+3
                  STA   ASMDEF+2(1:1)
                  LDA   FINTEMP+4
                  STA   ASMDEF+2(2:2)  INSERT * OCTAL IN PRT LINE
*
                  OUT   ASMDEF(LP)    PRINT ASSEMBLER DEFINED
```

```
                    JBUS  *(LP)
         *
DENFDSYM            EQU   *              SYMBOL IS DEFINED
         *
                    LDA   SYMTAB+3,3(4:5)  CHECK FOR CHAIN
                    CMPA  CHAINEND
                    JE    UPSYM1          IF NOT, GO ON TO NEXT
         *
                    STA   VALUE(4:5)   PREPARE VALUE FOR LOADER
                    LDA   SYMTAB+2,3(4:5)  ADDRESS OF SYMBOL
                    STA   VALUE(0:2)
                    LDA   VALUE
                    JMP   TAPEOUT        OUTPUT FIX-UP COMMAND
         *
UPSYM1              INC3  4
                    CMP3  NSYMBOL       CHECK END OF TABLE
                    JL    NEXTSYM1
         *
                    LDA   STARTADD
                    STA   VALUE(0:2)   STARTING ADDRESS
                    ENTA  2
                    STA   VALUE(3:3)   TYPE FOR STARTING ADDRESS
                    STZ   VALUE(4:5)   BYTES 4:5 ZERO
                    LDA   VALUE
                    JMP   TAPEOUT        OUTPUT STARTING ADDRESS
         *
                    JMP   FINISHBUF   CLEAR LAST BUFFER TO TAPE
         *
FINEXIT             JMP   *
         *
```

Evaluation

The MIXAL assembler which we have presented in this chapter is a relatively simple one, despite its length. A number of improvements can be made. However, the basic structure of the assembler is such that most improvements can be made by only local modifications to a few subroutines. The entire assembler will not need to be rewritten.

1. By changing only the GETFIELDS routine, the assembler could be changed from a fixed-format to a free-format assembler.
2. Literals were not included. However, the introduction of literals would involve only changing EVALSYM, to recognize a literal by its preceeding and terminating equal signs, adding code to FINISHUP to define them

and a decision on whether to store literals in the symbol table or in a separate literal table. Notice that the definition of literals as being limited to no more than nine characters would allow them to be stored in the symbol table, and distinguished by their leading equal sign. The trailing equal sign is not needed.

3. Local symbols (*i*H, *i*F, *i*B) would similarly require only a change in EVALSYM and DEFINESYM plus a local symbol table.

4. Additional error checking should be added to consider the problems of symbol table overflow, additional types of syntax errors, and programs which attempt to use more than 4000 words of memory.

5. The binary and floating point opcodes could be added.

6. The input program, output listing, and loader tape routines could be modified to allow input or output from tape, disk, or drum and to produce loader output on cards, tape, disk, or drum as desired by the programmer.

7. The FINISHUP subroutine could be extended to print a symbol table following the assembly program listing. With a nontrivial amount of new code, a cross reference listing could be added.

These are just a few of the changes which can be, or should be made. One of the major evaluation criteria is the ability of a programmer, other than its author, to understand a program, and be able to correctly modify it.

Another evaluation criteria is performance. This can be measured in terms of either memory size or speed. For a 4000-word MIX memory, the assembler occupies about 1600 words for its code and opcode table. This leaves over half of memory for the symbol table, allowing the symbol table to hold a maximum of about 600 symbols. Reducing the size of a symbol table entry to 3 words would increase this to 800 symbols.

Since card input, listing output, and tape output are all double buffered, and overlap most of the computation, the speed of the assembler is bounded mainly by the speed of the I/O devices. The assembler took 80.9 seconds to assemble itself (1579 cards) on a 1-microsecond-per-time-unit MIX computer, with a 1200-card-per-minute card reader, and a 1200-line-per-minute line printer. Of this time, 76.1 seconds were spent waiting for I/O devices. This means that only 5.8 percent of the total execution time was needed for the assembly of the program, the remainder of the time is all I/O. Assemblers are typically very I/O bound programs.

This simple measurement means that it would be very difficult to significantly speed up the assembler. A number of minor modifications can be made to speed up the assembler (such as a better symbol table search algorithm, better use of registers, and not saving registers which are not needed). But the effect of these changes on the total processing time would be minimal at best, and hence they are probably not worth the bother.

8.4 SUMMARY

The basic function of an assembler is to translate a program from assembly language into loader code for loading. The major data structures which assist in this translation are the opcode table, which is used to translate from symbolic opcode to numeric opcode, and the symbol table, which is used to translate programmer-defined symbols to their numeric values.

With these major data structures and subroutines to search and enter these tables, as necessary, to evaluate symbols, to evaluate expressions, to print lines, to handle errors, to buffer and block loader output, to read cards and get symbols, to initialize and terminate the assembler, the code for assembling each type of assembly language statement is relatively easy to write and understand.

The major problem for an assembler is forward references. These can be handled by either a two-pass assembler or a one-pass assembler. A one-pass assembler requires the loader to fix-up forward references.

Assemblers are a major topic for books on systems programming, and chapters on assemblers are included in Stone and Siewiorek (1975), Graham (1975), Hsiao (1975), and Donovan (1972). Gear (1974) and Ullman (1976) also discuss assemblers. The book by Barron (1969) has an extensive description of assemblers and how they work. For a look at the insides of a real assembler, try the Program Logic Manual for the assembler for the IBM 360 computers (IBM order number GY26–3716).

EXERCISES

a. Hand assemble the following MIXAL program. Use two passes. First construct the symbol table, then assemble the program into octal machine language.

```
MAXSYM          EQU   100
SYMBOL          ORIG  2*MAXSYM+2
*
SEARCH          STJ   ENDSEAR
                ST2   SAVSEAR(0:2)
                STA   0,1
                LD2   1,1
                INC2  2,2
2H              EQU   *
                DEC2  2
                CMPA  0,1:2
                JNE   2B
                ENT1  0,2
SAVSEAR         ENT2  *
```

```
ENDSEAR         JMP    *
        *
```

b. Hand assemble the above MIXAL program in one pass. Show the assembled code in octal. Chain all forward references in the address fields of instructions with forward references. Use +7777 as the end of the list of forward references to a symbol. Explain any errors discovered. Give the symbol table at the end of assembly.

c. A friend of mine complained that she had two MIX routines. One was prepared for fixed-format MIXAL; the other for free-format MIXAL. She wants to combine the two subroutines in one program. Which will have to be reformatted for a fixed-format assembler? Which will need reformatting for a free-format assembler?

d. A free-format assembler will often include the nonfree-format restriction that any label in the location field must begin in column 1. Can this restriction be relaxed? What are the problems?

e. What would be the result of using only one table for both the symbol table and the opcode table?

f. What information is kept in the symbol table of a one-pass assembler?

g. Assume that an assembler uses a linear search for a symbol table. Entries into the symbol table are made by adding to the end of the table. Symbols are added to the table whenever they occur in the label field. Multiply-defined symbols are allowed. If the first defined value of a multiply-defined symbol is wanted, how should the search routine search? What if the most recently defined value is desired?

h. Suppose it were very easy to read the time of day. Would this be useful in computing a hash function?

i. For a two-pass assembler, which of these functions must be done on pass 1, which must be done on pass 2, which can be done on either, and which must be done on both?

1. construct the symbol table.
2. output code to the loader.
3. scan for the opcode.
4. print the listing.
5. process ORIG pseudo-instructions.
6. search the symbol table.
7. update the program location counter.
8. treat an LDA different from an STA.
9. process a CON pseudo-instructions.
10. process the label field.

j. What can be done on the first pass of a two-pass assembler if a symbol in the location field has already been entered into the symbol table (i.e., it is multiply-defined)?

k. On which pass of a two-pass assembler would you detect the following types of errors?

1. undefined symbol
2. undefined opcode
3. multiply-defined symbol
4. ORIG to a forward reference
5. expression value too large for address field

l. Name three techniques for handling forward references in an assembler?

m. An assembler gives a listing of the symbol table before listing the assembly program and assembled code. How many passes is it?

n. Suppose you had available (already written) both a one-pass and a two-pass assembler for a particular machine, and suppose that any program accepted by one was also acceptable to the other. Give one advantage you might expect the one-pass assembler to have, and one advantage you might expect the two-pass assembler to have.

o. A one-pass assembler cannot handle forward references in expressions. Thus, the following is illegal in MIXAL.

```
X                    EQU    Y+1
Y                    EQU    0
```

A two-pass assembler can do this without problems, since on pass 1 it finds the value of Y, and on pass 2 it can compute the value of X, enter it in its symbol table, and use it in the remainder of the program. Does this mean that a two-pass assembler has no restrictions on forward references? If it does not, show an example to demonstrate a problem which even a two-pass assembler cannot handle.

p. An assembler is assembling for a relocating linking loader. What internal tables and data structures must it have that an absolute assembler need not have?

q. Suppose we want to extend MIXAL by adding the following new symbolic opcodes.

$$LDN* \quad * = A, \ 1, \ 2, \ 3, \ 4, \ 5, \ 6, \ X$$

These new opcodes should be treated like the LD*i*N opcodes. That is, both the opcodes should generate the same code and accept the same form of operand. How would we need to modify the existing MIXAL assembler to allow these new opcodes?

r. Consider a restricted MIX machine with only the A register and X register (no index registers). Eliminate all indexing and partial field considerations and all mnemonics involving index registers. Write a fixed-format assembler for this restricted assembly language. Allow only symbols or constants (no expressions) for operands.

9

SYSTEMS PROGRAMS

The loaders and assemblers of the last two chapters are only a few of the many systems programs which are used on most computers. Like most systems programs, their main purpose is to make the writing and running of other programs easier. However, they are far from being the best programming tools. As more and more programs are written, the usefulness of other system programs becomes evident.

Historically, as the desire for more sophisticated systems programs grew, so too did the capability of the computer systems available to support these programs. These larger computers are more capable of supporting the larger and more complex systems programs and their data structures. Today almost all large computers have at least one system program of each of the types described in this chapter, and many smaller computers do also. However, many of the smaller computer systems may not have sufficient memory, primary or secondary, to support some of these programs. This is generally the case for MIX machines. Since most programmers use many different machines in their careers, it is probable though that these systems will be available to you at some point in your programming.

9.1 MACRO ASSEMBLERS

When writing a large assembly language program, like the assembler of Chapter 8, it is not uncommon to encounter sections of repetitive coding. Consider, as an example, the error subroutines. Six small subroutines (MULDEF, BADSYM, UNOP, ILLFOR, EXPOV, ILLSYN) were all four statements long, of the form

```
STJ    *+3
JMP    ERROR
ALF    x
JMP    *
```

The letter x in the ALF statement varied according to the kind of error. Other instances of short pieces of repetitive code can be found in the assembler. It would ease the programming task if we could simply say that the section of code listed above is a schema, or form, called ERR. When we write ERR U, it would be the same as writing

```
STJ    *+3
JMP    ERROR
ALF    U              SUBSTITUTE THE U FOR x
JMP    *
```

This sort of a feature would allow us to write programs faster.

The standard means of eliminating repetitive code is to use subroutines. But often, as in the example above, the repetitive code is too short for subroutines to be effective in reducing the amount of code to be written. Remember also that calling a subroutine with p parameters will require at least $p + 1$ instructions, so if the code segment is short, a subroutine call may take more code than the code itself. In many cases, in fact, the repetitive code is itself a subroutine call, the repetition being caused by the use of a standard calling sequence.

The execution time for using a subroutine call to replace repetitive code must also be considered. From our simple analysis of the cost of using a subroutine (Section 6.4), it was obvious that although a subroutine can sometimes save space, it always takes more time to execute a subroutine than to just write the code out. In some cases this additional time is of crucial importance, as when the code will be executed millions of times.

Thus, what is needed is a means of reducing the repetitive writing of similar sections of code without introducing the cost of calling a subroutine. A *macro assembler* provides this facility. A *macro* is a named sequence of instructions. The macro assembler generates the sequence of instructions whenever it encounters the macro name. A macro name is thus an abbreviation for the sequence of instructions. (The name "macro" comes from thinking of the sequence of instructions as a macro-instruction.)

Macros are sometimes called *in-line* or *open* subroutines to distinguish them from the standard *closed* subroutine concepts of Chapter 6. When a subroutine is used, the code for the subroutine is located out of the way of the main line of code. Hence the subroutine is out of line. Since a subroutine is only to be entered at its entry point and its internal structure is of no concern to the rest of the program, a subroutine is closed, like a black box. A macro, on the other hand, places its code right where it is called, in-line, and it is part of the routine in which it occurs. Thus, its internal structure is part of that routine and open to that routine.

Macro usage

As with a subroutine, macro usage consists of two things: a *macro definition* and a *macro call*. The macro definition defines the name of the macro and the sequence of statements for which that name stands. The macro call causes *macro expansion* to occur, with the sequence of instructions for which the macro name stands replacing the macro name in the program. Also, as with subroutines, macros may have parameters. Actual parameters, given in each call, replace the formal parameters used in the macro definition during macro expansion.

MIXAL does not provide for macros. To illustrate how macros typically are used, we extend MIXAL to MACRO-MIXAL, a macro assembly language for the MIX computers, based on MIXAL. MACRO-MIXAL is upwards compatible with MIXAL; that is, any MIXAL program is also a legal MACRO-MIXAL program. Thus, all of the features and facilities of MIXAL are included in MACRO-MIXAL, and the syntax is almost the same.

The extensions to MIXAL in MACRO-MIXAL are to allow the definition and use of macros. These require the introduction of two new pseudo-instructions, MACR and ENDM. The MACR pseudo-instruction indicates the start of a macro definition, and the ENDM pseudo-instruction indicates the end of the macro definition.

A macro definition consists of three parts: a macro header, a macro body, and a macro trailer. The macro header is one assembly language instruction whose opcode field is the MACR pseudo-instruction. The label field of the macro header has the name of the macro and the operand field has a (possibly empty) list of formal parameters for the macro, separated by commas.

```
name              MACR p1,p2,. . .,pn
                  ⟨macro body⟩
                  ENDM
```

The macro body is composed of those assembly language statements which are to be assembled whenever the macro is called. The formal parameters may be used in the macro body wherever a symbol may appear. This includes the label field, the opcode field, or the operand field. The macro trailer is simply the ENDM statement.

Once a macro has been defined, it may be called by simply writing its name in the opcode field of an assembly language statement. Actual parameters are specified by listing them in the operand field, separated by commas. Any label is processed by entering it in the symbol table with a value equal to the value of the location counter at the time that the macro call was encountered.

As a simple example, assume that the value of the variable C must be incremented at several places in a program. The macro definition for this function might be

```
UPC          MACR
             LDA   C
             INCA  1
             STA   C
             ENDM
```

After this definition, the three lines of the macro body can be generated simply by writing UPC as an opcode. This macro has no parameters. A more general macro, which could be used for the same purpose, could make the name of the variable to be incremented a parameter.

```
UP           MACR  N
             LDA   N
             INCA  1
             STA   N
             ENDM
```

A call of this macro might look like

```
             UP    C
```

or

```
 LOOP        UP    COLUMN
```

This latter call is equivalent to writing the lines

```
LOOP         LDA   COLUMN
             INCA  1
             STA   COLUMN
```

Macros can be used to introduce new instructions. For example, the BSS pseudo-instruction can be used with a macro assembler which provides only the ORIG pseudo-instruction but does not provide the BSS, by defining the macro

```
BSS          MACR  N
             ORIG  N+*
             ENDM
```

Macro calls can be nested; that is, a macro may call another macro. A macro can be defined to save all registers upon entry to a subroutine by

```
ENTRY          MACR  NAME
               BSS   8              SPACE FOR REGISTERS
NAME           STA   *-8
               STX   *-8
               ST1   *-8
               ST2   *-8
               ST3   *-8
               ST4   *-8
               ST5   *-8
               ST6   *-8
               ENDM
```

When this macro is called, it immediately calls another macro, the BSS macro defined above. After the BSS macro is expanded, expansion of the ENTRY macro continues.

In addition to the introduction of two new pseudo-instructions, macros require one other change to the MIX assembly language. Notice that the name of a macro is defined by placing it in the label field. Hence it is possible to define a macro with a name of up to 10 characters. A macro call, on the other hand, requires putting the name of the macro in the opcode field of the assembly language instruction. Since the opcode field is only four characters wide, problems may arise. These problems may be solved in either of two ways. One method is to restrict macro names to four characters or less. This can make it difficult to use meaningful macro names, and so the alternative solution is more common: change to a free-format input. Most macro assemblers are free-format assemblers. This allows the length of macro names to be longer than the typically short opcode mnemonics. Assembly language statements are still composed of four fields: a label field, an opcode field, an operand field, and a comment field. A label, if present, begins in column 1 and continues to the first blank. Fields are separated by one or more blanks.

Parameter passing for macros is by name. The character string which defines the actual parameter is substituted for each occurrence of the formal parameter. The actual parameter in the macro call is not evaluated in any way until the expanded macro is assembled. This allows parameters to be used which would appear ill-formed if they were evaluated before substitution, as in the following example.

```
WEIRD          MACR  P1,P2
               P1    P2)
               ENDM
```

With this definition, the macro call

```
               WEIRD    MOVE,ARR(7
```

will yield the expansion

```
               MOVE  ARR(7)
```

which is perfectly correct, although neither the sequence P2) nor ARR(7 is a correct syntactic entity by itself.

Occasionally it is convenient to include commas or blanks within parameters. Extra measures must be taken if this is the case since commas normally separate parameters and blanks terminate a line. In these cases, the parameter is enclosed in parenthesis. When the parameter substitution is done, the outermost parentheses are removed before any substitution occurs. For example, consider the macro, XCH, defined by

```
XCH              MACR   P1,P2
                 LDA    P1
                 LDX    P2
                 STA    P2
                 STX    P1
                 ENDM
```

If we wish to use this macro to generate the assembly lines

```
                 LDA    X,1
                 LDX    Y,2
                 STA    Y,2
                 STX    X,1
```

we must call the macro as

```
                 XCH    (X,1),(Y,2)
```

If we were to write XCH X,1,Y,2, we would appear to be calling a macro of two parameters with four actual parameters.

The inclusion of blanks in a parameter is illustrated by the following macro, which performs an operation on each of the elements of the 100-element array X.

```
ALLX             MACR   OP
                 ENT1   99
2H               LDA    X,1
                 OP
                 STA    X,1
                 DEC1   1
                 J1NN   2B
                 ENDM
```

To add one to all the elements of the X array, we simply write

```
                 ALLX   (INCA 1)
```

which expands to

```
                 ENT1   99
2H               LDA    X,1
                 INCA   1
```

```
            STA   X,1
            DEC1  1
            J1NN  2B
```

To perform more complicated operations, we can define a macro and pass the name of that macro to ALL X as a parameter. To insure that all X are within the range from LOW to HIGH, we could define the macro

```
TSTR        MACR
            CMPA  HIGH
            JLE   *+2
            LDA   HIGH
            CMPA  LOW
            JGE   *+2
            LDA   LOW
            ENDM
```

and call the ALLX macro by

```
            ALLX  TSTR
```

This expands to

```
            ENT1  99
2H          LDA   X,1
            TSTR
            STA   X,1
            DEC1  1
            J1NN  2B
```

This in turn expands to

```
            ENT1  99
2H          LDA   X,1
            CMPA  HIGH
            JLE   *+2
            LDA   HIGH
            CMPA  LOW
            JGE   *+2
            LDA   LOW
            STA   X,1
            DEC1  1
            J1NN  2B
```

Some care must be taken with nested macros and local symbols. Consider what would have happened to ALLX TSTR, if TSTR had been defined as

```
TSTR        MACR
            CMPA  HIGH
```

```
              JLE    2F
              LDA    HIGH
2H            CMPA   LOW
              JLE    2F
              LDA    LOW
2H            EQU    *
              ENDM
```

When the ALLX macro and the TSTR macro are both expanded, the 2B in ALLX does not refer the the 2H in the ALLX macro, but rather to the second 2H in the expanded TSTR macro.

Macros are also very useful in defining data structures. The opcode table in the assembler, for example, had most of the entries of the form

```
              ALF    op
              op
```

Thus, the number of lines needed to define the opcode table could be reduced by half, with the definition of a macro such as

```
MACHOP        MACR   OP
              ALF    OP
              OP
              ENDM
```

Macro implementation

How are macros implemented? What changes to the assembler are necessary to allow macro processing? Several changes are needed, including both the modification of some existing code and the introduction of some new data structures.

The major new data structure is a macro table. The macro table contains the symbolic name of each defined macro and additional information to allow the body of the macro to be found. This can be done in several ways. One of the most straightforward is to have each entry of the macro table include the macro body. Thus, each macro table entry consists of the name of the macro, followed by the macro body. Macro bodies may differ in size, and so each entry must also include length information. This allows the macro table to be searched for a given macro name by using the length information to skip over macro bodies, looking only at macro names.

The variable length of macro table entries in the above scheme causes problems in searching the macro table. (The macro table must be linearly searched.) To allow more efficient search techniques, fixed-size macro table entries are desired. To this end, an alternative approach utilizes two data structures: a macro name table, and a macro body table. The macro name table contains entries which specify the macro name, its length, number of parameters, and so on, and a pointer to the beginning of the macro body in the macro body table. The macro body table is a large array in which macro bodies are stored as they are defined. This approach separates the fixed-length macro information (in the macro name table) from the variable-length macro information (in the macro body table).

Parameters can similarly be handled in several ways. The formal parameter names can be stored in the macro body table as the first N symbols of each macro body table entry, before the macro body itself. The macro name table entry would include N, the number of parameters. During expansion of the macro, every symbol in the macro would be compared against the list of formal parameters. If one is found, the actual parameter would be used instead. This approach minimizes the amount of work at macro definition time, but increases the work done at expansion time.

Another approach to parameters increases the work at definition time, in exchange for more efficient macro expansion. In this approach, each parameter is assigned a number, according to its position in the list of parameters in the macro header. When the macro body is being stored, during macro definition, the macro is scanned for formal parameters. If a formal parameter is found, it is replaced by a special character which is not otherwise allowed in the assembly language, followed by the number of the parameter. In MACRO-MIXAL, for example, notice that the character "$" is not used for any special purpose. If we simply declare that the $ is an illegal character (and check all input to be sure that a $ does not occur), then we can replace all occurrences of the first parameter by $A (the character code for A is 1), all occurrences of the second parameter by $B, etc.

As the macro is expanded, the assembler need only check each character in the macro to see if it is a $. When a $ is found, the next character can be used to index into the list of actual parameters for substitution. Using this convention, the macro definition

```
CALL2          MACR  SUB,PARM1,PARM2
               JMP   SUB
               NOP   PARM1
               NOP   PARM2
               ENDM
```

would be stored internally as

```
               JMP   $A
               NOP   $B
               NOP   $C
```

Notice that different methods of handling the substitution of actual parameters for formal parameters may result in subtly different results, in much the same way that the different subroutine calling conventions (call by value, call by reference, call by name) could give different results in some cases. Some of these differences may show up at the programmer level, such as not being allowed to use the character $, or not being allowed over 64 parameters (the maximum number which can be held in the one byte following a $). Other differences are more subtle. Consider the two macros XPL1 and XPL2, defined by

```
XPL1              MACR  A,B,C
                  A     *+1(0:2)
                  ENT1  *
                  XPL2  C
                  STA   B
                  ENDM
XPL2              MACR  N
                  LDA   N
                  INC1  C
                  ENDM
```

If the search for parameters is done at execution time, then the expansion of the macro call

```
XPL1  STA,X,Y
```

would result in substituting the actual parameters STA, X, Y for the formal parameters A, B, C. The expansion of the inner macro call to XPL2 would result in the C of the definition of XPL2 being recognized as a formal parameter of the macro XPL1. The assembly code generated by the macro expansion would thus be

```
STA   *+1(0:2)
ENT1  *
LDA   Y
INC1  Y
STA   X
```

If the parameter substitution is done when the macro is defined, replacing an occurrence of the ith parameter by $i, then the two macros would be stored as

```
XPL1
                  $A    *+1(0:2)
                  ENT1  *
                  XPL2  $C
                  STA   $B
XPL2
                  LDA   $A
                  INC1  C
```

Thus, a macro call XPL1 STA,X,Y would result in the expanded assembly code

```
STA   *+1(0:2)
ENT1  *
```

```
LDA   Y
INC1  C
STA   X
```

The symbol C in the XPL2 macro would not be substituted for, since it was not known to be a parameter at macro definition time when parameters were identified and replaced by the $i representation.

In addition to these basic concerns, other programming techniques can be used to improve the efficiency of a macro assembler. One common technique is the use of *compressed text*. When a macro definition is stored for later expansion, not all of the input text is stored. Remember that for a standard assembly language input statement, most of the 80-character input is comments or blank. A typical input card may have only 10 to 20 useful characters on it. Thus, when the card is stored in the macro body table there is no need to store the entire card. Only the label, opcode, and operand fields need be saved, and multiple blanks between fields can be reduced to only one blank between fields.

The use of compressed text has several results. First, it increases the number or size of macros which can be stored in the fixed amount of memory available for the macro body table by 4 to 10 times. Second, it increases the complexity of macro expansion. Consider that the card images that are to be manipulated now are no longer of fixed length, but rather are of variable length. This requires special programming techniques for the representation and manipulation of variable-length strings of characters. Typically, this is done by appending the length of the string to the front of it (just as the length of the loader blocks was contained in a header word at the first of each block), or the use of a special end-of-line character or characters at the end of the line. Still, the extra efficiency in the use of memory by the assembler is generally considered to be worth the additional cost of using variable-length strings.

A rough idea of how macros are implemented should now be apparent to you. As with everything else in programming, there are many ways of actually writing a macro assembler. One of the simplest is to add another pass to an existing assembler to expand all macros. Thus, an existing two-pass assembler can be converted into a three-pass macro assembler. The first pass expands all macros, the second pass defines the symbol table, and the third pass generates the loader output.

The macro expansion pass copies all assembly language statements except macro definitions and macro calls. A macro definition is entered into the macro name table, and the assembly language statements which follow are stored, in compressed text form, in the macro body table until an ENDM statement is encountered. When a macro call is found the body of the macro is copied out onto the secondary storage device which holds the copy of the program for input to pass 2 of the assembler. Parameter substitution is performed as the macro body is copied out for pass 2. Nested macros require some additional programming care.

A little thought shows that there is nothing in the second pass of a three-pass assembler (symbol table definition) which cannot be done in the first pass along with the macro expansion. Similarly, it is possible to create a one-pass assembler which assembles a macro assembly language program in one pass. Because of the complexity of these assemblers, however, they must be very carefully designed, written, and documented.

The concept of macros need not be applied only to assembly languages, but can be applied more generally to any arbitrary file of characters. PL/I programs have a limited form of macros.Some computer systems have a program called a *general purpose macro processor*, which will input a text file, possibly with macro definitions and macro calls, and will output the text file which results from expanding all macro calls. (In business offices, macros are generally called form letters.)

The ideas behind a general purpose macro processor are discussed in Strachey (1965), while Brown (1969) gives a survey of macro processors. Kent (1969) emphasizes the characteristics of the macro assembly language for the IBM System 360/370.

9.2 CONDITIONAL ASSEMBLY

A professional systems programmer often writes a program in such a way that it may be usable in a wider set of circumstances than is necessary. He knows that certain aspects of the environment in which the program is to be run may change. These changes may include device numbers or types, the amount of memory available, and so forth. In writing a program, this type of information is provided to the program in such a way that the program can be easily changed, if necessary. The EQU statement provides one mechanism for this type of programming. Unit numbers (like CR, LP, or TAPE in the assembler) or the size of large tables (like the symbol table of the assembler) are defined in terms of symbolic constants, rather than their (current) numeric values. This allows these values to be changed easily if the configuration of the computer changes.

Motivation for conditional assembly

The EQU statement often suffices for small changes, but more drastic changes may require complete changes in the way in which a program is written. Consider the assembler of Chapter 7. This assembler was written with a binary MIX computer in mind. This is reflected in the use of an octal representation for the listing of assembled instructions, and the limitations on the ranges of numbers which can be represented in one byte, two bytes, or an entire word. By just changing these few values and the code for generating listing output, we can have an assembler for a decimal MIX computer.

Typically, making these changes will result in two separate programs, one an assembler for a MIX 1009B, the other for a MIX 1009D. This requires twice as much storage space, and any changes or modifications to the assembler must be made in both programs. Experience with this arrangement indicates that after a while small changes will be made in one assembler but not in the other, so that the two supposedly equivalent programs become different.

Another problem may deal with the use of different algorithms depending upon some property of a variable. For example, in our discussion of the opcode table, we indicated that either a linear or a binary search can be used; the choice between these two algorithms is made on the basis of the size of the opcode table. When the search routine was written, however, we did not know the exact size of the opcode table, except that it had NUMBEROPS opcodes. It would be possible to write our search routine so that, at execution time, the value of NUMBEROPS would be tested, and if greater than 32 (say), a jump would be made to a binary search; if less than 32, a jump would be made to a linear search. However, the value of NUMBEROPS is fixed at assembly time and hence for any particular assembly the nonselected search algorithm would never be used; it would only take up valuable space.

Both of these problems, and others, can be solved using *conditional assembly*. Conditional assembly refers to the ability, during assembly, to have the assembler test a condition. On the basis of the results of that test, assembly language statements may either be assembled (as normal) or not assembled (treated as comments). The important concept in conditional assembly is that the test is done during assembly, not during execution.

A conditional assembly feature is added to an assembly language by the introduction of additional pseudo-instructions. Two things need to be specified: the test to be performed and the assembly language statements to be conditionally assembled or skipped. The complexity and sophistication of these types of statements varies widely.

A simple conditional assembly feature

Probably the simplest form of conditional assembly would be the provision of a single new pseudo-instruction of the form

```
IF      expression,expression
```

This pseudo-instruction, when encountered by the assembler, evaluates the first expression in the operand field. If this expression is zero, then the next n lines are skipped, where n is the value of the second expression. If the expression is nonzero, the n lines following the IF pseudo-instruction are assembled normally.

To illustrate the use of this new pseudo-instruction, consider the problem of modifying the assembler for both binary and decimal MIX computers. We define a variable BINARY which is 0 for a binary machine and 1 for a decimal machine

```
BINARY          EQU  0              BINARY ASSEMBLER
BINARY          EQU  1              DECIMAL ASSEMBLER
```

Then we can write

```
HLBYTE          CON   0              HIGH AND LOW FOR BYTE
                IF    BINARY-1,1
                CON   63             BINARY MACHINE
                IF    BINARY,1
                CON   99             DECIMAL MACHINE
```

If BINARY is zero, then BINARY−1 is nonzero, so the CON 63 is assembled. The second IF has a zero expression, however, so it skips 1 line, the CON 99 statement. Thus, if BINARY is zero, the above code is identical to

```
HLBYTE          CON   0
                CON   63
```

On the other hand, if BINARY is 1, the CON 63 is skipped and the CON 99 is assembled. Thus, the assembled code would be

```
HLBYTE          CON   0
                CON   99
```

Similar conditional code could be used in the other few places where an assembler for a binary MIX machine would differ from an assembler for a decimal MIX machine.

The implementation of a conditional assembly feature such as the above is very simple. To the one-pass assembler of Chapter 8, it would be necessary only to,

1. Add the new pseudo-instruction to the opcode and give it an opcode type of 7.
2. Add a jump to IFOP to the jump table of the main loop which separates out opcode types.
3. Add code to interpret the IF pseudo-instruction by first calling the EXPRESSION routine. If the value of the expression is nonzero, return control back to the end of the main loop. Otherwise evaluate the second expression and skip that many cards by calling READCARD repetitively. Then return to the end of the main loop.

```
IFOP            ENT1  HLWORD         FIRST EXPRESSION ANY VALUE
                JMP   EXPRESSION
                JANZ  ENDCASE        IF NONZERO, CONTINUE
*
*                      IF EXPRESSION WAS ZERO, SKIP N CARDS.
*                      FIRST DETERMINE N, PUT IN I1.
*
                ENT1  HLADDR         SKIP MAX OF 4000 CARDS.
                JMP   EXPRESSION
```

```
                STA    *+1(0:2)
                ENT1   *              MOVE A TO I1
SKIPCARDS       JMP    READCARD
                DEC1   1
                J1P    SKIPCARDS
                JMP    ENDCASE
*
```

More sophisticated conditional assembly

The simple form of conditional assembly introduced in the previous Section can easily be introduced into any assembler. However, it is unsatisfactory for a number of reasons. First, the requirement of providing the number of input cards to skip is, while simple for the assembler, troublesome for the programmer. The programmer must carefully count the number of cards to skip. If any changes are made in code which is conditionally assembled which may increase or decrease the number of cards, the programmer must remember to change the skip counts on the IF instructions also.

This problem is generally eliminated by introducing a new pseudo-instruction, ENDI. When an IF pseudo-instruction is encountered and the assembler decides to skip, it skips cards until it encounters an ENDI pseudo-instruction. If an ENDI is encountered when the assembler is not skipping due to conditional assembly, it is simply treated as a comment and ignored.

In addition, the form of the IF pseudo-instruction is generally more complex. Rather than allow only a test for zero or nonzero, conditional assembly often allows tests for zero, nonzero, positive, negative, nonpositive, or nonnegative of an expression. These could be written as

```
        IF    Z,expression
        IF    NZ,expression
        IF    P,expression
        IF    N,expression
        IF    NP,expression
        IF    NN,expression
```

In each case, the expression is evaluated. If the condition is true, then the following lines are assembled; if the condition is false, the lines which follow, up to and including the next ENDI, are skipped and treated as comments.

Even more complex conditional assembly forms allow the comparison of two expressions for equal, not equal, less than, less than or equal, greater than, and greater than or equal. In addition, it is sometimes possible to test for equality or nonequality of character strings (generally passed as parameters to macros).

Another type of conditional assembly allows a symbol to be tested for a defined or undefined characteristic. This is easily done by a simple search of the symbol table, and is most useful in macros, when a parameter may or may not be defined. For example, consider a macro to exchange the values of the A and X registers. This can be written as

```
AXCH            MACR
                STA    TEMPA
                STX    TEMPX
                LDA    TEMPX
                LDX    TEMPA
                JMP    *+3
TEMPA           CON    0          TEMPORARY SPACE
TEMPX           CON    0
                ENDM
```

However, notice that if this macro is ever called twice, the second call will result in the labels TEMPA and TEMPX being doubly defined. To avoid this we can write, assuming that the IFD pseudo-instruction will skip until an ENDI if the symbol is defined

```
AXCH            MACR
                STA    TEMPA
                STX    TEMPX
                LDA    TEMPX
                LDX    TEMPA
                IFD    TEMPA
                JMP    *+3
TEMPA           CON    0
TEMPX           CON    0
                ENDI
                ENDM
```

This macro will not generate the last three lines of code (the JMP and two CONs) if the symbol TEMPA is defined. This prevents multiply-defined labels from multiple uses of the macro.

Even more sophisticated pseudo-instructions can be added to an assembler to control what instructions are generated. These pseudo-instructions can result in only a minor change to the assembler, or can require additional passes for correct processing. Although each of these additional features may be very useful, and even necessary in some cases, they often make the use of such a sophisticated assembler much more expensive (in both time and memory) than a simpler assembler. The important concept is that a certain amount of control over what code is generated can be exercised at assembly time. The assembler itself can make decisions to include or exclude blocks of assembly language statements in order to generate more efficient, compact, or useful machine language programs.

9.3 COMPILERS AND HIGHER LEVEL LANGUAGES

Assemblers are used because programming in machine language is too boring, dull, and error-prone to be fun or cost-effective. Assemblers allow the programmer to express the specification of a program in a symbolic rather than a numeric form. This allows the programmer to create a program in a more convenient form, one closer to the way in which the algorithm for solving the problem was conceived.

Assembly language is still a very primitive, computer-oriented means of writing a program. To ease the programmer's task even more, higher-level languages have been defined. Algol, Cobol, PL/I, Fortran, Pascal, and Basic are all examples of higher-level languages. These languages attempt to be more human-oriented than computer-oriented, and, compared to assembly languages, succeed.

Still, all computer programs must be expressed in machine language in order to be executed. A *compiler* is a program which translates from a higher-level programming language into machine language. (Actually, of course, a compiler, like an assembler, translates into loader code and then a loader translates this loader code into machine language.) A compiler is a translator.

A higher-level language program is composed of a sequence of statements. Each statement corresponds to possibly many machine language (or assembly language) instructions. This is the major difference between the definition of an assembler (which is basically a one assembly language statement to one machine language instruction translator) and a compiler. A compiler may generate many machine language instructions for a statement in a higher-level language. Also, a program written in a higher-level language is relatively machine independent. It does not deal with bits, registers, or addresses, but rather with variables and statements which operate on these and more complex data structures.

The statements of a higher-level language are specified in two ways. First, each statement has its own *syntax*. The syntax of a statement defines the form or forms that a statement can take. For example, in Fortran the syntax of an assignment statement is

⟨variable name⟩ = ⟨expression⟩

The same type of statement in Algol or Pascal has a different form

⟨variable name⟩ := ⟨expression⟩;

The meaning of these two statements is the same, but the syntax is different. The items in brackets are *syntactic entities*, items whose syntax is also defined in the syntactic definition of a higher-level language.

In addition to syntax, a higher-level language defines for each statement its *semantics*, or meaning. The semantics of a statement or other syntactic unit define what that statement means when it is written in a program. The semantics of the assignment statement in Fortran are that the value of the expression on the right of the equal sign should be evaluated and the value of the variable named on the left of the equal sign is set equal to the value of the expression. (In fact, the semantics of the assignment statement are considerably more complex due to such things as type conversions between different types of variables and expressions.)

The problem for a compiler is to generate code which, when executed, correctly reflects the semantics of a program with correct syntax. To do so, a compiler has great latitude in the type of code it generates. A compiler has complete control over (and responsibility for) how storage is allocated for variables, how registers are used, subroutine calling sequences, code generation, and so on.

To compile a program, each statement passes through several phases. First, there is a lexical phase. This phase groups together characters from the input statement into variable names, operators, separators, and other lexical entities. One of the important classes of lexical entities is the class of *reserved words* or *keywords*. Keywords are used in the next phase of a compiler: the syntactic analysis. Syntactic analysis identifies the type and components of a statement and checks for errors in the form of the statement. This is also called *parsing*.

The result of the syntactic analysis determines the input to the semantic phase. In this phase further error checking occurs to insure that proper types of variables and expressions are used in that statement. Then the machine code to be executed is generated, and the compiler continues with the next statement. Code optimization routines may go back over the generated code and try to improve it by better register allocation and use of instructions.

Many different techniques are used to compile programs. The older languages, like Cobol and Fortran, generally use ad-hoc techniques which make heavy use of the keywords in the language. In Fortran, for example, every statement except the assignment statement starts with a keyword. Thus, a compiler need only check the first few characters of a statement. If it is a keyword, then the type of the statement has been identified; if it is not a keyword, then the statement is an assignment statement, and again its type has been identified. Once the type of the statement is identified, the expected syntax of the remainder of the statement is known, and can be used to direct the parsing. Basic is another language which requires each statement to begin with a keyword.

Other languages have been designed in such a way that special compiling techniques can be used with them. The compilers for these languages determine what code to generate from the sequence of lexical entities which the compiler sees. These compilers are called *syntax directed* compilers. Algol and Pascal are examples of these languages.

Compiling techniques and programming languages are subjects for study in themselves. We do not consider them in this book. The basic concepts are the same as with assemblers: the input program is read and an equivalent program in loader format is output, along with a listing of the input program. Some compilers are one-pass, load-and-go systems, while others take multiple passes to produce their output loader code. (Rumor has it that there exists a twenty-pass Cobol compiler.) Compilers allow programmers to concentrate more on the problem to be solved, instead of having to constantly consider the idiosyncrasies of the computer on which the problem is to be solved.

The books by Gries (1971) and Aho and Ullman (1973) are excellent and comprehensive treatments of how to write compilers. Less formal treatments are in Donovan (1972) and Graham (1977).

9.4 INTERPRETERS

All of the systems programs we have examined so far could be classified as translators, in that they only transform a program from one form to another; they do not add anything to the program which was not there before. A different class of programs is the class of *interpreters*. Where a translator only translates from one language to another, an interpreter actually executes the program. Most often an interpreter executes the machine language for some computer, or sometimes executes a higher-level language directly.

There are many reasons for using an interpreter. For a machine language interpreter, the machine which is being simulated may not have been built yet. Having a simulator or interpreter available allows the basic software (loaders, assemblers, compilers) to be written at the same time that the machine is being built. This allows the computer to be useful for programming months earlier than if software development had to wait until the hardware was available.

Another use for interpreters is to allow the evaluation of a proposed computer design before committing the resources needed to actually build one. If the design is not easy to program, or does not perform well on typical programs, it may need to be redesigned or discarded altogether.

Perhaps the largest use of interpreters, however, is for education. Since, as of this writing, there are no real MIX machines, the "computer" which you have been programming is most likely a simulator which interprets the MIX instruction set. The MIX machine is used because it is typical of a number of real machines (as we shall see in Chapter 10), but does not have the hard-to-explain properties of real computers that are caused by the realities of engineering.

In addition it is possible to add to an interpreter features which make the debugging of programs much easier than debugging on a real machine. Routines which dump simulated memory when a error is found, that trace the execution of certain instructions by printing the program counter, instruction being executed, and contents of the affected registers and memory locations, that stop the program when certain conditions occur (program counter equal to one of a set of values, a given memory location is read from or written to, a certain opcode is encountered), or that can even print the instructions which were executed just before any of the above conditions occurred; all these features can be programmed into an interpreter, but would be difficult to add to the hardware of a real computer. Also, these features are really only needed when a program is being debugged, not when it is being run in a production environment.

Writing an interpreter is relatively simple. Knuth (1968), in Volume 1 of his *The Art of Computer Programming* presents the basic idea by presenting an interpreter for MIX, written in MIXAL. The basic data structures are an array which is used to simulate MIX memory, and variables which simulate the MIX registers. The general flow of the the interpreter is to read an instruction from memory, decode the instruction according to its opcode, and then branch to short code segments which simulate each type of instruction in the MIX instruction set. If you have an opportunity, review Knuth's program. It is an example of the work of a master of the art of computer programming.

9.5 OPERATING SYSTEMS

You may have noticed that the number of programs which have been discussed is getting large, and we have not begun to discuss programs for solving differential equations, for playing chess, for computing your tax returns, for learning French, for compiling a list of all distinct words in Shakespeare's plays, and so on. As more and more programs are written and the procedure for executing them becomes more and more varied, it is necessary to write a program to organize and control the use of the computer. This program is called an *operating system*. An operating system is a large program, or collection of programs, whose only purpose is to make the use of the computer more convenient and more efficient.

The convenience occurs in many ways. The operating system performs services for the user of the computer. Most operating systems do all the I/O for their users. The I/O is automatically buffered and blocked to keep the I/O devices as busy as possible while relieving the user from having to write the code for this task for each new program.

In addition, this I/O is *device independent*. User programs perform I/O on named collections of data called *files*. A file generally looks to the user like a magnetic tape; it can be read, written, or rewound. The physical implementation may be a tape, or a card reader (for an input only file), or a line printer (for an output only file), or magnetic disk or drum. The user need not worry about which device his information is stored on, nor (for disk and drum) where on the device it is. The operating system maintains a symbol table, called a *file directory*, which maps symbolic file names onto numeric device unit numbers and (for disk and drum) track and sector numbers.

Another convenience offered to the user of an operating system is *control cards*. Without an operating system, an assembly language programmer must first load the bootstrap loader, then load the absolute loader, then the assembler, then the relocatable loader, then the assembled program. This can take a lot of work even for very simple programs. An operating system relieves the programmer of most of this work by defining a control card language which allows the most commonly requested uses of the computer to be specified with only one (or a few) control cards. For example, the control card

        MIXAL.

might cause the MIXAL assembler to be loaded and begin reading a program from the card reader, printing a listing on the line printer and putting loader code on a file called RUN. Then the control card

        RUN.

could load and begin execution of the assembled program. The *control card interpreter* is the part of the operating system which reads the control cards and causes the computer to perform the correct actions.

For small computers, this may be all the operating system which is needed. The operating system may be either a *batch* system, if it accepts its input from a card reader, or an *interactive* system, if it accepts its input from a terminal like a typewriter or CRT. For large computers, however, the operating systems become much more complex in an effort to use the computer as efficiently as possible. Typically, the cost of a large computer is $200 to $500 an hour. (Cost of the purchase price of the system divided by its expected lifetime plus operating expenses of power, paper, programmers, and people.)

To justify such large costs, the computer should be busy all the time. To increase the efficiency, such machines are often *multiprogrammed*; that is, several programs are executed together for short periods of time, to share the computer. The main idea is to execute one program until it has to wait for I/O, then, rather than sitting idly by, the computer begins to execute another program, until the I/O for the first program is complete; then it switches back to the first program. Later it will continue the second program where it was interrupted. The computer is so fast (and I/O is so slow) that often four to eight programs can be executed this way without any one program being executed any slower than if it had the computer to itself. An extreme case of this is a *time-sharing* system, where possibly 50 people, sitting at typewriter or CRT terminals, each give the computer commands to execute and each think that they have the computer all to themselves.

Like the subject of compilers, the subject of operating systems is a field of study in itself. A great deal of work has been and is being done concerning the services which an operating system should provide, how it should be designed, and how it should be implemented. The introductory texts by Madnick and Donovan (1974) and Tsichritzis and Bernstein (1974) have good treatments of general operating system problems and solutions. Wilkes (1968) concentrates on time-sharing systems.

9.6 OTHER SYSTEMS PROGRAMS

The major systems for a computer system are the loaders, assemblers, compilers and operating systems, but there are more.

A *text editor* is a system program for manipulating files of text. The text files may be programs, data, output, or any other set of textual material which is machine-readable. Typically, these programs are written for time-sharing systems, although a few have been written for batch systems. The objective of a text editor is to allow a user of the computer who has some text file to modify that file easily without the necessity of using cards.

A text editor is an interpreter. It inputs commands from the user and executes them, modifying the text file as instructed. Text editors allow characters and lines to be inserted, deleted, replaced, searched for, substituted for, and moved about in the file. Some editors allow macros of the basic editing commands to be defined and called allowing very complex editting functions to be done by a single macro command. A good text editor in a time-sharing system will allow programs to be written, compiled, debugged, corrected, and documented entirely in the computer.

Much of the use of text editors is for the writing of programs, but some uses are for simple text such as papers and books. This book was written, revised, and edited entirely on a computer. This allowed changes to be easily made as necessary. To assure an attractive appearance, another program, a *text formatter* was used. The text formatter read an input text file and produced a nicely formatted output file. The output file had proper indention and spacing, centered titles, automatic line counting for paging, and right-justification. Right-justification is the property of having all complete lines ending evenly at the right margin. This is fairly difficult to do on a typewriter but can be easily coded in a computer program with a little character manipulation.

Text formatters are generally driven by commands imbedded in the text to be formatted. These commands control spacing, margins, paging, paragraphing, indenting, centering, underlining, and so on. The more sophisticated text formatters allow macros of commands to be defined and used and some allow conditional formatting.

There are many more, useful systems programs. Most of these are not often treated in printed sources, but mainly are developed as needed for each new system. The book by Kernighan and Plauger (1976) is probably the best published treatment of systems programs and how they should be designed and coded.

9.7 SYSTEMS PROGRAMMING LANGUAGES

The vast majority of systems programs are written in assembly language. There are many reasons for this. One reason is simply historical—systems programs have always been written in assembly language—but the primary reasons are function and speed. A higher-level language, such as Fortran, generally does not allow the programmer to express easily those functions which are common to systems programs, such as character manipulation or the use of absolute addresses. Higher-level languages are generally meant to be machine independent, preventing the systems programmer from exploiting the particular features of the particular computer being used. This is especially critical in interrupt handling and I/O instructions.

Just as important is the fact that no compiler can generate code which is better than the code that the best assembly language programmer can write. Consider simply that any code which a compiler can produce can also be written by a programmer, but the programmer may be able to apply local or global optimizations to improve the speed of the code or to reduce its size. On many small computers, like MIX, the problem of limited memory space may be quite severe, and this is a constraint that compilers tend to be unable to consider.

There are also arguments against using assembly language. First, assembly language demands great attention to detail, which complicates the programming process. This makes assembly language programs difficult to write, debug, and understand. It is particularly difficult to try to read an assembly language program which has been written by another programmer. Second, assembly language is specific to a particular machine, which means that programs written in assembly language for one computer cannot be transported to a different computer; they must be completely rewritten.

Finally, although compiler-generated code may not be better than the best assembly language code produced by the best assembly language programmers, all programmers are not assembly language experts; most are average programmers writing average code. Compilers can often generate reasonably good, average code. Further, the real determining factor in efficient programming is not the coding but the algorithm design. A good algorithm, with average code, will far out perform a poor algorithm, with excellent code. For example, a binary search on a large table will take far less time than a linear search, no matter how well the linear search is coded.

These considerations have resulted in the development of a number of new languages, called *systems programming languages* (or machine-oriented languages, or systems implementation languages). These languages lie between the low-level assembly languages and the higher-level procedure-oriented languages. One early language was PL360 for the IBM 360 (and IBM 370) computers. It was designed by Wirth (1968) to include the advantages of both assembly language (in terms of control over generated code) and higher-level languages (in terms of ease of reading and coding). PL360 allows a program to be written in a syntax similar to PL/I or Algol, but allows anything which can be written in assembly language to be written in PL360.

Many other systems programming languages have been developed, including some, like the SIMPL language of Basili and Turner (1975) which are reasonably transportable; that is, they can be used on several different computers. A systems programming language exists for many current computers, so that many systems programs need no longer be written in assembly language. Knuth (1968) mentions PL/MIX, a systems programming language for the MIX computer which will be described in Chapter 9 of his set of books, *The Art of Computer Programming*.

9.8 SUMMARY

The first pieces of system software which are developed for a computer are the loaders and assemblers. As the use of a computer grows, the sophistication of the software generally does also. A macro assembler with conditional assembly features can make assembly language programming easier. Text editors, compilers, text formatters, and operating systems are programs which help the user of the computer to accomplish useful work without being forced to write assembly language programs. Systems programming languages can give the programmer the power of an assembly language but with the syntax of a higher-level language.

EXERCISES

a. What is the primary difference between a subroutine and a macro? Give an advantage of subroutines over macros and an advantage of macros over subroutines.

b. A macro

1. is an open subroutine.
2. is an inline subroutine.
3. is a closed subroutine.
4. is a reeentrant subroutine.
5. passes parameters by value.
6. passes parameters by name.
7. passes parameters by address.

c. Assume that we have a three-pass macro assembler. What is the most likely purpose for each pass?

d. Why isn't a macro checked for errors when it is first defined?

e. Some macro generators permit assembly language operations to be redefined as macros. How could this feature be used advantageously in debugging?

f. If an assembler allows recursive macro calls, what else must it allow? (For example: Nested macro definitions? Conditional assembly? Forward references in expressions? Default parameters?)

g. Explain how macros are implemented in an assembler. What new data structures are needed?

h. What is the name of the system software which,

   1.   makes one computer act like another?

   2.   translates Fortran into machine language?

   3.   translates MIXAL into machine language?

   4.   coordinates and controls the entire computer and its use?

i. What is an interpreter?

j. Some systems have a form of conditional loading (similar to conditional assembly) that works like this: Input to the loader is a collection of segments with defined entry points and externals (as discussed in Chapter 7). In addition, associated with each segment is a special bit. If this bit is on, then loading proceeds as normal. If this bit is off, then this segment is loaded only if there is a reference to an entry point of this segment by some other segment which is loaded.

This allows library subroutines to be included, and if they are never used, they will not be loaded into memory. For example, if the segment for a SQRT function is marked to be conditionally loaded, it will be loaded only if it is used by a segment which is loaded.

Notice that loading a segment which was marked for conditional loading may require that other conditionally loaded segments be loaded also.

How many passes would a loader need to be to implement conditional loading?

k. What are some advantages of higher-level languages over assembly languages? Of assembly languages over higher-level languages? How do systems programming languages fit in with these other languages?

l. Are there reserved words in MIXAL?

m. Why would programs be run on an interpreter rather than a real computer?

n. What is the purpose of control cards?

o. What is device independent I/O? What is a file?

p. Why can't a compiler generate better code than an assembly language programmer? How does a systems programming language approach this problem?

10

SOME COMPUTER ARCHITECTURES

As was admitted in the last chapter, there is no real MIX computer. MIX computers are simulated on other machines. However, the MIX computer is very similar to many existing computers. To illustrate this, we present here a description of some of the more common computers in use today. We do not attempt to teach you how to program in the assembly language of each of these computers; we present them for two reasons. First, after your extensive work with MIX, and the brief description of the computer given here, it should be obvious that, given about a week to familiarize yourself with a reference manual describing the hardware instruction set and the assembly language, you could be programming on any of these computers as well as you currently program for the MIX computer. Second, it is unlikely that you will only work on one computer in your life. Thus, this chapter will give you a familiarity with the different types of computers which currently exist. This will allow you to move easily from machine to machine, including new designs or machines which you have not seen before.

We begin with a brief history and survey of recent computers.

10.1 A HISTORY OF COMPUTERS IN THE UNITED STATES

The first commercial computer sold in the United States was the Univac I in 1951. The Univac I was produced by the Univac division of the Remington Rand Corporation (later to become Sperry Rand). The Univac I was a very sophisticated machine, for its time, and established Univac as the leader in the computer market. The Univac I was followed up by the Univac II in 1957 and the Univac III in 1960. These were all commercial machines aimed towards business data processing.

Univac was also building computers for the scientific research market. In 1952, the Univac 1103 was built, followed later by the 1107. These were early vacuum tube computers, and were eventually replaced by the larger, faster 1108 and 1106 in 1964. In 1970, the 1110 was announced. The Univac 1108 and 1110 are very powerful scientific computers which normally execute under the EXEC-8 operating system.

Univac was not the only computer manufacturer in the early 1950s, however. The International Business Machines Corporation (IBM) had for a long time sold punched card equipment as well as general office equipment. Their early 701 (1952) computer was later replaced by the 704 (1954) and the 709 (1957). These vacuum tube computers were superseded by the 7070 and the 7090 (1958) and 7094 (1962). The 7090 and 7094 computers were very popular and considered the best scientific computers of their day. The 1401 (1959) and 1410 (1960) were very successful for commercial data processing problems.

IBM, by 1960, could see the tremendous market which was developing for computers and computer services. They could also see that there was a wide range of uses for computers, so that one computer would not be able to meet the diverse demands of small businesses and large scientific computing. But each different computer required its own hardware, maintenance, and software. To try to limit the cost of producing different software and hardware for different computers, IBM in 1964 announced its System 360 family of computers. Originally six models (30, 40, 50, 60, 62, 70) were announced to handle the range of computing problems from small systems (the model 30), through medium sized systems (models 40 and 50), and on to larger systems (the models 60, 62, and 70). The entire family utilized the same hardware, architecture, and instruction set and I/O devices (with some exceptions). Any program which was programmed for one model could also be used on another model. Thus, IBM could provide excellent support for a large range of computing problems with one family of internally compatible computers.

This approach was immensely successful, with the 360 establishing itself as the major computer on the market. Some models were dropped and others added as technology and demand changed, but the basic architecture remained the same. A user could, if his workload increased, move up from his current model to the next larger model and still retain his existing software and I/O devices. Compilers, assemblers, loaders, and the operating systems (DOS/360 and OS/360) all run on all of the models (more or less). The larger models were simply faster and could support more services than the smaller models. Eventually fourteen models were produced (20, 22, 25, 30, 40, 44, 50, 65, 67, 75, 85, 91, 95, 195).

In 1970, IBM announced their 370 series (models 115, 125, 135, 138, 145, 148, 155, 158, 165, 168), which represented an evolutionary compatible improvement over the 360 family. Some problems of the 360 design were corrected, and some new features added. The technology of construction was changed so that the 370s are faster, but from an architectural point of view the 370s are simply a continuation of the 360 line.

Although the basic idea of using one family of computers to span the range of demand for computers is reasonable, economic realities make it nearly impossible to achieve in practice. The major problem is at the low end, where very simple, inexpensive systems are needed by small businesses. The IBM System/3 (1969) is aimed at this market and has been relatively successful. Recently the System/32 has been introduced as an even smaller system, aimed at situations where there is no resident programming staff (like the typical office). Similar demands for small to medium scientific computers resulted in the IBM 1620 and its successor the IBM 1130. The IBM 1800 and the follow-on System/7 were also aimed at process control and scientific laboratory requirements. The Series/1 (1977) is aimed at this market too.

At the other end of the computer market are the users of large scientific computers. The 370/168 is IBM's main machine in this area. One of the principal designers of the 360, Gene Amdahl, left IBM after the announcement of the 370 series. He formed his own company which is now producing its own computer, the Amdahl 470V/6. The Amdahl computer uses the same instruction set as the IBM 360/370 series (thus allowing software developed for the IBM computers to be run on the Amdahl computer), but is about twice as fast as the IBM 370/168 at a slightly lower price (from $4 million to $6 million, depending on the amount of memory wanted).

The forming of a competing company by ex-employees of a company is not unheard of in the computer field. As early as 1957, a group of Univac employees left Univac and formed their own company, Control Data Corporation (CDC). Their first computer was the CDC 1604 (1960), followed by the 3600 in 1963. These were medium-sized machines. In 1964, however, CDC announced their CDC 6600 computer, the largest and fastest computer system then available. The 6600 (and other 6000 series machines, the 6400, 6500, and 6700) was aimed at the large scientific computer market and particularly the need for massive computing power of the Atomic Energy Commission. In 1968, the 7600, successor to the 6600 was announced. The 7600 was 7 to 8 times faster (20 million instructions per second) than the 6600 and generally cleaned up some of the design problems of the 6600. The 6000 and 7000 series were renamed the Cyber 70 series in 1970, but this was mainly a marketing move.

In 1972, the chief designer of the CDC 6600, Seymour Cray, left CDC to form his own company (backed in part by CDC and Fairchild, a leading semiconductor component manufacturer). Cray Research, Inc., has now produced the CRAY-1 computer, a very large powerful scientific computer. Unlike the Amdahl computer, however, which is identical to IBM's 370 in architecture, the CRAY machine has an architecture and instruction set which, although vaguely similar, differs from the CDC computers. Thus, entirely new software will need to be developed.

Many other companies also manufacture computers. The Burroughs Corporation has built computers for many years. Their most popular large machine was the B5500, a successor to the B5000. The B5500 was succeeded by the larger, newer B6500, B7500, and B8500 computers. All of these machines were designed with both hardware and software in mind and represent architecturally different concepts from the standard register machines. The Burroughs machines are stack machines. A stack machine is particularly appropriate for executing code written in a high level language like Algol, so that no assembly language programming need be done on the Burroughs machines; there are no assemblers. All programming is done in a higher-level language, or an intermediate language called a systems programming language. Even the operating system, MCP (Master Control Program), is written in the systems programming language.

Univac, IBM, and Burroughs are all companies which have entered the computer field from the business side of computing, having been involved in office machines, forms, and service before producing computing equipment. The other side is, of course, the electronics field. General Electric, RCA, and Honeywell were all well-established electronics firms before entering the computer field.

General Electric produced three lines of computers: the 200 series, 400 series, and 600 series. Some significant software was developed for these systems. The Basic programming language was originally developed at Dartmouth College for a GE 235 computer, and has since spread to almost all computer systems. The 600 series, the larger computers in GE's product line, gave rise to the GECOS operating systems and the MULTICS operating system of MIT's Project MAC. However, GE's computer division consistently lost money, and so in 1970 GE withdrew from the commercial computer manufacturing market. Its computer division was sold to Honeywell, which has merged it into its own computer operations.

RCA was an early pioneer in computer technology, but never seemed to be able to take advantage of this position. Its major computer line, the Spectra 70 series, was compatible with the IBM System 360 family, having the same architecture and instruction set. Although there were some price/performance advantages to some of the RCA models, sales did not go well, and in 1972 RCA sold its computer division to Univac.

A more complicated history starts with the Scientific Data Systems (SDS) computer firm. This California-based company produced two lines of computers. The 900 series started in 1962 with the 910 and 920, and continued with the 930, 940, and 945 models. These computers were used for some of the early time-sharing systems. In 1965, to compete with IBM's System 360, SDS produced the Sigma line of computers. The Sigma 2 and Sigma 7 were superseded by the Sigma 3 and Sigma 5. The users of these computers thought highly of their design as medium-sized scientific computers.

In 1969, Xerox Corporation bought SDS, changing its name to Xerox Data Systems (XDS), in an attempt to enter the computer field. New computer models were introduced in 1973, the Xerox 530 to replace the Sigma 3 and the 550 and 560 to replace the Sigma 5. However, these did not sell well, and in 1975 Xerox withdrew from the computer field, selling its computer division to Honeywell.

The major problem in the medium and large computer market is, of course, competing with IBM. The most successful strategies have been to concentrate on a particular segment of the computer field, and not try to cover the entire market. This has been particularly successful in the minicomputer market where computers are used as laboratory and control devices.

The Digital Equipment Corporation (DEC), is the IBM of the minicomputer market. One of its most successful computers is the PDP-8 (1965). This small machine is extremely limited, but also very inexpensive. (Originally under $10,000 and now around $2,000). It has become, and remains, very popular. The PDP-11 (1969) has also become a very popular computer. These smaller computers complement the DEC-10, a large time-sharing computer whose roots lie in the PDP-10 and PDP-6 computers.

DEC is not the only minicomputer manufacturer, however; far from it. Data General (DG) started in 1968, by a group of ex-DEC employees, produces the NOVA line of minicomputers. Hewlett-Packard's 2116 developed in 1967 to compete with the PDP-8, was followed by the HP 2100 and HP 21MX computers. The Interdata Corporation's 7/32 computer is architecturally similar to an IBM 360. Minicomputers are also produced by General Automation, Varian, Prime, Modular Computer Systems, Computer Automation, Harris, Datum, Cincinnati Milacron, Lockheed Electronics, Tandem Computers, MITS, Texas Instruments, Raytheon Data Systems, and many more.

Even smaller computers, the microcomputers, are now being produced. The heart of these systems is a microprocessor which puts all the functions of a central processing unit on just one or a few semiconductor chips. The Intel 8080 and Motorola 6800 microprocessors seem to be the two most popular microprocessors. The Intersil IM6100 executes the PDP-8 instruction set, and the PDP-11 instruction set is available in an LSI-11 microprocessor. Microprocessors are being used in many applications where simple control functions can be easily programmed, and also by a growing number of people who build and program their own computers as a hobby.

This discussion gives you some familiarity with the names of common computers. Now, we briefly present the architecture of a selected set of common computers to give you a better understanding of their structure.

10.2 THE PDP-8

The PDP-8 is a small but easy to use and simple computer. It was first sold in 1965. Since then several versions have been manufactured as new hardware technology became available. The PDP-8/I, PDP-8/E, PDP-8/S, PDP-8/L and PDP-8/A are all models of this same computer. The PDP-8 is a product of the Digital Equipment Corporation. It is mainly used in dedicated data collecting or control functions, like running steel mills, medical laboratory experiments, or monitoring air pollution. The PDP-8/A is available with a CRT terminal for about $5,000.

Memory

The PDP-8 is a 12-bit binary machine. It uses two's complement arithmetic. With 12-bit addresses, up to 4096 words of memory can be addressed, so most PDP-8's have 4K of main memory. There are two registers in the PDP-8, the A

FIGURE 10.1   A PDP-8A computer, the most recent version of the very successful PDP-8 architecture. The two boards in the foreground are the central processor (left) and the memory (right). (Photo courtesy of Digital Equipment Corporation.)

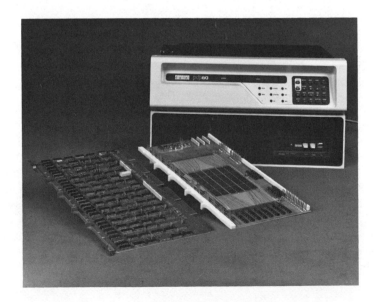

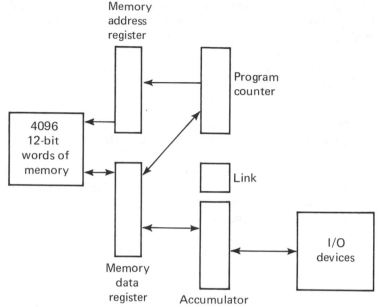

FIGURE 10.2 A block diagram of the PDP-8. All registers except the Link bit are 12 bits.

register (a 12-bit accumulator) and the Link bit. There is also a 12-bit program counter, but this is not directly accessible to the programmer. A block diagram of the PDP-8 is shown in Figure 10.2.

Instruction set

The PDP-8 has eight instructions. These can be grouped into three classes:

1. memory reference instructions
2. operate instruction
3. input-output instruction

For eight instructions, a 3-bit opcode is needed. In a 12-bit instruction, this leaves 9 bits to specify a memory address. But 9 bits will address only 512 words, so special addressing techniques must be used.

One technique is *indirect addressing*. One bit associated with each memory reference instruction specifies whether the address in the instruction is (0) the address of the memory location wanted (no indirection), or (1) the address of the address of the memory location (indirect addressing). Indirect addressing is at most *one* level. In order to specify the entire 4K memory, all 12 bits of a memory location are needed, so there is no bit left over in a 12-bit word to indicate if further indirection is needed.

FIGURE 10.3 Memory reference instruction format (PDP-8)

This leaves us with eight bits in the instruction with which to specify an address. One more bit is used to specify a *page*. Memory is considered to be split into 32 *pages*. The first page is addresses 0000 to 0177 (octal), the next page is from 0200 to 0377 (octal), 0400 to 0577 (octal), and so forth. In effect, a 12-bit address is broken into two parts: a 5-bit page number and a 7-bit location within a page.

Each memory reference instruction has one bit which is used to specify what page the address is on. This bit specifies that the address is either (0) on the *zero* page (locations 0000 to 0177) or on the *current* page (same page as the current instruction). The remaining seven bits in the instruction specify the location in the page. This scheme allows certain locations (zero page) to be accessed by any instruction (allowing global variables), while the current page can be used to store local variables.

The memory reference instruction format is given in Figure 10.3. To interpret the instruction at location P, the Z/C bit is examined. If Z/C is zero, the high-order five bits of the memory address are zero (zero page); if Z/C is one, the high order five bits of the memory address are the same as the high order 5 bits of the address P (current page). The low-order seven bits are the address field of the instruction. This specifies a 12-bit memory address. Now if the D/I bit is zero, then this is the effective address (direct addressing); if the D/I bit is one, then the contents of the memory address are fetched, and these contents are the effective address (indirect addressing). The effective address is used in all memory reference instructions.

There are six memory reference instructions:

Instruction	Mnemonic	Opcode	Time
Logical AND	AND	0	2
Two's complement add	TAD	1	2
Increment and skip if zero	ISZ	2	2
Deposit and clear accumulator	DCA	3	2
Jump to subroutine	JMS	4	2
Jump	JMP	5	1

The time for each instruction is the number of memory cycles needed. The actual time varies from 1.5 to 8 microseconds per memory cycle, depending upon the model. Indirect addressing adds another memory cycle, of course.

In more detail, the instructions are

AND   The contents of the effective address are ANDed with the A register.

ANDing is done bitwise. The result is left in the A register; memory is not changed.

TAD   The contents of the effective address are added to the A register. Addition is 12-bit, two's complement integer arithmetic. The result is left in the A register; memory is not changed. A carry out of the high-order bit (sign bit) will complement the Link bit.

ISZ   The contents of the effective address are incremented by one and put back in the same memory location. If the result of the increment is zero, the next instruction is skipped (i.e., the program counter is incremented by 2, rather than 1).

DCA   Store the contents of the A register in the effective address and clear the A register (i.e., set A register to zero). The original contents of the memory location are lost.

JMS   The address of the next location (program counter plus one) is stored at the effective address and the program counter is set to the effective address plus one.

JMP   The program counter is set to the effective address.

These instructions are a little different, but very similar to some instructions in the MIX machine. TAD is addition to the A register. DCA is a store into memory. AND is used for masking. JMP allows transfer of control. JMS stores the return address in the first word of the subroutine and starts execution at the next location; a JMP indirect through the entry point will return to the main program. The ISZ instruction is used for loops. The negative of the number of loop iterations wanted is stored in memory some place, then the ISZ instruction counts each loop. If the count is nonzero, the next instruction (a JMP to start of loop) is executed; when count is zero, we skip over the JMP and continue. For example, to multiply the A register by 10, (where X has −10, and Y is a temporary)

```
DCA    Y              /STORE A IN Y TO CLEAR IT
TAD    Y              /ADD OLD VALUE FROM Y TEN TIMES
ISZ    X              /X STARTS WITH NEGATIVE TEN
JMP    *-2            /REPEAT JUMP BACK TEN TIMES
...    ...            /A REGISTER NOW HAS TEN TIMES OLD A
```

There are still a large number of things we want to do as programmers. The Operate instruction is a special instruction which allows for many different functions. These functions are *encoded* in a very few bits. The operate instruction specifies operations which affect only the A register, Link bit, and program counter. Thus, the space used in memory reference instructions for specifying a memory address can be used for other purposes. There are two formats for the operate instruction; these are called group 1 and group 2 operate instructions.

For group 1:

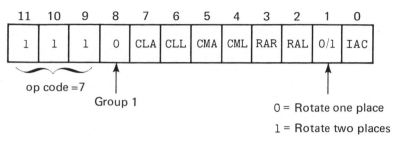

op code = 7

Group 1

0 = Rotate one place

1 = Rotate two places

Group 2

For group 2:

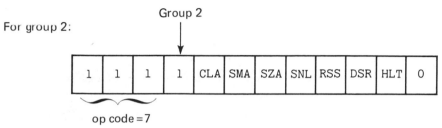

op code = 7

FIGURE 10.4   Format of the operate instruction of the PDP-8.

Bit 8 distinguishes between these two groups. The instruction format is shown in Figure 10.4.

The effect of the operate instruction is determined by which of the subinstructions are selected. Each subinstruction is selected by setting the corresponding bit to one. The subinstructions are:

CLA   Clear the A register; set it to zero.

CLL   Clear the Link bit.

CMA   Complement the A register (bit by bit, change 1 to 0 and 0 to 1).

CML   Complement the Link bit.

RAR   Rotate the A register right (one bit if bit 1 of the instruction is zero; two bits if bit 1 of the instruction is one). A rotate is a circular shift of the A register and Link bit. The Link bit is shifted into bit 11 of the A register, and bit 0 of the A register is shifted into the Link bit.

RAL   Rotate the A register left. Rotate one bit if bit 1 of the instruction is zero; two bits if bit 1 of the instruction is one.

RTR   Special mnemonic for rotating two bits right (sets bit 1 in the instruction).

RTL   Special mnemonic for rotating two bits left.

IAC   Add 1 to the A register.

SMA Skip on Minus A. If the A register is negative, skip the next instruction.

SZA Skip on Zero A. If the A register is zero, skip the next instruction.

SNL Skip on Nonzero Link. If the Link bit is one, skip the next instruction.

RSS Reverse Skip Sense. If this bit is one, the SMA, SZA, and SNL subinstructions will skip on the opposite condition. That is, SMA skips on positive or zero, SZA skips on nonzero, and SNL skips if the Link is zero.

OSR OR from the Switch Register. The contents of the switch register on the console are ORed into the A register.

HLT Halt.

These subinstructions can be combined independently of each other to form more complicated instructions. Thus,

CLA   Clear the A register.
CLA CLL Clear both the A register and the Link.
CLA CMA Clear the A register, then complement (set the A register to all ones).
CMA IAC Complement and add 1 (two's complement).
CLL RAL Clear Link; rotate one place left (multiply the A register by two; put sign bit in Link).
SMA SZA Skip if the A register is less than or equal to zero.
CLA SZA First, test if A is zero or not. Then clear A. If A was zero, skip next instruction.

This last example points out that the order in which the subinstructions are executed is very important. The PDP-8 interprets these instructions for group 1 as follows:

1. CLA and CLL (if selected of course)
2. CMA and CML
3. IAC
4. RAR, RAL, RTR, and RTL

For group 2,

1. Test SMA, SZA, SNL. If any of these are selected and the condition is true, set the Skip flag. If all selected conditions are false, clear the Skip flag. (If none are selected, the Skip flag is cleared.)
2. If RSS is selected, complement the Skip flag.
3. CLA
4. OSR
5. HLT

Notice that subinstructions can only be selected from one group, group 1 or group 2. These different groups cannot be combined in one instruction.
Possible combinations are

```
CLA,  CLL,  CMA,  CML,  IAC,  (RAR,  RAL,  RTR, or RTL)
SMA,  SZA,  SNL,  RSS,  CLA,  OSR,  HLT
```

Any subset of the instructions may be selected, but only one of the RAR, RAL, RTR, or RTL subinstructions may be selected per operate instruction.
Bit 0 of a group 2 operate instruction is always zero. Setting this bit to one (leaving bits 11, 10, 9, and 8 one) specifies an additional set of instructions which are executed by an Extended Arithmetic Element (EAE) for doing multiplies, divides, and shifts. The EAE is an optional feature of the PDP-8 (and costs extra).

Assembly language

Several assembly languages for the PDP-8 exist. One is the PAL-III assembler. It is extremely simple, since the assembler must run on such a small computer. Most assembly language statements are of the form:

    label,   opcode I operand   /comments

Any field may be omitted. A label, if it occurs, is the first symbol on the line and is followed by a comma. Symbols can be up to six characters long, must start with a letter, and cannot be opcodes or the letter I. The opcodes are any of the mnemonics presented in the last section plus a few extras. Additional mnemonic instructions have been added to the assembler for commonly used combinations of the operate instruction.

NOP	No instructions selected; no operation
SPA	SMA RSS (Skip on Positive A register)
SNA	SZA RSS (Skip on Nonzero A register)
SZL	SNL RSS (Skip on Zero Link)
SKP	RSS (Always skip)
CIA	CMA IAC (Complement and Increment A register)
LAS	CLA OSR (Load A register from Switch Register)
STL	CLL CML (Set Link)

Some mnemonics are also added for common I/O instructions and EAE instructions.
Comments are indicated by the slash and continue to the end of the card. Indirect addressing is indicated by the letter I. The symbol ".." (period) refers to the value of the location counter. Fields can be either symbols or octal numbers or the period.
Only two pseudo-instructions are recognized. The ORIG function in MIX is accomplished in the PDP-8 by an assembly language statement of the form,

    *nnnn

where *nnnn* is an octal number. This resets the value of the location counter to *nnnn*. The END function of MIX is simply a card with a $ on it for PAL-III. Constants can be defined by omitting an opcode, as

```
C100,          144    /CONSTANT 100
```

Remember that all constants are octal. There are no literals, local symbols, character strings (ALF), or EQUs.

The PAL-III assembler is a two-pass assembler (or three-pass if you want a listing). Only one symbol table is used, including opcodes and user symbols into this one table. (This is why you cannot use I or mnemonics for labels). The assembly language is admittedly very simple, but even so, it is an improvement over machine language and has enough features to allow reasonable assembly language programs to be written.

Programming techniques

Even though there are very few instructions on the PDP-8, there are enough. Below we list some of the fundamental programming techniques.

Loading

One major obvious lack is the absence of a load instruction. Loading the A register is done by first clearing the A register and then adding the storage location to be loaded. For example, to load the A register with the contents of location X, either

```
DCA    some place
TAD    X
```

or

```
CLA
TAD    X
```

Subtraction

Subtraction is done by complementing and adding. To subtract Y from X, and leave the difference in Z

```
CLA                    / A IS ZERO
TAD    Y               / 0 + Y = Y
CMA    IAC             / −Y
TAD    X               / X − Y
DCA    Z               / Z = X − Y,  A = 0
```

To subtract X from the A register can be done in two ways: (1) simple

```
DCA    TEMP            / SAVE A REGISTER
TAD    X               / X
```

```
        CMA    IAC        / -X
        TAD    TEMP       / A - X
```

or (2) clever

```
        CMA    IAC        / - A
        TAD    X          / X - A
        CMA    IAC        / -(X - A) = A - X
```

Comparisons

To compare two numbers X and Y, we use the old "subtract and compare difference to zero" trick.

```
        CLA
        TAD    Y          / A = Y
        CMA    IAC        / A = -Y
        TAD    X          / X - Y
        SNA
        JMP    EQUAL      / X-Y = 0,  X=Y
        SMA
        JMP    GREATER    / X-Y > 0,  X>Y
        JMP    LESS       / X-Y < 0,  X<Y
```

Loops

The ISZ instruction is the easy way to execute a loop. For example to search a list of numbers starting at location X, for one equal to the A register with the length of the list in the variable N

```
        DCA    TEMP       / SAVE A
        TAD    N
        CMA    IAC        / -N FOR ISZ
        DCA    LOOPN
/
LOOP,   TAD    X
        CMA    IAC        / -X
        TAD    TEMP       / A - X
        SNA    CLA        / SKIP IF NOT EQUAL, CLEAR A
        JMP    FOUND      / FOUND IT
        ISZ    LOOP       / MODIFY ADDRESS OF X
        ISZ    LOOPN      / TEST END OF LOOP
        JMP    LOOP
        ...    ...        / NOT FOUND IN LIST
```

Notice that we use the fact that the SNA test is done before the CLA to assure that the test is done correctly and that the A register is zero when we get back to LOOP. Also notice that we are using *address modification*. There are no index registers on the PDP-8, so addressing through a loop must be done either by modifying the address portion of an instruction (as above) or by indirection, as follows.

```
                DCA    TEMP         / SAVE A FOR COMPARISON
                TAD    N
                CMA    IAC
                DCA    LOOPN        / LOOP COUNTER = −N
                TAD    XADR         / ADDRESS OF LIST
                DCA    ADDR         / FOR INDIRECTION
    LOOP,       TAD    I ADDR       / INDIRECT LOAD
                CMA    IAC
                TAD    TEMP         / A REGISTER − X
                SNA    CLA
                JMP    FOUND
                ISZ    ADDR         / INCREMENT ADDRESS
                ISZ    LOOPN        / LOOP COUNTER
                JMP    LOOP
                ...    ...          / NOT FOUND IN LIST
```

where XADR has the address of X as its contents.

A special feature on the PDP-8 is *auto-indexing*. In page 0, locations 0010 through 0017 (octal) automatically increment their contents by one *before* they are used as the address of the operand when it is addressed indirectly. Thus, if we assign ADDR to location 0010 in the above code, we do not need the ISZ ADDR, since this will be done automatically. We do need to store, not the address of X, but one less than the address of X (since auto-indexing is done before using the address for indirection).

Subroutines

With as simple a machine as the PDP-8, subroutines are used a lot. Subroutine linkage is done by the JMS, which stores the return address in its operand and starts execution at the next location. For example, a subroutine to decrement one from the A register:

```
    DEC1,       NOP                 / WILL BE RETURN ADDRESS
                CMA    IAC          / −K
                CMA                 / − (−K) − 1
                JMP    I DEC1       / INDIRECT RETURN
```

The call is simply

```
                JMS    DEC1
```

We can make this a decrement and skip if zero by

```
    DSZ,        NOP                 / RETURN ADDRESS
                CMA    IAC
```

```
CMA
SNA
ISZ   DSZ         / INCREMENT ADDRESS IF ZERO
JMP   I DSZ
```

Parameters are almost always passed by reference, after the call to the subroutine, or in global variables on the zero page.

Input/output

The one instruction we have ignored so far is the Input/Output transfer (IOT) instruction. It has an opcode of 6 and two fields, a 6-bit device number and a 3-bit function field. A device can have up to eight different functions and each device can have any eight functions which are appropriate for that device. Each device normally has a one-bit *device flag*. If the flag is 0, the device is busy; if the flag is 1, the device is ready. The ASCII character code is used. Most I/O transfers go through the A register, one character at a time.

To illustrate the use of the input/output instructions, consider the functions of a Teletype input keyboard.

Function	Mnemonic	Explanation
0	KCF	Clear the flag, but do not start the device
1	KSF	Skip next instruction if flag is 1
2	KCC	Clear the A register and flag
4	KRS	Read a character from device into A register
6	KRB	Read a character into A register; clear flag.

For the Teletype printer,

Function	Mnemonic	Explanation
0	TFL	Set flag
1	TSF	Skip if Flag is 1
2	TCF	Clear Flag
4	TPC	Output character and start printing it.
6	TLS	Clear Flag and Output Character.

To input one character from the keyboard and echo print it on the printer

```
KCC              / CLEAR FLAG ON KEYBOARD
KSF              / WAIT UNTIL CHARACTER READ
JMP   .-1
```

FIGURE 10.5   Instruction format for opcode 6, I/O instructions.

110	device	function
11 9	8 3	2 0

```
KRB                    / READ CHARACTER INTO A
TLS                    / OUTPUT CHARACTER TO PRINTER
TSF
JMP    .-1             / WAIT UNTIL DONE
```

This program first clears the flag for the keyboard. Clearing the flag is a signal for the keyboard to input a character. When a key is hit on the keyboard, the keyboard reads the key, constructs the appropriate ASCII character code, and saves it in a buffer register. Then the flag is set. In the meantime, the CPU has been repetitively testing the flag, waiting for it to become set. When the flag is set, the CPU reads the character from the buffer register into the A register. Then it outputs this character to the buffer register for the printer, and clears the flag, telling the printer to print the character in its buffer register. The CPU waits until the printer signals that it has printed the character by setting the flag.

Normally, the program would try to overlap its input, output, and computing, of course.

Suppose we have several different I/O devices, *d1*, *d2*, *d3* and *d4*, and we want to do I/O on all of them simultaneously. We also have some computing to do. We can do all our I/O on each device one at a time or try to overlap them. Suppose we are inputting from *d1* and *d2* into buffers in memory and outputting from buffers to *d3* and *d4*. All of the devices operate at different speeds. If we program them as above for the Teletype we will spend most of our time in loops like

```
KSF                    / IS KEYBOARD READY
JMP    .-1
```

What we need is to test each device at regular intervals; if any device is ready, we will service it; if not, we will go compute for a while, and come back to check again later. The KSF and TSF commands are like Skip if ready, so we will say SKR *di* for device *di*. We can then write a subroutine

```
POLL,        NOP                   / RETURN ADDRESS
             SKR    D1             / IS D1 READY
             SKP                   / NO
             JMS    SERVD1         / YES, SERVICE IT.
             SKR    D2             / IS D2 READY
             SKP                   / NO
             JMS    SERVD2         / YES, SERVICE IT
             SKR    D3             / IS D3 READY
             SKP                   / NO
             JMS    SERVD3         / YES, SERVICE IT
             SKR    D4             / IS D4 READY
             SKP                   / NO
             JMS    SERVD4         / YES, SERVICE IT.
             JMP    I POLL
```

In our main program we can now add JMS POLL at regular intervals. The length of the interval depends upon how long we are willing to tolerate having an I/O device finish and not be served. In the worst case (must respond to each device finishing as soon as possible), this may be after each instruction.

```
DCA    TEMP
JMS    POLL
TAD    N
JMS    POLL
CMA    IAC
JMS    POLL

. . .
```

This is called *polling*. Although it is better than busy loop waiting (JBUS *), it takes a lot of time.

Interrupts do this polling in hardware. Each device has an interrupt request flag. The interrupt system can be either on or off. If it is off, execution is just as we have always thought it to be. If the interrupt system is on, however, the following changes take place (on the PDP-8).

After every instruction is executed, the CPU looks at all of the interrupt request flags. If they are all off, the CPU continues to the next instruction. If any flag is on, the CPU

1. executes a JMS 0, storing the program counter in location 0 and executing the instruction at location 1, and
2. turns the interrupt system off.

This allows the programmer to be informed immediately that one of the I/O devices needs attention. After the I/O device is serviced, and the programmer wishes to resume the computation which had been executing when the I/O interrupt occurred, it is necessary to only do a JMP I 0. Thus, an interrupt forces a subroutine jump to location 0.

The normal use of the interrupt system for I/O is,

1. Start all I/O devices.
2. Turn on the interrupt system. (On the PDP-8, the interrupt system is device 0, so I/O instructions are used to turn it on and off.)
3. Go do some computation, or twiddle your thumbs (JMP .) if you have nothing to do, while you wait for an interrupt.

When an interrupt occurs,

1. The address of the current instruction is stored in location 0. The interrupt system is turned off to prevent interrupting an interrupt.
2. The instruction in location 1 is executed. This is normally a JMP to an interrupt service routine.
3. Save all registers.

4. Determine what device caused the interrupt.
5. Service that device, possibly restarting it on something new (next character).
6. Check if any other devices want service too; if so, go back to 5.
7. Restore the registers.
8. Turn the interrupt system back on.
9. Return to the interrupted program by a JMP I 0.

The addition of an interrupt system to the design of a computer system is necessary if I/O is to be effectively overlapped with computation and other I/O. Almost all modern computers have an interrupt system. The major features of the interrupt system are that it can be turned on or off, and that interrupts cause a forced jump to some location in such a way that the interrupted program can be restarted without knowing that it was interrupted. Thus, the background computation can proceed correctly, without special programming being necessary because of the frequent interrupts of the CPU to service I/O devices.

The best source of more complete information on the PDP-8 is from its manufacturer, Digital Equipment Corporation. DEC publishes several manuals about the PDP-8. Of particular interest are the "Introduction to Programming" and "Small Computer Handbook" manuals.

EXERCISES

a. Describe the memory and registers of the PDP-8. What is the word size? What is the address size?
b. How is the memory of the PDP-8 logically organized? Describe the effective address calculation for a memory reference instruction.
c. The PDP-8 has only a 3-bit opcode. Does this mean that it only has eight instructions? If so, why are there more than eight mnemonics in the assembly language?
d. Are all of the instructions for the PDP-8 necessary, or could the number of instructions be reduced even more? For example, are the ISZ and JMS instructions really necessary? If not, why do you think they were included in the instruction set of the PDP-8?
e. What is the meaning of the PDP-8 instructions

   1. CMA,IAC
   2. SMA,CLA,IAC

f. We wish to test the high-order bit of the switch register on the PDP-8. One student wrote

         CLA,OSR,SMA,RSS
         ⟨JMP for sign bit on⟩

   Why does this not work?

g. The MIX computer is much more powerful than the PDP-8 because the MIX computer has a much larger instruction set. To show this, consider both the MIX code and the PDP-8 code needed to jump to NNEG if a location labeled TEA is nonnegative and jump to NGE if not. The MIX code is

```
LDA   TEA
JANN  NNEG
JMP   NGE
```

Write the PDP-8 code to do this same function. (Assume the A register may have any initial value.)

h. The last problem showed that the MIX computer is better than the PDP-8. However, for some purposes the PDP-8 may be better. Write the MIX code and the PDP-8 code which would add one to a variable TOPS and jump to LOOP if the resulting sum (which should be stored back in TOPS) is nonzero, or continues on at the next instruction (falls through) if TOPS is zero.

i. Write a subroutine for the PDP-8 to add the elements of an array. Call your subroutine SUM. Define an appropriate calling sequence. How does your code compare with the subroutine SUMMER in Chapter 6?

10.3 THE HP 2100

The HP 2100 (1972), manufactured by the Hewlett-Packard Company, is a new model of the HP 2116. The HP 2116 was brought out in 1967 to compete with the PDP-8. It was designed and built with the design of the PDP-8 in mind and hence has some similarities to the PDP-8. The designers tried to correct what were felt to be the major limitations of the PDP-8. Like the PDP-8, the HP 2100 is used mainly in process control and laboratory systems, but it also is used to provide simple time-sharing in Basic for up to 32 terminals.

The HP 2100 was produced in two models, the 2100A and the 2100S. These computers have generally been replaced by the newer 21MX computers (M-series, K-series, and E-series); however, these newer models are basically the same as the 2100 architecturally.

Memory

The HP 2100 is a 16-bit binary computer. It uses two's complement integer arithmetic. With 16-bit words, integers from $-32,678$ to $+32,767$ can be represented. Addresses are 15 bits, allowing up to 32K words to be addressed. Two 16-bit registers, the A and B registers, function as accumulators, while two one-bit registers, E (the Extend bit) and 0 (the Overflow bit) are also provided. The Extend bit acts the same as the Link bit on the PDP-8; the Overflow bit acts like the overflow toggle of the MIX computer.

FIGURE 10.6   Two of the HP 21MX series of computers from Hewlett-Packard. These small minicomputers are often used in dedicated
applications. (Photo courtesy of Hewlett-Packard Company.)

A number of internal registers are also used, including a program counter (P
register), a memory address register (M register), and a memory data register (T
register).

A special feature of the HP 2100 is that locations 0 and 1 of memory are the
A and B registers, respectively. Thus, a LDA 1 will load the A register with the B
register.

Instruction set

The instructions of the HP 2100 can be grouped into three classes of instructions:

1.   memory reference instructions
2.   register reference instructions
3.   input/output instructions

Other classes would include the extended arithmetic instructions (multiply, divide, shift) and the floating point instructions, available as options at extra cost.

Memory reference instructions are encoded as shown in Figure 10.8. Four
bits are used for the opcode, giving 16 different memory reference instructions.
Addressing of memory is accomplished by two techniques, indirection and
paging. Bit 15 of the instruction specifies either direct (D/I = 0) or indirect (D/I =
1) addressing. If indirect addressing is specified, the address given in the instruction is not the address of the operand, but the address of the address of the

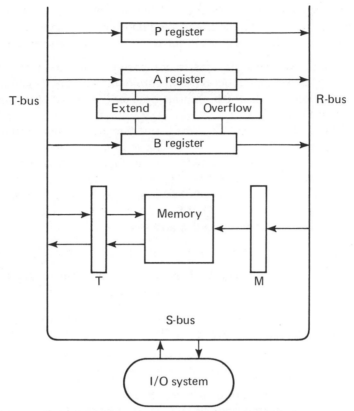

FIGURE 10.7 A block diagram of the HP 2100 computer. All registers are 16 bits, except the extend and overflow bits, and the 15-bit M register.

operand. Since only 15 bits are needed for an address, and the word in the indirect address is 16 bits, the high-order bit of that word is again taken as a direct/indirect bit. Indirect addressing can occur to any number of levels, and continues until bit 15 of the word fetched from memory is zero. When bit 15 is zero, the remaining bits specify the address of the operand.

Paging allows the 10 bits in the instruction to specify a 15-bit address. Bit 10 of a memory reference instruction specifies if the upper 5 bits of the address should be zero ($Z/C = 0$) or the same as the upper 5 bits of the program counter ($Z/C = 1$). This logically breaks memory up into 32 pages, each with 1024 words.

FIGURE 10.8 Memory reference instruction format for HP 2100.

D/I	opcode	Z/C	memory address

The 1024 words on the zero page or the 1024 words on the current page can be accessed directly at any time. The remaining pages must be accessed indirectly. The effective address calculation for the HP 2100 is thus as follows.

1. (Paging) The initial address is composed of the lower 10 bits of the instruction with an upper 5 bits of zero (if the Z/C bit of instruction is 0) or the upper 5 bits of the program counter (if the Z/C bit of the instruction is 1).

2. (Indirection) If the D/I bit of the instruction is zero, this initial address is the effective address; if the D/I bit is one, then the contents of the memory location addressed by the initial address is fetched.

3. (Multiple levels of indirection) As long as bit 15 of this fetched memory word is 1, the lower 15 bits are used as an address to fetch a new memory word. When bit 15 is finally 0, the lower 15 bits of the fetched memory word are the effective address.

The instruction set is then (expressing the opcode as an octal number)

02 AND   AND the contents of the effective address to the A register, leaving the results in the A register.

04 XOR   Exclusive-OR the contents of the effective address to the A register, leaving the results in the A register.

06 IOR   Inclusive-OR the contents of the effective address to the A register, leaving the results in the A register.

03 JSB   Jump to subroutine. Store the address of the next instruction in the effective address and jump to the effective address plus one.

05 JMP   Jump to the effective address.

07 ISZ   Add 1 to the contents of the effective address and store the sum back in the effective address. Skip the next instruction if the stored sum is zero.

10 ADA   Add the contents of the effective address to the A register.

11 ADB   Add the contents of the effective address to the B register.

12 CPA   Compare the contents of the effective address to the A register. Skip the next instruction if they are equal.

13 CPB   Compare the contents of the effective address to the B register. Skip the next instruction if they are equal.

14 LDA   Load the contents of the effective address into the A register.

15 LDB   Load the contents of the effective address into the B register.

16 STA   Store the contents of the A register into the effective address.

17 STB   Store the contents of the B register into the effective address.

Notice that these instructions are similar to the instructions for the PDP-8. However, the extra bit in the opcode field has allowed us to add another register (the B register) and some additional instructions (the IOR, XOR, CPA, CPB). Also by including a load instruction, we no longer need a deposit and clear, but can use a standard store instruction.

The register reference instructions come in two groups: the shift-rotate group and the alter-skip group. These instructions are formed by combining subinstructions. The format of these instructions is shown in Figure 10.9. Bit 11 controls whether the A or B register is used. For the shift-rotate group, bits 8–6 and 2–0 are 3-bit shift and rotate fields. The shifts and rotates are

mnemonic	bit pattern	meaning
*LS	000	Shift left one bit, end off.
*RS	001	Shift right one bit, end off.
R*L	010	Rotate left one bit, circular.
R*R	011	Rotate right one bit, circular.
*LR	100	Shift left one bit, then zero sign bit.
ER*	101	Rotate right one bit register and Extend bit. Bit 0 into E; E into 15.
EL*	110	Rotate left one bit, register and Extend bit. Bit 15 into E; E into bit 0.
*LF	111	Rotate left four bits.

The * is either A or B, depending upon which register is selected by bit 11. Since all of these combinations select some change on the selected register, a separate bit is used to disable or enable the selected shift. If the control bit disables the shift, then the register is not changed; the shift does not occur. (This provides a NOP if both shifts are disabled). Bit 9 is the disable/enable control bit for the shift/rotate of bits 8–6; bit 4 is the disable/enable control for bits 2–0.

Bit 5, if set to one, causes the Extend bit to be cleared; otherwise it is left alone. Bit 3, if set to one, will cause the CPU to skip the next instruction if the

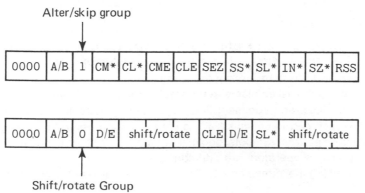

FIGURE 10.9   Alter/skip and shift/rotate instruction formats for HP 2100.

least significant bit (bit 0) of the selected register is zero; the next instruction is executed as normal if bit 3 is zero or bit 0 of the selected register is nonzero. These two functions (clear E; skip if low-order bit zero) occur after the shift function selected by bits 9, 8, 7, 6 and before the shift function of bits 4, 2, 1, 0.

These subinstructions can be combined according to the following:

(Any Shift/Rotate), CLE, SL*, (Any Shift/Rotate)

The register used in all the subinstructions in one register reference instruction must be the same, of course. The ability to select two shifts in one instruction allows a great deal of flexibility. For example, in one instruction we can rotate 1, 2, 3, 4, 5, or 8 bits left or right by combining the rotate one and rotate four functions appropriately. By combining end-off and circular shifts, a bit in a register can be selectively cleared, or tested by moving it into the E bit or low-order bit, and then moving it back, in the same instruction.

The alter-skip group provides the following subinstructions, where the * represents either A or B, as selected by bit 11.

CL*	Clear register
CM*	Complement register
SEZ	Skip on E zero
CLE	Clear E
CME	Complement E
SS*	Skip if register is positive
SL*	Skip if low-order bit is zero
IN*	Increment register
SZ*	Skip if register is zero
RSS	Reverse skip sense.

These subinstructions can be combined according to the following chart.

CL*, CM*, SEZ, CLE, CME,
SS*, SL*, IN*, SZ*, RSS

Subinstructions are executed left to right.

Assembly language

The assembler for the HP 2100 is a three-pass assembler like the assembler for the PDP-8. The first pass creates the symbol table, the second the output loader code, and the third a program listing.

The input to the assembler is free-format, consisting of a label field, opcode field, operand field, and comment field, delimited by spaces. The label field is optional; it must start in column 1 if it is present. The operand field may be an expression formed from symbols, decimal numbers, or "*" (the location counter value). Expression operators are addition and subtraction. Octal numbers are indicated by using the letter B as a suffix. Literals may also be used. Indirection is indicated by following the operand with a comma and the letter I, as

```
LABEL          LDA   SAM,I          INDIRECT ACCESS
```

Pseudo-instructions for the HP assembler include ORG (to define the origin of a program or reset the location counter), END, EQU, DEC (to define a decimal constant), OCT (to define an octal constant), and BSS (to reserve storage locations). Pseudo-instructions also exist for creating relocatable programs with entry points (ENT), and external symbols (EXT). Primitive conditional assembly and some listing pseudo-instructions are also provided.

Input/output

Programming for the HP 2100 is very similar to programming either the PDP-8 or MIX computers. The additional register allows some code to be simpler on the HP 2100 than on the PDP-8. The longer word length increases the range of numbers which can be represented, the number of opcodes, and the amount of memory which can be addressed. The major changes are in the I/O system.

Each I/O device has two bits to control I/O operations. One bit is called the control bit; the other is the flag bit. The setting of the control bit initiates an I/O operation; the control bit cannot be changed by the device. The flag bit is set by the I/O device when a transfer is complete. Normal I/O operation is to clear the flag and set the control bit to initiate the I/O operation. When the I/O device finishes the I/O operation, it sets the flag bit. Each device has its own interface card, with control and flag and buffer registers. Information is normally transferred between the A and B registers and the device interface buffer.

I/O instructions have four fields. The A/B bit selects either the A or B register; the H/C bit will clear the flag bit of the selected device if the H/C bit is one. The device field is a 6-bit field which indicates the selected I/O device. A 3-bit operation field specifies an I/O operation to be performed on the selected device. These are,

Mnemonic	Bit pattern	Meaning
HLT	000	Halt the computer
STF,CLF	001	Clear or set the flag (bit 9 says which)
SFC	010	Skip on flag clear
SFS	011	Skip on flag set
MI*	100	Inclusive OR interface buffer to register
LI*	101	Load interface buffer into register
OT*	110	Output from register to interface buffer
STC,CLC	111	Set or Clear (bit 11) the control bit

FIGURE 10.10   Input/output instruction format for HP 2100.

1000	A/B	1	H/C	function	device number

Input or output can be done under flag control using busy wait loops, as in MIX. For example, to output one character

```
LDA   CHAR        GET CHARACTER
OTA   DEVICE      OUTPUT CHARACTER TO DEVICE
STC   DEVICE,C    SET CONTROL AND CLEAR FLAG
SFS   DEVICE      SKIP WHEN FLAG IS SET
JMP   *-1         WAIT UNTIL FLAG SET
```

Input is similar. (Set control/clear flag, wait until flag is set by device, then load or merge character into A or B register.) Most I/O is character-by-character (ASCII character code) through the A and B registers. Polling can also be used.

Two major improvements were made over the PDP-8 I/O. In addition to the busy loop I/O technique illustrated above, the HP 2100 has an interrupt system. The PDP-8 had an interrupt system which would, when any device requested an interrupt, store the address of the next instruction is location 0, and begin execution at location 1. The interrupting device could be determined by polling.

The HP 2100 eliminates the need for polling by having a *vectored interrupt system*. Instead of all interrupts causing a forced transfer to a fixed address, each device on the HP 2100 interrupts to a different location. The device number indicates the address to interrupt to. Thus, device 20 interrupts to location 20; device 21 interrupts to location 21; and so on. The action which occurs when an interrupt occurs is somewhat different also. Instead of automatically executing a subroutine jump (as on the PDP-8), the contents of the interrupt location for the interrupting device is fetched and executed as an instruction. No registers are changed before the fetched instruction is executed. Typically, the instruction executed is a subroutine jump.

For example, if we have a JSB 300 in location 20, are executing the instruction at location 1734, and an interrupt request arrives from device 20, the execution proceeds as follows. The execution of the instruction at location 1734 continues until it is completed, since it had already begun. Interrupt requests are honored only between instructions, never in the middle of an instruction execution. The program counter is incremented to 1735. Now the computer pauses before fetching the instruction at 1735 to look for interrupt requests. Seeing a request from device 20, it fetches the contents of location 20, decodes it, and executes it (intending to continue at 1735 after this one instruction). The instruction at 20 is a jump to subroutine at location 300, so the program counter (with 1735 in it) is stored in location 300, and then reset to 301. Execution continues at location 301. Control can be returned to the interrupted program by an indirect jump through location 300.

Notice that, since each device interrupts to a different location, each device interrupt can be serviced immediately. There is no need to poll all the devices to determine which caused the interrupt. An additional feature of the HP interrupt system is its *priority interrupt structure*. On the PDP-8, the interrupt system is automatically turned off when an interrupt occurs. On the HP 2100, when an interrupt from device x is requested, interrupts from all higher numbered devices are disabled, but all lower numbered devices may still interrupt. Thus, a priority scheme is established where higher priority (lower device numbered) devices can interrupt lower priority (higher device numbered) devices. Generally, higher speed devices are given higher priority so that they will not have to wait for lower speed devices to be serviced before continuing.

An interrupt is requested anytime the interrupt system is on, and a flag is set. Setting the flag disables interrupt requests from lower priority devices. These requests are held *pending*. When the flag of a interrupting device is cleared, the next lower priority pending request becomes enabled and can cause a new interrupt for that device.

With a 6-bit device select field, up to 64 different device codes are possible. Some of these are used for special purposes. Device 0 is the interrupt system, device 1 is the overflow bit and switch register. Devices 4 and 5 are used to indicate interrupts caused by a power failure (4) or a parity error in memory (5).

The addition of a priority vectored interrupt system is one major feature of the HP 2100 I/O system. The other is the *direct memory access* (DMA) feature. High-speed I/O devices, such as disks, drums, and magnetic tapes, can sometimes transfer information faster than the computer can handle it if all information must go through the A or B register when being transferred between memory and the I/O device. At best, because of instruction fetches, incrementing pointers, the lack of index registers, comparisons, and such, only one word every seven memory cycles can be input or output. Even this takes all available CPU time. To change this situation, a special "device" is available on the HP 2100 which allows DMA transfer between memory and a high speed I/O device which bypasses the CPU completely.

A DMA processor is a special purpose processor which is built for one purpose and one purpose only, to transfer information between memory and an I/O device. To start a DMA transfer, the DMA device is told (a) which device is involved, (b) whether the transfer is an input or an output, (c) the address in memory for the transferred words, and (d) the number of words. The DMA processor then supervises fetching words from memory and sending them to the I/O device, or vice-versa, as fast as the I/O device and memory can handle them. This continues until all words are transferred (or an error occurs). While this is going on, the CPU may continue computing. (The I/O for MIX consists of DMA transfers). The I/O can proceed at the speed of the I/O device. The DMA device does *cycle-stealing* by using memory read-write cycles as necessary when the CPU is not using memory. If both the CPU and DMA want a word from memory at the same time, one of them must wait, and it is generally the CPU which does the waiting.

The HP 2100 is a considerable improvement over the PDP-8. It has a longer word length, additional register, more instructions, and more sophisticated I/O system, including a priority, vectored interrupt system and DMA transfers. These additional features are not free, however. A minimal HP 2100 system with CPU and 4K of memory costs around $6,000.

As with the PDP-8, the best source of further information is the manufacturer. Hewlett-Packard publishes the "Pocket Guide to the 2100 Computer," a manual which covers the basic hardware for the HP 2100 as well as the assembler, Fortran, Basic, and a simple operating system.

EXERCISES

a. Describe the memory of the HP 2100. What is its word size? What is its address size? Why are these two (word size and address size) different?
b. Describe the registers of the HP 2100.
c. What is the fundamental difference between the instruction set of the PDP-8 and the HP 2100?
d. How does the I/O system of the HP 2100 differ from the PDP-8?
e. What is DMA?
f. What is a vectored interrupt system?

10.4 THE PDP-11

The PDP-11, first announced in 1969, is not just one computer, but has developed over the years into a family of computers. All PDP-11 computers have the same instruction set. The various models may have different options available, are manufactured from different hardware technologies, use memories of different speeds, and cost different amounts. The models vary from the LSI-11 (less than $1,000), 11/04, and 11/10, at the small, slow, and cheap end, through the medium size 11/40, and 11/45 to the moderately fast 11/70 ($55,000), the top of the line. The 11/04 can have from 4K to 28K words of memory and is used mainly for process control and laboratory use. The 11/70 on the other hand can have up to 2 million words of memory and is used as a general purpose computing machine.

Memory and registers

Memory for the PDP-11 is designed to handle the desire to access both words and bytes. Memory consists of 16-bit words, each of which is composed of two 8-bit bytes, an upper (high-order) and lower (low-order) byte. Memory is *byte-addressable*, meaning that each byte has its own unique address. Words are addressed by the address of the low-order byte. Thus, addresses of sequential memory locations are 0, 2, 4, 6, 8, and so on. The word at location n (where n is an even number) is composed of the bytes with addresses n and $n + 1$. Addresses are 16 bits.

Each byte can hold an integer from 0 to 255 which can be either a small integer or a character code. The ASCII character code is most commonly used. Each 16-bit word can be either two characters or an integer number. Instructions treat 16-bit integers as either unsigned integers or signed two's complement

FIGURE 10.11   A PDP-11 computer system. The processor in this system is the PDP-11/35. Also shown is a set of peripherals including magnetic tape, disks, cassette tapes, paper tape reader, CRT, and printer. (Photo courtesy of Digital Equipment Corporation.)

numbers. Floating point numbers are represented by either two words (with sign, 8-bit excess 128 exponent, and 23-bit fraction) or four words (with sign, 8-bit excess 128 exponent, and 55-bit fraction). Floating point numbers are always normalized, so the leading one bit just after the binary point in the fraction is not stored.

FIGURE 10.12   Memory on the PDP-11 is byte-addressable. Words are two bytes, so word addresses are even.

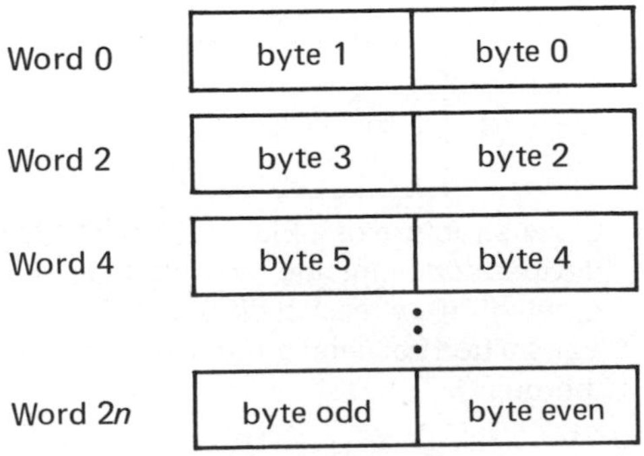

Word 0	byte 1	byte 0
Word 2	byte 3	byte 2
Word 4	byte 5	byte 4
⋮		
Word 2n	byte odd	byte even

The PDP-11 has eight (or seven or six) 16-bit general purpose registers. A general purpose register can be used as either an accumulator or an index register, or both, or anything else that a 16-bit register can be used as. The vagueness over the number of registers comes from the fact that two of these registers are used for special purposes: register 7 is the program counter, and register 6 is used as a stack pointer. Thus, although the instructions allow registers 6 and 7 to be used as any other register, they are normally not used as general purpose registers.

In addition to the general purpose registers, a collection of bits indicate the status of overflow, carry, and comparisons. These bits are grouped together and collectively called the *condition code*. The condition code consists of four bits (N, Z, V, C) which roughly are used to indicate the following information about the last CPU operation,

Z = 1 if the result was *zero*.
N = 1 if the result was *negative*.
C = 1 if a *carry* out of the high-order bit resulted.
V = 1 if there was an arithmetic *overflow*.

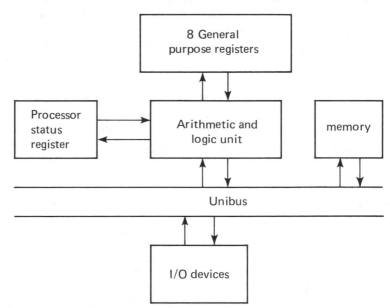

FIGURE 10.13   Block structure of a PDP-11. The CPU, memory, and all I/O devices communicate by using the UNIBUS. The UNIBUS is a set of 56 wires which allow data and addresses to be transmitted between any two devices, memories, or CPUs on the bus.

Instruction set

The PDP-11 has a very rich instruction set, which makes it that much more difficult to describe, and that much easier to program when the entire instruction set is understood. The instructions can be grouped into the following categories

1. double operand instructions
2. single operand instructions
3. jumps
4. miscellaneous

The double and single operand instructions may address memory. For the double operand instructions, two addresses need to be specified; for single operand instructions, only one address need be specified. Since memory addresses are 16 bits long, how can one instruction specify two 16-bit addresses in one 16-bit word? The answer is that it often does not, but the solution to the problem is actually somewhat more complex.

Instructions sometimes specify addresses in different ways. On the MIX computer, addresses could be direct, indexed, indirect, or combinations of these. Each different way of specifying the address is an addressing *mode*. The PDP-11 has eight addressing modes. A register is used with each addressing mode. Each address is thus six bits long, three bits to specify one of eight modes and three bits to specify one of the eight general purpose registers. These eight modes and their assembler syntax are

FIGURE 10.14 Instruction formats for the PDP-11.

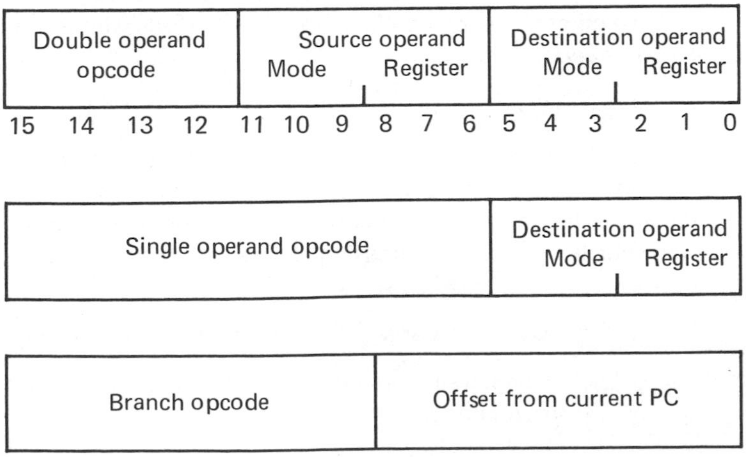

Double operand opcode	Source operand Mode Register	Destination operand Mode Register
15 14 13 12	11 10 9 8 7 6	5 4 3 2 1 0

Single operand opcode	Destination operand Mode Register

Branch opcode	Offset from current PC

Assembler syntax	Numeric mode	Meaning
Rn	0	General purpose register n.
(Rn)	1	The contents of register n is the address of the operand.
(Rn)+	2	The contents of register n is the address of the operand, and after the contents is used as an address it is incremented (auto-increment).
@(Rn)+	3	Indirect auto-increment.
−(Rn)	4	The contents of register n is decremented and then used as the address of the operand (auto-decrement).
@−(Rn)	5	Indirect auto-decrement.
X(Rn)	6	The contents of the *next word* in memory are added to the contents of register n to yield the address of the operand (indexing).
@X(Rn)	7	Indirection after indexing.

These eight modes allow for a great flexibility in programming. Operands can be registers, or pointed at by registers, or pointed at by the address in words pointed at by registers. In addition pointer registers can be incremented or decremented automatically to allow operations on tables, arrays, or character strings. The auto-decrement before and the auto-increment after were specifically designed for use with stacks. Using the program counter (register 7) in mode 6 allows addresses to be specified as *program counter relative*. The advantage of this mode is that the instruction need not be changed if the program is loaded in a different set of locations (relocated). Code with this feature is called *position independent code*.

Double operand instructions

One major group of instructions is the double operand instruction group. These instructions have two operands: a source and a destination. The high-order bit indicates if the operands are bytes or words. The source and destination fields each specify one of the addressing modes listed above and a register. The opcodes are

MOV	1	Copy the contents of the source to the destination.
CMP	2	Compare the source and destination and set the condition code.

BIT	3	AND the source and destination and set the condition code. Do not change either the source or destination.
BIC	4	Clear the bits in the destination which correspond to one bits in the source.
BIS	5	Set the bits in the destination that correspond to one bits in the source.
ADD/SUB	6	Add or subtract (bit 15 says which) the contents of the source to the contents of the destination, storing the result back in the destination.

Notice that the MOV instruction eliminates the need for load and store instructions to transfer information between memory and registers, and can even eliminate the need for using the registers in many cases. Consider that on the MIX computer, to copy from one location to another requires

```
LDA   P
STA   Q
```

On the PDP-11, this can be simply

```
MOV   P,Q
```

which assembles to two program counter relative indexed addressing modes, occupying three words of memory (one for the instruction and one for the index for each operand).

The single operand instructions

The single operand instructions use the same address modes as the double operand instructions but only operate on one operand. Most of these instructions are instructions which, on the PDP-8 or HP 2100, use one of the registers as an operand. On the PDP-11, one of the registers, or any memory location, can be the operand for the instruction.

CLR	Clear. Set the contents of the operand to zero.
COM	Complement the contents of the operand.
INC	Increment by 1 the contents of the operand.
DEC	Decrement by 1 the contents of the operand.
NEG	Negate the operand (complement and add one).
TST	Test the contents of the operand and set the condition code.
ASR	Arithmetic shift right.
ASL	Arithmetic shift left.
ROR	Rotate right.
ROL	Rotate left.

These shifts and rotates are all by one bit and include the carry bit.

ADC   Add carry.
SBC   Subtract carry.

These two instructions use the carry bit in the condition code and are used for multiple precision arithmetic.

Jump instructions.

All the test and compare instructions set the condition code. To jump on the outcome of a test, a branch (or jump) instruction is used. Separate branch instructions are available for almost every interesting condition code value. The format of the jump instruction includes five bits which determine the test to be used to determine if a jump should take place (branch on equal, not equal, plus, minus, and so on). The address to jump to is defined by an 8-bit offset (interpreted as an 8-bit signed two's complement number) plus the program counter. Thus, a branch instruction can transfer control up to 128 words backwards, or 127 words forwards. All branches are automatically position independent.

For longer transfers of control, the JMP instruction is used. Both the JMP and JSR (jump to subroutine) instructions allow their operands to be specified in any of the PDP-11 addressing modes. The JSR also specifies a register. The return address is put in the register and the previous contents of the register are pushed onto the stack pointed at by register 6. An RTS (return from subroutine) instruction reverses the operations, jumping to the address contained in a register and reloading the register from the top of the stack.

Miscellaneous instructions

This last classification includes HALT and WAIT (wait for an interrupt) instructions as well as an entire set of of instructions for setting or clearing the condition code bits. Additional instructions are used mainly with operating systems to cause and return from interrupts.

Assembly language

The assembly language for the PDP-11 is more similar to the assembly language for the PDP-8 than MIXAL. An assembly language statement still has four fields: label, opcode, operand, and comment. Input is free-format. A label is followed by a colon (:). Comments are preceded by a semicolon (;). Operand formats depend upon the type of opcode and the mode of the addressing. Double operand instructions are of the form

```
LOOP:          MOV   SRC,DST      ;COMMENT
```

where SRC is the source operand and DST is the destination operand. The assembler will automatically generate additional words for the indexed and indirect indexed addressing modes. All other instructions have only one operand. For branch instructions, the assembler automatically calculates the proper offset. The location counter is referenced by the period (.).

The pseudo-instructions for the PDP-11 are distinguished from machine instructions by all starting with a period. The assembler includes the normal pseudo-instructions

.GLOBL   Declares each symbol on its operand list to be either an entry point or an external. The assembler knows which, since entry points will be defined in this program, and externals will not.

.WORD   Acts like a CON for full word values

.BYTE   Acts like a CON for bytes.

.ASCII   Defines an ASCII character coded string.

.EVEN   Assures that the location counter is even (so that it addresses a word).

=   The equal sign is used for an EQU pseudo-instruction.

I/O and interrupts

The PDP-11 has no I/O instructions. I/O is performed in a manner which allows the normal instruction set to do all necessary I/O functions. This is done by assigning all I/O devices, not a device number, but an address, or set of addresses in memory. All I/O device control registers, buffer registers, and status registers are assigned addresses in the PDP-11. (In the HP 2100, the A and B registers were assigned addresses 0 and 1 in memory. The registers were not really in memory, but simply could be accessed by the addresses 0 and 1.) On the PDP-11, the upper 4K words of memory, from addresses 160000 to 177777 (octal) are reserved for I/O device addresses.

For example, if a PDP-11 has a card reader attached, that card reader has two registers associated with it, a control register and a data register. The control register will have address 177160, and the data register, address 177162. A line printer will have addresses 177514 (control and status) and 177516 (data). An RF11 disk uses the addresses from 177400 to 177416 for various status registers, word counts, track address registers, memory addresses, and so on.

I/O is performed differently for each device. For simple devices, however the interface is generally provided by two registers: a control register and a data register. For output a character is put in the data register (using the MOV or MOVB instructions). Then a bit is set in the control registers (using the BIS instruction). When a bit is cleared by the device, the output is complete. For higher-speed devices, DMA transfers are made.

The PDP-11 has a priority vectored interrupt system. Two types of interrupts can occur: I/O interrupts and *traps*. A trap is an interrupt caused by the CPU. In

the PDP-11, traps can occur for many reasons, including illegal opcodes, referencing nonexistent memory, using an odd address to fetch word data or instructions, power failure, and even some instructions. Traps cannot be turned off;
they will always cause an interrupt. I/O interrupts will only be recognized when
the priority of the I/O device exceeds the priority of the CPU.

The CPU priority is kept with the condition code bits in a special register
called the processor status. The processor priority is a three-bit number, allowing eight priority levels in the PDP-11. Each device has its own (fixed) three-bit
priority. An interrupt request from a device will be recognized if the device
priority is greater than the current CPU priority.

Interrupt processing on the PDP-11 is more complex than on the HP 2100.
Notice that there are no device numbers and that sequential memory addresses
refer to single bytes, while addresses are two bytes long and instructions may be
several words long. On the PDP-11, each device is assigned an interrupt location. Interrupt locations are in low memory, starting at address 4 and counting at
4-byte intervals up to address 192. Each interrupt location is two words (4 bytes)
and consists of a new processor status (priority and condition code) and an
address. The address is the address where control should be transferred when
an interrupt occurs. When an interrupt occurs, the current processor status and
program counter are pushed onto the stack pointed to by register 6. Then a new
processor status and a new value for the program counter are loaded from the
interrupt vector, in low core, for the interrupting device. Execution now continues at the new program counter. A special instruction, RTI (Return from Interrupt) is used to reload the old processor status and program counter when the
interrupt processing is over.

The PDP-11 has been a highly successful computer. Many people think that
it is one of the better designed computers in years, that it is easy to program and
easy to use. A number of relatively sophisticated programming techniques
(stacks, reentrant code, position independent code) can be routinely used on the
the PDP-11. The I/O system has been designed to allow I/O programming to be
a natural extension of ordinary programming, while the interrupt system provides
a fast means of handling I/O to achieve maximum response to external I/O
events.

Manuals published by Digital Equipment Corporation about the PDP-11
include processor handbooks for each of the models of the PDP-11. Separate
handbooks describe available software and peripheral devices. The PDP-11 is
also discussed in Gear (1974), Eckhouse (1975), and Stone and Siewiorek
(1975), which use the PDP-11 as an example machine to teach assembly language programming in the same way we have used the MIX computer.

EXERCISES

a. Describe the memory of the PDP-11. What is the word size? What is the
    address size?

b.   Why would the PDP-11 want each byte to be addressable, rather than each word?

c.   What are the registers of the PDP-11? What are their uses?

d.   Double operand instructons require two addresses per instruction. Why might this be better than a one address instruction set?

e.   Why do you think all pseudo-instructions for the PDP-11 start with a period?

f.   Why are recursive programs easy to write on the PDP-11?

g.   Describe the interrupt structure of the PDP-11.

10.5 THE IBM SYSTEM 360 AND SYSTEM 370

The IBM system 360 and system 370 line of computers is probably the most important computer system today, and no description of computer systems would be complete without including these machines. The 360 was announced in 1964, and is one of the first third-generation computers, using solid state circuitry with a low level of integration. The range of machines was an attempt to satisfy all customers with one basic architecture. This strategy has been successful for the most part.

The 370 series was brought out in 1970 to replace the aging 360 machines by newer computers with a compatible instruction set, but implemented in newer technology to give faster internal performance, increased reliability, and extended capabilities in some areas. For purposes of our discussion, the 360 and

FIGURE 10.15   An IBM Model 168. One of the most powerful computers available from IBM is shown here with a complete set of peripheral devices. (Photo courtesy of IBM Corporation.)

370 computers are identical. Most 360s have been replaced by 370s by now, so we will refer to the IBM 370. A small 370/115 system will cost about $250,000, while a 370/168 can cost as much as $5,000,000.

Memory and registers

As with the PDP-11, memory in the 370 is byte addressable. Memory is composed of 8-bit bytes, and memory size is generally quoted in units of bytes, not words. 370 systems have from a low of 64 kilo-bytes to a maximum of 16,384 kilo-bytes (16 mega-bytes) of memory. Each byte can hold an integer from 0 to 255, or one EBCDIC character.

Although memory is byte-addressable, it is generally used in larger quantities. A word on the 370 is 32 bits (4 bytes). Since memory is byte addressable, word addresses are all multiples of 4 (0, 4, 8, 12, 16, . . .). In addition, memory can be accessed by half-words (16 bits, 2 bytes, addresses multiples of 2), or double-words (64 bits, 8 bytes, addresses multiples of 8). Memory addresses are 24 bits long, allowing up to 16 mega-bytes of memory.

Number representation schemes on the 370 are many. The basic representation is two's complement integer. This representation can be used in a half-word or fullword memory unit. Bytes are treated as unsigned integers.

Floating point numbers in fullword memory units are stored as sign and magnitude numbers with a 7-bit excess-64 base 16 biased exponent, and a 24-bit fraction. A long floating point form increases the precision of the number to a 56-bit fraction. There is even an extended precision format which gives a 112-bit fraction (about 34 decimal places of accuracy).

The integer and floating point data representations on the 370 computers are normally found on general purpose computers. The integer format is used for counters and pointers. Floating point numbers are generally used in scientific computing. For commercial data processing, other data formats are useful, however. Since the 370 design was to be used for all computing functions, it includes other data representations. Strings of characters, from 1 to 256 characters (bytes) in length can be easily manipulated. Decimal numbers are represented in either of two formats. Packed decimal format uses four bits to represent one decimal digit. Two decimal digits can be packed in one byte. A sign and magnitude format is used with the sign stored in the low-order 4 bits of the last byte.

Another decimal format is the zoned decimal number format. This format is based on the Hollerith punched card character code, where most characters consist of one of the digit punches (0–9) and a zone punch (rows 0, 11 and 12). In the zoned decimal format, the lower four bits of each byte represent one decimal digit, while the upper four bits represent the zone punch. The sign is encoded in the upper four bits (zone) of the last byte.

The 370 has two sets of registers. The most commonly used set consists of 16 general purpose registers. These 32-bit registers, numbered 0 to 15, can be

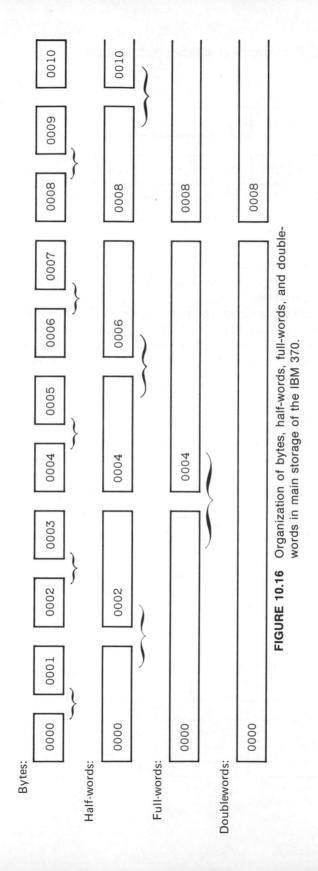

FIGURE 10.16 Organization of bytes, half-words, full-words, and double-words in main storage of the IBM 370.

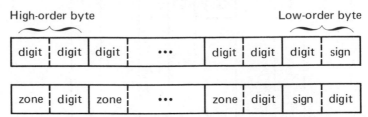

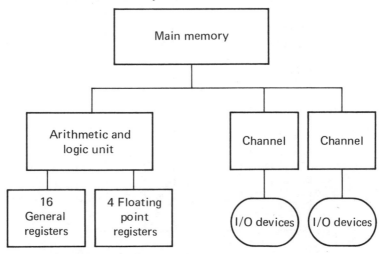

FIGURE 10.17 Representation of decimal numbers on the IBM 370 is in two formats, packed and zoned.

used as accumulators, index registers, pointers, and so forth. In addition, four 64-bit floating point registers (numbered 0, 2, 4, and 6) are used for floating point operations. Separate instructions control the use of the floating point and general purpose registers.

In addition to the general purpose and floating point registers, the 370 has a program counter (called the instruction address) and a condition code. These, along with other information, are stored in a *program status word* (PSW). The other information in the PSW deals mainly with interrupt enabling and disabling.

Instruction set

The designers of the 360 and 370 were faced with the same problem that other designers have: how to provide the largest set of useful instructions encoded into the least number of bits. This problem was solved in several ways.

FIGURE 10.18 Block structure of an IBM 360 or 370. Channels are special-purpose processors for performing input and output from memory.

First, an 8-bit opcode is used, providing up to 256 different instruction opcodes. In addition, different types of instructions are provided. Some instructions operate only on registers, others between memory and registers, still others between memory and memory. Since only 4 bits are needed to specify a register, and 24 bits are needed for a memory address, this results in instructions of *varying length*. Register-to-register instructions need only specify an opcode (one byte) and two registers (one byte), while memory-to-memory instructions take six bytes for opcode and two addresses.

Another technique used was to group the instructions according to function. Not all models include all instructions. For example, the small commercial models may not include the Floating Point Instructions, while the larger scientific machines may not include the decimal instructions. If these instructions are used on machines which are not equipped for them, they are treated as illegal instructions and a trap occurs.

The major problem for a computer designer is memory accessing. Since the 360/370 design was to be good for many years, it was designed with very large memory addresses, 24 bits. (Even so, some models have been modified to allow 32-bit addresses.) But if two 24-bit addresses are stored in an instruction, the instructions become very long. And, since few computer centers would have the funds to buy the entire 16 mega-bytes of memory, most of the addresses which were used would have up to 8 bits of leading zeros. Even if the maximum memory existed, few programs would need to use all of it.

These two contradictory goals (large address space, and short instructions) were solved by using a *base-displacement* addressing technique. All addresses are described by 16 bits: a 4-bit base register and a 12-bit displacement. The address is computed by adding the contents of the selected register to the displacement. The lower 24 bits of this sum is the memory address. (The extension to 32-bit addresses is obvious.)

Register 0 cannot be used as a base register. If register 0 is used as the base register, the contents of the register are ignored and a zero is used as the base address. Thus, the lower 4096 bytes may be accessed directly without setting a base register. To access any other byte in memory, it is necessary to use at least one register as a base register. Most commonly, one or two registers are used as base registers to allow access to instructions in the current subroutine (needed for local variable accessing and jump addresses), and one or two are used for accessing global variables, arrays, tables, and other data structures. Notice that this can reduce the number of generally available registers from 16 to 12 or 13.

The instruction formats for the different instructions are shown in Figure 10.19. The RX-formatted instructions, which include most memory reference instructions, allow indexing by any general register (except register 0) in addition to the base-displacement address calculation. Although we cannot discuss all of the instructions, here are some of them.

The load instructions copy information from memory to the registers. Loading instructions allow the general registers to be loaded with another register

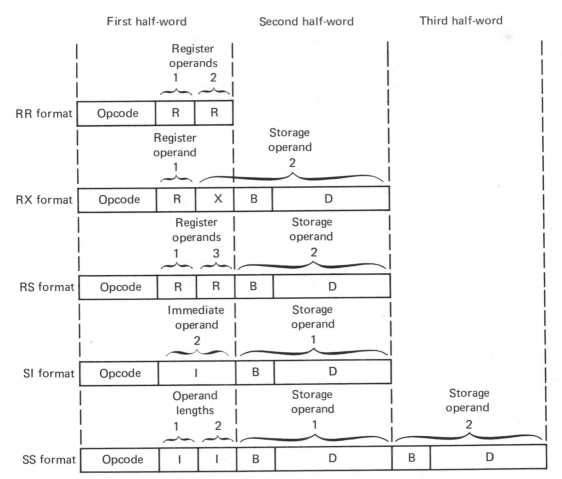

FIGURE 10.19 The five basic instruction formats of the IBM 360 and 370.

(LR), a fullword (L), a half-word with sign extension (LH), and load an immediate quantity, like an ENTA (LA). Additional loads between registers allow load complement (LCR), load and test, setting the condition code (LTR), load positive (LPR), and load negative (LNR). Multiple registers can be loaded from memory at once (LM), allowing all general purpose registers to be loaded with one instruction. Similar instructions allow the floating point registers to be loaded, single or double precision, from memory or a register, positive, negative, tested or rounded.

Storing can be done by character (STC), halfword (STH), fullword (ST), or multiple registers (STM).

Arithmetic operations can be between registers or memory, fullword or halfword, and include addition (A, AR, AH, AL), subtraction (S, SR, SH, SL), multiplication (M, MR, MH), division (D, DR), and comparisons (C, CR, CH, CL, CLR,

CLI). Multiplication and division involve double-length integers and so need double-length registers. This is done by grouping even and odd registers together as even-odd pairs. Register 0 is paired with register 1, register 2 with register 3, and so on. The comparison instructions set the condition code. Floating point arithmetic instructions operate on long or short floating point numbers in the floating point registers.

Jump instructions (called branch instructions) allow jumps to any address in memory on any setting of the condition code. Branch instructions also can be used to increment a register, compare against another register and branch if greater (BXH), or branch if less than or equal (BXLE), or decrement and branch if nonzero (BC, BCR). Subroutine jumps are made by a branch and link (BAL) instruction which puts the return address in a register.

Logical AND, OR and exclusive-OR instructions can be used on the general purpose registers for masking, as can a set of left or right, single or double (even-odd pairs), end-off shifts by any number of bits (0 to 63).

Decimal instructions all operate directly on numbers stored in memory and allow addition, subtraction, multiplication, division, and comparisons as well as instructions for converting between binary and packed decimal, and between packed decimal and zoned decimal. Fancy editing instructions allow leading zero suppression, check protection, and addition of commas and periods in decimal numbers for output.

Character strings can be manipulated by instructions which copy strings of bytes from memory to memory, that translate from one character code to another, or that search for particular characters.

Assembly language

The assembly language for the 370 is similar to the other assembly languages we have seen, but larger. The large number of different instructions, instruction formats, and data representations all make the assembler a very complex program. There are, in fact, at least six assemblers for the 370 assembly language, ranging from a two-pass load-and-go assembler to a four-pass assembler.

The basic assembly language statement format is the same as for a free-format MIXAL program. An optional label (up to eight characters, starting with a letter) may start in column one. The opcode field may be any of the symbolic mnemonic opcodes for 370 instructions, an assembler pseudo-instruction, or a macro call. The operand field format depends upon the opcode. The operand field may be followed by a comment field. All fields are separated by blanks. An asterisk in column 1 indicates a comment card.

One of the major problems in writing 370 programs is addressing. The base-displacement form of address calculation is a good hardware design but requires that the machine language programmer constantly calculate displacements. This is solved in assembly language by maintaining a base register table in the assembler. Whenever a symbol is used in an operand field where base-displacement in needed, the assembler searches the base register table for the base register closest to the symbol. The displacement from this base register is calculated, and code is generated using this displacement and base register. Entries are added to the base register table by the USING pseudo-instruction. It has the format

USING address,register

When this pseudo-instruction is encountered, it is entered into the base register table to allow that register to be used as a base register if necessary. A DROP pseudo-instruction will remove the register from the table. It should be used whenever the contents of base registers are changed. Remember that all this calculation is done at assembly time and affects only the generation of assembled code. If a programmer lies with his USING or DROP pseudo-instructions, the assembler will generate the code it thinks is correct, but this code will probably not execute correctly.

Other pseudo-operations include EQU, DC (a complex version of the CON statement), DS (a BSS statement), ENTRY and EXTRN (for relocatable programs), ORG, MACRO and MEND, listing control (define a title, start a new page, space), and many others.

The 370 assembly language, particularly its macro and conditional assembly features, is very powerful. A truly excellent programmer can write very sophisticated programs in 370 assembly language. The rest of us tend to ignore a large number of these features.

I/O and interrupts

Six classes of interrupts can occur in the 370. These are *I/O*, *external* (an interrupt from a clock or power failure), *program* (illegal opcode, addressing error, illegal data, overflow or underflow, or translation errors), *supervisor call* (a special instruction to allow programs to communicate with the operating system), *machine check* (hardware failure) and *restart* (operator pushes the restart button on the console). Each type of interrupt has two doublewords assigned to it in low core. When an interrupt occurs, a new PSW is loaded from the first doubleword assigned to this type of interrupt; the old PSW is saved in the other doubleword (old PSW).

Each type of interrupt has a priority associated with it. If two interrupts are requested at the same time, the higher priority request takes precedence. In addition, four bits in the PSW allow I/O, external, machine check, and program interrupts to be enabled or disabled separately. Supervisor calls and restart interrupts are always possible.

Another field in the PSW records information on the specific interrupt which occurred. The device number and channel number are stored for I/O interrupts.

In addition, the length of the last instruction is stored in the PSW to allow the computer to "back up" and try again if need be.

The I/O system of the 370 is quite sophisticated. All I/O is done directly to memory. This requires a processor, as on the HP 2100 and PDP-11, to control the transfer of information between the I/O devices and memory, to count the number of words transferred, and to keep track of the address where each word should go. On the HP 2100 and PDP-11, this was a relatively simple special-purpose processor. On the 370, this processor is more complex. It is called a *channel*. A channel on the 370 is a special purpose computer which can execute *channel programs*.

Channel programs, like CPU programs, are made up of instructions. The channel, after initiation by the CPU, executes a channel program by executing each instruction in the channel program, one after another. The channel program is stored in main memory along with normal CPU programs. The channel fetches each instruction from memory as necessary. The CPU initiates I/O activity by starting a channel with a Start I/O (SIO) instruction. When an SIO instruction is executed, the addressed channel loads the address of the first instruction in its channel program from location 72 in memory, and starts to execute its channel program. The CPU continues to execute programs independent of channel activity. Two other instructions, Test I/O (TIO) and Halt I/O (HIO), can be used by the CPU to interact with a channel.

A channel is a special purpose processor. Since it is meant to do I/O and nothing else, it does not need arithmetic instructions or conditional instructions or similar instructions which are necessary for computation. Each instruction to a channel is called a channel command word (CCW) and is a doubleword (see Figure 10.20). The fields of a CCW are its command code (read, write, read backwards, sense, control, and jump), a memory address of the memory buffer for the I/O transfer, a count of the number of bytes to transfer, and a set of flag bits. The flags contain various options including one to not store data during reads, to request an interrupt after each CCW (instead of only after the entire program is completed or an error occurs), and a *chain bit*. The chain bit in a channel command word is the opposite of a halt bit. As long as the chain bit in a CCW is on, the channel processor will continue to fetch the next doubleword in memory as a new CCW when the current CCW is completely executed. The first CCW which is encountered with a zero chain bit causes the channel processor to stop and request an interrupt of the CPU.

There are several different kinds of channels available. Multiplexor channels are used for slow-speed devices, while selector channels are used for high-speed devices. Channels, with their direct memory access and ability to execute relatively simple sequences of I/O actions, relieve the CPU of the need to keep complete track of all activity itself, just as a secretary allows an executive to be more effective by taking over some of the routine work.

"IBM System/370 Principles of Operation" (IBM Order number GA22-7000)

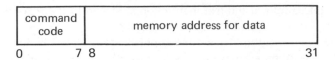

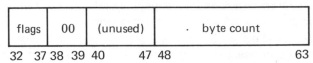

FIGURE 10.20   Channel command word format. The flags field includes a chain bit.

is the definitive reference on the 370 computers, while "IBM System/370 System Summary" (IBM Order number GA22-7001) gives a good overview of the different models, their features, and their peripherals. Several textbooks use the 360 and 370 computers to teach assembly language programming, including Struble (1975).

EXERCISES

a.   Describe the memory and registers of the IBM 370 family of computers. What is the word size? What is the address size? How is memory addressed?

b.   What is the difference between a System 360 model 30 and a System 370 model 168?

c.   Describe the effective address calculation for the 370.

d.   Describe the instruction set of the 370. Include the size of the opcode field, the instruction length, number representations, and types of operands for the different instructions.

e.   What are the USING and DROP pseudo-instructions for?

f.   How is I/O done on the 370? What is the advantage of this approach over the approach of the MIX or PDP-8 computers?

10.6 THE BURROUGHS B5500

The B5000, announced by Burroughs in 1961, is a radical departure from the architecture of most computers. Most computers are register-oriented, from the programmer's point of view, while the Burroughs' computers are stack-oriented (see Section 4.5). The B5000 was the first of this line of computers. The B5500 (1965) was a second edition which solved some of the problems of the B5000. More recent computer systems, including the B2700, B3700 and B4700, and the B2800, B3800, and B4800, have followed the same general architectural design,

FIGURE 10.21   A Burroughs B5500 computer system. The B5500 was a very successful computer system based on a stack architecture. (Photo courtesy of Burroughs Corporation.)

although with new technology. We describe here the B5500, as the classic model of a stack machine.

One point should be kept in mind during the discussion of the architecture of the B5500: there is virtually no assembly language programming for the B5500. In fact, there is no assembly language. This remarkable fact is a result of a conscious decision on the part of the designers of the Burroughs' computers. The designers saw the computer hardware as only a part of the overall computing system, composed of hardware and software. Thus, the B5500 was designed to efficiently execute higher-level languages, particularly Algol-like languages. Since it does this so well, there is no need for assembly language, and *all* code for Burroughs' computers is written in a higher-level language. This includes even the operating system, MCP.

With this in mind, we present a description of the Burroughs B5500.

Memory

The B5500 is a 48-bit machine with 15-bit addresses, allowing up to 32K words of memory. Each word can be either data or instructions. Data words can be interpreted in two ways. A 48-bit word can be interpreted as eight 6-bit characters; the character code is a variant of BCD.

Alternatively, the data word can be interpreted as a number. Numbers are represented in floating point notation, with a 6-bit exponent and a 39-bit fraction.

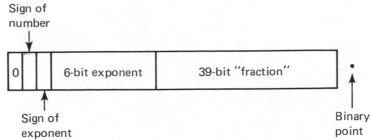

FIGURE 10.22 Representation of numbers on the B5500. All numbers, both floating point and integer, are represented in this floating point format.

Each portion of the number, exponent and fraction, has a separate sign bit, using sign and magnitude notation. "Fraction" is a misleading term for the 39-bit part, since the decimal point is assumed to be at the far right of the "fraction," making the 39-bit portion an integer, not a fraction. This integer portion is in the range 0 to 549,755,813,887. The exponent base is 8, so the range of representation is approximately 8^{-51} to 8^{+76} with about 12 places of accuracy. There is no integer number representation; integers are simply floating point numbers with a zero exponent.

Instruction set

The instruction set for the B5500 is composed of two separate sets: word mode instructions and character mode instructions. The computer operates in one of two modes; word mode or character mode, with separate instruction sets for both modes. One of the instructions in word mode switches the B5500 to character mode; one of the instructions in character mode switches to word mode. A one-bit flag register remembers the current mode. We consider word mode operation first.

Word mode

In word mode, the B5500 is completely stack-oriented. Each instruction which needs an operand or generates a result uses the stack for the source of its operands and the destination of its results. For example, the ADD instruction takes the two words at the top of the stack, removes them from the stack, adds them, and places their sum back on the top of the stack. The stack is stored in memory and pointed at by a special register, the S register.

This approach to designing the instruction set has several advantages. No operand address need be specified in the instruction. A stack machine is thus called a 0-address machine. This makes the instruction very short, since it need only specify an opcode. Thus, programs are very short, saving memory. No

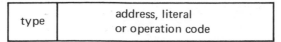

FIGURE 10.23   Instruction format for word-mode instructions. The two-bit type field selects either a literal (00), operand (01), descriptor (11), or operation (10); this determines the interpretation of the remaining 10 bits.

registers are needed to act as accumulators or counters; all functions are performed on the top of the stack.

The B5500 has 12-bit instructions, allowing 4 instructions to be packed into each word. There are four types of instructions, selected by two bits of the instructions. These four types of instructions are,

1.   Literals (00). This instruction type is composed of a 10-bit literal. This literal is a small integer in the range 0 to 1023 and is copied to top of the stack. This allows small constants and addresses to be put on the stack directly.

2.   Operand (01). This instruction type consists of a 10-bit address. The contents of the addressed location is copied onto the top of the stack. This is similar to a load instruction.

3.   Descriptor (11). This instruction type includes a 10-bit address which is copied to the top of the stack.

4.   Operation (10). The remaining 10 bits of the instruction specify an operation to be performed, generally on the top of the stack.

The operand and descriptor instructions are more complex than the above description indicates. Notice for example that the descriptor function would appear to be the same as the literal function. Also both descriptor and operand instructions specify addresses, but only a 10-bit address, despite the fact that addresses are 15 bits. The reason for this is that the 10-bit "addresses" are not addresses into memory but rather indices into an area of memory called the *Program Reference Table* (PRT).

The PRT contains constants and simple variables for the program as well as pointers to more complex structures, such as subprograms and arrays. All references to subprograms and arrays are made indirectly through the PRT. The PRT acts like a symbol table (but without the symbols), allowing each symbol in a program to be represented by its index into the PRT rather than a complete 15-bit address. The descriptor function places the absolute 15-bit address of its PRT index on the stack.

Operations

The operations which can be performed on the B5500 are typical of most computers. The top two elements of the stack can be added, subtracted, multiplied, or divided, with the result placed on the top of the stack. These operations

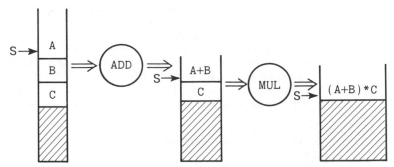

FIGURE 10.24   Stack operation on the B5500. All operations are done on the top elements of the stack, with the result being placed back on the stack. The S register points to the top of the stack.

can be either single or double precision. All of these operations are floating point operations, but since integers are represented as unnormalized floating point numbers, these same operations can also be used on integers or mixed integer and floating point numbers. A special integer divide instruction allows an integer quotient and remainder to be generated from two numbers.

Logical operations of AND, OR, equivalence (1 bit for each pair of identical bits, 0 bit for each pair of different bits), and negate operate on the top of the stack, placing the result on the top of the stack. Each word is treated as a string of 48 bits. These logical operations are useful in conjunction with the compare operators and for masking.

The compare operators compare the top two elements of the stack for equal, not equal, less, less or equal, greater, or greater or equal, whichever is selected, and places the result of the comparison (zero for false, nonzero for true) on the top of the stack. A special field compare instruction allows any two arbitrary fields of the top two elements of the stack to be compared.

Conditional jumps use the top of the stack to control jumping: jumping if true, not jumping if false. Unconditional jumps always jump. The address to which to jump is given on the top of the stack. Separate instructions exist for forward jumps and for backward jumps. The address on the stack is the offset (from the current instruction) of the instruction to which to jump. Since a jump will normally not be too far away, only the lower 12 bits of the stack address are used. This allows a jump to any instruction within 1023 words forward or backwards. In all cases the jump offset and logical value (for conditional jumps) are removed after the jump instruction is completed.

Storing operations require the value to be stored and the address of the location to be on the top of the stack. The value is stored in the memory location addressed, and normally both are removed from the stack. A special store operation allows the value to remain on the stack for further use, removing only the address from the stack.

A special set of instructions allows the top two elements on the stack to be interchanged, the top element to be duplicated, or the top element to be deleted.

An example of using the stack

To see how the stack structure of the B5500 affects its programming, consider the program to evaluate a simple arithmetic expression like,

```
( (B+W) * Y) + 2 + ( (M–L) * K)/Z
```

For the B5500, our program could look like

```
*
*       OPCODE      OPERAND          STACK CONTENTS
*

        OPERAND     W                W
        OPERAND     B                W        B
        ADD                          B+W
        OPERAND     Y                B+W        Y
        MUL                          (B+W)*Y
        LITERAL     2                (B+W)*Y        2
        ADD                          ((B+W)*Y)+2
        OPERAND     M                ((B+W)*Y)+2      M
        OPERAND     L                ((B+W)*Y)+2      M       L
        SUB                          ((B+W)*Y)+2      M–L
        OPERAND     K                ((B+W)*Y)+2      M–L        K
        MUL                          ((B+W)*Y)+2      (M–L)*K
        OPERAND     Z                ((B+W)*Y)+2      (M–L)*K      Z
        DIV                          ((B+W)*Y)+2      ((M–L)*K)/Z
        ADD                          (((B+W)*Y)+2)+((M–L)*K)/Z
```

This expression was programmed in Chapter 4 with 10 MIX instructions, while the above B5500 program takes 15 instructions. However, remember that MIX instructions are 31 bits in length, while B5500 instructions are only 12 bits. Thus, the MIX program took 310 bits compared to the 180 bits for the B5500 program. Also the MIX program required a temporary storage location, while the B5500 program needs no temporary storage, storing all intermediate results on the stack.

Character mode

One special control instruction for the B5500 changes the mode of execution to character mode. In character mode, the entire instruction is interpreted in a different manner. There is no stack. Two special registers point to two areas of memory called the source and the destination. Operations transfer from the source to the destination, compare the source to the destination, add or subtract the source to the destination (as decimal integers), and perform editing opera-

FIGURE 10.25 Instruction format in character mode. Each instruction has a 6-bit repeat count and a 6-bit opcode. All operations are between two memory areas, the source character string and the destination character string.

tions (like suppressing leading zeros). Two instructions are almost exactly like NUM and CHAR in MIX. The length of the character strings is included in each 12-bit instruction. Each instruction has a 6-bit repeat field and a 6-bit opcode field. This allows character strings to be any length from 0 to 63.

An interesting pair of special instructions is the BEGIN–LOOP/END–LOOP pair. When a BEGIN–LOOP opcode is encountered, a counter is initialized to the 6-bit repeat field in the instruction and the address of the BEGIN–LOOP instruction is remembered. When an END–LOOP instruction is executed, the counter is decremented. If it is still positive, the loop is repeated from the address following the BEGIN–LOOP instruction. If the counter is zero, the computer continues to the next instruction, following the END–LOOP instruction. These instructions allow loops on character strings without the need for an explicit counter, decrement, and conditional jump.

I/O and interrupts

The input and output of information is handled by channels executing a channel program. The I/O start instruction starts the channel executing a channel program which starts at memory location 8. An interrupt system is used to signal completion of I/O and also to handle exceptional conditions such as overflow or underflow (of numbers or of the stack), divide by zero, memory parity errors, and so on. A 7-bit interrupt code is used to indicate the type of interrupt occuring. Interrupts are vectored through locations in low memory. Registers are stacked when the interrupt occurs, allowing the interrupted program to be restarted after the interrupt is serviced.

EXERCISES

a. Describe the memory of the B5500.
b. What would be the advantage of building a machine which does not need assembly language programs?
c. Can *all* programming for a computer be done in a higher-level language, or must at least some program be written in machine language at least once? (Hint: consider loaders).
d. Why are there two modes of operation on the B5500?

e. Why are there no integer numbers on the B5500?

f. Write a program for the B5500 to calculate the expression, $Y + 2 *$ $(W + V) / 4 - 6 * (10 - W - V)$.

g. A stack machine allows instructions to be much shorter, since no address need be specified for arithmetic operations. Does this mean all programs are always shorter on a stack machine?

10.7 THE CDC 6600

In discussing the CDC 6600, it is important to make clear at the start that the 6600 was not designed for the same purpose as the other computers described in this chapter. The 6600 was built for the express purpose of delivering the greatest possible computing power for the solution of large scientific computing problems. As such it has succeeded very well. The 6600 and the later 6400, 6500, 6700, and Cyber 70 models are not meant for the business data processing problems which typically involve much I/O and little computation. They were designed for problems which involve large amounts of floating point calculations.

FIGURE 10.26   A CDC 6600. The 6600 is composed of 11 separate computers: one central processor and 10 peripheral processors. One peripheral processor is commonly used to drive the operator's console, shown in the foreground. (Photo courtesy of Control Data Corporation.)

The design goals resulted in a dramatic change in the basic architecture of the computer. The CDC 6600 is not 1 processor but 11 separate processors: 1 main central processor (CP) and 10 *peripheral processors* (PP). Each of these processors has its own memory, registers, and instruction set. The objective is quite simple: to relieve the central processor of all input/output, bookkeeping, and control functions. The entire operating system of the 6600 resides in the peripheral processors. This is an extension to the extreme of the same ideas which lead to the design of the channels on the 360/370 computers. The idea is to relieve the CP of the responsibility for operating system functions, allowing it to devote itself totally to computation. The 6600 is an expensive computer system, costing from $3,000,000 to $5,000,000.

The peripheral processors

Each of the peripheral processors is a 12-bit computer with its own 4K of memory and an 18-bit accumulator, the A register. Instructions are either 12-bits or 24-bits long and allow loading, storing, addition, subtraction, shifting, masking, and conditional jumps. A subroutine jump instruction stores the return address in memory and starts execution at the next instruction. Addressing modes allow 6-bit and 18-bit immediate operands, as well as direct and indirect addressing. All of these instructions access the PP's private 4K of memory. Additional instructions allow the PPs to copy words between central memory and its own memory.

The PPs have I/O instructions which allow each PP to do input or output on any I/O device, one word at a time. No interrupt system is used, so busy loop waiting, or polling, is needed for I/O. Remember, however, that when busy loop waiting is used, the entire computer system is not waiting, only the one PP doing that I/O. The other PPs can continue work.

The PPs are designed to perform I/O and operating system functions, not general computing. They normally execute only programs which are a part of the operating system. Thus, most programmers never have an opportunity to program the PPs. When the 6600 is discussed, most discussion centers on the central processor.

Central memory

The central processor was designed for scientific calculations. This implies floating point numbers and a desire for many digits of precision. This in turn implies a large word length. Correspondingly, the word length for central memory is 60 bits. Each 60-bit word can be copied to 5 12-bit PP words. Up to 256K words can be used on a 6600, since addresses are 18 bits.

A 60-bit word can represent integers, in a ones' complement notation, or 10 6-bit characters. The character code is of CDC's own design, called display code, but is only 6-bits per character, 64 characters. The characters provided are basically the same as those provided by the BCD character code.

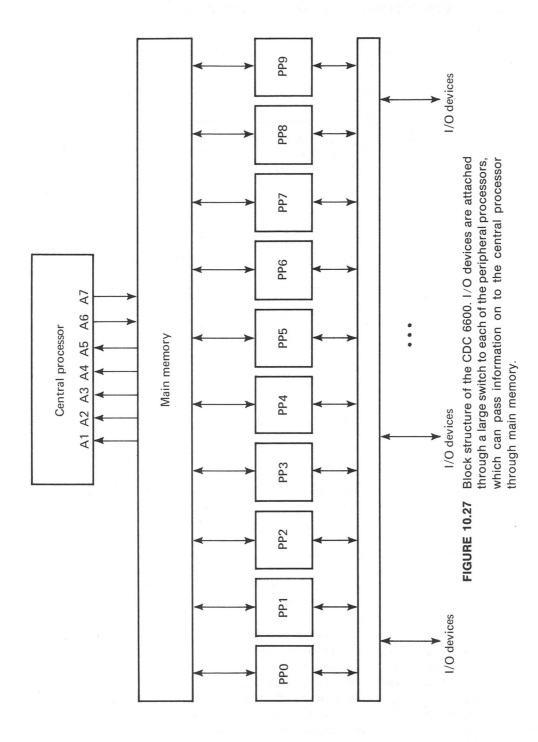

FIGURE 10.27 Block structure of the CDC 6600. I/O devices are attached through a large switch to each of the peripheral processors, which can pass information on to the central processor through main memory.

Main memory

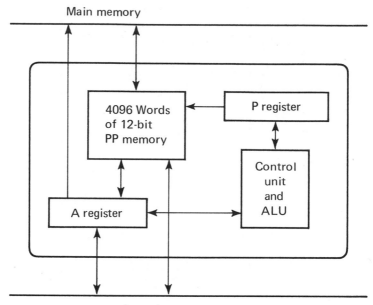

Input/output system

FIGURE 10.28   Block diagram of a peripheral processor (PP). There are 10 PPs, and each has its own registers and 4096 12-bit words of memory.

A 60-bit word can also be interpreted as a floating point number in ones' complement notation, with an 11-bit, ones' complement base 2 exponent (but with a complemented sign bit) and a 48-bit fraction with a binary point to the right of the fraction. Special floating point numbers are used to represent "infinite" and "indefinite" numbers. Infinite numbers result from operations causing exponent overflow, while indefinite numbers result from using infinite numbers in operations.

The 6600 has 24 (plus or minus one) programmable registers: 8 X registers (X0, X1, . . . , X7), 8 B registers (B0, B1, . . . , B7), and 8 A registers (A0, A1, . . . , A7). The X registers are the operand registers. These are 60-bit registers. All arithmetic operations are done on these registers. The B registers are 18-bit index registers; they can hold addresses, or "small" integers. The A registers are 18-bit address registers.

The A registers are used to do all loading and storing of the X registers. Whenever an address is loaded into any of A1, A2, A3, A4, or A5, the contents of that memory location in memory is loaded into X1, X2, X3, X4, or X5, respectively. Whenever an address is put into A6 or A7, the contents of X6 or X7, respectively, is stored into the memory word at that address. Memory is only loaded from or stored into as a result of setting one of the appropriate A registers (A1 though A5 for loading; A6 or A7 for storing) to an address.

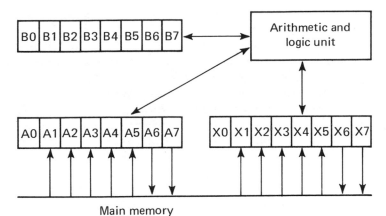

Main memory

FIGURE 10.29   The central processor of a CDC 6600. The A and B registers are 18-bit registers for holding counters and addresses; the X registers are 60-bit registers for holding integer, character, and floating point operands.

A few of the registers are special. A0 and X0 are not connected nor do they cause loading or storing. A0 is essentially an extra index register, while X0 is a "free" operand register. B0 is always zero. It is possible to "store" into B0 any value, but it will always be read out as zero. This is actually very useful, and many programmers go one step farther, initializing B1 to 1 and leaving it as 1 for the duration of their programs.

Instruction set

The 6600 has two types of instructions. The short form is 15 bits with an opcode field (6 bits), and three 3-bit register fields (i, j, and k). The register fields select one of the eight registers for the instruction. The opcode determines whether the A, X, or B registers should be used. The long form of instruction has

FIGURE 10.30   Instruction formats for the CDC 6600. Several instructions are packed into each word. The opcode defines the length of the instruction. K is an 18-bit constant; the other fields (i, j, k) select one of eight registers.

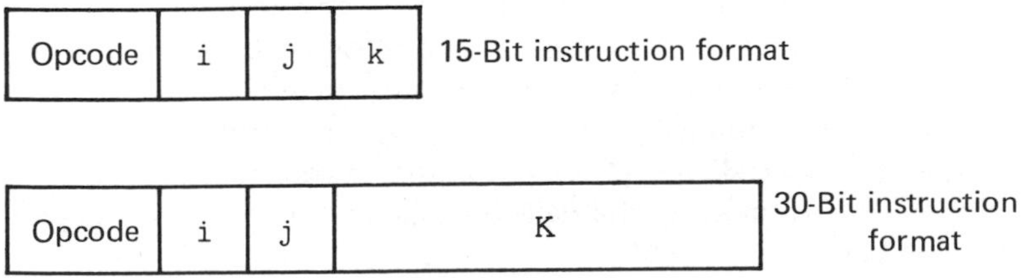

| Opcode | i | j | k | 15-Bit instruction format |

| Opcode | i | j | K | 30-Bit instruction format |

the same format, except the *k* field is an 18-bit ones' complement number, denoted as K. The K field most often holds an 18-bit address.

Having instructions of varying lengths is not unusual, but notice that both instruction lengths are smaller than the size of the basic addressable memory unit (in this case a 60-bit word), not larger, as in the PDP-11 and IBM 370. Multiple instructions are packed into each word. In the best case, four 15-bit instructions can be packed into one 60-bit word. Alternatively, two 30-bit instructions, or two 15-bit and one 30-bit instruction can be packed into one word. If, in writing a program, you encounter the situation of having three 15-bit instructions (or one 15-bit and one 30-bit instruction) in a word, and the next instruction is 30 bits, then the last 15 bits of the word are padded with a no-operation (NOP), and the next word gets the 30-bit instruction in its upper 30 bits. If an instruction is to be jumped to, it must be the first instruction in a new word. This can result in a word being padded with up to three NOPs.

The instruction set itself is quite simple. With only 6 bits for the opcode field, only 64 opcodes are possible. The instructions can be split into three groups: the set instructions, the jump instructions, and the computational instructions.

The set instructions are used to put values into the A, B, and X registers. The values are 18-bit quantities which result from addition or subtraction of the contents of A, B, and X registers, or (in the long format instructions) the number K. Any Ai, Bi, or Xi register can be set to

1. The contents of an A register plus K (Aj + K)
2. The contents of a B register plus K (Bj + K)
3. The contents of an X register plus K (Xj + K)
4. The contents of an X register plus the contents of a B register (Xj + Bk)
5. The contents of an A register plus the contents of a B register (Aj + Bk)
6. The contents of an A register minus the contents of a B register (Aj − Bk)
7. The sum of the contents of two B registers (Bj + Bk)
8. The difference of the contents of two B registers (Bj − Bk)

Remember that the B register involved can be B0, which is always zero. This allows any Ai, Bi, or Xi to be set to any Aj, Bj, Xj, K, −Bk or zero.

The contents of registers can be tested and a jump made on the result by the jump instructions. The jumps allow X registers to be tested for positive, negative, zero, nonzero, indefinite, or infinite values. If the condition is true for the selected X register, a jump is made to the address K given in the instruction. In addition, jumps can be made as the result of comparing any two B registers for equality, nonequality, greater than or equal, or less than. Since one of these registers can be B0, this allows jumps if a B register is positive, negative, zero, nonzero, nonnegative, or nonpositive. Two other jumps are an unconditional jump and a subroutine jump. A subroutine jump to location K from location P will result in a jump instruction to location P+1 being stored in location K, and execution continuing at K+1. A return to the calling program is effected by jumping to K (which jumps back to P+1).

The remaining instructions are the computational ones. These are the instructions which actually compute. They include boolean operations (AND, OR, and exclusive-OR of X registers and their complements), shifts (left or right, end-off or circular), addition, subtraction, multiplication, and division (both integer and floating point). Additional instructions help to multiply and divide double precision numbers and to convert between integers and floating point numbers.

The contents of X registers can be copied from register to register by ANDing or ORing the source register with itself. This is probably the most common use of the boolean instructions: to move values between registers.

A few miscellaneous instructions allow the CP to do nothing (NOP) or stop (PS).

And that is all the instructions for the 6600 (give or take a few). There are no load or store instructions (this is done by setting A registers), no character handling instructions (done by shifting and masking with the Boolean operations), and no I/O instructions (done by the PP's). The instruction set is very simple, possessing a kind of elegance for its simplicity. This makes the computer relatively easy to program (once you get used to it).

However, it should be admitted that although it is possible to program the 6600 in a very straightforward manner, this is seldom done. The main reason for this is that very large increases in speed can be obtained by careful use of registers, selection of operations, and ordering of instructions. Only the very sophisticated programmer can consider all of these factors and produce truly optimal code.

Assembly language and programming

Since there are two computers with two separate instruction sets for the CDC 6600 (CP and PP), two assemblers would be expected. However, since most of the code in an assembler is independent of the instruction set, only one assembler is used. A pseudo-instruction selects the PP opcode table for PP programs; normally the opcode table for the CP is used. This assembler runs on the CP, but not on the PPs. Thus, the PPs have no assembler for PP assembly language which runs on a PP. The CP assembler for PP assembly language is a *cross-assembler*, an assembler which runs on one computer and produces code to be executed on another computer.

The statement format for the 6600 assembly language is the same as for many other computers: free-format, composed of four fields: label, opcode, operand, and comment. The label field must start in column 1 or 2, if there is a label. (Labels are allowed to start in column 2 because the operating system uses the Fortran convention of using column 1 for carriage control information when a file is printed. Thus, if labels started in column 1, and the program were simply copied onto the printer, the first letter of each label would be interpreted as a carriage control character.)

The central processor assembler recognizes the special symbols A0, A1, . . .

A7, B0, B1, . . . , B7 and X0, X1, . . . , X7 as the names of the corresponding registers. The opcode field plus the form of the operand field are used to determine the opcode and assembled instruction. For example, all set instructions use the mnemonic "S" followed immediately by the register to be set. The type of set and the other registers involved are indicated by the form of the operand. The following examples might illustrate this

```
SA1   A1+B1      SET A1 TO THE SUM OF A1 AND B1. OPCODE = 54.
SA1   B2+B5      SET A1 TO THE SUM OF B2 AND B5. OPCODE = 56.
SX1   B2+B5      SET X1 TO THE SUM OF B2 AND B5. OPCODE = 76.
```

When an instruction is used with a constant (SB3 B3+1), the constant can be numeric (decimal or octal if suffixed by B), symbolic, * (location counter), or an expression. Expression operators are + − * and /, with * and / having precedence over + or −; otherwise evaluation is left to right. Literals are allowed.

A large number of pseudo-instructions are used. Each program is preceded by an IDENT pseudo-instruction (which identifies and names the program), and terminates with an END pseudo-instruction. DATA or CON pseudo-instructions can be used to define constants; DIS defines strings of characters (like ALF), and BSS reserves memory locations. ORG is used to set the location counter, but almost all programs are relocatable, so it is seldom used. ENTRY and EXT pseudo-instructions declare entry points and externals. The EQU defines a symbol for the symbol table. Conditional assembly and macro instructions are also available.

Some of the more unusual pseudo-operations include BASE, which can be used to define the base in which numeric constants are interpreted (octal or decimal); PPU which declares the program which follows to be a PP program and not a CP program; and OPDEF, which allows the programmer to define his own entries for the opcode table. The assembler is two-pass.

Programming the 6600 is somewhat different from programming other computers. All operations are done on registers and loading and storing operations are done in a somewhat unconventional manner. Most of these problems disappear as experience and familiarity with the machine are gained. The more important problems deal with the coordination of the CP and the ten PPs to allow a program to perform both computation and I/O as necessary. Since the CP can do no I/O, it must request the PPs to do all I/O for it. This leads to some interesting problems in operating system design, but is beyond the scope of this book.

As with most computers, the reference manuals published by the manufacturer provide the most authoritative description of the hardware and assembler for the computer. For the 6600, these are the "Control Data 6000 Series Computer Systems Reference Manual," and the "Compass Reference Manual". Another source is the excellent book by one of the designers of the 6000 series of computers, Thornton (1970), which describes the 6600 and its hardware design. Programming techniques for the central processor are described in the text by Grishman (1974).

EXERCISES

a. Describe the memory and registers of the CDC 6600 central processor. What is the word size? What is the address size?

b. The CDC 6600 central processor has no LOAD or STORE operations. How is information transferred between memory and the registers?

c. Both MIX and the 6600 have index registers; why doesn't the 370?

d. Since the 6600 has no interrupts, how does the computer know when devices have completed requested I/O operations? Which processor(s) in the 6600 actually do the I/O?

e. The 6600 peripheral processors (PPs) each have 4K of 12-bit words and an 18-bit accumulator. Why would they have an 18-bit accumulator when they have only 12-bit words?

f. IBM uses hexadecimal for the IBM 370, while CDC promotes octal for the 6600. Can you suggest reasons why?

10.8 THE INTEL 8080

One of the major concerns which must be considered in designing a computer is the available technology. Charles Babbage was unable to complete his Analytical Engine in the nineteenth century not because of faulty design, but simply because his design exceeded by almost a century the technology to implement his ideas. Within the last five years, however, the technology of electronic circuits has improved to the point that an entirely new type of computer is possible: the microcomputer.

The transistor started the semiconductor revolution, allowing computers to replace the bulky vacuum tubes with the smaller, faster, and more reliable solid state devices. Originally these devices (transistors, resistors, capacitors, diodes) were used as discrete components, but soon they were combined into combinations of devices produced as an entity. This is known as small-scale integration (SSI). SSI allowed several gates to be put on a single silicon chip. Medium-scale integration (MSI) increased the number of components that could be placed on a single chip, so that an entire register might be one chip. Most recently, large-scale integration (LSI) has allowed thousands of components to be put on a single chip. In particular, LSI makes possible the construction of an entire CPU on one chip. This includes the ALU, registers, and control logic. Separate chips can be used to provide memory and I/O driver circuits.

One of the first computers-on-a-chip, or microprocessors, to be developed was the Intel 8008. This was used to control an "intelligent" CRT terminal. The 8008 was replaced by the Intel 8080. The 8080 has more instructions than the 8008 and is faster, but is also upwards compatible, so any 8008 program will also run on the 8080. The 8080 has been upgraded to the 8080A and recently the 8085 has been announced. The 8085 is compatible with the 8080, but runs 50 percent faster.

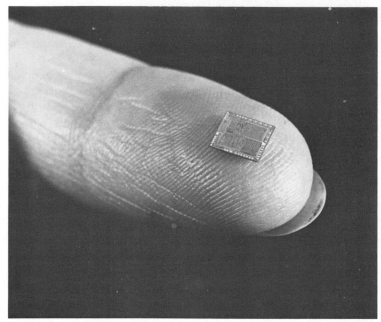

FIGURE 10.31 The Intel 8080 CPU. This small chip of semiconductor material includes all of the logic for the arithmetic and logic unit and control unit for the 8080. The entire chip is less than $\frac{1}{2}$ inch on each side. (Photo courtesy of Intel Corporation.)

The 8080 is certainly not the only microprocessor. The Motorola M6800 is another popular 8-bit microprocessor, while the Intersil IM6100 is a 12-bit PDP-8 compatible processor, and the LSI-11 microprocessor is a 16-bit PDP-11 compatible processor. Zilog Corporation makes the Z80 which is 8080-compatible but twice as fast and uses less power. RCA manufactures the COSMAC microprocessor; Data General manufactures the microNOVA microprocessor; and so on. We have chosen to describe the 8080, not because it is best, but only because it is well-known, widespread, and similar to many other microprocessors.

Memory

The 8080 is an 8-bit machine, so memory is made up of 8-bit bytes. Each byte has a separate address (byte-addressable). If 8-bit bytes were used as addresses, only 256 bytes would be addressable, so 16-bit addresses are used. This allows up to 65,536 bytes of memory to be used.

The 8080 chip does not have memory on it; memory is available on other chips, such as the 8102 chip with 1024 bits of memory. Typically, an 8080 will have from 4K to 16K bytes of memory. For dedicated applications, programs could be in read only memory (ROM) with only a small amount of read-write random access memory (RAM) for storing data and variables.

Registers

The 8080 has several registers. A 16-bit program counter contains the address of the next instruction, and a 16-bit stack pointer contains the address of the top of a stack in memory. The stack is used for subroutine return addresses and can also be used for temporary storage and parameters.

The 8-bit accumulator (A) is used for arithmetic functions. In addition there are six 8-bit general registers: B, C, D, E, H, and L. These registers can be used to store 8-bit bytes or used as register pairs (B,C), (D,E), and (H,L) to hold 16-bit

FIGURE 10.32   An Intel 8080 CPU chip. This photomicrograph shows the structure of a single chip which includes registers (upper left), an arithmetic and logic unit (lower half), and control circuits. (Photo courtesy of Intel Corporation.)

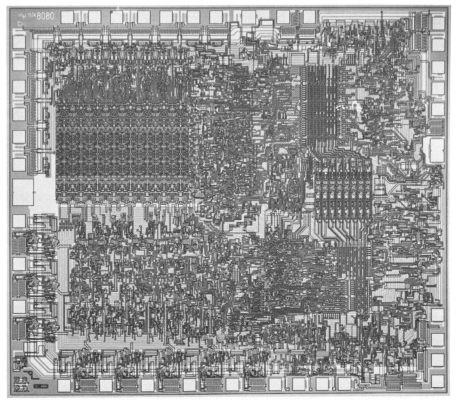

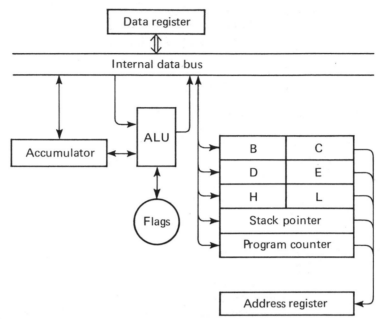

FIGURE 10.33 Block diagram of the Intel 8080. All communication between the CPU and memory or external devices is via the 8-bit data register and the 16-bit address register.

quantities, generally addresses. A set of five 1-bit flag registers are used as condition code indicators to signal when the result of an arithmetic operation is zero, negative, generates a carry, has even parity, or generates a carry out of bit 3 (for decimal arithmetic).

Data is stored as 8-bit binary integers and can easily be interpreted as signed two's complement or unsigned 8-bit integers. Double precision (16-bit) integers can be used by multiple-precision programming techniques and even floating point numbers could be simulated with proper programming, but generally programs work with signed or unsigned 8-bit or 16-bit integers.

Instructions

The 8080 instruction set uses an 8-bit opcode. This allows up to 256 different instructions, of which 12 are not used by the 8080. Many of these opcodes operate on the registers and so do not have operands. A few use the byte following the opcode for an 8-bit "immediate" constant, or the two bytes following the opcode for an address. Thus, an instruction may be one, two, or three bytes in length, depending upon the opcode.

The instructions can be divided into four types:

1. Data transfer instructions, which move data between registers and memory, or between registers and registers.

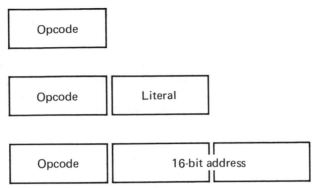

FIGURE 10.34   Instruction formats for the Intel 8080. Instructions can be one, two, or three bytes long, depending upon the opcode.

2.   Arithmetic instructions, which operate on the registers, or the registers and memory, leaving the result in the registers.
3.   Jump instructions, which may alter the flow of control in the program.
4.   Miscellaneous instructions, including I/O instructions, stack instructions, HALT and NOP instructions.

Notice that the above commands may reference memory. Memory can be addressed in several ways. First, it can be addressed directly. In this case the two bytes following the opcode specify the address of the memory location. Second, memory can be addressed indirectly through the register pairs (H,L), (B,C), or (D,E). Most commonly (H,L) is used as an address of a memory location.

Memory can also be accessed via the stack pointer and data may be in the instruction for immediate use. Immediate operands can be 8 or 16 bits, depending on the opcode. Thus, addressing modes include immediate, direct, and indirect (through a register). Not all addressing modes are possible with all instructions.

Data transfer instructions

The data transfer instructions include instructions to move data between any two registers, or between a register and memory. This allows both loads, stores, and the entering of immediate data.

Arithmetic instructions

Arithmetic instructions allow the contents of any register or memory location to be added or subtracted from the accumulator. Memory is addressed only indirectly through the (H,L) register pair, so to add the contents of an arbitrary memory location, x, to the accumulator would require first entering the address of x into (H,L) and then adding. Immediate adds and subtracts (increments and decrements) are also possible.

Remember that the accumulator is an 8-bit register, so all arithmetic is 8-bit arithmetic. To allow multiple-precision arithmetic to be programmed easily, the carry bit records the carry (for addition) or the borrow (for subtraction) out of the high-order bit. Instructions allow this carry to be added to the accumulator. Thus, to add two unsigned 16-bit integers, a program would first add the low-order 8-bit bytes of each operand, store the sum back in memory, and then add the two high-order 8-bit bytes and the carry from the low-order addition. If there was a carry from this addition, overflow has occurred.

The logical operators of AND, OR, and XOR are available also. These instructions operate between the accumulator and any register, memory [indirect through the (H,L) register pair], or immediate operand. Rotate instructions allow the contents of the accumulator to be rotated (circular shift) left or right one bit position, with or without the carry bit. The accumulator can also be complemented.

Another set of instructions allow any register or memory location [addressed indirect through the (H,L) register pair] to be incremented (by one) or decremented (by one). This is particularly useful for counters and index addresses.

Finally, the accumulator can be compared with any other register or memory location [addressed indirectly through the (H,L) register pair], or an immediate operand. The results of this comparison are used to set the condition flags.

Jump instructions

The jump instructions allow the program to jump, either conditionally or unconditionally, to any memory location. The jump address is contained in the two bytes following the jump opcode. Conditional jumps are based on the value of the condition flags, which may be set on the basis of a compare, addition, subtraction, or logical operation.

Subroutine linkage is performed by two special instructions, CALL and RET. These allow a subroutine to be called and later return. The return address of the call is automatically pushed by the CALL instruction onto the stack pointed to by the stack pointer register. The RET instruction then pops the top two bytes off the stack and jumps to that address to return from the subroutine call. This mechanism makes it easy to write recursive subroutines. The designers of the 8080 then went one step farther and allowed subroutine calls and returns to be conditional as well as unconditional. A subroutine call or return can be conditional on the value of the condition flags in the same way as the conditional jumps.

Miscellaneous instructions

In addition to being used by CALL and RET, the stack can be used directly. Specific instructions allow register pairs to be pushed onto or popped from the stack. The accumulator and condition flags can also be saved and restored using the stack. This allows convenient saving and restoring of registers in subroutines or interrupt handlers.

Instructions for halting the CPU and doing nothing (NOP) are also provided.

I/O operation

Four instructions control input and output. An IN instruction moves one 8-bit byte from an I/O device to the accumulator, while an OUT instruction moves one 8-bit byte from the accumulator to an I/O device. The device number is specified in the byte following the opcode, allowing up to 256 I/O devices. These instructions are similar to the MIX I/O commands, but there is one major difference: the MIX system provides the JBUS and JRED instructions to determine when the I/O devices are busy or ready; the 8080 has no such instructions.

There are several ways to solve this problem. One would be to assign two device numbers to each I/O device. The even device number would be used for control and status information and the odd device number for data. This effectively reduces the number of different I/O devices to 128, still a reasonably large number, and the additional control circuitry is not great.

Another approach that has been suggested is to assign I/O devices to memory addresses. Thus, when an address is sent from the CPU, ostensibly to memory, special circuitry separates the addresses into some which are sent on to the memory modules and others that are sent to I/O devices. For example, using the high-order bit to choose between memory addresses and I/O devices would allow up to 32,768 bytes of memory and 32,768 different I/O devices. This scheme is similar to the approach of the PDP-11.

There are two other I/O techniques which can be used with the 8080. For high-speed devices, DMA transfers can be made directly to memory. To avoid interference at the memory between the I/O device doing the DMA transfer and the CPU, it may be necessary to suspend all CPU operations during the transfer. This will be necessary only if the memory cycle time is too long to allow the memory units to service both the CPU and the DMA I/O device.

Finally, the 8080 has an interrupt structure. Two instructions allow the interrupt system to be turned on and off. When the interrupt system is on, and a request for an interrupt is made by an I/O device, the interrupt system is turned off and an interrupt phase is entered. The interrupting I/O device is requested to provide one 8-bit opcode to the 8080 processor. After this instruction is executed, the 8080 continues its normal instruction execution cycle.

The instruction supplied by an interrupting I/O device can be any 8080 instruction, but, of course, what is desired is a jump to an interrupt routine in such a way that control can be resumed at the interrupted instruction; that is, a subroutine jump to an interrupt routine. The problem is that all jumps and subroutine calls require an address, meaning that subroutine call instructions are three bytes in length. To remedy this problem, a special instruction has been included in the instruction set. This instruction, called a restart, has a 3-bit field in the 8-bit opcode which specifies one of the 8 addresses, 0, 8, 16, 24, . . ., 56. The restart instruction cause a subroutine call to the address specified by its 3-bit field. This pushes onto the stack the address of the interrupted instruction.

Typically then an interrupt instruction is a restart to one of the 8 restart addresses. At each of these addresses is a short program segment which saves registers and then jumps to another section of code to service the interrupt. After the interrupt has been serviced, the interrupt system is turned back on, and processing is returned to the interrupted instruction. By storing interrupt return addresses and registers on the stack, it is possible to allow interrupts to occur during interrupt handling subroutines.

Assembly language

Several assembly languages for the 8080 exist and more are being developed. One sizable market for the 8080, and other microprocessors, is the computer hobbyist. Since a complete 8080-based computer costs less than $500, many people are buying them for personal experimentation and use. Since assemblers are relatively straightforward to write (as shown in Chapter 8), many people are writing their own. We describe here the assembly language provided by Intel.

Each assembly language statement has four fields, as usual: the label field, the opcode field, the operand field, and the comment field. Input is free-format. The general form of an assembly language statement is:

```
LABEL:          OPCODE          OPERAND          ;COMMENT
```

The colon following the LABEL defines it as a label and not an opcode. One or more blanks must separate the opcode and its operand.

The operand field may or may not be needed, depending upon the opcode. It can contain a constant, a symbol, or an expression. Constants can be specified as decimal, octal, hexadecimal, binary, or an ASCII character. Symbols are one to five characters (the first character being alphabetic) and must appear as labels somewhere. The special symbol $ is the value of the current location counter. Expressions are constructed from constants and symbols and the operators of +, −, *, /, MOD (modulo), NOT, AND, OR, XOR, SHR (shift right), and SHL (shift left). Parentheses can be used to force the order of evaluation; otherwise evaluation is by precedence of operators, similar to most higher level languages.

Pseudo-instructions include

DB	Define a byte of data
DW	Define a word of data
DS	Reserve storage (like a BSS)
ORG	Define the location counter value
EQU	Define a symbol value
SET	Like EQU but the symbol can be redefined later
END	End of assembly

Conditional assembly is provided by IF and ENDIF pseudo-instructions. The expression in the operand field is evaluated, and if it is zero, the statements between the IF and the ENDIF are ignored. If the expression value is nonzero, the statements are assembled.

Macros are available by using the MACRO and ENDM pseudo-instructions for macro definition. The MACRO pseudo-instruction specifies the macro name (in the label field) and a (possibly empty) list of parameter names in the operand field. For an instruction set as primitive as the 8080, macros are very important for convenient programming.

Programming techniques

Most of the programming techniques for the 8080 are very similar to those of the PDP-8, although the instruction set is actually more powerful for the 8080. Complex instructions like multiplications and division are programmed either as macros or subroutines, as space and time demand. Array processing is easiest by keeping the base address in a register pair and incrementing or decrementing to move through the entire array. Subroutine calls use the stack for return addresses. Parameters can be passed in the registers, on the stack or in memory. The use of subroutines and macros is very important in the production of good assembly language programs.

EXERCISES

a. Describe the memory of the Intel 8080.
b. Why would the designers of the 8080 limit the word size to 8 bits?
c. Describe how multiple precision arithmetic would be coded on the 8080.
d. Compare the interrupt processing of the 8080 with the PDP-8 and HP 2100.
e. The assembler for the 8080 is a cross-assembler. Define what this means and why this would be the case.
f. Compare the I/O instructions of the 8080 with the I/O instructions of the MIX computer.

10.9 SUMMARY

By this point, we hope you are aware of both the basic similarities among computer systems and the points of difference. Each new computer should be considered for the following design points.

Memory and registers

What is the basic unit of memory (word, byte) and its size (8 to 128 bits)? What are the variations on this basic unit (bytes, halfwords, fullwords, double-words)? How big can memory be and what is the address size (8 to 32 bits)? What forms of data are represented (integers, floating point, decimal, character strings) and in what representation (ones' complement, two's complement, packed, zoned, etc.)?

What registers are available for use by the programmer, their size and usage (accumulators, index registers, floating point registers, general purpose registers, condition codes)?

Instruction set

What is the instruction set and its format? What addressing modes are available (direct, indirect, indexed, auto-increment or decrement)? Are the instructions three-address (A = B *op* C), two-address (A = A *op* B), one-address (register = register *op* A), or zero-address (all operations use the top elements of a stack and replace their results on the stack)? How is loading, storing, testing, and arithmetic handled? What jump conditions are available and how is a subroutine jump done? How man (bits, bytes, words) does each instruction format take?

Assembly language

What is the assembly language statement format? What is the maximum symbol length and any other restrictions on the naming of symbols? How are fields of the statement defined? What are the mnemonic opcodes and the pseudo-instructions? What forms of expressions are allowed? What is the symbol for the location counter?

I/O and interrupts

How is I/O performed (CPU, DMA, channels)? What are the I/O instructions? Is there an interrupt structure and what kind (vectored, priority)? What happens when there is an interrupt? Are some device numbers interpreted in a special way, and if so, what way?

These are the questions which need to be asked about a new computer. With a familiarity with the computers considered in this book, you should be able to both ask these questions and to understand their answers. Within a short period of time, you can then be programming in assembly language on any new computer that you find.

EXERCISES

a. The following computer companies were founded by ex-employees of other computer companies. Identify the company from which the founders of the following companies came.

1. Amdahl Corporation
2. Control Data Corporation
3. Data General Corporation
4. Cray Research, Inc.

b. The PDP-8 has a 3-bit opcode field and has eight instructions. The IBM 370 has an 8-bit opcode and has about 160 legal instructions (plus about 90 which are not used). The MIX machine has a 6-bit opcode field, but the list of instructions in Appendix B has almost 180 different instructions. Explain why MIX has more than 64.

c. Give the instruction execution cycle for a computer with interrupts.

d. Why would some machines have a conditional skip instruction (like the PDP-8), while other machines have a conditional jump instruction (like MIX).

e. What is the advantage of having a lot of registers in a computer?

f. Which of the following is a stack machine?
1. a 3-address computer
2. the IBM 360 or IBM 370
3. a 0-address computer
4. a 1-address computer
5. the MIX computer
6. a Burroughs B5500

g. What sort of machine would be able to execute code such as

```
LOAD    A
LOAD    B
LOAD    C
ADD
MPY
STORE   D
```

What does the above code compute?

h. Define microprogramming. Why is it a reasonable way to build computers?

i. Give the main reason for interrupts.

j. What is a branch initiated by the control unit in response to an error called?

k.   Fill in the blanks in the following table.

	MIX	PDP-8	HP2100	PDP-11	IBM 370	CDC 6600
Word Size (in bits)	___	___	___	___	___	___
Addressable Memory Unit	___	___	___	___	___	___
Integer Number Representation	___	___	___	___	___	___
Major Registers	___	___	___	___	___	___
Bits in Address	___	___	___	___	___	___
Opcode Size (in bits)	___	___	___	___	___	___

APPENDIX A

REFERENCES

1. Aho, A. V. and Ullman, J. D., "The Theory of Parsing, Translation and Compiling," Volumes 1 and 2, Prentice-Hall, Englewood Cliffs, New Jersey, 1973.
2. Barron, D. W., "Assemblers and Loaders," MacDonald-Elsevier, New York, 1969.
3. Basili, V. R. and Turner, A. J., A Transportable, Extendable Compiler, *Software, Practice and Experience*, Volume 5, Number 3, (July 1975), pp. 269–278.
4. Bell, C. G., and Newell, A., "Computer Structures: Readings and Examples," McGraw-Hill, New York, 1971.
5. Brown, P. J., A Survey of Macro Processors, *Annual Review of Automatic Programming*, Volume 6, Part 2 (1969), pp. 37–88.
6. Conway, M., Design of a Separable Transition Compiler, *Communications of the ACM*, Volume 6, Number 7, (July 1963), pp. 396–408.
7. Donovan, J. J., "Systems Programming," McGraw-Hill, New York, 1972.
8. Eckhouse, R. H., Jr., "Minicomputer Systems," Prentice-Hall, Englewood Cliffs, New Jersey, 1975.
9. Gear, C. W., "Computer Organization and Programming," Second Edition, McGraw-Hill, New York, 1974.
10. Graham, R. M., "Principles of Systems Programming," Wiley, New York, 1975.

11. Grishman, R., "Assembly Language Programming for the Control Data 6000 Series and the Cyber 70 Series," Algorithms Press, New York, 1974.
12. Gries, D., "Compiler Construction for Digital Computers," Wiley, New York, 1971.
13. Hsiao, D. K., "Systems Programming," Addison-Wesley, Reading, Massachusetts, 1975.
14. Ingermann, P. Z., Thunks, *Communications of the ACM*, Volume 4, Number 1 (January 1961), pp. 55–108.
15. Kent, W., Assembler Language Macroprogramming, *Computing Surveys*, Volume 1, Number 4 (December 1969), pp. 183–196.
16. Kernighan, B. W. and Plauger, P. J., "Software Tools," Addison-Wesley, Reading, Massachusetts, 1976.
17. Knuth, D. E., "The Art of Computer Programming, Volume One, Fundamental Algorithms," Addison-Wesley, Reading, Massachusetts, 1968; Second Edition, 1973.
18. Knuth, D. E., "The Art of Computer Programming, Volume Two, Seminumerical Algorithms," Addison-Wesley, Reading, Massachusetts, 1969.
19. Knuth, D. E., "The Art of Computer Programming, Volume Three, Sorting and Searching," Addison-Wesley, Reading, Massachusetts, 1973.
20. Madnick, S. E. and Donovan, J. J., "Operating Systems," McGraw-Hill, New York, 1974.
21. Morris, R., Scatter Storage Techniques, *Communications of the ACM*, Volume 11, Number 1 (January 1968), pp. 38–44.
22. Presser, L. and White, J. R., Linkers and Loaders, *Computing Surveys*, Volume 4, Number 3 (September 1972), pp. 149–168.
23. Rosen, S., Electronic Computers: A Historical Survey, *Computing Surveys*, Volume 1, Number 1 (March 1969), pp. 7–36.
24. Sloan, M. E., "Computer Hardware and Organization, An Introduction," SRA, Chicago, Illinois, 1976.
25. Stone, H. S. (Editor), "Introduction to Computer Architecture," SRA, Palo Alto, California, 1975.
26. Stone, H. S. and Siewiorek, D. P., "Introduction to Computer Organization and Data Structures: PDP-11 Edition," McGraw-Hill, New York, 1975.
27. Strachey, C., A General Purpose Macrogenerator, *Computer Journal*, Volume 8, Number 3 (October 1965), pp. 225–241.
28. Struble, G. W., "Assembler Language Programming, the IBM System/360 and 370," Addison-Wesley, Reading, Massachusetts, 1975.
29. Tanenbaum, A. S., "Structured Computer Organization," Prentice-Hall, Englewood Cliffs, New Jersey, 1976.
30. Thornton, J. E., "Design of a Computer, The Control Data 6600," Scott, Foresman and Company, Glenview, Illinois, 1970.

31. Tsichritzis, D. C. and Bernstein, P. A., "Operating Systems," Academic Press, New York, 1974.

32. Ullman, J. D., "Fundamental Concepts of Programming Systems," Addison-Wesley, Reading, Massachusetts, 1976.

33. Wilkes, M. V., "Time-Sharing Computer Systems," Second Edition, American Elsevier, New York, 1972.

34. Wirth, N., PL360, A Programming Language for the 360 Computers, *Journal of the ACM*, Volume 15, Number 1 (January 1968), pp 37–74.

APPENDIX B

THE MIX INSTRUCTION SET

The instruction set of the MIX computer is described below. The instructions are grouped by function. In describing the instructions, the following notation is used:

A	the A register
X	the X register
AX	the 10-byte double-length register composed of the A and X register, with the A register being the upper 5 bytes and the X register being the lower 5 bytes.
I1,I2,I3,I4,I5,I6	the 6 index registers
J	the J register
MEMORY[q]	the memory word whose address is q ($0 \leq q < 4000$)
REG[*]	the *th register, where REG[0] is A, REG[1] is I1, REG[2] is I2, REG[3] is I3, . . ., REG[6] is I6, and REG[7] is X
q → r	the contents of register or memory word q, or the value of the expression q, is copied to the register or memory word r
q(L:R)	the L:R bytes of memory word or register q
m	the effective address of the instruction being executed

P   the program counter
I   the instruction register; holds the instruction while it is
                           being executed

The instruction execution cycle for the MIX computer is:

1. (Fetch instruction) MEMORY[P] → I.
2. (Increment program counter) P + 1 → P.
3. (Calculate effective address) effective address(I) → m.
4. (Execute instruction) execute(I).
5. (Repeat until HLT instruction.) If the instruction was not a HLT, return to
    step 1.

The effect of execute (I) depends upon bytes 5 and 4 of the instruction
register I as follows. (All numbers are octal.)

For each instruction, the assembler mnemonic, octal numeric opcode and
field specifications are given, along with a short description of the instruction.
When the same instruction applies to the eight registers, A, X, I1, I2, I3, I4, I5,
and I6 in the same way, the symbol "*" is used to stand for the register to be
used. For mnemonics, the * should be replaced by A, 1, 2, 3, 4, 5, 6, X; for
opcodes by 0, 1, 2, 3, 4, 5, 6, 7, as appropriate.

Loading Instructions

LD*	10+*	L:R	MEMORY[m](L:R) → REG[*]
LD*N	20+*	L:R	−MEMORY[m](L:R) → REG[*]

Storing Instructions

ST*	30+*	L:R	if L=0, then REG[*](0:0) → MEMORY[m] (0:0) and REG[*](6−R:5) → MEMORY[m] (1:R); if L>0, then REG[*](5−R+L:5) → MEMORY[m](L:R)
STJ	40	L:R	if L=0, then "+" → MEMORY[m](0:0) and J(6−R:5) → MEMORY[m](1:R); if L>0, then J(5−R+L:5) → MEMORY[m](L:R)
STZ	41	L:R	+0 → MEMORY[m](L:R)

Arithmetic

ADD	01	L:R	A + MEMORY[m](L:R) → A; if the magnitude of this sum is too large, "ON" → Overflow toggle

SUB	02	L:R	A − MEMORY[m] (L:R) → A; if the magnitude of this difference is too large, "ON" → Overflow toggle
MUL	03	L:R	A × MEMORY[m](L:R) → AX
DIV	04	L:R	the quotient of AX / MEMORY[m](L:R) → A; the remainder → X; if the magnitude of the quotient is too large, or MEMORY[m] (L:R) = 0, then "ON"→ Overflow toggle

Immediate Instructions

INC*	60+*	00	REG[*] + m→REG[*]
DEC*	60+*	01	REG[*] − m→REG[*]
ENT*	60+*	02	m→REG[*]
ENN*	60+*	03	−m→REG[*]

Comparison Instructions

| CMP* | 70+* | L:R | if REG[*] (L:R)<MEMORY[m] (L:R), then "LESS" → Comparison indicator; if REG[*] (L:R) =MEMORY[m] (L:R), then "EQUAL" → Comparison indicator; if REG[*] (L:R)>MEMORY[m] (L:R), then "GREATER" → Comparison indicator |

Jumps

JMP	47	00	P → J and m→ P
JSJ	47	01	m→ P
JOV	47	02	if Overflow toggle = "ON", then "OFF"→ Overflow toggle and P → J and m → P
JNOV	47	03	if Overflow toggle ="OFF", then P → J and m → P; if Overflow toggle = "ON", then "OFF" → Overflow toggle
JL	47	04	if Comparison Indicator ="LESS", then P → J and m → P
JE	47	05	if Comparison Indicator = "EQUAL", then P → J and m → P
JG	47	06	if Comparison Indicator = "GREATER", then P → J and m → P
JGE	47	07	if Comparison Indicator = "GREATER" or

			Comparison Indicator = "EQUAL", then P → J and m → P
, JNE	47	10	if Comparison Indicator = "GREATER" or Comparison Indicator = "LESS", then P → J and m → P
JLE	47	11	if Comparison Indicator = "LESS" or Comparison Indicator = "EQUAL", then P → J and m → P
J*N	50+*	00	if REG[*] < 0, then P → J and m → P
J*Z	50+*	01	if REG[*] = 0, then P → J and m → P
J*P	50+*	02	if REG[*] > 0, then P → J and m → P
J*NN	50+*	03	if REG[*] ≥ 0, then P → J and m → P
J*NZ	50+*	04	if REG[*] ≠ 0, then P → J and m → P
J*NP	50+*	05	if REG[*] ≤ 0, then P → J and m → P
JBUS	42	N	if unit N is busy, then P → J and m → P
JRED	46	N	if unit N is not busy, then P → J and m → P

Input/Output Instructions

IN	44	N	if unit N is busy, then wait until it is not busy; then issue an input command to unit N with memory address m.
OUT	45	N	if unit N is busy, then wait until it is not busy; then issue an output command to unit N with memory address m.
IOC	43	N	if unit N is busy, then wait until it is not busy; then issue a control command to unit N with parameter m.

Shift Instructions

SLA	06	00	shift A left m bytes, end-off, zero fill
SRA	06	01	shift A right m bytes, end-off, zero fill
SLAX	06	02	shift AX left m bytes, end-off, zero fill
SRAX	06	03	shift AX right m bytes, end-off, zero fill
SLC	06	04	shift AX left m bytes, circular
SRC	06	05	shift AX right m bytes, circular

Miscellaneous Instructions

NUM	05	00	convert from decimal character code in AX to binary numeric in A

CHAR	05	01	convert from binary numeric in A to decimal character code in AX
HLT	05	02	halt the computer
NOP	00	00	do nothing, simply continue with the next instruction
MOVE	07	N	copy the N words at m, $m+1$, $m+2$, ..., $m+N-1$ to I1, I1+1, I1+2, ..., I1+N−1, one at a time, leaving I1 + N → I1

Floating Point Instructions

FADD	01	06	A + MEMORY[m] → A
FSUB	02	06	A − MEMORY[m] → A
FMUL	03	06	A × MEMORY[m] → A
FDIV	04	06	A / MEMORY[m] → A
FCMP	70	06	if A < MEMORY[m], then "LESS" → Comparison indicator if A = MEMORY[m], then "EQUAL" → Comparison indicator if A > MEMORY[m], then "GREATER" → Comparison indicator
FLOT	05	06	convert the integer number in A to a floating point number of the same value, and leave the floating point representation in A

Binary Instructions

AND	05	03	A *and* MEMORY[m] → A
ORR	05	04	A *or* MEMORY[m] → A
XOR	05	05	A *xor* MEMORY[m] → A
SLB	06	06	shift AX left m bits
SRB	06	07	shift AX right m bits
JAE	50	06	if A is even, then P → J and m → P
JAO	50	07	if A is odd, then P → J and m → P
JXE	57	06	if X is even, then P → J and m → P
JXO	57	07	if X is odd, then P → J and m → P

APPENDIX C

MIX SYMBOLIC OPCODES— ALPHABETIC ORDER

Notation: m is the computed effective address
(m) is the contents of location m

code	field	symbol	instruction
01	L:R	ADD	add (m) to register A
03	07	AND	logical and (m) into A
05	01	CHAR	A is converted to 10-byte decimal characters in AX
70	L:R	CMPA	compare A and (m), set comparison indicator
77	L:R	CMPX	compare X and (m), set comparison indicator
71	L:R	CMP1	compare I1 and (m), set comparison indicator
72	L:R	CMP2	compare I2 and (m), set comparison indicator
73	L:R	CMP3	compare I3 and (m), set comparison indicator
74	L:R	CMP4	compare I4 and (m), set comparison indicator
75	L:R	CMP5	compare I5 and (m), set comparison indicator
76	L:R	CMP6	compare I6 and (m), set comparison indicator
60	01	DECA	decrement A by m
67	01	DECX	decrement X by m

61	01	DEC1	decrement I1 by m
62	01	DEC2	decrement I2 by m
63	01	DEC3	decrement I3 by m
64	01	DEC4	decrement I4 by m
65	01	DEC5	decrement I5 by m
66	01	DEC6	decrement I6 by m
04	L:R	DIV	divide (m) into AX giving A (quotient) and X (remainder)
60	03	ENNA	enter negative of m into A
67	03	ENNX	enter negative of m into X
61	03	ENN1	enter negative of m into I1
62	03	ENN2	enter negative of m into I2
63	03	ENN3	enter negative of m into I3
64	03	ENN4	enter negative of m into I4
65	03	ENN5	enter negative of m into I5
66	03	ENN6	enter negative of m into I6
60	02	ENTA	enter m into A
67	02	ENTX	enter m into X
61	02	ENT1	enter m into I1
62	02	ENT2	enter m into I2
63	02	ENT3	enter m into I3
64	02	ENT4	enter m into I4
65	02	ENT5	enter m into I5
66	02	ENT6	enter m into I6
01	06	FADD	floating point add (m) to A
70	06	FCMP	floating point compare (m) to A, set comparison indicator
04	06	FDIV	floating point divide of A by (m)
05	06	FLOT	convert A from integer to floating point in A
03	06	FMUL	floating point multiply of A by (m)
02	06	FSUB	floating point subtract (m) from A
05	02	HLT	halt the MIX machine
44	N	IN	start input transfer from unit N
60	00	INCA	increment A by m
67	00	INCX	increment X by m
61	00	INC1	increment I1 by m
62	00	INC2	increment I2 by m
63	00	INC3	increment I3 by m
64	00	INC4	increment I4 by m
65	00	INC5	increment I5 by m
66	00	INC6	increment I6 by m
43	N	IOC	issue I/O control signal to unit N
50	06	JAE	jump to m if A is even
50	00	JAN	jump to m if A is negative
50	03	JANN	jump to m if A is nonnegative
50	05	JANP	jump to m if A is nonpositive

50	04	JANZ	jump to *m* if A is nonzero
50	07	JAO	jump to *m* if A is odd
50	02	JAP	jump to *m* if A is positive
50	01	JAZ	jump to *m* if A is zero
42	N	JBUS	jump to location *m* if unit N is busy
47	05	JE	jump to *m* if comparison indicator is equal
47	06	JG	jump to *m* if comparison indicator is greater
47	07	JGE	jump to *m* if comparison indicator is greater or equal
47	04	JL	jump to *m* if comparison indicator is less
47	11	JLE	jump to *m* if comparison indicator is less or equal
47	00	JMP	jump to *m*
47	10	JNE	jump to *m* if comparison indicator is not equal
47	03	JNOV	jump to *m* if overflow off, turn overflow off anyway
47	02	JOV	jump to *m* if overflow on, turn overflow off
46	N	JRED	jump to location *m* if unit N is ready
47	01	JSJ	jump to *m* (but do not change register J)
57	06	JXE	jump to *m* if X is even
57	00	JXN	jump to *m* if X is negative
57	03	JXNN	jump to *m* if X is nonnegative
57	05	JXNP	jump to *m* if X is nonpositive
57	04	JXNZ	jump to *m* if X is nonzero
57	07	JXO	jump to *m* if X is odd
57	02	JXP	jump to *m* if X is positive
57	01	JXZ	jump to *m* if X is zero
51	00	J1N	jump to *m* if I1 is negative
51	03	J1NN	jump to *m* if I1 is nonnegative
51	05	J1NP	jump to *m* if I1 is nonpositive
51	04	J1NZ	jump to *m* if I1 is nonzero
51	02	J1P	jump to *m* if I1 is positive
51	01	J1Z	jump to *m* if I1 is zero
52	00	J2N	jump to *m* if I2 is negative
52	03	J2NN	jump to *m* if I2 is nonnegative
52	05	J2NP	jump to *m* if I2 is nonpositive
52	04	J2NZ	jump to *m* if I2 is nonzero
52	02	J2P	jump to *m* if I2 is positive
52	01	J2Z	jump to *m* if I2 is zero
53	00	J3N	jump to *m* if I3 is negative
53	03	J3NN	jump to *m* if I3 is nonnegative
53	05	J3NP	jump to *m* if I3 is nonpositive
53	04	J3NZ	jump to *m* if I3 is nonzero
53	02	J3P	jump to *m* if I3 is positive
53	01	J3Z	jump to *m* if I3 is zero
54	00	J4N	jump to *m* if I4 is negative
54	03	J4NN	jump to *m* if I4 is nonnegative

54	05	J4NP	jump to *m* if I4 is nonpositive
54	04	J4NZ	jump to *m* if I4 is nonzero
54	02	J4P	jump to *m* if I4 is positive
54	01	J4Z	jump to *m* if I4 is zero
55	00	J5N	jump to *m* if I5 is negative
55	03	J5NN	jump to *m* if I5 is nonnegative
55	05	J5NP	jump to *m* if I5 is nonpositive
55	04	J5NZ	jump to *m* if I5 is nonzero
55	02	J5P	jump to *m* if I5 is positive
55	01	J5Z	jump to *m* if I5 is zero
56	00	J6N	jump to *m* if I6 is negative
56	03	J6NN	jump to *m* if I6 is nonnegative
56	05	J6NP	jump to *m* if I6 is nonpositive
56	04	J6NZ	jump to *m* if I6 is nonzero
56	02	J6P	jump to *m* if I6 is positive
56	01	J6Z	jump to *m* if I6 is zero
10	L:R	LDA	load A with (*m*)
20	L:R	LDAN	load A with negative of (*m*)
17	L:R	LDX	load X with (*m*)
27	L:R	LDXN	load X with negative of (*m*)
11	L:R	LD1	load I1 with (*m*)
21	L:R	LD1N	load I1 with negative of (*m*)
12	L:R	LD2	load I2 with (*m*)
22	L:R	LD2N	load I2 with negative of (*m*)
13	L:R	LD3	load I3 with (*m*)
23	L:R	LD3N	load I3 with negative of (*m*)
14	L:R	LD4	load I4 with (*m*)
24	L:R	LD4N	load I4 with negative of (*m*)
15	L:R	LD5	load I5 with (*m*)
25	L:R	LD5N	load I5 with negative of (*m*)
16	L:R	LD6	load I6 with (*m*)
26	L:R	LD6N	load I6 with negative of (*m*)
07	N	MOVE	move N words starting from *m* to (I1), add N to I1
03	L:R	MUL	multiply (*m*) by A giving AX
00	00	NOP	no operation
05	00	NUM	10-byte decimal in AX converted to binary in A
05	03	OCT	A is converted to 10-byte octal characters in AX
01	07	ORR	inclusive *or* of (*m*) with A
45	N	OUT	start output transfer from unit N
06	00	SLA	shift A *m* bytes left, end-off
06	02	SLAX	shift AX *m* bytes left, end-off
06	06	SLB	shift AX *m* bits left, end-off
06	04	SLC	shift AX *m* bytes left, circular
06	01	SRA	shift A *m* bytes right, end-off

06	03	SRAX	shift AX m bytes right, end-off
06	07	SRB	shift AX m bits right, end-off
06	05	SRC	shift AX m bytes right, circular
30	L:R	STA	store A into location m
40	L:R	STJ	store J register into location m
37	L:R	STX	store X into location m
41	L:R	STZ	store zero into location m
31	L:R	ST1	store I1 into location m
32	L:R	ST2	store I2 into location m
33	L:R	ST3	store I3 into location m
34	L:R	ST4	store I4 into location m
35	L:R	ST5	store I5 into location m
36	L:R	ST6	store I6 into location m
02	L:R	SUB	subtract (m) from A
02	07	XOR	exclusive *or* of (m) with A

APPENDIX D

MIX SYMBOLIC OPCODES— NUMERIC ORDER

Notation: *m* is the computed effective address
(m) is the contents of location m

code	field	symbol	instruction
00	00	NOP	no operation
01	L:R	ADD	add (m) to register A
01	06	FADD	floating point add (m) to A
01	07	ORR	inclusive *or* of (m) with A
02	L:R	SUB	subtract (m) from A
02	06	FSUB	floating point subtract (m) from A
02	07	XOR	exclusive *or* of (m) with A
03	L:R	MUL	multiply (m) by A giving AX
03	06	FMUL	floating point multiply of A by (m)
03	07	AND	logical *and* (m) into A
04	L:R	DIV	divide (m) into AX giving A (quotient) and X (remainder)
04	06	FDIV	floating point divide of A by (m)
05	00	NUM	10-byte decimal in AX converted to binary in A
05	01	CHAR	A is converted to 10-byte decimal characters in AX
05	02	HLT	halt the MIX machine

05	03	OCT	A is converted to 10-byte octal characters in AX
05	06	FLOT	convert A from integer to floating point in A
06	00	SLA	shift A m bytes left, end-off
06	01	SRA	shift A m bytes right, end-off
06	02	SLAX	shift AX m bytes left, end-off
06	03	SRAX	shift AX m bytes right, end-off
06	04	SLC	shift AX m bytes left, circular
06	05	SRC	shift AX m bytes right, circular
06	06	SLB	shift AX m bits left, end-off
06	07	SRB	shift AX m bits right, end-off
07	N	MOVE	move N words starting from m to (I1), add N to I1
10	L:R	LDA	load A with (m)
11	L:R	LD1	load I1 with (m)
12	L:R	LD2	load I2 with (m)
13	L:R	LD3	load I3 with (m)
14	L:R	LD4	load I4 with (m)
15	L:R	LD5	load I5 with (m)
16	L:R	LD6	load I6 with (m)
17	L:R	LDX	load X with (m)
20	L:R	LDAN	load A with negative of (m)
21	L:R	LD1N	load I1 with negative of (m)
22	L:R	LD2N	load I2 with negative of (m)
23	L:R	LD3N	load I3 with negative of (m)
24	L:R	LD4N	load I4 with negative of (m)
25	L:R	LD5N	load I5 with negative of (m)
26	L:R	LD6N	load I6 with negative of (m)
27	L:R	LDXN	load X with negative of (m)
30	L:R	STA	store A into location m
31	L:R	ST1	store I1 into location m
32	L:R	ST2	store I2 into location m
33	L:R	ST3	store I3 into location m
34	L:R	ST4	store I4 into location m
35	L:R	ST5	store I5 into location m
36	L:R	ST6	store I6 into location m
37	L:R	STX	store X into location m
40	L:R	STJ	store J register into location m
41	L:R	STZ	store zero into location m
42	N	JBUS	jump to location m if unit N is busy
43	N	IOC	issue I/O control signal to unit N
44	N	IN	start input transfer from unit N
45	N	OUT	start output transfer from unit N
46	N	JRED	jump to location m if unit N is ready
47	00	JMP	jump to m
47	01	JSJ	jump to m (but do not change register J)

47	02	JOV	jump to *m* if overflow on, turn overflow off
47	03	JNOV	jump to *m* if overflow off, turn overflow off anyway
47	04	JL	jump to *m* if comparison indicator is less
47	05	JE	jump to *m* if comparison indicator is equal
47	06	JG	jump to *m* if comparison indicator is greater
47	07	JGE	jump to *m* if comparison indicator is greater or equal
47	10	JNE	jump to *m* if comparison indicator is not equal
47	11	JLE	jump to *m* if comparison indicator is less or equal
50	00	JAN	jump to *m* if A is negative
50	01	JAZ	jump to *m* if A is zero
50	02	JAP	jump to *m* if A is positive
50	03	JANN	jump to *m* if A is nonnegative
50	04	JANZ	jump to *m* if A is nonzero
50	05	JANP	jump to *m* if A is nonpositive
50	06	JAE	jump to *m* if A is even
50	07	JAO	jump to *m* if A is odd
51	00	J1N	jump to *m* if I1 is negative
51	01	J1Z	jump to *m* if I1 is zero
51	02	J1P	jump to *m* if I1 is positive
51	03	J1NN	jump to *m* if I1 is nonnegative
51	04	J1NZ	jump to *m* if I1 is nonzero
51	05	J1NP	jump to *m* if I1 is nonpositive
52	00	J2N	jump to *m* if I2 is negative
52	01	J2Z	jump to *m* if I2 is zero
52	02	J2P	jump to *m* if I2 is positive
52	03	J2NN	jump to *m* if I2 is nonnegative
52	04	J2NZ	jump to *m* if I2 is nonzero
52	05	J2NP	jump to *m* if I2 is nonpositive
53	00	J3N	jump to *m* if I3 is negative
53	01	J3Z	jump to *m* if I3 is zero
53	02	J3P	jump to *m* if I3 is positive
53	03	J3NN	jump to *m* if I3 is nonnegative
53	04	J3NZ	jump to *m* if I3 is nonzero
53	05	J3NP	jump to *m* if I3 is nonpositive
54	00	J4N	jump to *m* if I4 is negative
54	01	J4Z	jump to *m* if I4 is zero
54	02	J4P	jump to *m* if I4 is positive
54	03	J4NN	jump to *m* if I4 is nonnegative
54	04	J4NZ	jump to *m* if I4 is nonzero
54	05	J4NP	jump to *m* if I4 is nonpositive
55	00	J5N	jump to *m* if I5 is negative
55	01	J5Z	jump to *m* if I5 is zero
55	02	J5P	jump to *m* if I5 is positive
55	03	J5NN	jump to *m* if I5 is nonnegative

55	04	J5NZ	jump to *m* if I5 is nonzero
55	05	J5NP	jump to *m* if I5 is nonpositive
56	00	J6N	jump to *m* if I6 is negative
56	01	J6Z	jump to *m* if I6 is zero
56	02	J6P	jump to *m* if I6 is positive
56	03	J6NN	jump to *m* if I6 is nonnegative
56	04	J6NZ	jump to *m* if I6 is nonzero
56	05	J6NP	jump to *m* if I6 is nonpositive
57	00	JXN	jump to *m* if X is negative
57	01	JXZ	jump to *m* if X is zero
57	02	JXP	jump to *m* if X is positive
57	03	JXNN	jump to *m* if X is nonnegative
57	04	JXNZ	jump to *m* if X is nonzero
57	05	JXNP	jump to *m* if X is nonpositive
57	06	JXE	jump to *m* if X is even
57	07	JXO	jump to *m* if X is odd
60	00	INCA	increment A by *m*
60	01	DECA	decrement A by *m*
60	02	ENTA	enter *m* into A
60	03	ENNA	enter negative of *m* into A
61	00	INC1	increment I1 by *m*
61	01	DEC1	decrement I1 by *m*
61	02	ENT1	enter *m* into I1
61	03	ENN1	enter negative of *m* into I1
62	00	INC2	increment I2 by *m*
62	01	DEC2	decrement I2 by *m*
62	02	ENT2	enter *m* into I2
62	03	ENN2	enter negative of *m* into I2
63	00	INC3	increment I3 by *m*
63	01	DEC3	decrement I3 by *m*
63	02	ENT3	enter *m* into I3
63	03	ENN3	enter negative of *m* into I3
64	00	INC4	increment I4 by *m*
64	01	DEC4	decrement I4 by *m*
64	02	ENT4	enter *m* into I4
64	03	ENN4	enter negative of *m* into I4
65	00	INC5	increment I5 by *m*
65	01	DEC5	decrement I5 by *m*
65	02	ENT5	enter *m* into I5
65	03	ENN5	enter negative of *m* into I5
66	00	INC6	increment I6 by *m*
66	01	DEC6	decrement I6 by *m*
66	02	ENT6	enter *m* into I6
66	03	ENN6	enter negative of *m* into I6

67	00	INCX	increment X by m
67	01	DECX	decrement X by m
67	02	ENTX	enter m into X
67	03	ENNX	enter negative of m into X
70	L:R	CMPA	compare A and (m), set comparison indicator
70	06	FCMP	floating point compare A and (m), set comparison indicator
71	L:R	CMP1	compare I1 and (m), set comparison indicator
72	L:R	CMP2	compare I2 and (m), set comparison indicator
73	L:R	CMP3	compare I3 and (m), set comparison indicator
74	L:R	CMP4	compare I4 and (m), set comparison indicator
75	L:R	CMP5	compare I5 and (m), set comparison indicator
76	L:R	CMP6	compare I6 and (m), set comparison indicator
77	L:R	CMPX	compare X and (m), set comparison indicator

APPENDIX E

MIX
CHARACTER
CODE

character	decimal	octal	character	decimal	octal
blank	00	00	N	15	17
A	01	01	O	16	20
B	02	02	P	17	21
C	03	03	Q	18	22
D	04	04	R	19	23
E	05	05	ϕ	20	24
F	06	06	Π	21	25
G	07	07	S	22	26
H	08	10	T	23	27
I	09	11	U	24	30
Θ	10	12	V	25	31
J	11	13	W	26	32
K	12	14	X	27	33
L	13	15	Y	28	34
M	14	16	Z	29	35

character	decimal	octal		character	decimal	octal
0	30	36		)	43	53
1	31	37		+	44	54
2	32	40		−	45	55
3	33	41		*	46	56
4	34	42		/	47	57
5	35	43		=	48	60
6	36	44		$	49	61
7	37	45		<	50	62
8	38	46		>	51	63
9	39	47		@	52	64
.	40	50		;	53	65
,	41	51		:	54	66
(	42	52		'	55	67

INDEX